ALL ASIAN
COOKBOOK

ALL ASIAN COOKBOOK

Japan • China • Korea • India • Malaysia • Singapore • Indonesia • Laos
Thailand • Burma • Cambodia • Vietnam • Philippines • Sri Lanka

JACKI PASSMORE

SPRING BOOKS

London · New York · Sydney · Toronto

ACKNOWLEDGEMENTS

In my teenage years I was the unofficial family cook — nothing adventurous, for we were a fairly large family living to a budget in the Queensland countryside, far removed from any of the influences that have resulted in this book — but those days in the family kitchen instilled in me a love of cooking and a desire to learn.

For me it all began in Brisbane several years later when, as students, my brother and I moved into a rooming house with a group of Asian students. Weekends and many evenings were spent scouring local markets for ingredients and cooking up a mass of exotic dishes of Burmese, Malaysian, Chinese, Japanese and Cambodian origin. Much was improvised, for in those days Oriental supply stores carried basic commodities only, but the results were memorable, and they sparked in me a determination to learn as much as I could about these exciting cuisines. To Jacob George, who became almost a part of our family, I owe special thanks for my humble beginnings as an enthusiast for Asian food.

Apart from the joy of seeing in print the labour of so many years, I have had the added pleasure of working with one of the most professional and talented of food photographers, Reg Morrison, who came to Hongkong to make these photographs with me. I could never hope to work with anyone more dedicated, yet so relaxed and easy to get along with. The results speak for themselves.

I would like to thank Kevin Weldon, managing director of Paul Hamlyn Pty Ltd, and all those in the company for the confidence they have showed in me by producing such a large and colourful book, and for their encouragement of my continuing work in this field.

I am indebted to my editors, Wendy and Peter Hutton, for putting so much effort into the recipes and manuscript. Wendy, who has a wide working knowledge of Southeast Asian cookery, lovingly worked over every recipe to ensure that each was clearly explained and did not lack for authenticity; Peter wrapped the whole work into a package for the printers — a job which anyone who is familiar with publishing will realise is a painstaking task. I could not have wished for a more competent and sympathetic editorial team.

Thanks also to my mother, sisters and brother, whom I have missed all these years and who I hope will learn something from their temporarily estranged daughter and sister through this book; and to all those friends who have helped, participated with and encouraged me through years of testing, sampling, writing, typing and searching for the answers to these cuisines.

And lastly, I owe special thanks to my friend and teacher Daljit Singh for introducing me to Indian cooking and convincing me that Asian cooking does not belong exclusively to Asians.

Jacki Passmore

TO PAUL
FOR ENJOYING ASIAN FOOD AS MUCH AS I DO

First published 1978 by Ure Smith
A division of Paul Hamlyn Pty Limited
176 South Creek Road, Dee Why West. Australia
2099

This edition published 1979 by the Hamlyn
Publishing Group Limited
London. New York. Sydney. Toronto
Astronaut House, Feltham, Middlesex, England

ISBN 0 600 30445 0

Printed in Singapore by Kyodo Printing Co., Pte, Ltd.

PREFACE

This book is the culmination of eight years of travel to collect recipes from all over the Far East, of testing them, adopting ideas and experimenting with ingredients that were all, in the beginning, totally alien to me, but that are now more familiar than many Western ingredients.

If politicians and peacemakers around the world should ever seek an ideal way to promote international goodwill and understanding, they might try food. Asians have a particular love of food, regarding it as one of life's greatest pleasures; the Chinese, perhaps even more than their neighbours, are truly dedicated to the enjoyment of eating. Living and working in Asia, among many who enjoy the very aspect of life that involves me so completely, has been a most rewarding experience.

I began collecting these recipes for myself. But now, having enjoyed them all, having entertained with them and made many friends through collecting them, I am happy to pass them on in the hope that others may derive as much pleasure from them as I have done and continue to do.

What has pleased me most about this project is that at no time has my nationality proved a barrier to learning from other people about the various cuisines, or to serving to friends the results of my endeavours in the kitchen. All but the most dedicated professional cooks were willing to divulge some of their most jealously guarded family recipes; and many also inundated me with helpful hints on cooking, preparing, eating and shopping for ingredients, even though language difficulties were sometimes frustrating — though never insurmountable! Many recipes were dictated in a variety of dialects, and were later painstakingly translated by friends.

Through a desire to please (rather than extreme confidence in my culinary abilities) I have never balked at serving Asian friends with dishes from their own countries. My Indian friends are treated to curries, Japanese relatives (I inherited some with my recent marriage) happily tuck into my versions of their favourite dishes, friends from Malaysia have had Laksa with all the trimmings — and I'm sure they enjoyed it more than they would meat and two veg. They may not have been the best meals these friends have ever been served, but every time I make this effort I am rewarded with evidence of even closer friendship then before.

I hope that through this book many others will also enjoy friendship through a mutual love of good eating.

J.P.

INTRODUCTION

The 505 recipes collected here present a broad view of the cuisines of eleven Asian countries ('Asia', in the context of this book, extents as far west as India; for reasons of space I have unfortunately had to omit the fascinating cuisines of countries in the Near and Middle East). Each section contains recipes belonging specifically to the country to which the chapter is dedicated, and includes the popular local specialities as well as a balanced selection of dishes fully representative of the country's culinary traditions. Where some national dishes are of similar origin or content — particularly in the case of Indonesia and Malaysia, where there are many overlapping ideas — I have omitted some from one chapter to use in the other so as to avoid repetition; similarly, I have loosely categorised recipes from areas north of India, including Kashmir and Pakistan, under 'Indian' purely for reasons of convenience.

Asian cooking in an average Western kitchen is not an impossibility. In fact, it is becoming increasingly easy to produce a wide variety of ethnic cuisines as the availability of specialised ingredients grows and expands. Obviously, one needs to stock up on the basics — herbs, spices and dried ingredients — and to consider alternative cooking methods, but nowadays many Western cooks are familiar with the Chinese *wok* and cleaver; curried dishes and various simmered foods can be cooked just as effectively in standard cooking pots as in the traditional *degchi;* while steaming can be done in any pan large enough to accommodate the food and the dish to hold it.

These recipes, just a small sample of the tens of thousands of recipes from these Asian countries, have been set out in an easy-to-follow format, illustrated in colour where possible, and giving many hints and guidelines for fast and easy Asian cooking. Through repeated testing in my kitchen I have been able to eliminate many of the time-consuming and often back-breaking preparatory tasks seen in most Asian kitchens, where the creative part is enjoyed by the cook and the hard work is usually done by the ever-present kitchen servants.

A blender and an interchangeable coffee grinder (reserved exclusively for dried spices) have been my replacement for at least one pair of hired hands — and why not, if they do the job well? Charcoal fires, *tandoor* ovens and similar traditional cooking facilities have proved dispensible. Gas is best for Chinese food, though it is also possible on an electric cooker, particularly with the new teflon-lined flat-bottomed *woks* being produced for the Western market. Grillers, barbecues (even electric ones), ovens and electric ranges are far easier to use than slow and messy charcoal fires.

Many of the exciting new tastes of Asia will be loved at the first mouthful; others, like the bland *dofu* (soft beancurd cake) used in Chinese and other cooking, may be an acquired taste, though one well worth acquiring. For the few ingredients that are difficult to obtain, information on substitutes and alternatives is provided in the comprehensive glossary, which also explains the many new ingredients you will encounter in these pages.

CONTENTS

Peking Duck (frontispiece, recipe page 156). Two Indian dishes: Prawns in Green Masala, and Prawn and Green Mango Curry (recipes page 17).

USEFUL INFORMATION

A FEW WORDS ON COOKING RICE

There are probably as many different ways of cooking rice in the Far East as there are types of grain. Chinese like their rice reasonably dry, short-grained, and would *never* cook it with salt. The Japanese and Koreans prefer it a little more moist, but still short-grained and saltless. Rice to be eaten with chopsticks should not separate easily but stick together enough to be manageable. Laotians prefer theirs fairly sticky, and work it into small balls to be eaten like bread. Their cooking method, too, varies from that used anywhere else in the Far East — prolonged steaming of soaked grain in bamboo baskets over low heat, usually requiring overnight soaking and around eight hours of cooking.

For *pillau* and *biriyani* long-grained rices are ideal. They have superb flavour (particularly the more expensive Basmati rice from India), and cook dry and separate. Salt is never omitted from an Indian rice dish, and the Burmese and Sri Lankans also prefer their rice well seasoned.

The two most commonly used rice-cooking methods are absorption, in which the rice is cooked with a carefully calculated amount of water that is completely absorbed into the grains, leaving them just moist enough to stick together; and (quite different from absorption) cooking in a large volume of water, which is drained off when the rice is done.

To cook rice by the absorption method, choose a heavy-based metal pan or a glazed clay pot. For long-grain rice, allow just under 2 cups of water for the first cup of rice, then 1 cup of water for every additional cup of rice; for short-grain rice, allow 1½ cups of water for the first cup of rice, and 1 cup of water for every additional cup of rice. Measure the rice into the pan or pot (the rice can be washed or not according to your preference), add the required amount of water, and bring to the boil. When bubbling, cover, reduce heat to the lowest point, and leave to steam gently until the rice is tender and quite dry (about 18 minutes).

To cook rice by the other method, put plenty of slightly salted water into a large saucepan with about 2 teaspoons of oil or butter (added to prevent the water boiling over and to keep the grains from sticking together). When the water is bubbling briskly, pour in washed rice and cook at moderately high temperature until the grains are cooked through. To test, squeeze a single grain between finger and thumb; if it is still slightly hard continue cooking, but do not cook until the rice is squashy. Drain well through a strainer, then rinse with boiling water and place the strainer over the saucepan, add a little water, cover, then leave on low heat for about 10 minutes to dry out. Stir occasionally with a chopstick.

Rice is often fried before cooking to give extra colour and flavour. It is preferable to wash it beforehand and to dry thoroughly by spreading on a tray and leaving in the sun. Fry until well oiled and lightly coloured, then add the liquid.

GUIDE TO WEIGHTS & MEASURES

A special note to North American readers

Lists of ingredients in this book have been designed to cater for cooks using either American Standard measures or metric measures, as can be seen from the following example:

> 1.5 kg (3 lb) chicken
> 3 cups water
> 2 large onions
> 5 tablespoons flour
> ½ cup milk

This listing can be read in two ways:

American	Metric
3 lb chicken	1.5 kilogram chicken
3 American cups water	3 metric cups water
2 large onions	2 large onions
5 American tablespoons flour	5 metric tablespoons flour
½ American cup milk	½ metric cup milk

It must be stressed that the quantities given in the American and metric ingredients listings are in proportion, but they are *not* exact conversions — the metric yield is approximately 10% greater than the equivalent American Standard yield. Therefore, to use this book successfully, follow American Standard quantities *or* follow metric equivalent, but do *not* use a mixture of the two.

The metric measuring cup specified in this book has a capacity of 250 millilitres (250 ml). Clearly graduated metric measuring cups and jugs can therefore be used for all liquid and dry cup quantities given in the recipes. Note that:

¼ metric cup	=	60 ml	
½ metric cup	=	125 ml	
¾ metric cup	=	185 ml	
1 metric cup	=	250 ml	= ¼ litre
2 metric cups	=	500 ml	= ½ litre
3 metric cups	=	750 ml	= ¾ litre
4 metric cups	=	1,000 ml	= 1 litre

The American Standard teaspoon and tablespoon can be used for measuring metric quantities. The American teaspoon has exactly the same capacity as the metric teaspoon specified in this book:

> 1 metric teaspoon = 5 ml = 1 American teaspoon

The American tablespoon is fractionally smaller than the metric tablespoon specified in this book. Therefore, use an American tablespoon *plus* one teaspoon for metric quantities.

MEASURES USED IN THIS BOOK

The metric weights and metric fluid measures used throughout this book refer to those of The Standards Association of Australia (AS 1325 1972). A good set of scales, a graduated Australian Standard measuring cup and a set of Australian Standard measuring spoons will be most helpful. These are available at leading hardware and kitchenware stores.
• The Australian Standard measuring cup has a capacity of 250 millilitres (250 ml).
• The Australian Standard tablespoon has a capacity of 20 millilitres (20 ml).
• The Australian Standard teaspoon has a capacity of 5 millilitres (5 ml).

New Zealand, Canadian and American weights and measures are the same except that the Australian Standard measuring tablespoon has a capacity of 20 millilitres (20 ml), whereas the New Zealand, Canadian and American Standard measuring tablespoons have a capacity of 15 millilitres (15 ml).

All spoon measurements given in this book are level spoonfuls.

Weight, volume and liquid measures

In all recipes, imperial equivalents of metric measures are shown in parentheses, e.g. 500 g (1 lb) lean beef. Although the metric yield of cup or weighed measures is approximately 10% greater, the proportions remain the same. For successful cooking use either metric weights and measures *or* imperial weights and measures — do *not* use a mixture of the two.

The following tables are extracted from conversion equivalents adopted by the Cookery Sector Committee of the Metric Conversion Board (Australia).

IMPERIAL			METRIC	
Liquid Measures	Cup Measures		Cup Measures	Liquid Measures
1 fl oz		is replaced by		30 ml
2 fl oz	¼ cup	,,	¼ cup	
	⅓ cup	,,	⅓ cup	
3 fl oz		,,		100 ml
4 fl oz (¼ pint US)	½ cup	,,	½ cup	125 ml
5 fl oz (¼ pint imp.)		,,		150 ml
6 fl oz	¾ cup	,,	¾ cup	185 ml
8 fl oz (½ pint US)	1 cup	,,	1 cup	250 ml
10 fl oz (½ pint imp.)	1¼ cups	,,	1¼ cups	
12 fl oz	1½ cups	,,	1½ cups	
14 fl oz	1¾ cups	,,	1¾ cups	
16 fl oz (1 pint US)	2 cups	,,	2 cups	500 ml
20 fl oz (1 pint imp.)	2½ cups	,,	2½ cups	

Mass (Weight)		Mass (Weight)
½ oz	is replaced by	15 grams (g)
1 oz	,,	30 g
2 oz	,,	60 g
3 oz	,,	90 g
4 oz (¼ lb)	,,	125 g
6 oz	,,	185 g
8 oz (½ lb)	,,	250 g
12 oz (¾ lb)	,,	375 g
16 oz (1 lb)	,,	500 g (0.5 kg)
24 oz (1½ lb)	,,	750 g
32 oz (2 lb)	,,	1000 g (1 kg)
3 lb	,,	1500 g (1.5 kg)
4 lb	,,	2000 g (2 kg)

INDIA

My good friend Mrs Daljit Singh introduced me to Indian cooking in 1970, shortly after my arrival in Hongkong. Daljit gives regular classes in Punjabi home cooking and has become something of an institution in expatriate circles. Her menus appear on tables all over Hongkong, and it is not unusual to hear men and women from various social backgrounds discussing their progress with her classes. To me these first lessons proved invaluable, for my growing interest in Indian cooking also encouraged my interest in other regional cuisines. But back to Indian food — and, of course, curry.

During the eighteenth century the British in India took a liking to curry (a word derived from the Tamil *kari,* which simply means 'sauce), and many of them returned home with recipes for making their own versions of India's chutneys, pickles and the many spice mixtures on which curries are based. These recipes were further modified by cooks catering for the less adventurous palates of those who had never been to India or the Far East, until the 'curry' that became part of the bland British culinary tradition was but a pallid relative of the original. Often made with poor grade or leftover meats, a few spoonfuls of insipid commercial curry powder, chopped apple and dried raisins, this poor cousin was nevertheless eagerly adopted by Western cooks and for many years remained the accepted 'curry' fare in Western homes. Only recently have discriminating cooks dared to refute the fallacies that a *real* curry cannot be made by anyone but an Indian, and that the best curries can only be found in India.

The art of curry making has two main principles: spice mixture and cooking method. An Indian cook would never use a commercial curry powder as we know it, but blends a mixture of fresh dried spices to suit each dish, heats them to bring out the full flavour, and grinds them to a powder just before using. The spices are then fried, releasing their heavenly aromas to penetrate deep into the main ingredients and the sauce. *Garam masala,* a mixture of at least six common dried spices, but which can be made up of many, many more, is the nearest thing in India to curry powder. It is used with other spices selected to produce a particular flavour that best enhances the ingredients, or it may be sprinkled over a finished dish as we might add salt and pepper. Fresh curry pastes and specific blends of dried spices for popular national dishes are also sold in India.

But curries do not constitute the entire Indian cuisine. There are masses of delicious dry spiced vegetable and meat dishes; poultry and mutton roasted in an enclosed pan over a slow fire (a method known as *dum*); a host of different kinds of breads, rice and lentil dishes; and the endless variations that make the vegetarian cuisine the diet of more than half of India's population.

To travel through India from north to south is to discover the vast diversity of Indian cooking. More than four hundred years ago the Mogul emperors brought to the mountainous north the richness and lavish presentation of Persian culinary traditions, blending meats (most often lamb and poultry) with dried fruits and nuts in sweet creamy sauces flavoured with rose and lime essences and decorated with gossamer-thin sheets of beaten silver. Charcoal-grilled kebabs of finely ground mutton, exotic *biriyani* and *pillau* loaded with nuts, meats and spices, flat breads and dry roasted meats were all adopted. Today in Kashmir and the Punjab this Persian element is still evident in thick (but rarely hot) sauces seasoned with almost every known spice and enriched with cream and yoghurt, tantalising sweetmeats made with milk and sugar, the use of lamb and chicken, and plentiful kebab dishes. These are served with various griddle-cooked or deep fried breads of white wheat flour and wholemeal flour, seasoned rice dishes or plain boiled rice. *Tandoor*-cooked poultry, seafood and breads are important here. White spongey *naan* is slapped damp onto the hot clay walls of the *tandoor* oven to bake, and is then prised off with a metal hook to be served piping hot. Whole small chickens, sausage-shaped kebabs of minced lamb, and whole flat fish are marinated in a selection of fragrant spices and tenderisers, dyed bright orange-yellow with a powdered food colouring, and threaded onto metal skewers suspended in white-hot *tandoor* ovens over a bed of glowing charcoal to roast until dry and crisp on the surface, tender and succulent inside.

Centuries ago the Parsis of Iran brought to western central India their own cooking ideas. Many of their traditional dishes, like Dhansak (Mutton and Lentil Stew) and the subtly seasoned scrambled-egg dish Akuri, are still popular today. Here too the Portuguese Indians of Goa developed their own cooking style and regional dishes. To the east, Bengali cooks have yet another set of ideals based on the pungent mustard oil they use in much of the cooking, and on an abundance of seafood from the bountiful Bay of Bengal.

Farther south the Arabian Sea coastline of Kerala is lined with coconut groves heavy with fruit. The creamy milk blends with aromatic herbs to make smooth, slightly sweet curries with seafood and vegetables. Across the southern regions of India vegetarianism predominates. Dishes are stingingly hot with an abundance of fresh chillies, aromatic with fresh herbs, lemon grass, fresh coriander, garlic and onions, and flavoured with such spices as fenugreek, cummin and small brownish-black mustard seeds. A popular soup accompanying many such dishes is the watery but fiery Rasam from which the British derived their beloved Mulligatawny Soup, named from the Tamil *mooloogoo* (pepper) and *thani* (water). Coconut milk and grated coconut find their way into many dishes, including the popular fresh coconut chutney. Boiled white rice is the staple, and even the breads are made from rice flour: Dosa, an enormous pancake of ground rice flour and lentils, is fried crisp and served with fresh chutneys and *sambar,* a spicy, watery sauce; and Iddly, small round cakes of steamed rice and lentil batter cooked over a steamer in a special pot with shallow indentations. Vaday, similar to a doughnut, is made with ground len-

Shrimp Rice (recipe page 35), Spiced Chickpeas (recipe page 38), and Dhal Special (recipe page 37).

tils. Small fried wholewheat breads or Puri, often served in the Punjab, are also made here and are served with a spiced potato filling.

Vegetarian meals are usually served on a *thali*, a circular metal tray holding several small dishes filled with an assortment of watery curries (at least one of which will be made with lentils), a dish of yoghurt and a mound of boiled white rice, often with crisply fried lentil wafers (Poppadam) at the side. The food is eaten with the fingers. Rice is scooped into a ball and mingled with as much curry sauce as possible.

The 'sacred cow' remains so in India. Its flesh is never eaten, but its milk is always on the table in the form of rich, buttery sweets, creamy sauces, home-made cheeses cooked in spicy curries, and yoghurt. The Indians have a high regard for the nutritional and digestive values of plain yoghurt and serve a dish with almost every meal, make it into Lassi (whipped yoghurt drinks, which come sweet or salted), and use it to thicken and enrich sauces and to tenderise meats. Milk products add yet more protein and flavour to protein-rich northern cooking, and compensate for the lack of meat protein in the vegetarian diet.

Cooking in India is done mostly in a deep-sided metal pot or *degchi* with a flat lid on which coals can be heaped for *dum* cooking. Earthenware pots or heavy-based metal cooking pots can be used for curry cooking. Sweets made with reduced milk are prepared in a *karahi* (similar to a Chinese *wok*), which is also used for deep frying. Breads are cooked on a very slightly curved iron griddle or *tawa*, for which a heavy-based frying pan is a suitable substitute. The clay oven or *tandoor* used for *tandoori* cooking has no equal in the Western domestic kitchen, so recipes for these dishes have been tested in a normal range oven, with the assistance of the grill and a charcoal barbecue.

Indian food is eaten with the fingers, using bread and rice, or with a spoon and fork; knives are rarely necessary. Plain dinner plates or shallow bowls are used, and the main dishes are served in separate bowls, never on a bed of rice. Rice and bread are handed around and the extra portions kept warm in covered pots near the table. A selection of side dishes including fried or roasted Poppadam, fried Bombay Duck, pickles and preserved or fresh chutneys, can be served in small bowls. Tepid water (rather than iced, which increases the tingle of hot foods in the mouth) is the common beverage with a meal, and other drinks include sweet or salt Lassi, milky Falooda, plain fresh milk or coconut milk, all of which work wonders on a curry-seared mouth and calm the digestive system after a highly seasoned meal.

MILK PRODUCTS

Milk and its derivatives are used extensively throughout India to add richness and protein to the diet. Several types of preparation are employed, resulting in such products as mild cottage cheese *(paneer)*, a reduced cream used mainly as an enricher *(khoya)* and another more crumbly type of cream used primarily in the making of sweetmeats *(malai)*. Milk is also extensively consumed in the form of curds or yoghurt *(dahi)*. Clarified butter *(ghee)* is the principle cooking me-

dium, although in some regions oil is preferred. *Ghee*, which gives a subtle nutty flavour and rich taste to both sweet and savoury dishes, can be purchased in tins.

The preparation of *khoya* and *malai* involves time-consuming reduction of whole fresh milk. Thick or clotted cream can be used as a substitute for *malai*, unless otherwise specified in a recipe, while a thick mixture of full cream milk powder and water can be used instead of *khoya*. The following methods may be used for preparing *paneer*, *khoya* and *malai*.

Paneer: Prepare plain yoghurt, or use commercial unflavoured yoghurt. Pour into a muslin bag and suspend over a drip tray for at least 3½ hours until all the liquid has drained off. Pour the thick curds into a square tin and press a board or plate on top, weighted sufficiently to compress the curds. Leave overnight to harden.

Khoya: Pour fresh milk into a saucepan, bring to the boil, then reduce heat and simmer until all the water has evaporated leaving a thick cream; 2½ cups of milk makes about 90 g (3 oz) *khoya*. A substitute can be made by mixing full cream powdered milk with just enough water to make a dry paste. This should be lightly fried in *ghee* before using to remove the rather raw taste.

Malai: Pour milk into a wide saucepan and bring to a brisk boil. Turn heat down slightly and boil until a skin forms. Remove this with a slotted spoon and set aside. Keep repeating this procedure until all the cream has been removed. Drain it well and crumble; 2½ cups of milk produces about 60 g (2 oz) *malai*.

SPICES

With the exception of a few freshly made curry pastes purchased from local markets, few Indian cooks would consider using commercial curry powders or pastes in their cooking. Instead, each household is equipped with a spice grinder, either an electric appliance or the time honoured 'curry stone', a granite grinding stone and pestle. Whole fresh spices are ground just before using for maximum freshness. The most commonly used spice blend is garam masala, *which is used in conjunction with other spices, or is used as a condiment and sprinkled on a cooked dish.* Chat masala *is a tart flavoured spice combination particularly good with vegetable dishes. Recipes for these two spice mixes are given below. They may be made in quantity and keep well in an airtight container.*

GARAM MASALA

60 g (2 oz) black peppercorns
60 g (2 oz) cummin seeds
60 g (2 oz) coriander seeds
25 large black cardamoms, peeled
15 g (½ oz) cloves
15 g (½ oz) ground cinnamon

Blend these to a fairly fine powder and pour into a jar with a tight fitting lid. The spice mixture will be even more fragrant if the peppercorns, cummin and coriander are lightly toasted under the griller before grinding.

CHAT MASALA

30 g (1 oz) cummin seeds
1 tablespoon salt
pinch of asafoetida
3 teaspoons chilli powder
2 tablespoons dried green mango powder *(amchur)*
1 tablespoon crushed dried mint
2 teaspoons dried ginger powder

Lightly toast cummin with salt and asafoetida. Grind all ingredients to a fine powder and pour into a jar with a tight fitting lid.

FRIED VEGETABLE DUMPLINGS

PAKORA

2 large potatoes
2 medium onions
5 spring onions
1 green chilli
1 medium eggplant, or 185 g (6 oz) spinach or cabbage
2 tomatoes
185 g (6 oz) gram flour *(besan)*
2 tablespoons self-raising flour
2 teaspoons salt
2 teaspoons *garam masala*
3 cm (1¼ inch) piece fresh ginger, minced
oil for deep frying

Peel potato, parboil and cut into very small dice. Finely chop onions, spring onions, chilli, eggplant, spinach or cabbage, and tomatoes. Mix with gram flour, self-raising flour, salt, *garam masala* and ginger. Mix to a smooth batter, adding just enough water to make it dropping consistency. Heat oil for deep frying and drop walnut-sized pieces of the batter into the oil and cook to a deep golden brown.

Drain well, then serve with mint chutney.

CRISP VEGETABLE SNACKS

SAMOOSA

frozen spring roll wrappers
2 large potatoes, boiled
60 g (2 oz) cauliflower, finely chopped
90 g (3 oz) frozen peas
2 tablespoons finely chopped fresh coriander leaves
2.5 cm (1 inch) piece fresh ginger, minced
1 small onion, minced
3 cloves garlic, minced
1 teaspoon chilli powder
½ teaspoon turmeric powder
2½ teaspoons *garam masala*
salt
black pepper
2 teaspoons lemon juice
oil for deep frying

Thaw wrappers and wrap in a damp cloth until needed. Dice cooked potato finely and put into a basin. Drop chopped cauliflower and peas into a bowl of boiling water and leave aside for 5 minutes. Drain well. Mix cauliflower and peas with potatoes and all remaining ingredients except oil and wrappers.

Cut spring roll wrappers into 4 cm (1½ inch) strips and fold one end over diagonally to make a triangular-shaped pocket. Fill with a spoonful of the mixture. Fold the whole strip over and over to finish with a triangular-shaped cake. Stick end down with a little water or prepare a starch with cornflour and boiling water and use this to glue the flaps.

Heat oil and deep fry Samoosa until golden. Drain and serve with coriander or mint chutney.

FRIED MEAT SNACKS

MEAT SAMOOSA

frozen spring roll wrappers
250 g (½ lb) minced beef or mutton
¼ cup water
1 clove garlic, minced
1 small onion, minced
1 cm (½ inch) piece fresh ginger, minced
2 teaspoons *garam masala*
1 teaspoon chilli powder
1 teaspoon black mustard seeds
½ teaspoon turmeric powder
salt
black pepper
1 heaped tablespoon chopped fresh coriander leaves
2 tablespoons frozen peas (optional)
2 teaspoons lemon juice
2 tablespoons *ghee*
oil for deep frying

Thaw wrappers and wrap in a damp cloth until needed. Cook minced meat in water until the liquid has completely dried up. Fry minced garlic and onion in *ghee* for 3 minutes. Add ginger, meat and *garam masala* and fry for a further 3 minutes. Add remaining ingredients and heat through thoroughly. Leave to cool.

Cut spring roll wrappers into 4 cm (1½ inch) strips and fold one end over diagonally to make a triangular-shaped pocket. Fill with the mixture and continue folding in this triangular shape until all folded. Stick the end down with a little water or prepare a starch with cornflour and boiling water and use to glue the flaps.

Heat oil and deep fry Samoosa until golden. Drain and serve hot with mint chutney.

SCRAMBLED EGGS PARSI STYLE

AKURI

6 large eggs
salt
black pepper
pinch of turmeric powder
3 tablespoons *ghee*
1 large onion
1 green chilli
3 tablespoons fresh coriander leaves
1 fresh red chilli, thinly sliced

Beat eggs lightly with salt, pepper and turmeric pow-

der. Mince or finely chop onion, chilli and coriander. Heat *ghee* in a frying pan and add chopped ingredients to the pan. Fry for 3 minutes on moderate heat, then reduce heat slightly and pour in beaten egg.

Cook, stirring frequently, until egg is just set. Check seasoning. Garnish with thinly sliced chilli and serve with fresh buttered toast.

COLD LENTIL CAKES IN YOGHURT SAUCE

250 g (½ lb) yellow lentils, soaked overnight
1 medium onion
2 teaspoons salt
2 teaspoons *garam masala*
½ teaspoon chilli powder
2 teaspoons baking powder
pinch of asafoetida (optional)
ghee or oil for deep frying
2½ cups plain yoghurt
1 tablespoon thick cream (optional)
salt
pepper
sugar
2 teaspoons finely chopped mint

Rinse lentils and drain well. Put into a heavy duty grinder and grind to a smooth paste. It may be necessary to add a little water to prevent machine clogging. Mince onion and add to the lentil paste with salt, *garam masala*, chilli powder, baking powder and asafoetida (if used). Mix thoroughly, then form the paste into walnut sized balls using wet or greased hands. If needed add a little plain flour or gram flour *(besan)* to bind.

Heat oil and drop in several balls at a time. Deep fry to a light golden brown. Lift out and drain thoroughly. Fry a second time for about 2 minutes on moderate heat and drain well.

Whip yoghurt with cream (if used) and season with salt, pepper and sugar to taste. Place lentil cakes in a serving dish and pour on the yoghurt sauce. Garnish with chopped mint. Chill slightly, leaving for at least 1 hour before serving to allow lentil cakes to soften.

MULLIGATAWNY SOUP

The origin of Mulligatawny soup was the thin and fiery pepper water, mooloogoothani, *which accompanies most south Indian meals. Under British influence it evolved into this richer, thicker soup containing coconut milk and diced meat.*

250 g (½ lb) chicken
5 cups chicken stock
1 large onion
3 cloves garlic
2 fresh red chillies, thinly sliced
2 tablespoons *ghee*
1 tablespoon coriander, ground
¼ teaspoon fenugreek, crushed
1 teaspoon cummin, ground
1 teaspoon turmeric powder
1 bay leaf

2.5 cm (1 inch) stick cinnamon
2 black cardamoms
2 cloves
salt
pepper
¾ cup thick coconut milk

Place chicken and stock in a large saucepan with sliced onion. Bring to the boil and simmer for 30 minutes. Mash garlic and chillies and fry in *ghee* for 2 minutes. Add all remaining spices and fry for 2 minutes. Add to the pot and continue cooking until chicken is tender.

Lift out chicken and cut into small dice. Return to the soup. Season to taste and stir in thick coconut milk. Heat through.

MASALA STUFFED FISH

1 whole flat fish weighing 625 g (1¼ lb) (John Dory, pomfret or turbot)
3 green chillies
60 g (2 oz) desiccated coconut
1 cm (½ inch) piece fresh ginger
3 cloves garlic
2 teaspoons lemon juice
¼ teaspoon fennel seeds, lightly crushed
1 teaspoon salt
pinch of white pepper
½ teaspoon chilli powder
1 tablespoon chopped fresh coriander leaves
6 shallots
oil for shallow frying
tomato and lemon wedges
onion slices or rings

Clean fish and trim fins. Carefully cut away backbone working through the stomach opening.

Grind all seasoning ingredients including coriander leaves and shallots to a paste and stuff into the fish. Sew up carefully or secure opening with toothpicks.

Heat oil and fry fish on both sides to a golden brown. Turn once only. Lift onto a serving plate and garnish with tomato and lemon wedges and onion.

BAKED FISH WITH CREAMED TOMATO SAUCE

750 g (1½ lb) snapper, bream or other meaty fish
3 tablespoons *ghee*
1¼ teaspoons fenugreek, ground
4 cloves garlic, crushed
2.5 cm (1 inch) piece fresh ginger, minced
1 tablespoon coriander, ground
2 teaspoons cummin, ground
1½ teaspoons chilli powder
¾ teaspoon turmeric powder
6 medium tomatoes, peeled
¾ cup water or fish stock
½ cup thick cream
¼ cup plain yoghurt
salt
black pepper
lemon juice

Baked Fish with Creamed Tomato Sauce (recipe this page).

Clean fish, remove scales and clip fins. Wipe dry.

Heat *ghee* in a small saucepan. Fry fenugreek, garlic and ginger in the *ghee* for 3 minutes, then add coriander, cummin, chilli and turmeric. Fry for 2 minutes, stirring frequently.

Chop tomatoes finely and add to the pan with water or stock. Cover and simmer until sauce is thick and creamy. Add cream and yoghurt and season to taste with salt and black pepper. Keep warm.

Sprinkle fish with salt, pepper and lemon juice and place in a lightly oiled oven-proof dish. Cover with a piece of foil and bake in a moderately hot oven for 15 minutes. Remove foil and cook for a further 5 minutes. Remove from the oven. Pour on hot sauce and return to the oven for 5 minutes before serving.

FISH KEBABS

500 g (1 lb) meaty white fish
1 cm (½ inch) piece fresh ginger, minced
2 tablespoons boiling water
¾ cup plain yoghurt
1 teaspoon fennel seeds, crushed
1 teaspoon cummin, ground
¼ teaspoon black pepper
1½ teaspoons chilli powder
pinch of ground cloves
2 curry leaves (optional)
1 teaspoon salt
1 large onion
1 green pepper
2 limes
lime or lemon juice
dry green mango powder *(amchur)*
ghee

Cut fish into 2 cm (¾ inch) cubes. Pour boiling water over ginger and leave for 10 minutes, then strain liquid over fish. Leave for 20 minutes. Mix yoghurt with fennel, cummin, pepper, chilli powder, clove powder, crumbled curry leaves (if used) and salt and rub into the fish pieces. Marinate for 2 hours.

Cut onion into thin slices and pull into rings. Cut pepper into thin circles. Cut lemons into wedges and place with onion and pepper on a serving plate. Thread fish onto skewers and brush with a little melted *ghee*. Roast over a charcoal fire or under the griller until cooked through but do not overcook. Sprinkle with dried mango powder and place on the plate with onion, pepper and limes. Serve hot.

GOAN CURRIED FISH

750 g (1½ lb) white fish fillets
1 tablespoon lemon juice
5 dried chillies, soaked
1 teaspoon cummin seeds
3 teaspoons coriander seeds
60 g (2 oz) grated fresh or desiccated coconut
6 cloves garlic
1 small onion

2 medium onions
3 cm (1¼ inch) piece fresh ginger
4 tablespoons *ghee* or 3 tablespoons coconut oil
¾ teaspoon turmeric powder
2 green chillies, thinly sliced
1 tablespoon finely chopped fresh coriander leaves
1½ tablespoons tamarind
1½ cups water
salt
sugar to taste

Cut fish into 5 cm (2 inch) pieces and sprinkle with lemon juice.

Grind ingredients from chillies to small onion to a paste. Thinly slice medium onions and shred ginger. Fry in *ghee* or oil for 4 minutes, then put in spicy coconut paste and fry for 2 minutes. Add turmeric, sliced chillies and chopped coriander. Infuse tamarind in water, strain and add to pan. Bring to the boil, reduce heat and simmer for 15 minutes.

Add sliced fish and cook gently for about 6 minutes. Season to taste with salt and sugar. Serve at once.

FISH IN COCONUT SAUCE

625 g (1¼ lb) thin fillets of white fish
2 large onions
2 green chillies
2.5 cm (1 inch) piece fresh ginger
4 cm (1½ inch) stalk lemon grass
3 cloves garlic
2 teaspoons dried shrimps, soaked
45 g (1½ oz) desiccated coconut
1 cup thick coconut milk
2 tablespoons coconut oil or vegetable oil
2 heaped tablespoons finely chopped fresh coriander leaves
1 cup thin coconut milk
lemon juice or tamarind water
salt

Cut fish fillets into 5 cm (2 inch) squares and place in a dish. Thinly slice one onion and set aside. Mince ginger, lemon grass, garlic, dried shrimps and desiccated coconut to a fairly smooth paste and add thick coconut milk. Pour over the fish and marinate for 1 hour.

Heat oil and fry sliced onion until lightly coloured. Add fish pieces and cook briefly, then pour on thin coconut with coriander and marinade. Cover and simmer on low heat until fish is cooked. Lift out fish with a slotted spoon and place on a serving dish.

Continue to simmer sauce until thick and creamy. Season to taste with lemon juice or tamarind water and add salt. Pour over the fish and serve at once.

CRAB KORMA

4 medium raw crabs
30 g (1 oz) desiccated coconut
2 teaspoons cummin
1½ tablespoons coriander

1 teaspoon fennel
pinch of powdered cinnamon
1 teaspoon turmeric
1 tablespoon white poppy seeds
3 cloves garlic
5 dried chillies, soaked
1 cm (½ inch) piece fresh ginger
1 small onion
¾ cup plain yoghurt
2 tablespoons *ghee* or coconut oil
4 cloves
1 teaspoon black peppercorns, lightly crushed
4 black cardamoms, lightly crushed
2.5 cm (1 inch) stick cinnamon
1¼ cups water
salt
lemon juice
chopped fresh coriander leaves

Wash crabs and chop into large pieces. Crack claws. Grind desiccated coconut, cummin, coriander, fennel, cinnamon, turmeric and poppy seeds to a powder. Grind garlic, chillies, ginger and onion to a paste. Mix spice powder and onion paste with yoghurt.

Heat *ghee* and fry cloves, peppercorns, cardamoms and cinnamon stick for 1 minute. Add crabs and cook, turning frequently, for 2 minutes. Add seasoning paste and cook, stirring, until the seasonings are dried up and clinging to the crab. Pour in water and simmer until crabs are cooked.

Lift out crab and place on a serving dish. Continue to simmer sauce until well reduced. Season to taste with salt and lemon juice and stir in coriander leaves. Pour over the crab and serve.

PRAWN AND GREEN MANGO CURRY

375 g (¾ lb) raw peeled prawns
2 large green mangoes
45 g (1½ oz) freshly grated or desiccated coconut
3 teaspoons coriander, ground
½ teaspoon chilli powder
6 dried chillies, soaked
2 tablespoons water
2 medium onions
3 tablespoons *ghee,* or 2 tablespoons coconut oil
2 curry leaves
2 cups water
¾ teaspoon turmeric powder
salt
fresh coriander leaves
⅓ cup thick coconut milk (optional)

Rinse prawns and remove dark veins, if any. Peel and slice mangoes. Grind coconut, coriander, chilli powder and chillies to a paste, adding water.

Thinly slice onions. Fry onions in *ghee* or coconut oil for 2 minutes, then add curry leaves and the coconut paste. Continue to fry until oil begins to rise to the surface. Add the prawns and mango, water, turmeric and salt and simmer on moderately low heat until cooked.

Garnish with fresh coriander leaves. For a thicker curry, stir in coconut milk and heat through.

PRAWNS IN GREEN MASALA

750 g (1½ lb) raw prawns, in shells
2 medium onions
2 cloves garlic
2.5 cm (1 inch) piece fresh ginger
1 teaspoon fennel
½ teaspoon cummin
2 green chillies
5 tablespoons chopped fresh coriander leaves
1 teaspoon salt
2 tablespoons *ghee* or coconut oil
¾ cup water

Peel prawns, leaving heads and tails on. Slice one onion thinly and make a seasoning paste by grinding remaining onion with all other ingredients except *ghee* or oil.

Fry sliced onion in *ghee* or oil until soft, then add seasoning paste and fry for 4 minutes. Add water and simmer until sauce is thick and smooth. Put in prawns and cook for about 5 minutes, or until tender. Do not overcook. Check seasonings and serve at once.

Thinly sliced fish fillets may also be cooked in this sauce.

YOGHURT CHICKEN

DAHI MURGH

1.5 kg (3 lb) chicken
1 teaspoon turmeric
1 tablespoon coriander, ground
1 teaspoon cummin
1½ teaspoons chilli powder
½ teaspoon fenugreek seeds, ground
1 large onion, minced
2 cloves garlic, minced
2.5 cm (1 inch) piece fresh ginger, minced
1½ cups plain yoghurt
4 tablespoons *ghee*
1 large onion
3 cloves garlic
3 black cardamoms, peeled
3 cloves
2.5 cm (1 inch) stick cinnamon
salt
black pepper
lemon juice
fresh coriander leaves or mint, chopped

Wipe chicken and cut into large pieces. Place in a bowl and rub with turmeric. Make a paste with spices, onions, garlic and ginger. Mix with the yoghurt, pour over the chicken and leave to marinate for 2 hours. Turn several times.

Heat *ghee* and fry sliced onion and garlic until soft. Add cardamoms, cloves and cinnamon stick. Add marinated chicken and cook until well coloured. Add any remaining marinade and enough water to just cover the chicken. Cover and simmer until tender. Season to taste with salt, pepper and lemon juice.

Garnish with fresh coriander or mint.

CHICKEN CURRY

1 kg (2 lb) chicken pieces
2 large onions
5 cloves garlic
2.5 cm (1 inch) piece fresh ginger
3 tablespoons *ghee*
2 black cardamoms
4 cloves
5 cm (2 inch) stick cinnamon
2 bay leaves
2 blades mace
1 tablespoon coriander, ground
1 teaspoon cummin, ground
¾ teaspoon turmeric powder
½ teaspoon chilli powder
water or light chicken stock
salt
black pepper
1 teaspoon *garam masala*
2 tablespoons finely chopped fresh coriander leaves
lemon juice

Cut chicken pieces into 5 cm (2 inch) cubes. Thinly slice onions and garlic and shred ginger. Heat *ghee* and fry onions until soft. Add garlic and ginger and cook for 1 minute, then put in chicken pieces and fry until well coloured.

Add all the spices and stir on moderate heat for 5 minutes. Add enough water or light chicken stock to just cover. Bring to the boil and simmer until chicken is very tender and liquid almost evaporated. Add salt and pepper to taste and pour in more water or chicken stock to just cover. Simmer for a further 20 minutes, then sprinkle in *garam masala*, coriander leaves and add lemon juice to taste.

CHICKEN IN WHITE CURRY

MURGH MUSSALAM

1.5 kg (3 lb) chicken
salt
black pepper
2 tablespoons *ghee*
1 large onion, minced
4 cloves garlic, crushed
2.5 cm (1 inch) piece fresh ginger, minced
1 tablespoon coriander, ground
3 cloves, crushed
1 teaspoon black peppercorns, crushed
2 teaspoons cummin, ground
2 bay leaves
60 g (2 oz) white poppy seeds, soaked overnight
2 cups water
½ cup thick cream
chilli powder
1 tablespoon finely chopped fresh coriander leaves

Clean chicken and wipe dry. Cut into large pieces and rub with salt and pepper. Melt *ghee* in a heavy pan and fry onion and garlic for 3 minutes on moderate heat. Add ginger and spices and fry for a further 3 minutes.

Put in chicken and cook until well coloured. Add bay leaves.

Grind poppy seeds to a smooth paste. Add ½ cup water to the pot and simmer until dried up, then add remaining water and poppy seeds and simmer until the sauce is thick and creamy and chicken tender. Stir in thick cream and add salt, pepper and chilli powder to taste.

Garnish with chopped coriander leaves.

CHICKEN KASHMIR

DUM MURGHI KASHMIR

This chicken is cooked in two stages: marinated and roasted, then rubbed with a spice paste and fried.

1.5 kg (3 lb) chicken
6 cloves garlic
2.5 cm (1 inch) piece fresh ginger
1 green chilli
1 tablespoon lemon juice
1 teaspoon *garam masala*
1 teaspoon chilli powder
½ teaspoon salt
¼ teaspoon turmeric powder
½ cup plain yoghurt
½ teaspoon sugar

Clean the chicken and wipe dry. Grind all ingredients except yoghurt and sugar to a paste, then stir in yoghurt and sugar. Rub over the chicken, inside and out. Leave for 2 hours to absorb the flavours. Roast in a moderate oven until almost cooked through, then remove from oven and leave to cool completely.

Curry paste:
1 large onion
4 cloves garlic
2.5 cm (1 inch) piece fresh ginger
6 cloves
1 teaspoon black peppercorns
2.5 cm (1 inch) stick cinnamon
1 heaped teaspoon fennel seeds
2 tablespoons coriander
6 black cardamoms
1 teaspoon cummin
45 g (1½ oz) ground almonds
1 teaspoon salt
¼ cup plain yoghurt
¼ teaspoon saffron powder
2 tablespoons boiling water
1 teaspoon *garam masala*
1 tablespoon finely chopped fresh coriander leaves
4 tablespoons *ghee*

Mince onion with garlic and ginger. Grind all spices to a fine powder and mix with onion paste. Add almonds, salt, yoghurt and saffron steeped in boiling water. Rub this mixture over the chicken.

Add *ghee* to the pan and cook chicken, basting frequently with *ghee* and the sauce, until chicken is done.

Sprinkle with *garam masala* and chopped coriander leaves before serving.

Chicken Kashmir (recipe this page).

TANDOORI CHICKEN

6 chicken thighs
1 small onion, grated
3 cloves garlic, minced
juice of 1 lemon
2 teaspoons salt
3 dried chillies
1 teaspoon turmeric powder
1 teaspoon fenugreek seeds, ground
3 teaspoons coriander
1½ teaspoons cummin
1½ teaspoons black mustard seeds
2 teaspoons chilli powder
½ teaspoon red colouring powder
¾ cup plain yoghurt
softened *ghee*
dried green mango powder *(amchur)*
lemon wedges
onion rings

Prick chicken thighs with a skewer and remove skin. Rub with a mixture of grated onion, garlic, lemon juice and salt. Leave for 20 minutes.

Grind chillies with remaining spices and mix with red colouring powder and yoghurt. Rub this mixture well into the chicken, cover and leave overnight.

Brush with *ghee* and bake in a moderately hot oven or under a moderate grill until cooked through. Brush with more *ghee* during cooking.

Sprinkle with mango powder and serve with lemon wedges and onion rings.

TIKKA CHICKEN

This recipe is a simplified version of Tandoori chicken.

750 g (1½ lb) chicken breasts
1 medium onion
3 cloves garlic
2.5 cm (1 inch) piece fresh ginger
¼ cup plain yoghurt
2 teaspoons white vinegar
2 teaspoons chilli powder
2 teaspoons coriander, ground
1 teaspoon cummin, ground
½ teaspoon turmeric powder
salt
lemon juice
garam masala
onion rings
lemon wedges
lettuce leaves

Cut chicken into 5 cm (2 inch) squares and press flat.

Grind onion, garlic and ginger to a paste and mix with yoghurt. Add vinegar and spices and rub well into the chicken. Leave for 3 hours to marinate.

Sprinkle with salt and thread onto skewers. Place under a hot grill or over a charcoal barbecue to cook until tender with crisp surface.

Sprinkle with lemon juice and *garam masala* and serve on a bed of lettuce leaves surrounded with onion rings and lemon wedges.

COCONUT CURRIED CHICKEN

1.5 kg (3 lb) chicken
salt
2 medium onions
1 clove garlic
1½ teaspoons chilli powder
2 tablespoons desiccated coconut, ground
1 teaspoon turmeric powder
4 cm (1½ inch) piece fresh ginger, shredded
1 tablespoon dried shrimps, soaked
10 cm (4 inch) stalk lemon grass, quartered
2 tablespoons coconut oil
2 cups thin coconut milk
6 small new potatoes
salt
lemon juice
fresh coriander leaves, finely chopped

Clean and wipe chicken and cut into large pieces. Season with salt. Grind onions and garlic to a paste and add chilli, coconut, turmeric and ginger. Grind dried shrimps and add to the seasoning with lemon grass. Heat oil and fry seasoning paste for 3 minutes, stirring constantly. Add chicken and cook until well coloured.

Pour on coconut milk, cover and simmer until chicken is tender. Peel potatoes, add to the curry and continue cooking until soft and the sauce has thickened. Add salt and lemon juice to taste and garnish with chopped coriander leaves.

CURRIED EGGS

8 large eggs
2 tablespoons *ghee*
5 shallots, thinly sliced
2 cloves garlic, crushed
1 green chilli, chopped
1 cm (½ inch) piece fresh ginger, shredded
2 teaspoons dried prawns, soaked and ground
½ teaspoon fennel seeds
1 teaspoon fenugreek seeds, lightly crushed
1 teaspoon turmeric powder
1½ cups thin coconut milk
½ cup thick coconut milk
lemon juice
salt
pepper
1 tablespoon finely chopped fresh coriander leaves

Place eggs in a pan of cold water and boil for 10 minutes. Run eggs under cold water, peel, cover with cold water and set aside. Heat *ghee* and fry shallots and garlic until soft. Add chilli, ginger, dried prawns, fennel and fenugreek and fry for 4 minutes, stirring frequently. Sprinkle on turmeric and add whole or halved boiled eggs. Turn to coat evenly with the seasonings, and fry for 3 minutes.

Pour on thin coconut milk and simmer for 10 minutes, then add thick coconut milk and season to taste with lemon juice, salt and pepper. Heat through and stir in chopped coriander.

EGG MASALA

6 large eggs
2 green chillies
1 cm (½ inch) piece fresh ginger
60 g (2 oz) desiccated coconut
2 teaspoons cummin
1 tablespoon coriander
1 large onion
2 tablespoons *ghee*
1 teaspoon black mustard seeds
1 teaspoon turmeric powder
2 large tomatoes, chopped
1 cup water
tamarind water or lemon juice
salt
pepper

Place eggs in a pan of cold water and boil for 10 minutes. Cover with cold water and set aside.

Grind chillies and ginger to a paste then grind with coconut, cummin and coriander. Thinly slice onion and fry in *ghee* until soft. Add seasoning paste and fry for 2 minutes. Sprinkle on mustard seeds and turmeric and add tomato and water. Bring to the boil and simmer for 10 minutes. Season to taste with tamarind water or lemon juice, salt and pepper.

Peel eggs and cut in halves, lengthways. Place in the masala and simmer for 3 minutes.

DHANSAK WITH BROWN RICE

This delicious lamb and lentil stew is the traditional Parsi Sunday meal. It is normally served with a rice dish made brown with fried onions, although side dishes of meat or prawn kebabs also accompany Dhansak for large elaborate dinners.

375 g (¾ lb) mixed lentils (black, yellow, red,
    chickpeas, etc)
750 g (1½ lb) lamb shoulder or leg
90 g (3 oz) pumpkin
125 g (¼ lb) spinach
1 large onion
3 tablespoons chopped fresh coriander leaves
2 teaspoons turmeric powder
2 teaspoons salt
4 dried chillies, soaked
2 teaspoons tamarind
3 tablespoons boiling water
2.5 cm (1 inch) piece fresh ginger
6 cloves garlic
2 green chillies
3 cloves
5 cm (2 inch) stick cinnamon
3 green cardamoms
1 teaspoon black mustard seeds
1 tablespoon ground coriander
2 teaspoons ground cummin
3 tablespoons chopped fresh coriander leaves
salt
pepper
1 large onion, finely chopped
3 tablespoons *ghee*

If using hard lentils like black or green lentils or chickpeas, soak overnight, then boil for 3 hours to soften. Place all lentils, well washed, into a saucepan and add meat cut into 1 cm (½ inch) dice. Cover with water to 8 cm (3 inches) above the level of the ingredients and bring to the boil. Simmer for at least 1 hour.

Peel and slice pumpkin, chop spinach and slice onion. Add pumpkin, spinach, coriander leaves, onion, turmeric and salt to the pan and cook until meat and lentils are tender. Remove meat and place in another pan. Mash lentils with vegetables or put in a blender to puree.

Grind seasonings (from dried chillies to green chillies) to a paste. Soak tamarind in water and add to paste together with cloves, cinnamon, cardamom and mustard seeds. Add ground coriander and cummin.

Heat *ghee* and fry seasonings for 4 minutes, then add fresh coriander, salt, pepper and finely chopped onion. Cook for a further 3 minutes, then put in lamb and cook until well coloured. Add lentil puree and adjust seasoning to taste. Heat through.

Keep warm while rice is prepared.

Brown Rice:
315 g (10 oz) long grain rice
2 large onions
2 tablespoons *ghee*
4 cloves
2 black cardamoms
5 cm (2 inch) stick cinnamon
salt
sugar
pepper

Wash rice and drain well. Chop onions finely and fry in *ghee* until very well coloured. They should be very dark brown, almost black. Add spices and rice and cover with water to 3 cm (1¼ inch) above the rice. Cover and bring to the boil. Simmer until cooked through. Season to taste with salt, pepper and sugar.

LAMB IN SPINACH PUREE

750 g (1½ lb) leg or shoulder of lamb
3 tablespoons *ghee*
3 cloves garlic, crushed
2.5 cm (1 inch) piece fresh ginger, grated
4 black cardamoms, crushed
1 tablespoon coriander, ground
½ green chilli, finely chopped
2 teaspoons black mustard seeds, ground
1 teaspoon turmeric powder
1½ cups water
2 teaspoons salt
750 g (1½ lb) fresh or frozen leaf spinach
pinch of freshly grated nutmeg
1½ teaspoons sugar
1 tablespoon white poppy seeds, ground
¼ cup plain yoghurt
salt
½ cup thick cream

Trim meat and cut into 4 cm (1½ inch) cubes. Heat *ghee* in a casserole or heavy saucepan and fry garlic for 2 minutes. Add ginger, crushed cardamoms, coriander, chilli and mustard seeds and fry on moderate heat for 2 minutes. Add meat and sprinkle on turmeric. Stir to coat meat thoroughly with the spices and cook for 5 minutes.

Pour on ½ cup water, cover pot and cook for 20 minutes. Add remaining water and salt and cook, covered, until lamb is tender and most of the liquid absorbed.

Drain frozen spinach, or wash and drain fresh spinach, discarding stems. Chop finely and put into a saucepan with nutmeg, sugar, poppy seeds and yoghurt. Cover and cook until tender. Add salt to taste and blend to a puree in a liquidiser. Add to the meat and heat through, stirring to mix the two sauces well. Add thick cream and reheat.

Check seasoning and serve hot.

BRAISED LAMB WITH FRUIT AND NUTS

750 g (1½ lb) boned young lamb, leg or shoulder
3 cups water
1 tablespoon lemon juice
2 bay leaves
5 cm (2 inch) stick cinnamon
4 tablespoons *ghee*
5 cm (2 inch) piece fresh ginger, shredded
6 cloves garlic, crushed
2 large onions, minced
6 green cardamoms, crushed
2 tablespoons coriander, ground
3 cloves
1 tablespoon white poppy seeds
45 g (1½ oz) ground almonds
1 teaspoon black pepper
2 tablespoons finely chopped fresh mint
¾ cup plain yoghurt
2 teaspoons *garam masala*
1 teaspoon chilli powder
salt
45 g (1½ oz) raisins, soaked
30 g (1 oz) sultanas, soaked
45 g (1½ oz) blanched, slivered almonds
¼ teaspoon saffron
1 tablespoon boiling water
1½ teaspoons rose water (optional)

Place trimmed lamb in a pot and add water, lemon juice, bay leaves and cinnamon. Cover and bring to the boil, then reduce heat and simmer for about 1 hour until very tender. Skim several times during cooking. Remove meat and reduce liquid to about ¾ cup.

Heat 3 tablespoons *ghee* and fry ginger, garlic and onions until soft. Grind cardamoms, coriander, cloves, poppy seeds, almonds and black pepper to a powder and add to the pan. Fry for 3 minutes, stirring frequently. Add mint and yoghurt and simmer until sauce is thick and creamy.

Add the meat and spoon the sauce over it. Braise until heated through and well seasoned. Add reserved stock and simmer uncovered, until the liquid is completely absorbed or evaporated. Sprinkle on *garam masala,* chilli powder and salt.

Melt remaining *ghee* and fry drained fruit and nuts gently for 5 minutes. Add to the pan. Mix saffron with boiling water and rose water. Pour over the meat and heat through, or cover and place in a moderate oven for 15 minutes.

KEBABS OF MINCED LAMB

SHEEK KEBAB

750 g (1½ lb) boneless lamb, finely minced
¼ teaspoon saffron powder
2 tablespoons water
2 teaspoons cummin, ground
1 large onion, minced
3 cloves garlic, crushed
2½ tablespoons finely chopped fresh coriander leaves
1½ teaspoons salt
3 tablespoons *ghee*
dried green mango powder *(amchur)*
lettuce leaves
lime wedges
onion rings

Mix all ingredients except 1 tablespoon *ghee* and dried green mango powder together and knead until smooth. Divide into 5 cm (2 inch) balls and flatten each into a sausage shape. Insert a flat metal skewer along each kebab, press firmly onto the skewer and roll across the bottom of a plate to give an even shape.

Melt remaining *ghee* and brush each kebab lightly. Cook under a hot grill or on a charcoal barbecue until well browned on the surface and cooked through. Brush with more *ghee* during cooking to keep moist. Remove from heat and sprinkle with mango powder.

Serve with lime wedges and onion rings on a bed of lettuce leaves.

LAMB AND POTATO CURRY

500 g (1 lb) lean lamb, shoulder or leg
250 g (½ lb) peeled potatoes
oil for deep frying
2 large onions
2 black cardamoms
¼ teaspoon fennel seeds
1 tablespoon coriander, ground
¾ teaspoon turmeric powder
2.5 cm (1 inch) piece fresh ginger
4 cloves garlic
2 green chillies
½ cup plain yoghurt
3 tablespoons *ghee*
1½ teaspoons black mustard seeds
½ teaspoon chilli powder
salt
black pepper
garam masala
fresh coriander leaves, finely chopped

Trim lamb and cut into 4 cm (1½ inch) cubes. Cut potatoes into 2 cm (¾ inch) dice. Heat oil and fry potatoes until well coloured. Remove and drain well.

Slice onions thinly. Grind seasonings from carda-

Kebabs of Minced Lamb (recipe this page).

moms to chillies to a fairly smooth paste and rub into the meat cubes. Place in a dish and pour on yoghurt. Leave for 2 hours to marinate.

Heat *ghee* and fry lamb until well coloured. Add any remaining marinade, sliced onion and cover with water. Bring to the boil, cover and simmer until meat is very tender. Add fried potatoes and mustard seeds and season with chilli powder, salt, pepper and *garam masala* to taste. Heat through, transfer to a serving dish and garnish with chopped coriander leaves.

MUTTON WITH FRIED OKRA

BHINDI GOSHT

500 g (1 lb) lean mutton, shoulder or leg
2 medium onions
3 tablespoons *ghee*
3 cloves garlic
2.5 cm (1 inch) piece fresh ginger
2 heaped teaspoons *garam masala*
1½ cups water
2 teaspoons salt
375 g (¾ lb) small okra
oil for deep frying

Trim mutton and cut into 2.5 cm (1 inch) cubes. Slice onions thinly and fry in *ghee* until soft. Mince garlic and ginger and add to the pan. Fry for 3 minutes, then put in meat and cook until well coloured. Sprinkle on *garam masala* and cook for 3 minutes, then pour on water and bring to the boil. Reduce heat and simmer until meat is tender. Season with salt.

Trim tops of okra and cut each in halves. Heat oil and deep fry the okra until slightly crisp. Lift out and drain well. Place in the pan with meat and heat through for 4 minutes.

Sliced eggplant may be added in place of okra. Sprinkle with a little salt and leave for 10 minutes then wipe dry and fry as above.

SAVOURY MINCED MEAT

RESHMI KIMA

250 g (½ lb) boneless mutton
6 cloves garlic
1 small onion
2.5 cm (1 inch) piece fresh ginger
½ cup water
2 tablespoons *ghee*
1 teaspoon salt
1 teaspoon *garam masala*
pinch of chilli powder
pinch of black pepper
1 tablespoon finely chopped fresh coriander leaves

Mince mutton with garlic, onion and ginger. Boil with water until all liquid has dried up and meat is well coloured. Add *ghee*, salt, *garam masala*, chilli powder and black pepper and fry for 5 minutes, stirring frequently. Add coriander and mix in well.

Serve with Chupati or fresh toast as a snack or breakfast dish.

MINCED MUTTON WITH PEAS

KEEMA MUTTAR

500 g (1 lb) minced mutton
1 large onion
3 cloves garlic
1 cm (½ inch) piece fresh ginger
3 tablespoons *ghee*
1 teaspoon chilli powder
1½ teaspoons *garam masala*
1 teaspoon black mustard seeds
½ teaspoon turmeric powder
3 medium tomatoes
185 g (6 oz) frozen peas
¾ cup water
salt
pepper
1 tablespoon finely chopped fresh coriander leaves

Boil mutton in a little water until cooked through and all liquid dried up. Set aside. Finely mince onion with garlic and ginger. Fry in *ghee* until soft, then add minced meat, chilli powder, *garam masala*, mustard seeds and turmeric. Fry for 3 minutes, stirring constantly.

Peel tomatoes and chop finely; add to the pan with peas. Pour in water and bring to the boil. Cover, reduce heat and simmer for 15 minutes. Season to taste with salt and pepper and stir in coriander leaves.

MUTTON KORMA

750 g (1½ lb) lean shoulder of mutton
2 large onions
2 cloves garlic
4 tablespoons *ghee*
2.5 cm (1 inch) piece fresh ginger
1 tablespoon coriander, ground
2 teaspoons cummin, ground
3 cloves
3 black cardamoms
5 cm (2 inch) stick cinnamon
2 teaspoons chilli powder
pinch of asafoetida (optional)
1 tablespoon white poppy seeds, soaked overnight
2 bay leaves
¾ cup plain yoghurt
salt
pepper
¾ cup thick cream
1 tablespoon raisins, soaked
3 tablespoons blanched almonds
1 teaspoon rose water
1 teaspoon saffron powder
2 tablespoons boiling water

Trim mutton and cut into 5 cm (2 inch) cubes. Slice onion thinly and crush garlic. Fry in 3 tablespoons of *ghee* until soft. Shred ginger and add to the pan with mutton cubes. Fry until well coloured, turning frequently. Add coriander and all spices to bay leaves and stir on moderate heat for 3 minutes.

Pour in yoghurt and stir to coat the meat thoroughly and mix with the spices. Cover and simmer until meat is tender and liquid completely absorbed. Splash in a little water and add salt and pepper. Add thick cream and raisins and cover again. Continue to simmer until meat is very tender and sauce thick. Add a little more water if needed.

Fry almonds in 1 tablespoon *ghee* until golden and stir into the sauce. Add rose water and saffron mixed with boiling water. Heat through for 10 minutes on low heat.

MUTTON IN COCONUT CURRY

750 g (1½ lb) mutton shoulder
1 teaspoon salt
3 cups thin coconut milk
4 cloves garlic, sliced
1 cm (½ inch) piece fresh ginger, shredded
6 dried chillies, soaked and mashed
½ teaspoon turmeric powder
10 cm (4 inch) stalk lemon grass, quartered
4 curry leaves
¾ teaspoon fenugreek seeds, crushed
5 cm (2 inch) stick cinnamon
1 medium onion, sliced
1 cup thick coconut milk
salt
lemon juice
1 tablespoon coconut oil or *ghee*

Trim mutton and cut into 2.5 cm (1 inch) cubes. Sprinkle with salt and place in a saucepan. Pour on thin coconut milk and add garlic, ginger and mashed chillies. Colour with turmeric powder and add half each of lemon grass, curry leaves, fenugreek seeds and cinnamon stick. Add sliced onion, reserving a little for garnish. Cover and simmer until lamb is tender, stirring occasionally.

Add thick coconut milk and season to taste with salt and lemon juice. Heat *ghee* and fry remaining lemon grass, crumbled curry leaves, fenugreek seeds, cinnamon stick and onion for 4 minutes. Stir into the curry and cook for a further 15 minutes on low heat.

MUTTON KOFTA CURRY

500 g (1 lb) boneless shoulder of mutton
1 thick slice bread
¼ cup milk
1 medium onion
5 cloves garlic
1 teaspoon chilli powder
2 teaspoons *garam masala*
1 teaspoon salt
gram flour *(besan),* as needed
1-2 eggs
ghee for deep frying
3 large onions
2.5 cm (1 inch) piece fresh ginger
2 tablespoons *ghee*
1 tablespoon coriander, ground
2 teaspoons *garam masala*
1 teaspoon chilli powder
2 medium tomatoes

¼ cup plain yoghurt
¾ cup water
salt
pepper
sugar
½ cup thick cream
2 tablespoons finely chopped fresh coriander leaves
chilli powder

Mince or chop mutton until very smooth. Soak bread in milk then squeeze out and add to the meat with minced onion and 2 cloves garlic. Stir in chilli powder, *garam masala* and salt and bind with eggs and enough gram flour to hold the mixture together. Knead to a smooth paste and form into small balls, then flatten each slightly.

Heat *ghee* and drop in several meatballs at a time. Cook to a rich golden brown. Lift out and drain well.

Thinly slice one large onion and mince remaining onions and garlic with ginger. Heat 2 tablespoons *ghee* and fry sliced onion until soft. Add minced onion, ginger and garlic and fry for 3 minutes, stirring. Add coriander, *garam masala* and chilli powder and simmer for 3 minutes.

Peel tomatoes and chop finely. Add to pan with yoghurt and water. Bring to the boil, reduce heat and simmer for 10 minutes. Add salt, pepper and sugar to taste and stir in cream and coriander leaves. Add fried meatballs and simmer until heated through.

Garnish with chilli powder.

BEEF VINDALOO

1 kg (2 lb) beef steak (chuck, round or knuckle) or
1½ kg (3 lb) oxtail
3 tablespoons coriander
1 tablespoon cummin
6 cloves
5 cm (2 inch) stick cinnamon
1½ teaspoons black peppercorns
2 teaspoons fenugreek seeds
1 teaspoon fennel seeds
6 dried chillied, soaked
8 cloves garlic
1 large onion
2.5 cm (1 inch) piece fresh ginger
¼ cup white vinegar
3 tablespoons *ghee*
2 bay leaves
2 cups beef stock
salt to taste

Trim meat and cut into 5 cm (2 inch) cubes. Set aside. Grind spices from coriander to fennel to a fine powder. Grind chillies with garlic, onion and ginger. Mix spice powder with vinegar and rub well into the meat. Pour on the onion paste and leave meat to marinate for 2 hours.

Heat *ghee* and fry meat until very deeply coloured. Add bay leaves and stock bring to the boil, then simmer until meat is very tender. Season to taste with salt and leave overnight if time permits. Reheat before using.

If using oxtail, cut into sections and prepare in the same way, cooking until the meat falls from the bones.

CRISP FRIED BEEF IN TOMATO AND CHILLI SAUCE

500 g (1 lb) frying steak
1 teaspoon salt
pinch of pepper
3 tablespoons *ghee*
1 large onion, thinly sliced
2 fresh red chillies
2 cloves garlic
1 cm (½ inch) piece fresh ginger
1½ teaspoons *garam masala*
1 teaspoon cummin seeds, toasted
1 teaspoon mustard seeds, toasted
3 large tomatoes, peeled
¼ cup beef stock
salt
lemon juice

Cut beef steak into thin slices and sprinkle with salt and pepper. Heat *ghee* and fry beef slices several at a time until very dark brown and slightly crisp. Set aside, keeping warm.

Drain off most of the *ghee* and add onion. Fry until very soft. Grind chillies, garlic and ginger to a paste and add to the pan, frying for 3 minutes. Sprinkle on *garam masala,* cummin and mustard seeds and fry for 1 minute.

Chop tomato finely and add to the pan with stock and salt to taste. Simmer for 5 minutes, then return beef slices and cook for a further 15 minutes on low heat, covered tightly. Sprinkle with lemon juice to taste.

MIXED TANDOORI KEBABS

125 g (¼ lb) chicken breast
6 chicken livers
3 kidneys
250 g (½ lb) boneless lamb, leg or shoulder
125 g (¼ lb) calves liver
onion rings
wedges of lime or lemon

Marinade 1:
½ cup plain yoghurt
3 cloves garlic
2.5 cm (1 inch) piece fresh ginger
2 teaspoons cummin, ground
½ teaspoon salt
pinch black pepper
2 cloves, crushed
2.5 cm (1 inch) stick cinnamon, broken
1 medium onion, grated
3 teaspoons lemon juice

Marinade 2:
3 teaspoons lemon juice
pinch of salt
pepper
sugar
1 small onion, minced
1 clove garlic, minced
onion rings
lime or lemon wedges

Cut chicken into thin strips. Quarter livers and kidneys. Slice lamb thinly and cut into strips. Cut liver into 2 cm (¾ inch) cubes.

Mix ingredients for both marinades. Rub Marinade 1 into chicken and lamb, and Marinade 2 into livers and kidneys. Colour both with a little Tandoori food colouring powder, if available.

Leave for 1 hour, then thread alternate types of meat on skewers and brush with a little *ghee*. Roast over a charcoal barbecue until cooked through, or cook under the grill.

Serve with onion rings and wedges of lime or lemon.

SPICED PORK

ASSAD

750 g (1½ lb) pork shoulder
salt
2.5 cm (1 inch) piece fresh ginger
8 cloves garlic
1 teaspoon turmeric powder
¼ teaspoon white pepper
3 tablespoons *ghee*
5 cm (2 inch) stick cinnamon
3 cloves
6 dried chillies
2 blades mace
1½ cups water

Wipe pork and trim. Rub with a little salt. Grind ginger and garlic to a paste with turmeric and pepper and rub into the pork. Heat *ghee* and fry meat until well coloured all over.

Transfer to a deep pot and add spices and water. Cover and bring to the boil. Simmer until meat is completely tender. Lift out and drain. Slice thickly before serving.

GOAN MEAT CURRY

SORPOTEL

This is a famous dish from Goa which should be prepared several days in advance to bring out the full flavour.

750 g (1½ lb) pork, slightly fatty
250 g (½ lb) pigs liver (in one piece)
1 tablespoon coriander
1½ teaspoons cummin
1 teaspoon black peppercorns
3 tablespoons malt vinegar
1 teaspoon turmeric powder
3 green chillies
4 cloves garlic
1 cm (½ inch) piece fresh ginger
3 tablespoons *ghee*
2 teaspoons tamarind or lemon juice to taste
sugar
salt

Cut pork into reasonably large pieces and place in a saucepan with the piece of liver. Cover with water to just above the level of the meat and bring to the boil.

Braised Lamb with Fruit and Nuts (recipe page 22).

Reduce heat and simmer for about 1½ hours until pork is tender. Remove meat, retaining the stock. Cut meat and liver into 1 cm (½ inch) dice.

Toast coriander, cummin and peppercorns under the griller for 3 minutes, then grind to a fine powder. Mix with vinegar and add turmeric. Mince chillies with garlic and ginger and fry in *ghee* for 3 minutes. Add spice powder and meat and fry until meat is well coloured.

Add the reserved stock and tamarind or lemon juice, and boil for 45 minutes, or until meat is very tender and liquid well reduced. Season to taste with sugar and salt and heat through again. Leave to cool, then cover and refrigerate for at least one day, but preferably up to three days before using.

Reheat before serving.

PORK ON STRAW POTATOES

625 g (1¼ lb) pork tenderloin
2 medium onions
8 cloves garlic
2.5 cm (1 inch) piece fresh ginger
2 tablespoons *ghee*
5 cm (2 inch) stick cinnamon
2 bay leaves
1 teaspoon salt
¼ teaspoon black pepper
4 large potatoes
oil for deep frying
½ teaspoon *garam masala*
fresh coriander leaves

Slice meat into thin steaks and flatten each with a meat mallet. Slice onions thinly. Pound garlic and ginger to a paste and rub well into the meat. Heat oil and fry onions until dark brown. Lift out, drain well and set aside.

Fry meat until well coloured, then add cinnamon, bay leaves, salt and pepper. Add enough water to just cover the steaks and simmer until very tender. Turn several times during cooking.

Peel potatoes and cut into matchstick pieces. Soak in cold salted water for 5 minutes. Drain and dry on a kitchen towel. Heat oil and deep fry straws until well coloured and crisp. Lift out and leave to cool, then return to the oil to fry for a further ½ minute.

Arrange potato straws on a serving dish. Lift steaks from the pan and place on the potatoes. Add any remaining sauce and sprinkle on *garam masala*. Garnish with fresh coriander.

CURRIED LIVER

375 g (¾ lb) lambs liver
1 medium onion
2 cloves garlic
2 green chillies
2 tablespoons *ghee*
½ teaspoon turmeric powder
2 teaspoons *garam masala*
2 cloves
2 bay leaves

pinch of white pepper
2 medium tomatoes, peeled
salt
¼ cup cream or thick coconut milk
1 tablespoon finely chopped fresh coriander leaves

Trim liver and cut into thin slices. Peel and thinly slice onion, garlic and chillies. Heat *ghee* and fry liver and sliced ingredients for 4 minutes. Sprinkle on turmeric and *garam masala* and add cloves, bay leaves and white pepper. Sprinkle on a very little water and add thinly sliced tomato. Simmer until tomato is soft and liver lightly cooked. Add salt to taste and pour on cream or coconut milk. Stir well and heat through.

Stir in coriander leaves and serve at once.

BRAISED PUMPKIN

625 g (1¼ lb) pumpkin
3 cloves garlic
3 dried chillies, soaked
1 medium onion
1 large onion
2 tablespoons *ghee*
1 teaspoon salt
¼ teaspoon black pepper
1 teaspoon tamarind
2 tablespoons boiling water
¾ cup water
1 tablespoon chopped fresh coriander leaves

Peel and slice pumpkin. Grind garlic, chillies and medium onion to a paste. Slice large onion thinly and fry in *ghee* until soft. Add pumpkin pieces and fry until lightly coloured, then add seasoning paste and stir on moderate heat for 2 minutes.

Season with salt, pepper and tamarind mixed with boiling water. Cover with water and bring to the boil. Simmer uncovered until pumpkin is tender, allowing most of the liquid to evaporate. Adjust seasonings, adding a little sugar if necessary.

Garnish with chopped coriander leaves.

SPINACH WITH COTTAGE CHEESE

SAAG PANEER

1.5 kg (3 lb) fresh spinach or
    500 g (1 lb) frozen spinach
3 tablespoons *ghee*
185 g (6 oz) prepared *paneer* (see page 12)
1 clove garlic
1 cm (½ inch) piece fresh ginger
1 tablespoon chopped fresh coriander leaves (optional)
½ teaspoon chilli powder
¼ teaspoon freshly grated nutmeg
½ cup thick cream
salt
pepper

Wash fresh spinach in several lots of cold water and shake out excess liquid. Shred and simmer with 1 tablespoon *ghee* and a very little water until completely tender. If using frozen spinach, place the unthawed block in a pan with 1 tablespoon *ghee,* cover and simmer until thawed. Remove lid and cook until most of the liquid has evaporated.

Cut *paneer* into 2.5 cm (1 inch) cubes. Grind garlic, ginger and coriander (if used) to a paste and add chilli and nutmeg. Heat remaining *ghee* and fry seasoning paste for 2 minutes. Add *paneer* cubes and fry until lightly coloured, then put in spinach and heat through. Stir in cream and check seasoning. Heat through before serving.

For a smoother sauce, blend spinach with cream in a liquidiser before adding to the pan to heat.

SPICED POTATOES

ALOO CHAT

500 g (1 lb) potatoes, peeled
2½ tablespoons *ghee*
1 large onion, minced
2 cloves garlic, minced
2 teaspoons *chat masala* (see page 13)
1 teaspoon turmeric powder
1 teaspoon chilli powder
1½ teaspoons salt
1 bay leaf, crumbled
½ teaspoon freshly ground black pepper
1 fresh red chilli, finely chopped
1 tablespoon finely chopped fresh coriander leaves

Cut potatoes into 2.5 cm (1 inch) cubes. Heat *ghee* and fry potato until well coloured and slightly crisp. Add onion and garlic and cook for 1 minute. Sprinkle on spices and add bay leaf. Cover pan and cook on low heat until tender. If needed, sprinkle on a little water. Shake the pan to turn potatoes. Do not open saucepan until done.

Serve with a sprinkling of black pepper and garnish with chopped chilli and coriander leaves.

MASALA POTATO WITH OKRA

2 large potatoes
250 g (½ lb) okra
3 green chillies
1 tablespoon fresh coriander leaves
1 large onion
1 large tomato
2 cloves garlic
1 cm (½ inch) piece fresh ginger
2 tablespoons *ghee*
2 teaspoons *chat masala* (see page 13)
½ teaspoon turmeric powder
1 cup water
sugar
salt

Peel potatoes and cut into 2.5 cm (1 inch) cubes. Wash okra and remove stems, slit lengthways. Cut green chillies into thin slices, removing seeds for milder taste. Chop coriander and slice onion and tomato. Crush garlic and shred ginger.

Heat *ghee* and fry sliced onion for 2 minutes. Add garlic and ginger and fry for a further 2 minutes, then sprinkle on *chat masala* and turmeric. Stir on high heat for 1 minute.

Add potatoes and okra and pour on water. Add chopped coriander leaves and tomato. Season to taste with sugar and salt and bring to the boil. Reduce heat and simmer until potatoes and okra are tender.

Serve with the sauce or cook until the liquid has almost evaporated.

EGGPLANT CURRY

500 g (1 lb) eggplant
1 teaspoon salt
1 teaspoon saffron powder
3 tablespoons *ghee* or oil
4 shallots, thinly sliced
3 cloves garlic, thinly sliced
2.5 cm (1 inch) piece fresh ginger, thinly sliced
8 dried chillies, toasted
2 teaspoons mustard seeds, toasted
2 teaspoons fish floss or dried shrimps, ground
10 cm (4 inch) stalk lemon grass
½ teaspoon fenugreek seeds, lightly crushed
1½ cups thin coconut milk
lemon juice
salt

Wipe eggplant and remove stems. Slice diagonally into 1 cm (½ inch) slices. Sprinkle with salt and leave for 10 minutes to draw bitter juices. Wipe off liquid and sprinkle slices with saffron powder.

Heat *ghee* or oil and fry eggplant until well coloured. Drain well. Fry shallots and garlic for 1 minute, then add ginger and chillies with all seasonings and stir on moderate heat for 1 minute. Pour in coconut milk and bring to a gentle boil. Simmer for 5 minutes. Add eggplant and cook until tender.

Season to taste with lemon juice and salt.

VEGETABLE CUTLETS IN CURRY SAUCE

500 g (1 lb) potatoes
½ teaspoon chilli powder
2 teaspoons salt
½ teaspoon pepper
2 teaspoons *garam masala*
3 tablespoons finely chopped fresh coriander leaves
2 eggs
gram flour *(besan)*
oil or *ghee*

Curry Sauce:
1 large onion
2.5 cm (1 inch) piece fresh ginger
4 cloves garlic
2 teaspoons *garam masala*
½ teaspoon fennel
3 tablespoons *ghee*
3 tomatoes
¾ cup cream
½ teaspoon turmeric powder
chilli powder

Peel potatoes and boil until soft. Drain and mash. Add chilli powder, salt, pepper, *garam masala* and coriander and bind the mixture with egg and gram flour. Shape into cutlets.

Heat about 2.5 cm (1 inch) oil or *ghee* in a pan, and fry cutlets until golden brown. Turn to colour evenly. Lift out and drain well.

Prepare Curry Sauce. Mince onion with ginger and garlic. Add *garam masala* and fennel and fry in *ghee* for 4 minutes, stirring frequently. Peel tomatoes, chop finely and add to the pan. Fry for 4 minutes. Add about 4 tablespoons water and bring to the boil, then reduce heat and stir in cream. Season to taste with salt and pepper and add turmeric. Stir well. Place vegetable cutlets in the sauce and heat through.

Transfer to a serving dish and garnish with chilli powder.

CREAM CURRY OF MUSHROOMS, PEAS AND TOMATO

SHABNAB

185 g (6 oz) canned champignons
185 g (6 oz) frozen green peas
6 medium tomatoes
3 tablespoons *ghee*
1½ teaspoons *garam masala*
¼ teaspoon fennel
pinch of salt and pepper
⅓ teaspoon turmeric powder
¾ cup thick cream
1 tablespoon finely chopped fresh coriander leaves
½ teaspoon chilli powder (optional)

Drain champignons. Thaw peas. Drop tomatoes into boiling water, count to eight and lift out. Peel and cut into wedges, discarding seeds if preferred.

Heat *ghee* and fry *garam masala* and fennel for 1 minute. Add tomato and fry until slightly softened. Add champignons and peas and cook briefly, then season with salt and pepper. Add turmeric and cream and simmer until heated through.

Stir in chopped coriander leaves and garnish with a sprinkling of chilli powder.

STUFFED LADIES FINGERS

BAHMIA

375 g (¾ lb) large okra
2 medium tomatoes
1 tablespoon brown sugar
2 tablespoons lemon juice
2 teaspoons fennel seeds, coarsely ground
¾ teaspoon turmeric powder
1 tablespoon coriander, ground
1 tablespoon *ghee*
salt
chilli powder
2 tablespoons beef stock

Wash okra, trim tops and cut a slit along each piece. Peel and finely chop tomato and mix with brown sugar, lemon juice and spices. Stuff the mixture into the okra and place in a fireproof dish.

Melt *ghee* and add to the dish. Sprinkle on salt and chilli powder and add beef stock. Cover and cook in a moderate oven or over moderate heat until the okra are tender, then remove lid and continue cooking until the pan juices are absorbed.

DRY VEGETABLE CURRY

250 g (½ lb) cauliflower
3 medium potatoes
2 medium onions
125 g (¼ lb) green beans
2.5 cm (1 inch) piece fresh ginger
2 tablespoons *ghee*
1½ teaspoons salt
2 tomatoes
¾ teaspoon turmeric
½ teaspoon chilli powder
½ teaspoon mustard seeds
2 teaspoons *garam masala*

Break cauliflower into florets and rinse in cold water. Peel and cube potato. Slice onions thickly. Cut beans into 5 cm (2 inch) pieces. Shred ginger. Heat *ghee* and fry onions and ginger for 2 minutes. Add potato and cook until lightly coloured. Add cauliflower and beans with salt and cook briefly. Peel and slice tomato and add to the pan with turmeric, chilli powder and mustard seeds. Cover and cook until the vegetables are tender but retain some crispness.

Sprinkle on *garam masala* and cook, uncovered, until the liquid has dried up completely. Stir carefully to avoid breaking the vegetables.

TOMATO PUREE

TAMATAR BURTHA

4 large tomatoes
2 large onions
1 clove garlic
1 green chilli
1 heaped teaspoon cummin, ground
1 teaspoon mustard seeds, toasted
1½ tablespoons *ghee*
1 tablespoon finely chopped fresh mint or coriander leaves
salt
sugar

Peel tomatoes and chop. Mince or finely chop onions, garlic and chilli. Heat oil and fry onion paste for 2 minutes, then add tomato with cummin and mustard. Simmer, stirring continually, until the mixture becomes a smooth sauce. Add a very little water if needed.

Stir in chopped mint or coriander leaves and season to taste with salt and sugar.

AUBERGINE PUREE
BRINJAL BURTHA

375 g (¾ lb) aubergines
2 medium onions
3 cloves garlic
2 tablespoons *ghee*
1 cm (½ inch) piece fresh ginger
2 teaspoons cummin, ground
1½ teaspoons *garam masala*
1½ teaspoons salt
2 spring onions, finely shredded
fresh coriander or mint leaves, finely chopped

Wipe eggplant and place under a moderate grill to cook until the skin is very dark and flesh completely soft. Peel off skin, discard stems and mash pulp or puree in a liquidiser.

Mince onions and garlic and fry in *ghee* for 2 minutes. Add minced ginger and eggplant puree and season with cummin. Simmer for 5 minutes on moderately low heat, then sprinkle on *garam masala* and salt. Add spring onion and cook for another 2 minutes.

Garnish with chopped coriander or mint.

YOGHURT SALAD WITH ONION AND MINT
RAITA

2 cups plain yoghurt
3 spring onions, minced
2 tablespoons finely chopped fresh mint
½ teaspoon salt
1 teaspoon sugar
¼ teaspoon black pepper
½ teaspoon cummin, ground

Beat yoghurt until smooth then stir in all remaining ingredients. Beat for 1 minute then refrigerate. Add 2 tablespoons thick cream for a richer sauce. Serve as a side dish with any main course.

Yoghurt side dishes may include any of the following ingredients: finely chopped tomato or pineapple, grated cucumber, cooked peas with mint, cooked finely diced potato, grated apple, chopped banana, or they can simply be flavoured with spices.

TOMATO AND ONION SALAD
LACHUMBER

3 medium tomatoes
2 medium onions
3 green chillies
vinegar or tamarind water
salt
sugar

Peel and finely chop tomatoes and onions. Slice chillies thinly, discarding seeds. Mix vinegar or tamarind water, salt and sugar to taste and pour over the vegetables. Leave to stand for 1 hour before serving.

Serve as a side dish with any main dishes.

WHOLEWHEAT UNLEAVENED BREAD
CHUPATI

Makes about 12.

250 g (½ lb) wholewheat flour *(atta)*
about ¾ cup warm water
ghee

Sieve flour into a bowl and add enough water to make a soft, workable dough. Knead for at least 6 minutes until dough is very soft and will lift from the board without sticking. Cover with a damp cloth and leave for 1 hour.

Divide dough into twelve pieces and roll into balls. Roll each piece out very thinly in a circular shape with a floured rolling pin. Stack between greaseproof paper.

Heat a heavy frying pan or hot plate and cook the Chupati on each side until brown flecks appear. Transfer to a hot grill until the Chupati blow up like a balloon. Spread with a little *ghee* then wrap in a cloth until needed.

CHUPATI STUFFED WITH SEASONED POTATO

Chupati dough (see preceding recipe)

Filling:
185 g (6 oz) mashed potato
3 teaspoons coriander, ground
1 teaspoon cummin, ground
1 teaspoon salt
2 tablespoons finely choppped fresh coriander leaves
ghee

Prepare Chupati dough and break into 16 pieces. Roll each out very thinly on a floured board.

Mix potato with seasonings, adding a very little *ghee* to make a smooth paste. Spread the paste thickly over half the Chupati, leaving a narrow border. Damp this border and press another Chupati on top. Heat a heavy frying pan or hot plate and cook Chupati on both sides until dark brown flecks appear. Transfer to a hot grill to make them puff up slightly. Brush with a little *ghee* and wrap in a cloth until needed.

WHOLEWHEAT BREADS
PARATHA

Makes about 10.

250 g (½ lb) wholemeat flour *(atta)*
lukewarm water
ghee
large pinch of salt

Sieve flour into a bowl and add lukewarm water to make a slightly stiff dough. Add salt and a little *ghee* and work the dough for 4 minutes. Divide into ten pieces and roll each out to about 20 cm (8 inch) discs. Brush with a little warmed *ghee* on one side. Cover with a damp cloth and leave for at least ½ hour.

Pleat the bread at two sides to form a pleated sausage shape then twist into a circle. Roll out or press flat with buttered fingers. Bake on a hot plate or heavy frying pan over moderate heat until brown and slightly crisp underneath. Turn and cook top. Place under a hot grill to make the bread puff up slightly.

Brush with more *ghee* and wrap in a cloth until needed.

PARATHA STUFFED WITH CAULIFLOWER

GOBI WALLA PARATHA

Paratha dough (see preceding recipe)

Filling:
250 g (½ lb) cauliflower
1½ teaspoons salt
1 fresh red chilli, minced (optional)
ghee
½ teaspoon *garam masala*

Prepare Paratha dough and leave for ½ hour, covered with a damp cloth.

Break into about 18 pieces and roll out each into a disc about 2 mm (1/16 inch) thick.

Finely chop cauliflower. Fry with salt and chilli in 2 tablespoons *ghee* until soft. Sprinkle on *garam masala*. Leave to cool.

Cover half the bread discs with the stuffing and place a second disc over the top. Seal edges by pinching together, using a little water to stick. Roll out again very gently, taking care the dough does not tear. Brush with *ghee* and cook on each side on a hot plate or heavy frying pan. Transfer to a hot grill to crisp each side and make the breads puff up very slightly. Spread with more *ghee* and wrap in cloth until needed.

FRIED UNLEAVENED WHOLEWHEAT BREAD

PURI

Makes about 14.

315 g (10 oz) wholewheat flour *(atta)*
1 teaspoon salt
1 tablespoon softened *ghee*
warm water
ghee or oil for deep frying

Sieve flour into a bowl and add salt and softened *ghee*. Work in with the fingers until the mixture is crumbly. Add enough warm water to make a stiff dough. Knead for 6 minutes.

Pull off pieces of dough and shape into walnut-sized balls. Roll out on a lightly floured board with a floured rolling pin until very thin. Stack between sheets of greaseproof paper until ready to cook.

Heat *ghee* or oil to smoking point. The oil must be very hot for these or they will not puff up properly. Drop in one Puri at a time. Quickly splash the top with the hot fat or oil and push the bread under the oil. It should puff up like a balloon soon after going into the pan. Cook briefly on one side, then turn and cook the other side briefly. They must not be overcooked.

Lift out and drain well on absorbent paper. Keep warm in a low oven until needed.

LEAVENED WHITE BREAD

NAAN

Makes 4-5.

250 g (½ lb) plain flour
1¼ teaspoons baking powder
½ teaspoon sugar
pinch of salt
⅓ - ½ cup plain yoghurt
1 tablespoon vegetable oil
1 egg

Sieve flour into a bowl and add baking powder, sugar and salt. Mix in ⅓ cup yoghurt, vegetable oil and the egg. Work with the fingers into a smooth, soft dough. Add extra yoghurt if the dough still feels slightly stiff. Knead for 5 minutes, then cover with a damp cloth and leave in a warm place to rise for 4 hours.

Heat a hotplate or heavy-based frying pan. Divide the dough into 4-5 pieces and with wet fingers pull into an elongated triangular shape. Wet one side and stick this down on the pan. Cook on moderate heat for about 1½ minutes, then turn pan over so the top of the bread is exposed directly to the heat. Cook until dark brown flecks appear and the bread is springy to the touch.

Keep in a cloth or covered box until needed.

LEAVENED YOGHURT YEAST BREAD

KULCHA

Yoghurt Yeast:
60 g (2 oz) plain flour
1½ tablespoons warm plain yoghurt
1½ teaspoons white sugar
4 black peppercorns (optional)
1½ tablespoons warm water

Mix ingredients together, beating well. Leave in a warm place overnight. Discard peppercorns.

Yeast Bread:
250 g (½ lb) plain flour
2¼ tablespoons yoghurt yeast (see above)
1 tablespoon sugar
1 teaspoon salt
2¼ tablespoons *ghee*
¼ - ⅓ cup warm milk
ghee or oil for deep frying

Sieve flour into a bowl and add remaining ingredients. Work to a soft dough, adding more milk if needed. Knead vigorously for 7 minutes, then cover with damp cloth and leave in a warm place for 2½ hours.

Wet hands and knead again for 3 minutes. Roll out

into 15 cm (6 inch) discs and leave, covered with a damp cloth, to rise again for about ½ hour.

Heat *ghee* or oil and fry Kulcha one at a time until golden and cooked through. Drain well and wrap in a cloth until needed. This makes about 6 Kulcha.

MUTTON BIRIYANI

375 g (¾ lb) lean mutton
¼ cup plain yoghurt
2 teaspoons lemon juice
4 teaspoons *garam masala*
1 teaspoon turmeric powder
4 cloves garlic
1 large onion
2.5 cm (1 inch) piece fresh ginger
3 tablespoons *ghee*
375 g (¾ lb) long grain rice
2 medium onions, thinly sliced
5 cm (2 inch) cinnamon stick, broken
4 cloves
2 blades mace
3 bay leaves
½ teaspoon chilli powder
3 hardboiled eggs
1 tablespoon blanched almonds, fried in *ghee*

Trim mutton and cut into 3 cm (1¼ inch) cubes. Place in a bowl and pour on yoghurt and lemon juice. Sprinkle on 2 teaspoons *garam masala* and the turmeric. Finely mince garlic, onion and ginger and add to the meat. Stir well and leave to marinate for 1 hour.

Put marinated mixture into a pan, cover with water and boil for 1½ hours. Drain, reserving stock.

Heat *ghee* and fry rice until each grain is well oiled. Add onion, cinnamon, cloves, mace and bay leaves. Fry for 3 minutes then add drained meat and fry until well coloured. Pour in mutton stock and add water, if needed, to make up 3¼ cups. Add chilli powder and bring to the boil. Cover and reduce heat to lowest point. Leave to cook until rice is tender and liquid completely absorbed.

Sprinkle on *garam masala* and stir meat into the rice. Cut hardboiled eggs into wedges and decorate the rice with egg and almonds. Serve hot.

PRAWN BIRIYANI

BIRIYANI JHINGA

750 g (1½ lb) raw prawns in shells
4½ cups water
1 large onion
6 cloves garlic
2.5 cm (1 inch) piece fresh ginger
4 dried chillies, soaked
1 teaspoon cummin
1 teaspoon black peppercorns
5 cm (2 inch) stick cinnamon
6 cloves
3 black cardamoms, crushed
¼ teaspoon saffron powder
1 tablespoon boiling water
3 tablespoons *ghee*

375 g (¾ lb) long grain rice
4 large tomatoes
salt
rose water (optional)

Remove heads and shells from prawns, leaving tails on. Place shells and heads in a pot with water. Cover pot, bring to the boil and then reduce heat and simmer for 1 hour. Strain, reserving liquid.

Pound onion, garlic, ginger and chillies to a paste. Grind cummin and black peppercorns coarsely. Mix in broken cinnamon stick, cloves and cardamoms. Mix saffron with boiling water.

Melt *ghee* in a large pan and fry rice until grains are well coated with the *ghee*. Add onion paste and mix well, fry for 3 minutes, stirring constantly, then add spice mixture and stir thoroughly. Add reserved stock which should measure 3¼ cups. Bring to the boil and cook until rice is almost tender and liquid absorbed. Add prawns, sliced tomato and salt to taste and continue to cook, tightly covered, until rice is tender and grains dry and well separated. Prawns should be pink and cooked through.

Splash on rose water and stir before serving.

MUTTON STOCK PILLAU WITH SHRIMP AND PEAS

750 g (1½ lb) mutton bones
5 cups water
1 medium onion
4 cloves
2 cloves garlic
2 bay leaves
5 cm (2 inch) stick cinnamon
375 g (¾ lb) long grain rice
3 tablespoons *ghee*
1 large onion, thinly sliced
3 cloves garlic, thinly sliced
4 black cardamoms, crushed
2 medium tomatoes, sliced
salt
pepper
185 g (6 oz) raw shrimp, peeled
185 g (6 oz) frozen peas
30 g (1 oz) blanched, slivered almonds
30 g (1 oz) raisins, soaked
1 teaspoon rose water (optional)

Chop up mutton bones and boil for 1 hour with water, onion stuck with cloves, garlic, bay leaves and cinnamon stick. Strain stock and reduce or add water to make up to 3¼ cups.

Wash rice in cold water and drain well. Heat *ghee* in a heavy saucepan and fry thinly sliced onion and garlic until soft. Add rice and stir until all grains are well coated with *ghee*. Add cardamoms, tomato, salt, pepper and the 3¼ cups stock. Cover and bring to the boil, then reduce heat and cook until the water is absorbed and the rice is beginning to soften. Stir in shrimps and peas. Cover and continue to cook until rice is tender and shrimp and peas cooked. Stir in nuts and drained raisins and place in a hot oven for 10 minutes.

Splash on rose water and stir the dish thoroughly before serving.

CHICKEN PILLAU

375 g (¾ lb) long grain rice
750 g (1½ lb) chicken
2 medium onions
3 cloves garlic, minced
6 tablespoons *ghee*
4 cm (1½ inch) piece fresh ginger, minced
½ cup plain yoghurt
2 teaspoons salt
½ teaspoon ground black pepper
2 bay leaves
5 cm (2 inch) stick cinnamon
4 black cardamoms, crushed
pinch of freshly grated nutmeg
2 fresh red chillies
4 shallots

Wash rice in cold water and drain well. Cut chicken into 2.5 cm (1 inch) cubes. Slice one onion and mince the other. Heat 5 tablespoons *ghee* and fry sliced onion until soft. Add minced onion and garlic and fry for 2 minutes, then put in chicken pieces and cook until well coloured.

Add ginger and yoghurt, stirring well. Pour rice into the pan and add salt, pepper, bay leaves, cinnamon, cardamoms and nutmeg. Cover to 3 cm (1¼ inches) above the level of the rice with water or light chicken stock. Cover and bring to the boil. Reduce heat and simmer until the rice is tender and chicken cooked through.

Fry sliced chillies and shallots in 1 tablespoon *ghee* or oil for 2 minutes and stir into rice.

SHRIMP RICE

375 g (¾ lb) long grain rice
1 large onion
4 tablespoons *ghee*
2 cloves garlic
2.5 cm (1 inch) piece fresh ginger
250 g (½ lb) raw shrimps, peeled
½ teaspoon ground black pepper
3 cloves
5 cm (2 inch) cinnamon stick
2 green cardamoms, crushed
1 teaspoon salt
¼ cup thick coconut milk or thick cream
1 bay leaf
fresh mint or coriander leaves
red or green chilli, sliced

Wash rice and soak in cold water for 40 minutes. Drain well. Slice onion thinly and fry in *ghee* until soft. Add minced garlic and ginger and fry for 1 minute, then put in shrimps and cook until pink. Add rice and stir on moderate heat until all grains are well coated with the *ghee*. Add pepper, cloves, cinnamon, cardamoms, salt and coconut milk or thick cream. Pour on water to reach 3 cm (1¼ inches) above the level of the rice. Add bay leaf. Cover and bring to the boil, then reduce heat and cook until rice is tender and liquid absorbed.

Stir rice well, cover and place in warm oven for 15 minutes. Garnish with mint or coriander leaves and sliced chilli.

YELLOW RICE

345 g (11 oz) long grain rice
¾ teaspoon saffron strands
1 tablespoon boiling water
5 cm (2 inch) stick cinnamon
4 cloves
3 black cardamoms
3 cups water
2 tablespoons *ghee*
30 g (1 oz) raisins
30 g (1 oz) blanched almonds

Soak rice in cold water for ½ hour. Drain well. Steep saffron in boiling water and grind to release the colour. Pour rice into a saucepan and add saffron water, cinnamon, cloves and cardamoms. Pour on water and bring to the boil. Cover, reduce heat and simmer until rice is tender and liquid absorbed. Transfer to a hot oven for 10 minutes.

Fry raisins and blanched almonds gently in *ghee* for 2 minutes. Stir into the rice and serve at once.

LEMONS PICKLED IN SALT

500 g (1 lb) small lemons
5 cm (2 inch) piece fresh ginger
6 green chillies
2 tablespoons chilli powder
500 g (1 lb) coarse salt

Wash and dry lemons and cut into quarters. Grind ginger and chillies to a paste and mix with chilli powder and salt. Place lemons in a large jar, add the seasonings and cover tightly. Shake jar to distribute seasonings and leave in a sunny place for 2-3 weeks, undisturbed, or place in a very low oven for 2 days, then store in a warm cupboard.

Leave for about 2 months before using.

FRESH MINT CHUTNEY

90 g (3 oz) fresh mint
1 small onion
1-2 green chillies, seeds removed
2 teaspoons sugar
salt
lemon juice

Wash mint and pick off leaves, discarding stems. Chop leaves finely. Mince onion and chillies and mix with mint, adding sugar and salt and lemon juice to taste. Pound all together to a smooth paste or puree in the liquidiser.

Serve with Samoosa or Pakora.

CORIANDER CHUTNEY

125 g (¼ lb) fresh coriander leaves
1 teaspoon salt
3 cloves garlic
1 cm (½ inch) piece fresh ginger
1-2 teaspoons sugar
lemon or lime juice

Wash coriander leaves and shake out water. Chop finely, then pound to a paste with remaining ingredients, adding lemon juice to taste. This can be prepared in the blender.

Keep refrigerated in an airtight container for up to 3 days.

COCONUT CHUTNEY

125 g (¼ lb) grated fresh coconut, or
  90 g (3 oz) moistened desiccated coconut
1 tablespoon white poppy seeds, ground
1 heaped tablespoon finely chopped fresh coriander
  mint or leaves
¾ teaspoon mustard seeds
pinch of chilli
pinch of saffron powder
1 teaspoon cummin, ground
salt
sugar
lemon juice

Pound coconut with poppy seeds and coriander or mint leaves to a coarse paste. Add mustard seeds, chilli and saffron and cummin and mix well. Season to taste with salt and pepper and add lemon juice to moisten.

Store in an airtight container in the refrigerator for up to 5 days.

MANGO PICKLE

AAM KA ACHAR

2 kg (4 lb) small unripe mangoes
2 tablespoons fenugreek seeds
3 teaspoons turmeric powder
½ teaspoon asafoetida
12 dried red chillies, soaked
500 g (1 lb) coarse salt
2 cups mustard oil

Cut mangoes in halves, lengthways, cutting through the stone which will still be soft if mangoes are sufficiently unripe. Mix spices with salt and about 4 tablespoons oil and cover one half of each mango with a thick layer of the paste. Press the other half on top. Arrange all stuffed mangoes in a wide-necked jar and sprinkle on any remaining spices. Cover jar and leave for 1 day.

Heat remaining mustard oil to lukewarm and pour onto the mangoes. Seal jars again and leave in a warm sunny place for 10 days, or place in a very low oven for 2 days, then keep in a warm cupboard for 1 month.

Store in a cool dry cupboard when ready.

SPICED LENTIL SAUCE

185 g (6 oz) whole black lentils
2 cups water
1 teaspoon salt
¾ teaspoon turmeric powder
1 green chilli, sliced
2 tablespoons ghee

1 large onion, finely chopped
2 cloves garlic, crushed
2 teaspoons garam masala
pinch of chilli powder
2 tablespoons finely chopped fresh coriander leaves

Soak lentils overnight in cold water. Drain and place in a saucepan with water, salt, turmeric and chilli. Bring to the boil, then reduce heat and simmer until lentils are tender. Add a little more water if needed. Heat ghee and fry onion and garlic until soft. Add garam masala and chilli powder and fry briefly.

Stir into the lentils and add fresh coriander leaves. Reheat before serving.

DHAL SPECIAL

250 g (½ lb) red or yellow lentils
2 medium onions
2 cloves garlic
1 green chilli
3 tablespoons ghee
1 tablespoon coriander, ground
1 teaspoon turmeric powder
1 teaspoon cummin, ground
salt
pepper
¼ cup thick cream
2 teaspoons coriander seeds
4 shallots, thinly sliced
1 tablespoon ghee

Wash lentils and cover with water to about 4 cm (1½ inches) above the level of the lentils. Bring to the boil and cook until very soft, then drain well, reserving the liquid.

Mince onions, garlic and chilli and fry in ghee for 3 minutes. Add spices and fry for 2 minutes, then pour in lentil mixture and heat through. Mash to a smooth puree and season to taste with salt and pepper. Stir in cream and some of the reserved liquid if too thick. The Dhal should have the consistency of a thick soup.

Fry coriander seeds and sliced shallots in ghee for 1 minute and stir into the Dhal.

DHAL CURRY WITH COCONUT

220 g (7 oz) red lentils
1¾ cups thin coconut milk
1 tablespoon dried shrimp, soaked and coarsely ground
½ teaspoon saffron powder
1 green chilli, thinly sliced
2.5 cm (1 inch) stalk lemon grass, finely chopped
1 cup thick coconut milk
salt
black pepper
2 curry leaves
4 shallots, sliced
chilli powder
1 tablespoon ghee

Wash lentils well and soak in cold water to cover for 2 hours. Drain well and put into a saucepan with thin coconut milk, dried shrimp, saffron, chilli and lemon grass. Bring to the boil, then cover and leave to simmer until lentils are almost tender. Add thick coconut milk, salt and pepper and continue to cook until done.

Crumble bay leaves and fry in *ghee* with sliced shallots for 2 minutes. Stir into the Dhal and add chilli powder to taste. Heat through briefly.

SPICED CHICKPEAS
KABLI CHANNA

625 g (1¼ lb) canned chickpeas
1 large onion
5 cm (2 inch) piece fresh ginger
2 cloves garlic
3 tablespoons *ghee*
1 teaspoon pomegranate seeds, ground, or
   1 tablespoon lemon juice
1½ teaspoons *garam masala*
¾ teaspoon dried green mango powder *(amchur)*
2 green chillies, sliced
2 large tomatoes, peeled
3 tablespoons chopped fresh coriander leaves
salt
black pepper
chilli powder (optional)

Drain chickpeas, reserving a little of the liquid. Slice onion thinly. Shred or grate ginger and crush garlic. Fry onion, ginger and garlic in *ghee* until soft then add pomegranate seeds (if using lemon juice do not add at this point), *garam masala* and mango powder. Stir on moderate heat for 1 minute then put in drained chickpeas. Stir until well coated with the spices. Add sliced chillies and pour in the reserved chickpea liquid and enough water to just cover. Bring to the boil, reduce heat, and simmer for 10 minutes.

Chop tomatoes coarsely and add to the pan with coriander leaves, salt, pepper and lemon juice (if used). Continue to cook for a further 15 minutes.

Garnish with chilli powder. Leave overnight if time allows, and reheat before serving, for extra flavour.

STEAMED YOGHURT SWEET
BARPHI DAHI

4 cups fresh whole milk
125 g (¼ lb) sugar
1 cup plain yoghurt
12 blanched, slivered almonds
15 g (½ oz) raisins
1 tablespoon *ghee*

Bring milk to boil and continue to cook until reduced by half. Stir in sugar and cook until dissolved. Beat yoghurt and add to the milk mixture. Pour into a buttered fireproof dish and cover with foil. Place in a dish of water in a moderately hot oven and cook until the pudding sets.

Fry almonds and raisins in *ghee* and sprinkle over the pudding. Cook for a further 5 minutes. Serve hot or well chilled.

RICE PUDDING
KHEER

90 g (3 oz) short grain rice
3¼ cups fresh whole milk
2 green cardamoms
75 g (2½ oz) sugar

Wash rice and soak for ½ hour in cold water. Bring milk to a rolling boil and pour in drained rice and cardamoms. Cover and simmer until rice is completely soft.

Stir in sugar and continue cooking for 5 more minutes. Serve hot or cold.

FRIED SWEET BATTER CURLS
JALEBI

250 g (½ lb) plain flour
2 teaspoons baking powder
1 heaped teaspoon saffron powder
2 tablespoons warm water
oil or *ghee* for deep frying
185 g (6 oz) sugar
1½ cups water
1 teaspoon rose water

Sieve flour and baking powder into a basin. Infuse saffron in warm water and pour over the flour. Add enough water to make a smooth batter which is thick enough to squeeze through a forcing pipe. Leave for 30 minutes.

Heat oil or *ghee* and fill forcing bag with the batter. Pipe swirls of batter into the oil and lift out after about 1½ minutes. They should be crisp and well puffed out. Drain on absorbent paper.

Pour sugar and water into a saucepan and bring to the boil. Simmer for 5 minutes, then remove from heat and splash in rose water. Leave to cool. Arrange Jalebi in a serving dish and pour on the syrup. Chill slightly before serving.

COCONUT TOFFEE
NARIAL KI BARFI

125 g (¼ lb) desiccated coconut
155 g (5 oz) sugar
½ - ¾ cup water
1 green cardamom, ground
pink food colouring

Moisten coconut slightly with water. Pour sugar and water into a small saucepan and cook on low heat without stirring until the syrup is sticky. To test if ready dab a little onto the back of a wooden spoon. Press a finger onto it and draw away. When thin threads of toffee are formed between spoon and finger, syrup is the correct consistency. Add moistened coconut and stir until mixture is thick. Stir in cardamom.

Spread half onto a greased tray and colour the other half pink. Pour on top and press flat. Mark out squares before completely set and cut when cold.

HALVA WITH PISTACHIOS

375 g (¾ lb) sugar
1¼ cups water
315 g (10 oz) full cream milk powder
5 tablespoons *ghee*
¾ teaspoon powdered cardamom
45 g (1½ oz) pistachios

Pour sugar and water into a saucepan and bring to the boil. Cook until lightly coloured and beginning to thicken. Beat in milk powder and *ghee* and continue beating over moderate heat until the mixture is smooth. Lower heat very slightly and stir until the mixture resembles a thick, light brown fudge and leaves the sides of the pan.

Finely chop or crush two-thirds of the pistachios and stir into the Halva. Heat through, then spoon into a greased tray 23 cm (9 inches) square, and spread out smoothly. Decorate the top with remaining pistachios and leave to cool. When set cut into squares.

BUTTERY PEA FLOUR FUDGE

MYSORE PAK

440 g (14 oz) *ghee*
125 g (¼ lb) gram flour *(besan)*
315 g (10 oz) sugar
¾ cup water

Melt one-third of the *ghee* and fry flour until lightly coloured. Melt remaining *ghee* and set aside.

Pour sugar and water into a saucepan and bring to the boil. Cook without stirring until very sticky and beginning to darken. Test if right by dabbing a little on the back of a wooden spoon. Press a finger on and pull away. The toffee should form into long firm threads between finger and spoon.

Add fried flour and melted *ghee* and cook on moderate heat, stirring continually, until very thick.

Pour into a buttered square tray and press flat. Cut into squares when set and serve when completely cold.

MILK BALLS IN SUGAR SYRUP

GULAB JAMON

185 g (6 oz) full cream milk powder
2 tablespoons *ghee*
125 g (¼ lb) self-raising flour
1 teaspoon baking powder
vegetable oil for deep frying
315 g (10 oz) sugar
1¾ cups water
1½ teaspoons rose water

Mix milk powder with *ghee* and work to a crumbly texture. Add self-raising flour and baking powder and mix well, crumbling with the fingers. Mix in a very little water to make a very stiff dough. Wrap in a damp cloth and leave for 3 hours.

Break the dough and rub hard on a floured board into fine crumbs. Add sprinkling of water and form mixture into walnut-sized balls. Heat oil and deep fry balls to a light golden brown. Shake pan during cooking to colour the balls evenly. Lift out and drain well.

Pour sugar and water into a saucepan and bring to the boil. Simmer until very slightly sticky. Splash in rose water and add milk balls. Leave milk balls to soak in the syrup for at least ½ hour before serving. Serve warm or chilled.

CREAM BALLS IN CREAM SAUCE

RAS MALAI

125 g (¼ lb) full cream milk powder
30 g (1 oz) self-raising flour
⅓ cup whole milk
250 g (½ lb) white sugar
1¼ cups water
3 cups milk
½ cup thick cream
1½ teaspoons rose water
1 tablespoon blanched, chopped almonds

Mix milk powder and self-raising flour with up to ⅓ cup milk, adding milk gradually to make a dough which just holds together. Wrap in a damp cloth and leave for 3 hours.

Break the dough and crumble with the fingers, then with wet hands form into walnut-sized balls.

Pour sugar and water into a saucepan and bring to the boil. Add cream balls and simmer for 15 minutes, shaking pan to turn the balls. Splash in about 1 tablespoon ice water, which should make the balls puff out a little. Lift out and leave to cool.

Bring milk to the boil and add enough of the sugar syrup to sweeten to taste. Return cream balls and leave in this liquid for another 3 hours.

Remove the cream balls again and boil milk until well reduced. Stir in cream and add rose water and chopped nuts. Return balls and allow to cool before serving. This is best served slightly chilled.

CREAM BALLS IN SUGAR SYRUP

RAS GULLA

cream balls from Ras Malai (see above)
375 g (¾ lb) white sugar
2 cups water
1 teaspoon cornflour
1 teaspoon rose water

Prepare the cream ball dough and shape into balls as directed. Pour sugar and water into a saucepan and bring to the boil. Simmer for 5 minutes, then put in the cream balls. Simmer for 15 minutes until the balls rise to the surface and are slightly expanded. Mix cornflour with a little cold water and stir into the syrup to thicken very slightly.

Remove from the heat and stir in rose water. Chill before serving. Serve the cream balls with a little of the syrup.

CARROT DESSERT

GAJAR HALWA

750 g (1½ lb) carrots
8 cups milk
3 tablespoons full cream milk powder
5 cm (2 inch) stick cinnamon
125 g (¼ lb) raisins, soaked
3 black cardamoms, crushed lightly
½ teaspoon saffron powder
1 tablespoon boiling water
3 tablespoons *ghee* or butter
2 tablespoons honey
185 g (6 oz) sugar, or to taste
90 g (3 oz) blanched, slivered almonds
1½ teaspoons rose water
silver leaf to decorate (optional)

Scrape carrots, rinse, then grate finely. Put into a saucepan and pour on milk. Add milk powder and cinnamon stick. Bring to the boil and cook, stirring frequently, until the mixture has thickened and carrot is beginning to become very soft. Add drained raisins, cardamoms and saffron mixed with boiling water and continue to cook, stirring continually, until the mixture becomes a thick paste.

Add *ghee*, honey and sugar and cook again, stirring, until thick. Stir in blanched almonds and rose water. Spoon into a lightly buttered dish and smooth the top. Decorate with silver leaf if available. Leave to cool before serving, or serve hot.

Carrot Dessert (recipe this page), and Cream Balls in Cream Sauce (recipe page 39).

SRI LANKA

Sri Lanka, the 'Resplendent Isle', previously known as Ceylon, has one of the world's more colourful cuisines. Here flowers and brightly coloured local herbs and nuts are not merely decoration, but are part of the food itself, and the table is bright with fresh tropical fruits, buttery cakes and sweetmeats, multi-hued curries, spicy rice and spongey breads. Sri Lankan food, like that of so many Southeast Asian countries, has absorbed much from its visitors: South Indian, Dutch, Malay, Portuguese and English have all passed through this beautiful island, and many lent their own recipes, spices and cooking methods to an already rich and varied cuisine.

Curries are inevitably the centre of any meal, and come in many flavours and colours. They are described after their seasonings rather than the main ingredients: white curries, mild and creamy from coconut milk; red curries, bright scarlet from loads of pounded dried chillies; and curries black as night. These black curries, not particularly appealing to the eye, but heavenly to eat, are most typical. The colour comes from coriander, cummin and fennel which, with other dried spices added to suit the ingredients, are roasted to a very dark brown before being ground on a stone spice grinder and then mulled for an age in a clay pot *(chatty)* with the other ingredients over a glowing charcoal fire. Curries cooked in these traditional pots have a mellowness which somehow cannot quite be achieved in metal cooking pots, though these are adequate if you are not lucky enough to own a *chatty* or two.

With these curries come Appe and Appum, known also as Hoppers, the substitute for bread and toast in a country where rice is the staple grain. Hoppers are cup-shaped pancakes made with a batter of fermented rice flour. Cooked in small pans shaped like a miniature Chinese *wok,* they are crisp and lightly golden on the sides, with soft spongey centres. They are served with a fiercely hot, tart onion *sambol.* Iddi Appe look like little bundles of steamed strings of rice flour, whence their name String Hoppers. These are served at breakfast with mild coconut curries and a *sambol* made with freshly grated coconut.

Sri Lankan food is meant to be eaten with the fingers, using the rice or hoppers to mop up the various curry sauces. All the food, including watery coconut-based soups, is served at the same time. One heaps rice and a spoonful of each accompanying dish onto the plate, adding a few spoonfuls of the hot *sambol* that will always be present. The meal ends with fresh fruit rather than sweets or desserts, the many delicious sweetmeats and rich puddings that Sri Lankan cooks have devised being served between meals and on special occasions.

The word *mallung* means 'mixed up', and has become the name of many dishes using a mixture of ingredients, often with grated coconut added. The green vegetable Mallung included in this small selection of Sri Lankan recipes came from a Dutch acquaintance who lived for many years in Sri Lanka, where her Sunday curry lunches were legend in her circle.

CHILLI SAMBAL

SEENI SAMBOL

4 large onions
5 cloves garlic
2.5 cm (1 inch) piece fresh ginger
5 tablespoons coconut oil
3 black cardamoms
2 cm (¾ inch) cinnamon stick
2 teaspoons curry powder or *garam masala*
½ teaspoon turmeric powder
2 teaspoons chilli powder
1 piece toasted Bombay Duck, ground
3 tablespoons dried prawns, powdered
1 teaspoon salt
1 teaspoon sugar
3 teaspoons vinegar
3 tablespoons tamarind
½ cup boiling water
¼ cup thick coconut cream
1 green chilli

Mince or finely chop onions, garlic and ginger and fry in oil until soft. Grind cardamoms and cinnamon stick and add to the pan with powdered spices, Bombay Duck, dried prawns, salt, sugar and vinegar. Stir on moderate heat for 5 minutes.

Steep tamarind in boiling water. Mash pulp and add with tamarind water to the pan. Bring to the boil and stir to mix well with other ingredients. Add coconut cream and simmer on low heat for 20 minutes.

Blend to a smooth puree and stir in thinly sliced chilli. Store in airtight jars until needed. Will keep in the refrigerator for several weeks. Serve as a side dish with meat, vegetable or rice dishes.

BEEF IN COCONUT CREAM

1 kg (2 lb) beef steak
1½ tablespoons coriander
1½ teaspoons cummin
½ teaspoon fenugreek seeds
2 large onions
8 cloves garlic
3 tablespoons *ghee*
5 cm (2 inch) stick cinnamon
1 tablespoon white vinegar
½ teaspoon turmeric powder
2 teaspoons chilli powder
3 curry leaves
¼ cup thick coconut milk
salt
2 tablespoons finely chopped fresh coriander leaves

Trim meat and cut into 5 cm (2 inch) cubes. Toast coriander, cummin and fenugreek under the grill or in a dry pan for 2 minutes. Grind to a fine powder.

Mince onion and garlic and fry in *ghee* until lightly coloured. Add cinnamon and meat and cook until well browned. Add ground spices, vinegar, turmeric, chilli powder and curry leaves and stir well. Add enough water or beef stock to cover meat. Bring to the boil, then reduce heat and simmer until meat is very tender.

Stir in coconut milk and add salt to taste. Heat through for 4-5 minutes and garnish with coriander.

LIVER CURRY

250 g (½ lb) calves liver
3 large onions
3 cloves garlic
10 cm (4 inch) stalk lemon grass
6 dried chillies, soaked
3 tablespoons *ghee*
1 cup beef stock
1 teaspoon coriander, ground
1 teaspoon cummin, ground
½ teaspoon fennel, ground
¼ cup thick coconut milk
salt
pepper

Slice liver thinly. Slice 2 onions thinly and mince the remaining one with garlic and lemon grass. Mash chillies.

Heat *ghee* and fry sliced onions until lightly coloured. Add onion paste and chillies and fry for 5 minutes. Put in sliced liver and cook until just coloured with no pink showing.

Pour in stock and add spices. Simmer until liver is tender. Stir in coconut milk and season to taste with salt and pepper. Cook for another 4-5 minutes then serve.

GREEN VEGETABLES WITH COCONUT

MALLUNG

500 g (1 lb) mixed green vegetables
3 tablespoons vegetable or coconut oil
4 green chillies
75 g (2½ oz) freshly grated or desiccated coconut
3 teaspoons powdered dried prawns or fish floss
¾ teaspoon saffron powder
1 large onion
6 curry leaves (optional)

1 teaspoon salt
½ cup water
lemon juice
salt

Wash and coarsely shred vegetables, such as cabbage, spinach, beans, kale, etc.

Heat oil and fry slit green chillies for 5 minutes. Pour off most of the oil. Add vegetables and all ingredients except lemon juice and salt. Cover and simmer until vegetables are tender and coconut moist.

Add lemon juice and salt to taste.

SPICY COCONUT PUDDING

VATTALAPPAM

2 large eggs
2 cups milk
3 tablespoons full cream milk powder
½ cup thick coconut milk
3 green cardamoms, crushed
½ teaspoon grated fresh nutmeg
½ teaspoon cinnamon powder
½ cup black molasses
2 tablespoons brown sugar

Beat eggs lightly. Mix milk with milk powder and coconut milk and heat until just beginning to boil. Add spices and stir in molasses. Mix thoroughly. Pour into the beaten eggs and pour into a dish. Set in a basin of water in a moderate oven and cook for about 1 hour, or until pudding is set. Sprinkle on brown sugar and raise heat to crisp the top. Serve warm or cold.

COCONUT RICE

315 g (10 oz) long grain rice
3 tablespoons *ghee*
5 shallots, thinly sliced
2 green cardamoms
1¾ cups chicken stock
1 cup thick coconut milk
salt

Wash rice and dry well. Heat *ghee* and fry shallots and cardamoms with rice for 3 minutes, stirring continually. Add chicken stock and coconut milk and sprinkle on a little salt. Cover and simmer until rice is tender and liquid absorbed. Add more salt to taste.

Stir rice and leave, covered, for a further 10 minutes.

BURMA

The heart of the Burmese cuisine is curry, but a curry quite different from that of nearby India. Where most Indian curries start with a complex blending of dried spices, those of Burma have their beginnings in a paste of pounded fresh onions, ginger, garlic, chillies and turmeric root as the main seasoning ingredients, supplemented by *ngapi* (the pungent, salty dried prawn paste similar to Malaysian *blacan*), lemon grass, and lemon juice or vinegar to give a slightly sour taste.

Colourful crisp salads made with imaginative combinations of vegetables, cold meats and seafoods are also very much a part of any Burmese meal; so too are lightly cooked vegetables garnished with aromatic sauces based on the much-used *ngapi*. Local long-grain rice is served boiled with all meals, except when noodles are the main dish. Burmese cooks also pride themselves on delicious rice dishes flavoured with dried fish, coconut and spices and served with an array of appetising accompaniments that are the hallmark of a good Burmese meal: hot and spicy pickles, dried prawns *(balachuang)*, finely ground fried chickpeas, chopped fresh coriander leaves and spring onion, dry fried onion and garlic, and fried dried chillies are served in small dishes to be added according to individual taste.

Mohinga, a delicious soup served over a thin rice vermicelli, is one of Burma's most popular dishes. It is served everywhere, often by hawkers with portable charcoal cookers atached to one end of a bamboo carrying pole and the ingredients arranged in a box at the other end. Mohinga should be served with several crisp, crunchy accompaniments.

Burmese food is traditionally eaten with the fingers from small bowls, but a fork and spoon can be used. A full meal consists of a bowl of hot boiled rice, a soup and several curry dishes, together with a salad and a number of accompaniments. The meal should be a balanced blending of ingredients, textures, colours and tastes calculated to enliven the palate.

No special cooking equipment is needed. Curries can be cooked in normal Western-style pots, and a *wok* can replace the *dar-o* (similar in shape to a *wok*, but with deeper, less sloping sides). Wet seasonings can be prepared in a heavy-duty blender; add oil to prevent the machine clogging, but only if the seasonings are later to be fried in oil.

FISH CURRY

500 g (1 lb) white fish fillets
2 large onions
12 cloves garlic
3 tablespoons oil
5 cm (2 inch) piece fresh ginger, sliced
1 stalk lemon grass, quartered
1 teaspoon turmeric powder
½ teaspoon dried shrimp paste
1 tablespoon vinegar
1 large tomato
2 tablespoons fish sauce
2 tablespoons chopped fresh coriander leaves

Slice fish and wipe dry. Slice onions and chop garlic. Fry onions and garlic in oil until soft. Add ginger, lemon grass, turmeric, dried shrimp paste and vinegar and simmer for 2 minutes. Slice tomato and add to the pot with fish sauce. Heat through.

In another pan fry fish pieces in a little oil until lightly coloured. Put fish in the curry and add a very little water. Cover and cook on low heat for 5-7 minutes. Stir in chopped coriander and serve at once.

PRAWN CURRY WITH BAMBOO SHOOTS

1 kg (2 lb) raw prawns
250 g (½ lb) canned bamboo shoots, drained
2 medium onions
8 cloves garlic
5 cm (2 inch) piece fresh ginger, sliced
2 tablespoons *ghee* or oil
1½ teaspoons turmeric powder
3 medium tomatoes, chopped
1 cup fish stock or water
½ cup thick coconut milk
fish sauce
fresh red chilli

Peel prawns and devein. Leave heads on, or remove if preferred. Cut bamboo shoots into matchstick pieces. Slice onions thinly and chop garlic. Fry onion, garlic and ginger in *ghee* or oil until soft and very lightly coloured. Reduce heat and put in turmeric and chopped tomatoes. Cook briefly, then add fish stock or water and bring to the boil. Put in prawns and bamboo shoots and simmer until cooked.

Add thick coconut milk and heat through, then flavour to taste with fish sauce. Garnish with sliced red chilli.

CHICKEN CURRY

CHET GLAY HIN

750 g (1½ lb) chicken
½ teaspoon turmeric powder
1 heaped tablespoon mild curry powder
1 teaspoon crumbled dried chillies
½ teaspoon cinnamon powder
½ teaspoon allspice powder
3 tablespoons oil
4 cloves garlic, crushed
6 shallots or 2 small red onions, finely chopped
2 cm (¾ inch) piece fresh ginger, minced
2½ cups water
2 curry leaves

Fish Curry (recipe this page), and Cucumber Salad (recipe page 47).

salt
pepper
lemon or lime juice
chilli 'flowers' or shredded chilli

Chop chicken into large pieces and put in a bowl.
Sprinkle on turmeric, curry powder, chilli, cinnamon
and allspice. Stand for 10 minutes, turning several
times.

Heat oil and fry chicken until well browned. Push to
one side of the pan and fry garlic, onions and ginger for
3 minutes. Pour in water, stir well, add curry leaves and
simmer until chicken is tender and sauce well reduced.
Season to taste with salt, pepper and lemon or lime
juice.

Arrange chicken pieces in a serving dish. Spoon on
the sauce and decorate with shredded chilli or 'flowers'
made by shredding the ends of red chillies and dropping them in ice water to curl the 'petals'.

BURMESE CHICKEN IN COCONUT MILK

KWAY SWE

750 g (1½ lb) chicken
1 teaspoon salt
¼ teaspoon white pepper
4 cups water
1 teaspoon turmeric powder
2 large onions, minced
8 cloves garlic, minced
2.5 cm (1 inch) piece fresh ginger, minced
2 green chillies, seeded and chopped
2 tablespoons oil
1½ cups thick coconut milk
fish sauce or salt
fresh coriander leaves, chopped
fresh red chilli, sliced
hardboiled egg, chopped
onion, sliced

Skin chicken and cut into pieces. Rub with salt and
white pepper. Put into a saucepan and cover with
water. Add turmeric and boil until the meat begins to
fall from the bones. Lift out, reserving stock, and pull
off all meat. Discard bones and cut meat into bite sized
cubes.

Pound onion, garlic, ginger and chillies to a paste
and fry gently in oil for 5 minutes. Add chicken pieces
and fry until coloured, then add stock to cover and
thick coconut milk. Simmer until the sauce is slightly
thickened and oily. Flavour to taste with fish sauce or
salt and stir in chopped coriander and sliced chillies.

Serve with small dishes of extra chopped coriander,
chillies, hardboiled egg and sliced onion.

SKEWERED BEEF

AME HUAT

500 g (1 lb) lean rump, sirloin or topside steak
5 cm (2 inch) piece fresh ginger, shredded
1 tablespoon coriander, ground

2 teaspoons cummin, ground
2 teaspoons salt
1 teaspoon turmeric powder
1 teaspoon fennel, crushed
⅔ cup thick coconut milk
oil

Cut beef into very thin slices, then into long, narrow
strips. Pound ginger, coriander, cummin, salt and turmeric to a paste and mix in fennel, coconut milk and
about 4 tablespoons oil. Put beef slices into a flat dish
and pour on the marinade. Leave for at least ½ hour.
Turn occasionally.

Thread strips of beef onto bamboo or metal skewers,
brush with a little more oil and grill or roast over a charcoal fire until dark brown and slightly crisp. Brush with
more oil during cooking to keep meat moist.

Serve with a hot chilli sauce or fish sauce.

ROAST PORK CURRY

625 g (1¼ lb) roast pork
1 medium onion
8 cloves garlic
5 cm (2 inch) piece fresh ginger, chopped
8 shallots, or 2 small red onions
1 medium tomato
½ teaspoon turmeric powder
½ teaspoon dried shrimp paste
1 fresh red chilli, finely chopped
1 teaspoon chilli powder
1 teaspoon salt
2 tablespoons oil
1 teaspoon tamarind
¾ cup boiling water
fish sauce
tomato slices
fresh red chilli, shredded

Cut pork into 5 cm (2 inch) cubes. Chop onion and
garlic and pound to a paste with ginger. Slice shallots or
red onions and tomatoes thinly. Rub pork pieces with a
mixture of turmeric and mashed shrimp paste mixed
with a little water. Leave for 10 minutes.

Put pork pieces, onion paste, sliced onions, chopped
chilli and chilli powder in a pan. Add salt and oil and
fry for 5 minutes on high heat. Splash on a little water
to prevent sticking. Add tomato, crumbled tamarind
and boiling water. Cover and cook until meat is tender
and has absorbed the seasonings and liquid. Splash on
fish sauce to taste.

Serve with a garnish of tomato slices and shredded
red chilli.

NOODLES WITH FISH SAUCE

MOHINGA

750 g (1½ lb) cold cooked rice vermicelli
750 g (1½ lb) white fish
2 stalks lemon grass, quartered
8 cups water
1 teaspoon turmeric powder
salt

2 tablespoons fish sauce
5 cm (2 inch) piece fresh ginger, shredded
6 cloves garlic, crushed
10 spring onions, shredded
220 g (7 oz) Chinese or white cabbage, chopped
155 g (5 oz) celery leaves, chopped
2 medium onions, finely chopped
2 tablespoons tamarind
¼ cup boiling water
chilli sauce or minced red chilli
fresh coriander leaves, finely chopped
hardboiled eggs
fried fish or shrimp cakes (see below)
wedges of lemon or lime
banana or ginger flowers, shredded (optional)

Soak vermicelli in cold water. Slice fish and put into a large saucepan with lemon grass and water. Bring to the boil and cook until fish is tender, then lift fish out and continue boiling stock for a further 15 minutes.

Flake fish and put into another saucepan. Strain stock over fish, discarding any bones and lemon grass. Season with turmeric, salt, fish sauce, ginger and garlic and cook for 30 minutes on low heat. Add spring onions, cabbage, celery and finely chopped onion and cook until vegetables are tender. Keep hot.

Drain vermicelli and divide between six large bowls. Soak tamarind in boiling water and mash pulp. Slice hardboiled eggs and prepare fish or shrimp cakes, if used. Add a little tamarind pulp and water, chilli sauce or minced red chilli, chopped coriander, egg slices, fish or shrimp cakes, lemon or lime wedges and shredded flowers to each bowl. Pour on a generous serving of the piping hot fish sauce.

Fried Fish or Shrimp Cakes:
250 g (½ lb) white fish fillets or raw shrimp
1 teaspoon salt
1 teaspoon sesame oil
2 spring onions
2 egg whites
cornflour
oil

Chop fish or shrimps and pound to a smooth paste. Season with salt, sesame oil and finely chopped spring onions and knead to a smooth paste. Bind with egg-white and a little cornflour and mash for 1 minute. Heat about 2.5 cm (1 inch) oil and put in walnut-sized balls of the mixture which have been lightly coated with cornflour. Fry over moderate heat until lightly coloured. Drain well.

BURMESE RICE

375 g (¾ lb) long grain rice
10 cm (4 inch) stalk lemon grass, chopped
2¾ cups water
1 medium onion, minced
3 cloves garlic, minced
1½ teaspoons turmeric powder, or
   ¼ teaspoon powdered saffron
75 g (2½ oz) dried shrimp or salted dried fish, soaked
2 fresh red chillies, minced
3 tablespoons oil

1½ tablespoons fish sauce
1 tablespoon lemon or lime juice
salt
shallots, sliced
fresh chilli, sliced

Wash rice and pour into a deep saucepan. Add lemon grass and water. Bring to the boil, then cover and reduce heat to very low. Cook until rice is tender and liquid absorbed.

Grind onion, garlic, turmeric or saffron, drained shrimp or fish and chilli to a paste, adding oil, fish sauce and lemon or lime juice. Stir seasonings into the rice, add salt to taste and cook, stirring with a chop-stick, for a further 4 minutes. Remove from heat and allow to stand, covered, for 10 minutes.

Spoon into a serving dish and garnish with sliced shallots and chilli.

PRAWN AND BAMBOO SHOOT SALAD

315 g (10 oz) canned bamboo shoots
250 g (½ lb) raw prawns
4 shallots
2 green chillies
2 fresh red chillies
salt
white pepper
lemon juice
fresh coriander leaves, chopped

Drain bamboo shoots and slice thinly, then cut into matchstick pieces. Drop prawns into boiling water and simmer for about 6 minutes until cooked. Cool, then peel. Thinly slice shallots and chillies. Put bamboo shoots, prawns (halve if large), onion and chillies into a salad bowl. Add salt, white pepper and lemon juice to taste and garnish with chopped coriander.

CUCUMBER SALAD

THANHAT

3 large cucumbers
¼ cup white vinegar
salt
1 heaped tablespoon white sesame seeds
¼ cup seasame oil
3 large onions
6 cloves garlic
1 teaspoon turmeric powder
1-2 teaspoons sugar
white vinegar to taste

Peel cucumbers and cut into 5 cm (2 inch) pieces, then remove seeds and cut flesh into fingers. Put into a saucepan with vinegar and cover with water. Add a little salt, cover and simmer until cucumber is slightly tender and transparent. Drain well.

Toast sesame seeds in a dry pan until they pop, then set aside. Heat about 1 tablespoon sesame oil in a frying pan and fry thinly sliced onion and garlic until very dark brown. Set aside. Add remaining oil, turmeric,

sugar and enough vinegar to make a tasty dressing. Stir over gentle heat until sugar is dissolved. Allow dressing to cool.

Arrange cucumber pieces in a salad bowl. Pour on salad dressing and garnish with onion, garlic and sesame seeds.

SHRIMP AND VEGETABLE SALAD

375 g (¾ lb) raw shrimp
salt
2 cups water
½ teaspoon white pepper
1 small cucumber
2 medium tomatoes
8 lettuce leaves
8 spring onions, chopped
2 tablespoons lemon or lime juice
1 tablespoon fish sauce
2 teaspoons sugar
1 fresh red chilli, thinly sliced

Peel and devein shrimp and rinse in warm salted water. Drain. Bring salted water to the boil and put in shrimp. Boil for 2 minutes, then lift out and drain well. Reserve 2 tablespoons water. Season shrimp with salt and white pepper and cool completely.

Peel cucumber and shred finely, or slice very thinly. Quarter tomatoes. Shred lettuce. Arrange lettuce on a serving plate and top with shrimp, cucumber and spring onions. Surround with tomato pieces.

Prepare dressing by mixing reserved stock with lemon or lime juice, fish sauce and sugar. Add salt and pepper to taste. Pour over the salad and scatter on sliced chilli. Serve slightly chilled.

VEGETABLE CURRY

500 g (1 lb) mixed vegetables
3 large onions
4 cloves garlic
2 green chillies
2 teaspoons dried shrimp paste
4 tablespoons oil
40 g (1½ oz) powdered dried prawns
2 cups chicken stock
salt
white pepper

Choose vegetables such as eggplant, cauliflower, pumpkin, red or green pepper, peas, green beans. Cut vegetables into fairly small pieces and rinse in cold water. Drain. Slice onions, garlic and chillies thinly. Crumble shrimp paste.

Heat oil and fry onions until soft. Add garlic, chillies, shrimp paste and powdered prawns and cook for 2 minutes. Put in vegetables and stir over moderate heat for 3 minutes, then pour in stock, cover and simmer for 10 minutes. Vegetables should be cooked but retaining crispness. Season with salt and white pepper.

STUFFED EGGPLANT

3 medium eggplants
220 g (7 oz) raw prawns or shrimp
1 large onion
5 cloves garlic
2 fresh red chillies
2.5 cm (1 inch) piece fresh ginger
10 cm (4 inch) stalk lemon grass
1 teaspoon turmeric powder
1 teaspoon dried shrimp paste
2 teaspoons salt
2 teaspoons oil

Put eggplants into a saucepan and cover with water. Bring to the boil and simmer for about 10 minutes until softened. Drain and cool.

Peel and chop prawns or shrimp. Mince onion, garlic, chillies, ginger and lemon grass and mix with shrimp, turmeric, crumbled shrimp paste and salt. Cut eggplants in halves lengthways and scoop out pulp, taking care not to break through the skin. Chop eggplant pulp and mix with all other ingredients.

Put oil into a small saucepan and saute all ingredients on moderate to low heat for 5 minutes, stirring constantly. Fill the shells with the mixture, rounding the tops neatly. Bake in a hot oven or over coals for about 6 minutes.

SEMOLINA CAKE

185 g (6 oz) fine semolina
5 cups fresh milk
2 cups thick coconut milk
2 eggs
440 g (14 oz) white sugar
2 black cardamoms, ground
30 g (1 oz) roasted slivered almonds
15 g (½ oz) toasted white sesame seeds

Put semolina into a dry saucepan and cook over moderate heat until a light golden brown. Stir frequently and shake pan to prevent the semolina burning. Remove from heat and allow to cool.

Pour milk and coconut milk into another saucepan and heat through. Beat eggs and sugar until light and smooth. Stir in cardamom and almonds. Pour milk and coconut over the cooled semolina and cook on moderate to low heat until very thick. Stir constantly to prevent sticking or lumps forming. Stir in egg batter.

Pour into a greased 25 cm (10 inch) square cake tin and smooth top. Sprinkle on sesame seeds. Cover with aluminium foil and cook in a tin of water in a moderate oven for 1¼ hours. Leave to cool completely and when cold cut into diamond-shaped pieces.

Stuffed Eggplant (recipe this page).

THAILAND

My first Thai meal was had in the idyllic setting of a *klong*-side restaurant in Bangkok. Apart from the tart and fiery Tom Yam Kung, a highly popular Thai soup served in a charcoal-heated hotpot, I inadvertently ordered several quite mildly seasoned dishes which I enjoyed tremendously but which left me completely unprepared for the hot dishes that subsequent meals were to include. An openair seafood restaurant, a barn-like place where one perches on rickety stools, revealed succulent lobsters and enormous fresh mussels bubbling in steaming pots of sauce from which wafted the scent of lemons, fresh coriander and chillies. Oysters came in a greyish-looking sludge with a strong fishy taste and so many chillies that I'm sure it could have been left out in the hot sun for a week without going rancid. Travelling farther afield I discovered roadside foodstalls selling Kai Yang (a delicious dry peppered chicken grilled over charcoal embers), raw fish marinated in coconut milk and lime juice, and magnificent seafood salads.

Eating Thai food is a multiple experience. Taste buds, eyes and nose are all completely involved with the heady aromas, brilliant colours, sour, sweet, pungent and stingingly hot tastes — often all jumbled together in a single dish. The roots, leaves, flowers, stems and seeds of a multitude of local herbs and shrubs go into Thai cooking: small whole limes and fragrant lime leaves, lemon grass, *kha* (a mild ginger root known as *laos* or *lengkuas* in Indonesia and Malaysia), tiny sourish wild figs, the roots, leaves and ground dried seeds of coriander, many types of mint, fresh basil, crunchy lotus stems and roots, water chestnuts, the flowers of banana and ginger plants. Some dry spices are used, but most often wet seasonings are the base for curries and soupy sauces. Red, green and yellow seasonings are prepared with combinations of red and green chillies, garlic, lemon grass and fresh herbs; fresh turmeric root gives a bright yellow colour and a subtle pungency; miniature green birds-eye chillies can be found floating in many a Thai dish (innocuous enough to look at, they are unspeakably hot!).

Decorative Thai salads bring together cold shredded meats with crisp vegetables uncommon to a Western salad but very much part of the Thai cuisine: water chestnuts, lotus roots and stems, unripe papaya and mango, bamboo shoots, and garnishes of shredded dried seafoods and crushed peanuts. Unusual too are combinations like Preo Wan (Shrimp and Cucumber in Tomato Sauce) or Ma Hou (Pork-stuffed Oranges).

In Thailand one is invited to 'eat rice' — meaning a full meal of which rice is always the central dish. Long-grain rice is usually cooked by the absorption method *(see page 8)*. A Thai meal will consist of a soup, an assortment of main dishes (several with sauce) and one or two side dishes, depending on the number of guests, but these are always considered secondary to the rice. Food may be eaten from plates with a fork and spoon, or from bowls using chopsticks, whichever is preferred. In northern Thailand food is usually served in the *khan toke* style on a small round brass table at which guests sit cross-legged on cushions; a traditional *khan toke* meal consists of five different dishes and rice.

Beef and poultry are the most commonly used meats in Thailand and are cooked by boiling, barbecueing and frying. Eggs, fresh vegetables and fruit, seafood and noodles make up the balance of the savoury dishes. The Thais also enjoyed a vast range of delicious cakes and desserts. Making desserts in Thailand is a complex art requiring as much artistic ability as cooking skill. Mung-bean flour, rice, coconut, palm sugar and fresh fruits are used to create delightful cakes or carved to represent blossoms or whole miniature fruits; slivers of fresh fruit are moulded in coconut-milk jellies; all are served with a natural flamboyance typical of the Thais. Flowers in profusion decorate tables, and long trains of sweet-perfumed jasmine blossoms hang over doorways and around the necks and wrists of girls waiting on the tables.

Kapi, a version of the dried prawn paste used endlessly in Southeast Asian countries, and the fish sauce, *nam pla*, flavour many Thai dishes; both give a distinct taste and salty flavour, and are used in sauces, curries, soups and salad dressings. *Nam prik* is a pungent hot sauce made with dried fish or shellfish, shrimp paste, garlic and chillies ground to a paste, slightly sweetened with palm sugar and made slightly acid with lime juice; this *prik* (hot) sauce accompanies mildly seasoned dishes to give them the heat and pungency demanded by the Thais.

FISH SAUCE

NAM PLA

Nam Pla is a strongly flavoured salty fish sauce produced by fermentation of dried fish. It is used constantly in Thai food in the same way that soya sauce is used in Chinese cooking — to add flavour and a salty taste to dishes. Vietnamese nuoc mam is a similar sauce, as is the salty fish sauce labelled 'Fish Gravy' available in the West. If Fish Gravy is not available, the following recipe produces a good substitute. It can be prepared in advance for convenience, and kept for several weeks in a sealed container without loss of flavour.

12 anchovy fillets, or
   4 tablespoons salted anchovy essence
1-2 teaspoons sugar
2 tablespoon light soya sauce

Pound anchovy fillets to a smooth paste. Add a little water, then blend in sugar and soya sauce. Blend in a liquidiser to make a smooth sauce. Pour into a jar and seal tightly.

Pork-stuffed Oranges (recipe page 60).

THAI HOT SAUCE

NAM PRIK

Some dishes served in Thailand are of a relatively mild flavour and are served with tasty hot sauces similar to the sambals of Malaysia and Indonesia. This particular sauce goes well with meat, vegetable, noodle or rice dishes and is a good standby. It can be prepared up to 2 weeks in advance and improves in flavour after standing for several days.

2 tablespoons dried shrimps, soaked
3 teaspoons salt
1 teaspoon brown sugar
4 cloves garlic
6 anchovy fillets, or 1 tablespoon salted anchovy essence
1 tablespoon light soya sauce
4-5 fresh red chillies
lemon or lime juice

Pound all ingredients, except lemon or lime juice, to a smooth paste. Sprinkle on juice to taste and stir into the sauce. Spoon into a jar and seal tightly.

FISH FRIED WITH GINGER SAUCE

PLA PRIU WAN LHING

Pla Kapong is a fish caught in the klongs *(water canals) which run through Bangkok and across much of the Thai countryside. Bream or snapper make a good substitute for this meaty fish.*

Pla Kapong fish, weighing about 625 g (1¼ lb)
2 tablespoons oil
1 teaspoon salt
2 tablespoons cornflour
oil for frying

Sauce:
2 tablespoons white vinegar
5 cm (2 inch) piece fresh ginger, shredded
2 tablespoons sugar
1 teaspoon salt
¼ teaspoon monosodium glutamate (optional)
½ cup water
1 fresh red chilli, finely chopped
4 spring onions, finely chopped
1 tablespoon oil
cornflour
pickled ginger
cucumber slices

Clean fish and wash inside and out. Dry thoroughly. Rub with oil and salt, then coat with cornflour.

Heat about 5 cm (2 inches) oil in a *wok* or frying pan and fry fish, turning once or twice, until golden brown and slightly crisp. Test with a skewer in the thickest part to see if fish is cooked through. When done, lift out and keep warm.

Mix vinegar with ginger, sugar, salt and monosodium glutamate (if used). Stir in water and bring to the boil in a small saucepan. Simmer on moderate heat for 4-5 minutes.

Saute red chilli and spring onions in oil and add to the sauce. Thicken with a little cornflour mixed with cold water and stir sauce until it clears and thickens.

Put fish on an oblong serving plate and pour on the piping hot sauce. Garnish with pickled ginger and cucumber.

MARINATED FISH

This can be served as a delicious appetiser, or as a main course with salad and rice dishes.

6 small fillets of whiting, trout or sole
3 tablespoons lime juice
2 tablespoons fish sauce or light soya sauce
⅔ cup thin coconut milk
2 spring onions
1 green chilli
lettuce leaves

Cut fish fillets into thin strips and place in a bowl. Cover with a marinade of lime juice, fish sauce or soya sauce and coconut milk. Cover dish with plastic film and stand for 24 hours in a cool place.

Shred spring onions and chilli. Drain fish. Arrange lettuce leaves in six glass cocktail bowls and top with a serving of the fish. Garnish with shredded chilli sauce and spring onion. A little more lime juice may be sprinkled on before serving.

Alternatively, line a serving dish with lettuce, arrange fish on top, garnish with the onion and chilli and pour marinade over the dish.

THAI SWEET SOUR FISH

375 g (¾ lb) fish fillets
1 teaspoon salt
¼ teaspoon white pepper
cornflour
2 medium onions
60 g (2 oz) canned bamboo shoots, drained
1 green pepper
½ cup light chicken stock or water
2 medium tomatoes
2 fresh red chillies
2.5 cm (1 inch) piece fresh ginger
3 pieces canned baby corn, halved
3 cloves garlic
oil for frying
fresh coriander leaves or mint

Sauce:
⅓ cup white vinegar
75 g (2½ oz) sugar
½ teaspoon salt
2 tablespoons fish sauce or light soya sauce
1 teaspoon chilli powder
½ cup fish stock
2 teaspoons cornflour

Slice fillets into 5 cm (2 inch) pieces. Season with salt, pepper and coat lightly with cornflour. Let stand while sauce is prepared.

In a small saucepan combine all sauce ingredients

except cornflour. Bring to the boil, then thicken with cornflour mixed with a little cold water. Stir on high heat until sauce thickens and clears. Set aside. If desired, a little red food colouring may be added to the sauce.

Cut onions, bamboo shoots and green peppers into 2.5 cm (1 inch) squares. Put in a saucepan, pour on stock or water and bring to the boil. Simmer for 2 minutes. Slice tomatoes and chilli and shred ginger. Add to the pot with baby corn and crushed garlic and simmer for a further 2 minutes. Add to the sweet and sour sauce.

Heat oil and fry fish slices for 3 minutes on each side. Drain and arrange on a serving dish.

Reheat sauce and pour piping hot sauce and vegetables over the fish. Garnish with mint leaves or coriander sprigs.

BUTTERED FISH

SOON TIM YEE

This is the very first Thai dish I ever tasted. Its mild flavour gave me a totally wrong impression of the cuisine, and I was surprised to discover later just how very hot most Thai dishes are.

375 g (¾ lb) fish fillets (cod, whiting, beam)
1 teaspoon salt
¼ teaspoon white pepper
cornflour
185 g (6 oz) butter
½ cucumber, peeled
2 tomatoes
60 g (2 oz) canned bamboo shoots, drained
2 slices pineapple
2.5 cm (1 inch) piece fresh ginger, shredded
1 small onion, minced
1 fresh red chilli, finely chopped
½ teaspoon coriander, ground
1 clove garlic, crushed
½ cup water or fish stock
1 teaspoon sugar
2 teaspoons fish sauce or light soya sauce
fresh coriander leaves, chopped
lemon slices

Slice fish fillets thinly. Season with salt and pepper, then coat very lightly with cornflour. Heat butter and fry fish on moderate heat for 2 minutes on each side. Drain and set aside, leaving butter in pan.

Cut vegetables into thin slices and soak cucumber and bamboo shoots in cold water. Cut pineapple into small wedges.

Add ginger, onion, chilli, coriander and garlic to the pan and saute for 2 minutes. Drain vegetables, add to pan, and saute for 4 minutes, stirring constantly. Pour in stock or water and season with sugar and fish or soya sauce. Simmer for 3-4 minutes, stirring occasionally. Season to taste with salt and pepper.

Return fish to the pan and reheat. Lift onto a warmed serving dish and cover with the vegetables, pineapple and sauce. Garnish with shredded coriander and surround with lemon slices.

TOMATO SAUCE PRAWNS

GOONG SAI TONG

6 raw king prawns, in shells
3 large tomatoes
1 onion
6 cloves garlic
2 tablespoons oil or butter
1 tablespoon tomato paste
2 teaspoons dried shrimp paste
2 cm (¾ inch) piece fresh ginger, minced
2 teaspoons sugar
½ teaspoon white pepper
2 teaspoons salt
½ cup water
lemon juice
fresh coriander sprigs

Drop prawns into a large pot of boiling, slightly salted water and cook for 5 minutes. Remove and allow to cool slightly. Remove heads and discard. Slice prawns in half lengthways and set aside.

Chop tomatoes, onion and garlic finely and fry in oil or butter in a small saucepan. Add tomato paste after 3 minutes and season with shrimp paste, ginger, sugar, pepper and salt. Pour in water and cook on low heat for 3-4 minutes until sauce thickens slightly.

Arrange halved prawns in a shallow pan and pour on sauce. Simmer on low heat for 3 minutes, adding a little more water if the liquid dries up too quickly.

To serve, arrange two prawn-halves on each plate and spoon on a little tomato sauce. Sprinkle on lemon juice to taste and garnish with a sprig of coriander.

SHRIMPS IN SWEET COCONUT CURRY

Makes six appetisers or one main dish.

220 g (7 oz) raw shrimp, peeled
1 cup thick coconut milk
2 teaspoons lime juice
2 green chillies
2 cloves garlic
1 large onion
1 tablespoon oil
1½ tablespoons brown sugar
2 tablespoons desiccated coconut
1 tablespoon mild curry powder
salt
pepper
lettuce leaves

Pour coconut milk and lime juice over shrimp and marinate for 10 minutes. Chop chillies, garlic and onion finely and fry in oil until soft. Add brown sugar, coconut and curry powder with a little water to prevent sticking and stir on moderate heat for 3 minutes. Add shrimps and marinade and cook gently until shrimps are pink and tender. Season with salt and pepper to taste.

Line shallow glass bowls or serving plate with lettuce and spoon on the shrimp curry. Serve warm or chilled.

SHRIMP BALLS WITH MEAT AND MUSHROOMS

RADHED RUCHI

375 g (¾ lb) raw shrimp
1 egg white
salt
cornflour
4½ cups water
220 g (7 oz) chicken breast meat
220 g (7 oz) pork meat, lean
white pepper
2 tablespoons oil
8 shallots or 2 small red onions, minced
1 tablespoon fish sauce or light soya sauce
250 g (½ lb) fresh mushrooms,
    or 12 dried mushrooms, soaked

Peel and clean shrimps and mince finely. Add egg white, 1 teaspoon salt and enough cornflour to form a thick paste. Form into walnut-sized balls. Coat lightly with cornflour.

Bring water to a rapid boil and put in shrimp balls. Turn heat down slightly and cook until they rise to the surface, then boil for a further 3 minutes. Lift out with a slotted spoon and cool slightly. Reserve liquid. Chop chicken and pork into 2 cm (¾ inch) cubes and season lightly with salt and pepper.

Heat oil and fry meat with minced onion until meat is well coloured. Pour on fish sauce or soya sauce and ½ cup reserved stock and simmer until meat is tender. Wipe mushrooms, remove stems and add to the pan. Simmer on medium heat for 2 minutes, then add shrimp balls and another ½ cup of reserved liquid. Cook briefly, then thicken sauce with a little cornflour mixed with cold water.

Spoon meat, mushrooms and sauce into a serving dish and surround with the shrimp balls.

SHRIMPS AND CUCUMBER IN TOMATO SAUCE

PREO WAN

250 g (½ lb) medium raw shrimp
salt
cornflour
oil for deep frying
185 g (6 oz) cucumber
1 medium onion
2 fresh red chillies
4 tomatoes, chopped
1 tablespoon fish or light chicken stock
1 tablespoon sugar
1 teaspoon dried shrimp paste
1½ teaspoons chilli powder
fresh coriander leaves, chopped

Peel and devein shrimp and remove heads. Season with 1 teaspoon salt and coat lightly with cornflour. Heat oil and deep fry shrimp for about 3 minutes until golden brown. Lift out and drain well.

Wipe cucumbers and cut into pieces about 2 cm (¾

inch) square. Peel onion and chop coarsely. Remove seeds from chillies and slice.

Heat 2 tablespoons oil in a pan and fry onion, chilli and cucumber until soft. Add tomatoes and cook for 3 minutes on low heat. Pour in stock and add sugar, shrimp paste and chilli powder. Stir well, then add salt to taste. Toss in fried shrimp and heat through.

Spoon onto serving plate. Thicken sauce, if necessary, with a little cornflour mixed with cold water, then pour over the shrimps. Garnish with fresh coriander leaves.

PRAWNS IN SPICED COCONUT SAUCE

12 large raw prawns
1 large onion
2 tablespoons oil
2 stalks lemon grass, chopped
2 fresh red or green chillies, sliced
2.5 (1 inch) piece fresh ginger, shredded
2 tablespoons fish sauce or light soya sauce
1 cup thick coconut milk
2 medium tomatoes, peeled and chopped
1 teaspoon sugar
½ teaspoon white pepper

Remove shells from prawns, leaving tails and heads intact. Remove dark veins and slit prawns down the underside from the head to tail.

Chop onion finely and fry in oil until soft. Add lemon grass, sliced chillies and ginger and saute for 2 minutes, then add fish sauce or soya sauce with coconut milk. Add tomatoes to the pan, with a little water. Cook on low heat until tomato is soft and sauce well flavoured.

Add prawns and simmer for about 5 minutes till tender. Season with sugar and white pepper.

STUFFED CRAB SHELLS

POO JAA

6 small raw crabs
100 g (3½ oz) pork, minced
4 spring onions, chopped
1-2 fresh red chillies, finely chopped
2 cm (½ inch) piece fresh ginger, minced
2 cloves garlic, crushed
100 g (3½ oz) fresh mushrooms or champignons,
    chopped
1 teaspoon salt
¼ teaspoon white pepper
3 eggs
2 tablespoons plain flour
cornflour
oil
155 g (5 oz) lettuce, shredded

Drop crabs into plenty of boiling water and cook for 5-6 minutes. Lift out, put under cold water to cool, then break shells open underneath. Scoop out meat and discard inedible parts. Shred crabmeat and set aside. Clean shells by brushing gently. Rinse with warm, salted water. Dry carefully. Crack open legs and claws to extract meat. Mix crabmeat with minced pork, spring onions, chillies and ginger. Blend in garlic and mushrooms. Season with salt and pepper and bind with 2 eggs and the flour.

Fill crabshells with the prepared mixture, press down firmly and round off. Coat top of mixture with cornflour and brush with the remaining egg, lightly beaten. Heat 8 cm (3 inches) oil in a large pan and deep fry stuffed crab shells, several at a time, for 4-5 minutes.

Drain well, allow to cool slightly, then arrange on a bed of lettuce to serve.

CRABMEAT AND PORK ROLLS

PRATAT LOM

185 g (6 oz) fresh crab meat
250 g (½ lb) pork shoulder or leg
75 g (2½ oz) canned bamboo shoots, drained
10 dried black mushrooms, soaked
2 tablespoons vegetable oil
2 cloves garlic, finely chopped
1½ teaspoons salt
½ teaspoon white pepper
2 teaspoons coriander, ground
½ tablespoon fish sauce, or light soya sauce
2 teaspoons cornflour
2 dozen frozen spring roll wrappers, or rice paper
    wrappers
oil for deep frying

Sauce:
3 tablespoons fish sauce or light soya sauce
1 tablespoon white vinegar
3 green chillies

Shred crab meat. Finely mince or dice pork. Slice bamboo shoots and black mushrooms into thin threads.

Heat oil and fry minced pork with garlic until cooked through. Add bamboo shoots and mushrooms, frying on moderate heat for 5 minutes before adding shredded crabmeat. Season with salt, white pepper, coriander and fish sauce or soya sauce. Remove from heat, sprinkle on cornflour and stir well. Allow to cool thoroughly before preparing rolls.

Place a spoonful of the filling on each wrapper and roll up, turning ends in securely. Well the outside edge with water and stick doen firmly. Heat oil to smoking point and drop in rolls, several at a time. Cook quickly to a light golden brown, then lift out and drain.

To prepare sauce, slice chillies and mix with other ingredients. Pour into several small bowls and serve with the fried rolls.

COLD LOBSTER SALAD

2 lobsters, to yield about 500 g (1 lb) meat
1 tablespoon oil
6 shallots or 1 medium red onion, thinly sliced
1 clove garlic, crushed
½ cup thick coconut milk
1 small green pepper
1 small green pear or apple
90 g (3 oz) roasted peanuts, coarsely chopped
2 tablespoons fish sauce or light soya sauce
1½ teaspoons salt
1 teaspoon sugar
¼ teaspoon white pepper
2 tomatoes
1 thick slice pineapple
1 fresh red chilli, thinly sliced

Drop lobsters into boiling, slightly salted water and cook for 7-8 minutes. Drain and cool under cold running water. Cut shells open and extract meat. Chop meat into 2.5 cm (1 inch) cubes.

Heat oil in a small saucepan and saute shallots or red onion and garlic for 2 minutes. Pour in coconut milk and remove from heat.

Shred green pepper and pear or apple finely, add to the sauce with peanuts, fish sauce or soya sauce, salt, sugar and pepper. Mix well. Quarter or slice tomatoes and cut pineapple into small wedges.

Arrange lobster meat in the centre of a serving dish or salad bowl. Surround with pineapple and tomato pieces and pour on the sauce. Garnish with shredded chilli and serve slightly chilled.

MUSSELS WITH THAI HERBS

HOY MANGPOO OB MOR DIN

4 dozen fresh mussels, cleaned and scraped
6 cups water
6 lemon or lime leaves
1 lemon rind
2 stalks lemon grass
1 tablespoon salt
3 fresh red chillies, sliced
3 spring onions, chopped

Bring water to the boil in a deep pot. Add lemon leaves, rind, lemon grass and salt. Put in mussels, cover pot and bring to the boil. Cook, shaking pot from time to time, until mussels open. Drain, reserving half the stock. Put mussels in a deep serving dish, discarding ones which have not opened.

Strain reserved stock, discarding leaves, rind and lemon grass. Bring to the boil. Add chilli and spring onions and boil for 2 minutes. Pour over mussels and serve immediately.

SPICED OYSTERS

YAM HOY NANG LOM

4 dozen very small or 2 dozen medium sized oysters
2 tablespoons oil
8 spring onions or 6 shallots, finely chopped
4 cloves garlic, minced
2.5 cm (1 inch) piece fresh ginger, minced
3 teaspoons dried shrimp paste
90 g (3 oz) salted fish, soaked and ground
2 tablespoons sugar, or to taste
2 teaspoons fish sauce or light soya sauce

½ teaspoon white pepper
1½ teaspoons chilli powder
1 heaped tablespoon chopped fresh coriander leaves
¾ cup water
lemon juice
lemon wedges

Heat oil and saute onion, garlic and ginger for 3 minutes. Mix shrimp paste with ground salted fish, sugar, fish or soya sauce, pepper, and chilli powder. Add to the pan and saute for 2 minutes. Stir in chopped coriander leaves and water, then simmer on moderate heat for 2 minutes. Add oysters and cook for 5 minutes. Thicken sauce with a little cornflour, if necessary.

Spoon into a serving dish and sprinkle on lemon juice to taste. Surround with lemon wedges.

FRIED CHICKEN WITH SWEET BASIL AND CHILLI

315 g (10 oz) chicken breast
60 g (2 oz) chicken liver and giblets (optional)
2 tablespoons vegetable oil
4 tablespoons very small green birds-eye chillies or
    6 green chillies, sliced
1 small bunch fresh sweet basil leaves
2 tablespoons parsley, finely chopped
2 tablespoons fish sauce

Chop chicken breast, liver and giblets into very small dice. Heat oil and fry chicken on moderate heat for 3 minutes, then add chillies, half the basil and the chopped parsley. Cook, stirring frequently, for 5 minutes. Splash on fish sauce and stir briefly.

Spoon chicken and herbs onto a serving dish and surround with remaining sweet basil leaves.

CHICKEN IN PEANUT AND COCONUT SAUCE

KAI PENANG

1.5 kg (3 lb) chicken
2 teaspoons salt
½ teaspoon white pepper
2 cloves garlic, crushed
1½ cups thick coconut milk
2 tablespoons cummin seeds, ground
1 tablespoon coriander, ground
3 teaspoons light soya sauce
3 fresh red chillies, finely chopped
2 teaspoons sugar
1 teaspoon dried shrimp paste
2 heaped tablespoons roasted peanuts, coarsely ground
lemon or lime juice
fresh coriander leaves, chopped
fresh red chilli, shredded

Clean chicken and wipe dry. Rub with salt, pepper and crushed garlic. Put in a deep pot and pour on coconut milk. Cover and simmer on low heat for 1 hour. Lift out chicken, cool and cut into bite-sized pieces. Set aside, keeping warm.

Reheat sauce and add all remaining ingredients except lemon or lime juice and garnish. Simmer for 2 minutes. Return chicken and cook until chicken is very tender.

Arrange chicken pieces on a serving dish, sprinkle with lemon or lime juice and pour on sauce. Garnish with chopped coriander leaves and shredded red chilli.

THAI CHILLI CHICKEN

KAI TOM KHA

500 g (1 lb) chicken breast
½ teaspoon salt
¼ teaspoon white pepper
1½ cups thin coconut milk
2 green chillies, sliced
2 fresh red chillies, sliced
10 cm (4 inch) stalk lemon grass
2 tablespoons chopped fresh coriander leaves
¾ cup thick coconut milk
1 tablespoon fish sauce or light soya sauce
lime or lemon juice

Clean chicken and cut into pieces about 4 cm (1½ inches) square. Season with salt and pepper. Pour thin coconut milk into a large saucepan and add chicken pieces. Bring almost to the boil, then cover, turn heat down and simmer until chicken is almost cooked.

Add sliced chillies, lemon grass and coriander and continue cooking until chicken is very tender. Pour in thick coconut milk and fish sauce or soya sauce and season to taste with lime or lemon juice. Stir well, then spoon into a serving dish.

BEEF AND WATER CHESTNUTS

PRA RAM LONG SONG

375 g (¾ lb) round, topside or knuckle beef
2 tablespoons oil
6 cloves garlic, crushed
10 shallots or 3 small red onions, sliced
1 teaspoon coriander seeds
2 cups thin coconut milk
2 teaspoons dried shrimp paste
1 teaspoon sugar
5 dried chillies, crushed
10 cm (4 inch) stalk lemon grass, chopped
125 g (¼ lb) roasted peanuts, crushed
salt
pepper
220 g (7 oz) canned water chestnuts, drained and sliced
½ cup thick coconut milk
fresh coriander or mint sprigs

Slice beef and cut into 5 cm (2 inch) squares.

Heat oil and fry garlic, onions and coriander for 2 minutes. Push to the side of the pan and fry beef slices

until well browned. Pour in thin coconut milk and add shrimp paste, sugar, chillies, lemon grass and peanuts. Mix well and bring almost to the boil. Turn heat down and simmer for 10-12 minutes. Season to taste with salt and pepper and keep warm.

Boil sliced water chestnuts in slightly salted water for 2 minutes, then drain and add to the curry with thick coconut milk. Heat through, then spoon into a serving dish. Garnish with coriander or mint.

BEEF IN COCONUT SAUCE WITH CABBAGE

NUA KUB NAM MAPRAW

375 g (¾ lb) lean beef (sirloin, round, topside)
½ teaspoon salt
2 teaspoons dark soya sauce
2 cups thin coconut milk
4 dried chillies, crumbled
2.5 cm (1 inch) piece fresh ginger, shredded
3 cloves garlic, crushed
8 shallots or 2 small red onions, sliced
1 heaped tablespoon roasted peanuts, crushed
1 tablespoon brown sugar
1½ teaspoons cornflour
500 g (1 lb) Chinese cabbage or white cabbage
2 medium carrots
2 fresh red chillies, sliced

Cut beef into thin strips. Season with salt and soya sauce and leave to stand for 10-15 minutes.

Pour 1¼ cups cocoonut milk into a saucepan and add crumbled chillies, ginger, garlic and sliced onion. Bring almost to the boil, then add marinated meat. Turn heat down, cover, and simmer until meat is tender. Stir in roasted peanuts, brown sugar and add salt to taste. Thicken sauce with cornflour mixed with a little cold water. Remove from heat and set aside, keeping warm.

Wash cabbage and cut into 8 cm (3 inch) pieces. Scrape or peel carrots and slice very thinly. Cook carrots in boiling, slightly salted water for 2-3 minutes then drain. Put cabbage in a pan with a little salt and remaining coconut milk. Simmer on low heat until cabbage is cooked, but still slightly crisp.

Arrange cabbage in a serving dish, top with carrots and the cooked beef. Pour on sauce. Garnish with sliced red chillies.

BEEF CURRY

KAENG NUA

1 kg (2 lb) stewing steak (flank, round, chuck, knuckle)
5 black cardamoms
4 cloves
1 teaspoon black peppercorns
1 heaped teaspoon chilli powder
1 tablespoon coriander, ground
2 teaspoons cummin
2 teaspoons dried shrimp paste
1 tablespoon lemon or lime juice

3 tablespoons oil
2 large onions, chopped
4 cloves garlic, crushed
2.5 cm (1 inch) piece fresh ginger, shredded
¾ cup beef stock
2 tomatoes, sliced
2 bay leaves
1½ teaspoons salt
1½ cups water
1 cup thick coconut milk
2 fresh red chillies, sliced

Cut stewing steak into 5 cm (2 inch) cubes. Peel cardamoms and grind to a powder with cloves, peppercorns, chilli powder, coriander and cummin, then make into a paste with shrimp paste and lemon or lime juice.

Heat oil and fry onions, garlic and ginger for 4 minutes. Push to the side of the pan and fry meat until well browned. Pour in stock, add sliced tomatoes, bay leaves and salt. Cook on moderate heat, uncovered, until liquid has been absorbed, then stir in seasoning paste and stir on high heat for 2 minutes.

Add ½ cup water and cook on high heat until water has evaporated, then add thick coconut milk and remaining water. Cover, turn heat down and simmer until meat is soft. Add sliced chillies, adjust seasoning and continue cooking until meat is very tender.

BEEF WITH VEGETABLES IN OYSTER SAUCE

SUB GUM NGOU YUK

250 g (½ lb) lean topside, sirloin or rump steak
¾ teaspoon salt
90 g (3 oz) green beans
1 large green pepper
3 medium tomatoes
75 g (2½ oz) canned bamboo shoots, drained
3 tablespoons oil
1 tablespoon dark soya sauce
2 tablespoons oyster sauce
2 teaspoons sugar
1 cup beef stock
1 teaspoon cornflour
fresh coriander leaves, chopped
spring onions, shredded

Slice beef into pieces about 5 cm (2 inches) square and 1 cm (½ inch) thick. Season with salt.

Cut beans into 5 cm (2 inch) pieces. Wipe peppers, remove seeds and stems and cut into 2.5 cm (1 inch) squares. Quarter tomatoes, removing seeds. Slice bamboo shoots thinly.

Heat oil and brown meat well. Add vegetables and soya sauce and saute for 3 minutes, stirring frequently. Pour on oyster sauce, sugar and stock, cover and cook on moderate heat for 5 minutes, stirring from time to time.

Mix cornflour with a little cold water and stir into the sauce. Cook until sauce thickens and clears. Lift meat slices from the sauce and arrange on a serving dish. Surround with vegetables and pour on sauce. Garnish with chopped coriander and shredded spring onion.

Beef in Coconut Sauce with Cabbage (recipe this page).

CHILLI BEEF

NUA PAD PRIK

375 g (¾ lb) beef steak (rump or sirloin)
1¼ teaspoons salt
½ teaspoon black pepper
2 tablespoons oil
4 cloves garlic, crushed
2 green chillies, sliced
1 fresh red chilli, sliced
1 teaspoon sugar
1 tablespoon fish sauce
1 heaped tablespoon chopped basil or fresh coriander
  leaves

Trim off fat and slice beef into pieces about 5 cm (2 inches) square and 1 cm (½ inch) thick. Season with salt and pepper.

Heat oil and fry crushed garlic, then add beef and fry on both sides until well browned. Add chillies, fish sauce and sugar. Stir, and simmer on moderate heat for 5 minutes, turning meat occasionally. Stir in chopped herbs and spoon onto a serving dish.

PORK OMELETTE

RUM

Makes 1 serving.

1½ tablespoons vegetable oil
1 clove garlic, minced
60 g (2 oz) lean pork, minced
3 teaspoons light soya sauce
monosodium glutamate (optional)
6 slices green chilli
2 eggs
spring onion, chopped
salt
pepper
fresh coriander sprigs
tomato and cucumber slices

Heat oil in a small saucepan and fry garlic for 1 minute. Add minced pork and saute on moderate heat until browned. Season with soya sauce and monosodium glutamate (if used) and stir in chilli slices. Remove from heat.

Beat eggs lightly and pour into lightly oiled omelette pan. Cook on moderate heat until egg begins to set. Spread minced pork and chopped spring onions over the omelette. Season to taste with salt and pepper and cook for a further minute.

Roll up and lift onto a heated plate. Garnish with a sprig or two of coriander and surround with tomato and cucumber slices.

PORK-STUFFED ORANGES

MA HOU

6 large oranges
1½ tablespoons oil
8 cloves garlic, minced
6 spring onions, finely chopped
1-2 fresh red chillies, chopped
1 heaped tablespoon roasted peanuts, crushed
625 g (1¼ lb) lean pork, minced
1 teaspoon dried shrimp paste
2 teaspoons light soya sauce
1½ teaspoons coriander, ground
1½ teaspoons salt
½ teaspoon white pepper
1 teaspoon sugar
oil
6 sprigs of mint

Cut oranges in half and scoop out most of the flesh, leaving a 1 cm (½ inch) layer attached to the skin.

Heat oil and saute garlic and spring onion for 2 minutes. Add chilli and peanuts and cook for a further 2 minutes, stirring frequently. Stir in minced pork, shrimp paste, soya sauce, coriander, salt, pepper and sugar. Cook, stirring occasionally, on moderate heat until meat is cooked through.

Stuff mixture into oranges, pressing in firmly. Round off tops and place oranges in a large baking pan or oven-proof tray. Brush with a little oil. Bake in a pre-heated moderate oven (180°C/350°F/Gas Mark 4) for 15 minutes, brushing with a little more oil during cooking.

Serve two orange halves on each plate, decorating each pair with a sprig of mint.

SLICED PORK SERVED WITH HOT SAUCES

MOO THOD KATIEM PRIK

375 g (¾ lb) pork tenderloin
½ teaspoon salt
¼ teaspoon white pepper
2 tablespoons butter and oil, mixed
3 cloves garlic
1 cm (½ inch) piece fresh ginger, minced
2 fresh red chillies, minced
1½ teaspoons cummin, ground

Sauces:
1. Fresh red chilli, ginger, onion and salt.
   Pound to a smooth paste.
2. Garlic, tomato, salt, sugar and chilli powder.
   Chop tomato and garlic finely and mix with remaining ingredients.
3. Sliced fresh red chilli, onion and soya sauce.
   Mix ingredients together.
Note: The amounts of each ingredient should be judged according to taste.

Slice pork thinly, rub with salt and pepper and fry in the butter and oil over moderate heat until lightly browned. Remove from pan and set aside, keeping warm.

Chop garlic finely and fry for 2 minutes in the same pan with ginger, chilli and cummin. Return meat and turn in the seasonings for 2 minutes, cooking on low heat until meat is tender. Add a sprinkling of water to keep meat moist.

Arrange meat slices on a serving plate. Pour sauces into tiny bowls and serve with the meat.

THAI RICE

500 g (1 lb) long grain rice
1 large onion
1 fresh red chilli
3 tablespoons oil
2.5 cm (1 inch) piece fresh ginger, minced
1 *pandan* leaf (optional), or
    4 curry leaves
5 cm (2 inch) stick cinnamon
2 teaspoons salt
5½ cups thin coconut milk
fresh red and green chilli
fried dried fish (optional)

Wash rice in cold water, drain and allow to dry for about ½ hour. Mince onion and chilli. Pour rice into a large heavy-based saucepan and pour in oil. Stir on high heat for 2 minutes until rice grains are thoroughly coated. Stir in remaining ingredients except fresh chillies and dried fish.

Cover saucepan tightly and cook on very low heat for about 15 minutes, until all liquid is absorbed into the rice and each grain is soft and tender. Discard *pandan* or curry leaves and cinnamon stick.

Spoon rice into a deep serving dish. Garnish with shredded red and green chilli and threads of fried dried fish, if available.

FRIED THAI NOODLES

MEE KROB

4 Chinese dried mushrooms, soaked in cold water for ½
    hour
155 g (5 oz) chicken meat
60 g (2 oz) chicken livers
75 g (2½ oz) Chinese roast pork (*cha siu*)
60 g (2 oz) cabbage or Chinese cabbage
2 squares hard beancurd (optional)
60 g (2 oz) canned bamboo shoots
vegetable oil
1 kg (2 lb) fresh Chinese egg noodles, parboiled
1 cm (½ inch) piece fresh ginger, minced
2 cloves garlic, crushed
6 spring onions, chopped
2 fresh red chillies, thinly sliced
60 g (2 oz) beanshoots
75 g (2½ oz) raw shrimp, peeled
1 tablespoon fish sauce
1½ teaspoons chilli powder
1 teaspoon salt
¼ teaspoon monosodium glutamate (optional)
½ cup chicken stock
2 teaspoons cornflour

Chop chicken, livers and pork into 1 cm (½ inch) dice. Wash and chop cabbage, shake out water. Cut beancurd into 0.5 cm (¼ inch) dice. Drain bamboo shoots and slice thinly.

Heat 2 tablespoons oil and stir-fry noodles for 3-4 minutes, then remove to a warmed plate. Add ginger and garlic to the pan and cook 1 minute. Add spring onions, sliced chillies, beanshoots and shrimp and saute for 2 minutes. Remove and keep warm. Heat a little more oil and saute cabbage, bamboo shoots and beancurd for 2 minutes.

In another pan, fry meat until lightly coloured, then season with fish sauce, chilli powder, salt and monosodium glutamate (if used). Pour on stock, bring to the boil and cook for 5 minutes, until meat is tender. Thicken gravy with cornflour mixed with a little cold water. Pour meat over vegetables, adding beanshoots and shrimp. Mix well then spoon over noodles.

Serve with Chinese brown vinegar or chopped chilli mixed with soya sauce.

Note: Prepare half the above amount if served with other dishes.

GREEN PAPAYA SALAD

250 g (½ lb) hard green papaya (pawpaw)
125 g (¼ lb) green beans
2 medium tomatoes
¼ cup thick coconut milk
2 tablespoons fish sauce or light soya sauce
2 cloves garlic, crushed
2 tablespoons roasted peanuts, crushed

Peel papaya and grate. Cover with cold water. Remove strings from beans and cut into 2.5 cm (1 inch) lengths. Cook in slightly salted water until done, but still crisp. Drain and refresh with cold water. Put tomatoes into boiling water, count to seven, then lift out and peel. Cut into thin wedges. Drain papaya.

Arrange papaya, beans and tomato wedges in a salad bowl. mix coconut milk with fish sauce or soya sauce and stir in crushed garlic. Pour onto the salad and toss a little.

Sprinkle on crushed peanuts. Garnish, if desired, with sprigs of fresh coriander.

STUFFED EGGPLANT

KAYANTHI HNAT

1 dozen very small eggplants
salt
250 g (½ lb) raw shrimp, peeled
185 g (6 oz) chicken breast
1 medium onion
4 cloves garlic
1 tablespoon chilli powder
1 teaspoon turmeric powder
1 tablespoon parsley or chopped fresh coriander leaves
oil for deep frying
1 egg
3 tablespoons cornflour
3 tablespoons plain flour

Wipe eggplants and cut off tops. Scoop out centres and chop into small dice. Season with a little salt and set

aside. Fill eggplants with salted water and stand for 3-4 minutes.

Chop shrimp and chicken into small dice and finely chop onions and garlic. Add chopped eggplants and season with chilli powder, turmeric and chopped parsley or coriander. Bind with 2 tablespoons oil and stir in 1½ teaspoons salt. Knead to a smooth paste. Drain eggplants, wipe out and stuff with the meat filling.

Make a thick batter with the egg, cornflour and flour, adding a little salt and cold water. Beat till smooth.

Heat oil and when at smoking point, lower heat slightly. Coat eggplant with the batter and drop into the oil, several pieces at a time. Cook for about 7 minutes, lift out and cool slightly.

Just before serving return to hot oil for a further 3 minutes. Drain and serve hot.

ASSORTED VEGETABLE SOUP

7 cups chicken stock or water
90 g (3 oz) dried fish, soaked and ground
2 teaspoons dried shrimp paste
185 g (6 oz) white melon or squash
1 medium cucumber
6 dried mushrooms, or 8 pieces 'cloud ear' fungus, soaked in cold water for ½ hour
1 green chilli
5 cm (2 inch) piece fresh ginger, thinly sliced
12 sweet basil leaves (optional)
8 cm (3 inch) stalk lemon grass, chopped
salt
fish sauce

Bring stock or water to the boil in a large saucepan and add dried fish and shrimp paste. Boil for 10 minutes.

Cut peeled melon into large cubes. Peel cucumber and slice thickly. Drain mushrooms and remove stems, or drain fungus and cut in halves. Remove seeds from chilli for milder flavour, and slice. Add vegetables to the stock and season with chilli, ginger, basil leaves (if used), and lemon grass. Boil for 10 minutes.

Adjust seasoning with salt and fish sauce to taste.

DUCK SOUP WITH WATER CHESTNUTS

PET TOM KAP KAOLOT

375 g (¾ lb) duck, boned
1 set duck giblets (optional)
10 cm (4 inch) stalk lemon grass
8 cups water
2 tablespoons oil
3 small red onions or 6 shallots, minced
1-2 cloves garlic, minced
2½ teaspoons coriander, ground
½ teaspoon cummin, ground
½ teaspoon white pepper
155 g (5 oz) canned water chestnuts, drained and sliced
1 tablespoon fish sauce
fresh coriander leaves, chopped

Chop duck into 2.5 cm (1 inch) cubes. Place meat, giblets and lemon grass in a large saucepan and pour on water. Bring to the boil, cover and cook for 1 hour. Strain soup, reserving meat and stock. Discard lemon grass and giblets.

Heat oil and fry minced onions and garlic for 2 minutes, then add coriander, cummin and pepper. Fry for 2 minutes, stirring constantly. Add the duck and fry on high heat until meat is well browned. Toss in sliced water chestnuts and season with fish sauce. Brown slightly, then pour in reserved stock after skimming off fat. Bring to the boil, turn heat down and simmer for 10 minutes.

Garnish with chopped coriander before serving.

BAMBOO SHOOT AND PORK RIB SOUP

KAENG NO MAI

375 g (¾ lb) pork ribs
155 g (5 oz) canned bamboo shoots, drained
1 tablespoon oil
2 cloves garlic, crushed
1 medium onion, finely chopped
1 teaspoon coriander, ground
1 tablespoon fish sauce
2 teaspoons sugar
1 teaspoon salt
½ teaspoon white pepper
4½ cups beef or chicken stock
spring onions, thinly sliced

Divide ribs and chop into 4 cm (1½ inch) pieces. Drain bamboo shoots and slice thinly.

Heat oil and fry garlic, onion and coriander for 1 minute. Add pork ribs and fish sauce and stir on high heat until pork pieces are well browned. Add sugar, salt and pepper and pour on stock. Bring to the boil, turn heat down and simmer for about 45 minutes until meat is very tender. Strain. Add bamboo shoots and cook for a further 2-3 minutes.

Pour into soup bowls and garnish with spring onions.

SOUR PRAWN SOUP

TOM YAM KUNG

Probably the most famous Thai soup. This sour, hot dish is normally cooked at the table in a charcoal-heated copper pot.

6 cups fish or chicken stock
1 lemon or lime
4 lemon or lime leaves (or one lemon rind)
2 stalks lemon grass, each cut into 4 pieces
2 cloves garlic, crushed
2 fresh red chillies, finely chopped
1 tablespoon fish sauce
2 teaspoons coriander, ground
3 teaspoons chilli powder (or to taste)
2 teaspoons salt

Sour Prawn Soup, Duck Soup with Water Chestnuts, and Bamboo Shoot and Pork Rib Soup (recipes this page).

½ teaspoon white pepper
¼ teaspoon monosodium glutamate (optional)
750 g (1½ lb) medium prawns
lemon or lime juice
6 spring onions, finely chopped

Slice lemon or lime into quarters. Combine all ingredients except prawns, lemon or lime juice and spring onions in a charcoal boiler or a large saucepan and bring to a rapid boil. Cook for 10 minutes on moderate heat then take to the table, bring to the boil again and cook for a further 10 minutes.

Add whole prawns, unpeeled, and cook for 7 minutes. Squeeze in lemon or lime juice to taste and garnish with spring onions.

PORK AND MUSHROOM SOUP WITH SHRIMPS

KAENG KUNG KAP HET

2 tablespoons oil or butter
2 cloves garlic, crushed
½ teaspoon white pepper
½ teaspoon coriander, ground
½ teaspoon cummin, ground
½ teaspoon chilli powder
1 bay leaf
3 teaspoons fish sauce
125 g (¼ lb) sliced roast pork (*cha siu*)
1½ teaspoons salt
6 cups beef or chicken stock
100 g (3½ oz) peeled shrimp, precooked
100 g (3½ oz) canned straw mushrooms or
    champignons, drained
fresh coriander leaves, chopped

Heat oil or butter and fry crushed garlic with pepper, coriander, cummin, chilli powder and bay leaf for 2 minutes. Add fish sauce, roast pork and salt. Stir for 2 minutes on moderate heat, then pour in stock and bring to the boil. Turn heat down and simmer for 10 minutes. Add shrimp and mushrooms and cook for a further 6 minutes.

Garnish with chopped coriander before serving.

THREE KINDS OF CHICKEN

The origin of this unusual and totally unrelated name remains a mystery.

2 tablespoons roasted peanuts
sliced spring onions
1 lemon or lime
1½ tablespoons dried shrimps
4 cm (1½ inch) piece fresh ginger
1 tablespoon birds-eye chillies
10 cm (4 inch) stalk lemon grass, chopped

Cut lime or lemon into thin slices, then into tiny pieces. Slice ginger. Arrange all ingredients in separate piles on a serving platter or in small bowls on a tray.

Serve as an appetiser, or as nibblers with drinks.

TAPIOCA PUDDING

2 eggs
2 cups thick coconut milk
pinch of salt
100 g (3½ oz) pearl tapioca
45 g (1½ oz) sugar
90 g (3 oz) palm sugar or brown sugar
¾ cup water

Separate eggs and mix yolks with coconut milk, salt and washed tapioca. Cook on moderate heat until the tapioca is softened and pudding thick. Stir in sugar and whipped egg whites and spoon into small oiled moulds. Leave to set, then chill.

Dissolve sugar in water and bring to the boil. Simmer for 3 minutes, then strain and leave to cool.

To serve, turn the puddings out onto small dessert plates and pour on some of the sugar syrup.

FRIED COCONUT CAKES

MOK SI KAO

100 g (3½ oz) palm sugar or brown sugar
3 cups water
250 g (½ lb) rice flour
1 egg
2 teaspoons baking powder
pinch of salt
125 g (¼ lb) grated fresh coconut or desiccated coconut
oil for deep frying

Dissolve sugar in water over moderate heat. Leave to cool. Make a paste of rice flour, egg, baking powder, salt and coconut. Pour in syrup and beat to make a smooth batter. Leave for 20 minutes.

Heat oil to smoking point, then lower heat and drop in large spoonfuls of the batter. Fry to a deep golden colour. Remove and drain well. Cool before serving.

Sliced banana, apple, jackfruit or pineapple may be added to the batter.

COCONUT JELLY WITH FRUIT

1 heaped tablespoon powdered *agar agar*
1 large ripe banana
1 thick slice pineapple
1 ripe mango
1 cup thick coconut milk
2 cups thin coconut milk
pinch of salt
125 g (¼ lb) sugar

Dissolve *agar agar* in a little warm water. Peel and slice banana, pineapple and mango. Arrange fruit attractively in small lightly oiled jelly moulds.

Mix one-third of the *agar agar* with thick coconut milk and a little salt and bring almost to the boil. Put pan in a basin of boiling water to keep from setting. Mix remaining *agar agar* with thin coconut milk, salt and sugar and bring almost to the boil. Strain over the fruit and leave to set. When cold place in the refrigerator until firm. Pour on thick coconut milk and leave to set. Chill well before serving.

Turn out onto dessert plates and decorate with flowers.

COCONUT PANCAKES

KHAN UM KLUK

2½ cups thin coconut milk
100 g (3½ oz) rice flour
3 eggs
125 g (¼ lb) sugar
90 g (3 oz) desiccated coconut
green and pink food colouring
pinch of salt
oil
¼ cup desiccated or grated coconut

Make a thin batter with coconut milk, rice flour, eggs and sugar. Beat for 5 minutes, then fold in 90 g desiccated coconut. Divide the batter into three portions. Colour one pink, one bright green and leave one plain. Add a little salt to each and beat well. Leave for at least 20 minutes.

Wipe a 15 cm (6 inch) omelette pan with an oiled cloth and heat through. When ready, pour in a thin layer of batter and swirl pan to thinly cover the bottom. Cook pancake on moderate heat until flecked with brown underneath. Flip over and cook other side. Roll up in the pan and slide onto a plate. Cook all pancakes and stack the different colours in groups on a serving plate.

Garnish with desiccated or grated coconut and serve warm or cold.

VIETNAM

Vietnamese food is as pleasing on the eye as it is on the stomach. It is never overpowering, each dish having just the right touch of sauce and condiments to bring out the flavours of the main ingredients. The Vietnamese cook, like her Thai and Japanese counterparts, holds beauty of presentation almost as high in her esteem as taste. Salads are arranged decoratively on flat platters, dark meats are placed on beds of lettuce and other salad greens, clear sauces contain slivers of carrot, garlic and crushed peanuts, vegetables and meats are carved and sliced with precision. A badly presented meal rates poorly in a Vietnamese household where the women, who from youth are taught the skills of home and kitchen and who involve themselves in this work with great devotion, often spend hours on the preparation of an evening meal just for the family.

Rice is the staple food. It is served boiled, or made into thin flat noodles cooked in various ways. Predominant flavouring ingredients are a salty fish sauce *(nuoc mam)*, garlic and fresh coriander leaves. The soup dish known as Pho (the origin of Fur in Laos and Cambodia) consists of noodles, thin slices of meat, a scattering of fresh beanshoots and a little chopped spring onion in a thin meat or seafood broth, to which flavourings are added at the table according to individual taste. Vendors hawk this light and tasty snack throughout the day in the countryside and the cities, setting up their portable cookers to warm up bowls of Pho for passersby.

Vietnamese cuisine includes a profusion of salads. Lettuce and shredded cabbage with beanshoots, sliced onion and shredded cold meat and seafoods, salad greens with cooked tripe and shrimp, roasted dried cuttlefish with sliced cucumber, eggplant, mint and spring onions — these are just some of the unusual combinations. Dressings are variations on the basic fish sauce with the addition of lime juice, sliced chillies, crushed peanuts, sugar and shredded pickled vegetables. Many types of cooked meat and meatballs are served with plates of salad ingredients to be rolled into small packets for eating with the fingers. These include tiny crisply fried rolls of minced chicken in clear rice-paper wrappers (Cha Gio) and fried minced pork balls (Nem). Barbecued beef, pork and chicken and roasted slivers of fish are also served in this way. Beef Seven Ways is a traditional celebration spread comprising, as the name suggests, beef cooked in seven different styles (using different cooking techniques as well), each dish being distinctively yet subtly seasoned with local herbs and flavourings.

Two dishes displaying the artistry of Vietnamese cooks and epitomising the delicacy and refinement of their seasonings are Chao Tom, peeled sugarcane sticks coated with a layer of minced shrimp and roasted over a charcoal fire; and a dish which incorporates freshly fried prawn crisps with small squares of rice noodle pastry, a sprinkling of dry fried meat, crushed peanuts and chopped fresh coriander.

In the colourful Central Market in Saigon bowls of Pho and sticks of Chao Tom can be bought from itinerant traders who set up in any available space with collapsable stools and a portable charcoal fire for a day's (or even just a few hours') trading. Here I also sampled several kinds of succulent Vietnamese sausage sandwiched into crisp white French-style rolls — good bread (often eaten with noodle dishes) and good coffee are two of the better legacies of the French colonial era. A local restaurant nearby provided me with a taste of some of their excellent salad dishes (and instructions for making them, written in Vietnamese), and I finished my meal with a creme caramel that would have made a French master chef proud. Later I was pleased to be invited into a number of homes where I was offered many traditional Vietnamese recipes, used for generations, which were subsequently translated for me by Cathie, an employee of one of the Saigon embassies and my self-appointed and much-appreciated guide.

Vietnamese food has recently become very popular in Hongkong, with new restaurants opening up all over town, and it is a joy to rediscover many of the dishes I last tasted some years ago in my travels through Vietnam. Little oil is used in this light and slimming food. Fat pork may be used for extra flavour and for its rich oil, but most meats and vegetables are simmered in water with perhaps a minimum of seasoning, most seasonings being added only when cooking is complete. Thit Bho To (Soya Sauce Pork), for example, has soya sauce and a dusting of white pepper added before serving, and Mein Gai (Noodles with Chicken) is a very mildly flavoured noodle soup also seasoned at the table with white pepper. The food is not difficult to prepare and requires a minimum of special equipment. In fact, a small portable charcoal barbecue is the only extra equipment suggested, for the flavour of charcoal-barbecued meats is far tastier than that of meats cooked under a grill.

Cooked dishes are all taken to the table at the same time, and no-one worries too much if the dishes (except the rice) do not stay hot. Many, including the salad rolls, are served cold. Chopsticks are used with small rice bowls, and soup noodles are served in larger bowls with a spoon and chopsticks. *Nuoc mam* and pounded fresh chilli paste are always on the Vietnamese table. Desserts are rarely served after meals, but are taken frequently as between-meal snacks. Thick and sweet French-style coffee or Chinese tea are the favoured drinks.

AROMATIC FISH

375 g (¾ lb) white fish fillets (turbot, sole, plaice)
2 egg whites
1 heaped tablespoon cornflour
vegetable oil
6 shallots, or 3 small red onions, thinly sliced
4 cloves garlic, crushed
1 heaped teaspoon fennel seeds, slightly crushed

Sugar Cane Sticks coated with Shrimp (recipe page 68).

1 dried red chilli, crushed
juice of 1 lime or lemon
2 teaspoons sugar
⅔ cup water
2 teaspoons fish sauce
sprigs of *daun kesom* or mint

Cut fish into 6 cm (2½ inch) squares. Beat egg whites lightly and brush over fish, then coat lightly with cornflour. Heat 2.5 cm (1 inch) oil in a frying pan and fry fish to a deep golden brown. Lift out and drain. Keep warm.

Pour off all but 1 tablespoon oil and fry sliced onions with garlic, fennel seeds and dried chilli for 3 minutes. Add lemon or lime juice, sugar and water. Bring to the boil, stir, then simmer for 3 minutes. Return fish slices, splash in fish sauce and cook on low heat for 5 minutes.

Lift fish onto a serving dish, pour on a little of the sauce and garnish with sprigs of fresh *daun kesom* or mint.

SUGAR CANE STICKS COATED WITH SHRIMP

CHAO TOM

6 pieces fresh sugar cane, peeled (each about 23 cm or 9 inches long)
750 g (1½ lb) fresh raw shrimp, peeled and cleaned
¼ teaspoon white pepper
3 teaspoons fish sauce
2 egg whites
2 tablespoons oil
8 spring onions, finely chopped

Sauce:
3 teaspoons brown sugar
1 tablespoon sugar cane juice (available canned), optional
2 tablespoons fish sauce
3 teaspoons roasted peanuts, crushed
3 cloves garlic, minced
1 fresh red chilli, minced

Trim about 10 cm (4 inches) of one end of each sugar cane stick to make that end slightly thinner than the rest of the stick. Wipe dry.

Mince or chop shrimp finely and season with white pepper and fish sauce. Bind with egg white and knead to a smooth paste. Press a thin layer onto the trimmed end of each stick. Make the thickness of the shrimp about 1 cm (½ inch), squeezing firmly onto the sticks. Brush with oil and put under grill or roast over a charcoal fire for about 6-7 minutes until lightly cooked. Brush with oil from time to time during cooking.

Remove from fire, dip into chopped spring onions, coating lightly. Press onions onto the shrimp paste and return to the grill or fire for another 1 minute, turning frequently.

Mix sugar with sugar cane juice (if used) and fish sauce and stir until sugar dissolves. Blend in peanuts, garlic and chilli and stir in a little water. Serve in small bowls with the sugar cane sticks.

Note: bamboo or metal skewers could be used if sugar

cane is not available, although the flavour of the dish will not be as good.

FRIED PRAWNS WITH GREEN ONION

TOM KHO TAU

12 spring onions
375 g (¾ lb) raw prawns
3 tablespoons oil
1 tablespoon fish sauce
2 teaspoons sugar
1 lettuce
mint sprigs

Chop spring onions into 4 cm (1½ inch) pieces. Peel and devein prawns, leaving heads and tail fins intact, if preferred. Wash and pat dry. With a small sharp knife make deep incisions down the backs of prawns which will make them curl during cooking.

Heat oil in a large frying pan and fry prawns and spring onions for 3-4 minutes. Splash on fish sauce. Add sugar and stir on moderate heat for another 2 minutes.

Shred lettuce or wipe leaves. Arrange in a serving dish. Top with cooked prawns and garnish with sprigs of mint.

SALT AND PEPPER CRABS

CUA RANG MUOI

6 medium raw crabs
2 tablespoons sea salt
3 tablespoons vegetable oil
8 cloves garlic, crushed
6 spring onions, chopped
3 teaspoons black peppercorns, slightly crushed
fresh red and green chilli, shredded
fresh coriander sprigs

Crack undershell of crabs and scoop out inedible parts. Wash and drain, then using a heavy knife or cleaver cut each crab into about 4 pieces, leaving legs and claws attached. Put crabs in a large saucepan and cover with cold salted water, and leave to stand for 30 minutes. Drain crabs, rinse with cold water, drain again and allow to dry.

Heat oil in a large pan and fry crushed garlic for 2 minutes. Add crabs and saute for 5-6 minutes. Add spring onions to the pan with peppercorns and a little sea salt. Continue to saute until crabs are cooked through, adding a very little water to keep meat moist.

Serve garnished with shredded chilli and coriander sprigs.

CHICKEN CITRONELLE

750 g (1½ lb) chicken pieces (breasts and thighs)
1 stalk lemon grass, finely chopped

1½ cups boiling water
3 egg whites
cornflour
oil
8 spring onions, shredded
4 cloves garlic, crushed
1 small lettuce
2 teaspoons salt
½ teaspoon white pepper
2 teaspoons sugar
fresh coriander leaves

Cut chicken into 5 cm (2 inch) pieces. Steep lemon grass in boiling water for 30 minutes. Sprinkle chicken with cornflour and brush with beaten egg white.

Heat 2.5 cm (1 inch) oil in a frying pan and when almost at smoking point put in chicken pieces and fry until crisp and golden. Turn once or twice. Lift out and drain, keeping warm.

Pour off all but 2 tablespoons oil. Fry spring onion and garlic for 3 minutes. Return chicken to the pan and pour on lemon grass and water. Bring to the boil, turn heat down and simmer, covered, until chicken is tender.

Wash lettuce and arrange on a large serving plate. Lift out chicken pieces and place on the lettuce. Season sauce with salt, pepper and sugar and thicken with a little cornflour. Pour over the chicken and garnish with coriander leaves.

BARBECUED CHICKEN

GA UOP CHAO NUONG

6 large chicken thigh joints
2 teaspoons salt
½ teaspoon white pepper
10 cm (4 inch) stalk lemon grass, finely chopped
4 cloves garlic, crushed
lemon or lime juice
90 g (3 oz) brown sugar
⅔ cup water

Remove skin from chicken and prick all over with a sharp skewer. Make a seasoning paste with salt, pepper, lemon grass, garlic and lemon or lime juice and rub well into the chicken pieces. Stand for 30 minutes.

Mix brown sugar and water in a small saucepan, and bring to the boil, stirring to dissolve sugar. Simmer for 5 minutes. Brush sugar syrup over chicken pieces and stand for a further 10 minutes. Brush again and put under the grill or over a charcoal barbecue to cook until done. Brush every few minutes with the syrup and turn occasionally. The chicken will be a shiny golden-brown with dark brown flecks and a rich barbecued flavour.

PORK WITH COCONUT MILK

THIT BHO TAU

500 g (1 lb) piece boneless pork, leg or shoulder
1½ tablespoons brown sugar
⅓ cup water
2 tablespoons fish sauce

½ teaspoon white pepper
1½ cups thin coconut milk

Trim excess fat from pork and place whole piece in a large saucepan with enough water to cover. Bring to the boil and cook for 45 minutes. Lift out and drain well. Cool, then slice thinly.

Combine sugar and water in a saucepan and bring to the boil. When sticky put in slices of pork and coat each with the syrup. Splash on fish sauce and season with white pepper. Pour in coconut milk, cover and simmer on moderate heat until pork is tender and sauce thick and creamy.

PORK MEATBALLS SERVED WITH SALAD

NEM NUONG

The traditional way to serve various tasty meat balls, fish purees, tiny spring rolls, stuffed beef rolls and slivers of barbecued beef is in a salad roll which is dipped into a tasty sauce. The bite-sized portions of meat or spoonsful of puree are rolled in a leaf of lettuce after first topping with a selection of herbs, often a small portion of rice vermicelli, some crushed peanuts and pickled vegetable. Usually the lettuce roll is then rolled in a sheet of transparent edible rice paper. The same manner of preparation is followed in Laos and Cambodia where herbs like mint, daun kesom, basil and dill are accompanied by a variety of pungent or bitter-tasting leaves picked from the forest or back garden.

Pork Meatballs:
375 g (¾ lb) finely minced pork
2-3 spring onions
2 cloves garlic
2.5 cm (1 inch) piece fresh ginger, grated
2 egg whites
2 teaspoons salt
½ teaspoon white pepper
1½ tablespoons oil

Salad:
24 lettuce leaves
24 rice papers, about 15 cm (6 inches) in diameter
155 g (5 oz) cooked rice vermicelli
bunch mixed fresh herbs (mint, *daun kesom,* basil)
155 g (5 oz) beanshoots
1 small cucumber, about 12 cm (5 inches) long
¼ giant white radish
1 carrot
1 star fruit (optional)

Sauce:
60 g (2 oz) roasted peanuts, crushed
2 fresh red chillies, chopped
3 cloves garlic, chopped
4 sprigs mint, chopped
2 tablespoons lime or lemon juice
3 tablespoons fish sauce
1 cup thin coconut milk

Prepare sauce first. Pound peanuts, chillies and garlic to a reasonably smooth paste. Add chopped mint, lime or

lemon juice, sugar and fish sauce. Stir in coconut milk and pour sauce into several small bowls. Set aside.

Next prepare pork meatballs. Mince spring onions, garlic and ginger finely and mix to a smooth paste with pork and remaining ingredients. Form into walnut-sized balls and put on a piece of muslin cloth over a steamer. Cook for 10 minutes over briskly boiling water. Remove from heat and set aside, keeping warm.

Wash lettuce and dry leaves. Stack on a plate with rice paper which has been slightly dampened by wiping with a wet cloth. Cut vermicelli into 5 cm (2 inch) pieces. Break mint and other herbs into small sprigs, rinse and shake out water. Put on the plate with lettuce and rice papers. Steep beanshoots in boiling water for 2 minutes. Drain and rinse in cold water. Drain again. Thinly slice cucumber and star fruit. Shred radish and carrot. Arrange vegetables and fruit on a serving plate.

If a portable hot plate or barbecue is available, barbecue pork meatballs at the table, otherwise prepare salad plates and put on the table with the bowls of sauce. Saute the meatballs quickly in a frying pan with a little oil. Take to the table while hot.

Wrap one or two meatballs in lettuce leaf and rice paper sheet after garnishing with some of each of the vegetables and herbs. Dip into the sauce.

SWEET AND SOUR PORK VIETNAM STYLE

SUON XAO CHUO NGOT

625 g (1¼ lb) meaty pork spare ribs
1 egg
1 heaped tablespoon plain flour
1 heaped tablespoon cornflour
2 teaspoons sugar
1½ teaspoons salt
½ teaspoon pepper
vegetable oil
3 cloves garlic, crushed
2 tablespoons fish sauce
12 lettuce leaves
small bunch mint
1 tablespoon finely chopped parsley or fresh coriander
  leaves
1 medium tomato, sliced
1 medium cucumber, sliced

Sauce:
½ cup white vinegar
90 g (3 oz) sugar
½ cup light beef or chicken stock
2 fresh red or green chillies, finely chopped
1 teaspoon black peppercorns, crushed
1 teaspoon cornflour
red food colouring (optional)

Divide ribs and chop each into 5 cm (2 inch) pieces. Wash and dry thoroughly. Beat egg and mix with flour and cornflour, sugar, salt and pepper and enough water to make a smooth, not too thick batter. Coat ribs.

Pour 5 cm (2 inches) oil into a wide pan, and heat to smoking point. Fry ribs on high heat until well crisped and deep golden brown. Remove from pan and drain off most of the oil. Add garlic and fry for 1 minute,

then return ribs and season with fish sauce. Cook, stirring frequently for 3 minutes, then turn heat off and let stand while sauce is prepared.

Mix vinegar, sugar and stock in a small saucepan and bring to the boil. Add chillies and peppercorns and thicken with cornflour mixed with a little cold water. Add red food colouring, if desired, and cook until sauce thickens and clears. Pour over ribs and simmer for a further 2 minutes.

Wash lettuce leaves and wipe dry. Line a serving plate with the leaves and arrange pork ribs on top. Sprinkle with finely chopped parsley or coriander leaves. Garnish with sprigs of mint, and surround with tomato and cucumber slices.

SOYA SAUCE PORK

THIT BHO TO

500 g (1 lb) pork belly, with skin
3 cloves garlic, chopped
6 spring onions, chopped
2.5 cm (1 inch) piece fresh ginger, shredded
3-4 tablespoons light soya sauce
2 teaspoons white pepper

Cut pork into large pieces. Put in a deep pot. Add garlic, onions and ginger to the pot. Cover pork with cold water, bring to the boil, then turn heat down and simmer for 2-2½ hours. Pork should be very tender and skin reduced to a jelly-like consistency.

Lift pork out and cut into strips. Arrange in a serving dish. Sprinkle with soya sauce and white pepper.

BEEF ROLLS STUFFED WITH BITTER MELON

BO NUONG KIM TIEN

375 g (¾ lb) sirloin, rump or topside steak
⅓ teaspoon Chinese five-spice powder
3 teaspoons peanut oil
salt
white pepper
185 g (6 oz) canned or fresh bitter melon
melted lard or oil
lettuce leaves
1 heaped tablespoon roasted peanuts, crushed

Cut meat into thin slices, then into strips about 4 cm x 8 cm (1½ inches x 3 inches). Mix five-spice powder with oil, salt and pepper and rub into the meat. Leave for 10 minutes to absorb flavours.

Cut melon into pieces 4 cm x 1 cm (1½ inches x ½ inch). Roll a strip of meat around each piece of melon and secure with a toothpick. Grill over a charcoal fire or under a moderate hot griller until cooked through. Turn frequently and brush with a little lard or oil during cooking.

Wash lettuce, dry and arrange on a serving plate. Place cooked meat rolls on top and sprinkle with crushed peanuts. Serve hot or warm as an appetiser or main dish.

Fried Rice (recipe page 72), Soya Sauce Pork, and Sweet and Sour Pork Vietnam Style (recipes this page).

BARBECUED BEEF WITH SALAD

500 g (1 lb) lean beef (rump, sirloin, topside)
4 cloves garlic
4 shallots or 8 spring onions
10 cm (4 inch) stick lemon grass, finely chopped
2 teaspoons salt
3 teaspoons sugar
3 tablespoons oil

Salad:
24 lettuce leaves
24 sheets rice paper, dampened slightly
125 g (¼ lb) fresh beanshoots
1 small cucumber
1 star fruit (optional)
1 small bitter melon (optional)
90 g (3 oz) pickled carrot and radish *
90 g (3 oz) cooked rice vermicelli
4 spring onions, finely chopped
small bunch mint, fresh coriander and *daun kesom*

Sauce 1:
2 tablespoons vinegar or lime juice
3 tablespoons thin coconut milk
2 tablespoons sugar (or to taste)
1 teaspoon salt
½ teaspoon black pepper
1 heaped tablespoon roasted peanuts, crushed

Mix all ingredients together in a small saucepan and simmer for 1 minute. Put in a small bowl.

Sauce 2:
3 tablespoons fish sauce
2 tablespoons thin coconut milk
1 fresh red chilli, minced
3 cloves garlic, crushed
1 tablespoon sugar (or to taste)
1 tablespoon lemon or lime juice
1 heaped tablespoon pickled carrot and radish,
  shredded finely *

Mix ingredients together. Pour into a small bowl.

Cut beef into very thin slices, then into strips about 2.5 cm (1 inch) wide and 5 cm (2 inches) long. Mince garlic and shallots or spring onions and make into a paste with lemon grass, sugar, salt and oil. Rub this seasoning paste well into the meat strips and stand for several hours to absorb flavours.

Wash lettuce, dry well and arrange on a serving plate with rice paper. Steep beanshoots in boiling water for 2 minutes. Rinse with cold water, drain again and put with the lettuce. Slice cucumber and star fruit thinly. Shred bitter melon (if used). Drain and thinly slice or shred pickled vegetables.

Press vermicelli into a flat dish, weight with a heavy dish and when it forms into a flat cake lift out and cut into 5 cm (2 inch) squares. Put on a serving plate and sprinkle with chopped spring onion. Wash mint, co-riander and *daun kesom*. Break into small sprigs and shake to remove excess water.

Arrange vegetables, fruit, pickles and herbs on an-other serving plate. Heat a portable barbecue, hot plate or an electric frying pan at the table and barbecue meat to taste. Lightly oil the hot plate before cooking.

Prepare salad rolls and select pieces of cooked meat from the barbecue to roll up with the salad, vegetables and herbs. Dip into the one of the sauces before eating. Alternatively, barbecue all meat and bring to the table on a plate for diners to help themselves.

* To make pickled carrot and radish, peel and grate or shred finely and steep in a mixture of vinegar, salt and sugar until softened.

VIETNAMESE BEEF STEW

THIT BO KHO

500 g (1 lb) beef steak (chuck, round, topside)
375 g (¾ lb) shin beef or flank
2 tablespoons mint leaves, chopped
2 tablespoons fish sauce
2 teaspoons sugar
½ teaspoon white pepper
3 tablespoons vegetable oil
5 cm (2 inch) piece fresh ginger, thinly sliced
1 tablespoon mild curry powder
4½ cups water
spring onion or shallots, shredded

Cut beef and shin, or flank, into pieces about 5 cm (2 inches) square. Season with chopped mint, fish sauce, sugar and pepper and marinate for 30 minutes, turning occasionally.

Heat oil in a large saucepan and fry meat until well browned. Add ginger and curry powder. Saute for 3-4 minutes. Pour in water and bring to the boil. Cover, turn heat down and simmer for about 2 hours until meat is very tender.

Garnish with shredded spring onion or shallots.

FRIED RICE

COM CHIEN DUONG CHAU

315 g (10 oz) long grain rice
90 g (3 oz) fat pork, diced
90 g (3 oz) raw shrimps, chopped
vegetable oil
2 eggs, lightly beaten
½ teaspoon white pepper
salt to taste
fresh coriander or spring onions, chopped

Wash rice and put into a heavy-based saucepan. Cover with water to 4 cm (1½ inches) above the level of the rice. Stand for 10 minutes, then put over high heat and bring to the boil. When water begins to bubble, turn heat down to lowest point and cook with saucepan tightly covered until rice is tender. Let stand for 10 minutes, then remove lid and stir rice with a chopstick. Spread on a tray to cool before frying.

Heat 2 tablespoons oil in a large frying pan. Fry pork for 3-4 minutes, stirring frequently. Add shrimp and cook 2 minutes. Add a little more oil if necessary and fry egg in a thin omelette until set. Lift out, cool and shred.

Heat pan again and fry cooled rice for 3 minutes, stirring to coat grains with the oil. Add meat and shrimps and continue to stir on moderate to high heat for 3 minutes. Season with white pepper and add salt to taste. Stir in shredded egg and transfer to a serving dish. Garnish with chopped coriander or spring onions.

ASPARAGUS AND CRABMEAT SOUP

NUOC DUNG GA MUNG CUA

4½ cups chicken or fish stock
2 teaspoons fish sauce
¼ teaspoon white pepper
pinch of monosodium glutamate (optional)
9 spears canned asparagus, drained
185 g (6 oz) shredded crab meat
3 egg whites
2 spring onions, chopped
fresh red and green chilli, shredded

Bring stock to the boil, season with fish sauce, white pepper and monosodium glutamate (if used). Cut asparagus into 6 cm (2½ inch) pieces, and add to the stock with crab meat. Simmer on low heat for 2 minutes. Beat egg whites lightly and stir into the soup. The egg should form white threads in the soup. Cook for another minute.

Garnish with chopped spring onion and shredded chilli.

NOODLES WITH ASSORTED MEATS IN SOUP

BANH CANH TOM CUA

125 g (¼ lb) boiled pork belly with rind
12 spring onions
4½ cups stock
155 g (5 oz) raw prawns or shrimp, peeled
125 g (¼ lb) thick egg noodles or spaghetti, cooked
90 g (3 oz) crab or lobster meat, cooked
monosodium glutamate (optional)
salt
white pepper
sprigs of fresh coriander
1 heaped tablespoon fried onion flakes (see page 125)

Cut pork into 2.5 cm (1 inch) cubes. Clean spring onions and cut into 2.5 cm (2 inch) lengths.

Boil stock, then add prawns or shrimp and cook until they turn pink. Add noodles, crabmeat or lobster and pork and boil for 2-3 minutes. Season with monosodium glutamate (if used), salt and pepper to taste and add spring onions and coriander sprigs. Boil for a further 1-2 minutes.

Pour into soup tureen and garnish with fried onion flakes. Serve with small bowls of fish sauce or other hot sauces and a pot of white pepper.

VIETNAMESE NOODLE SOUP

PHO

3 litres (14 cups) water
2 kg (4 lb) beef shank or rib bones
750 g (1½ lb) flank steak
3 spring onions
5 cm (2 inch) piece fresh ginger
1 teaspoon black peppercorns
salt or fish sauce to taste
500 g (1 lb) beanshoots
500 g (1 lb) *hor fun* noodles
3 spring onions
fish sauce
chilli sauce
fresh coriander leaves or chillies, chopped

Pour water into a large pot. Add bones and cubed flank steak. Trim spring onions, slice ginger and add to pot with peppercorns. Cover and boil for 5 hours on moderately low heat. Season to taste with salt or fish sauce.

Discard beef bones, lift out meat and tear into shreds. Drop beanshoots into boiling water for 1 minute to soften. Lift out and drain well. Place noodles in the water and cook until softened, then drain. Trim and slice spring onions finely.

Place a portion of shredded beef, beanshoots, noodles and spring onion into each soup bowl. Add a ladleful of the rich soup stock. Serve fish sauce, chilli sauce and bowl of chopped fresh coriander leaves or chilli on the side.

CHICKEN SOUP WITH NOODLES

MEIN GAI

½ small chicken, about 500 g (1 lb)
60 g (2 oz) chicken giblets (optional)
4½ cups chicken stock or water
125 g (¼ lb) rice vermicelli, or thick egg noodles
4 spring onions, chopped
3 shallots or 1 small red onion, chopped
2 tablespoons oil
6 dried black mushrooms, soaked in cold water for ½ hour
1 tablespoon fish sauce
salt
white pepper
lemon slices
fresh red or green chilli, shredded

Put chicken in a saucepan with giblets (if used), and cover with chicken stock or water. Boil until meat is tender. Lift out, drain and cool, then shred meat thinly. Reserve stock. Drop noodles into the stock, simmer until softened, then strain and return stock to the saucepan.

Fry spring onions and shallots or red onion for 2-3 minutes. Add shredded chicken and fry briefly, then return to the stock. Bring to the boil. Shred mushrooms and add to the soup. Season with fish sauce and salt and white pepper to taste.

Simmer for 5 minutes, then pour into a soup tureen and garnish with lemon slices and shredded chilli. Serve with fish sauce.

CHICKEN ROLLS WITH SALAD

CHA GIO

Chicken Rolls:
24 sheets transparent rice paper or spring roll wrappers, each 15 cm (6 inches) square
250 g (½ lb) chicken meat
30 g (1 oz) transparent vermicelli (optional)
4 spring onions, chopped
2 cloves garlic, crushed
2 cm (¾ inch) piece fresh ginger, grated
4 dried black mushrooms, soaked in cold water for ½ hour
2 egg whites
2 teaspoons cornflour
2 teaspoons fish sauce
¼ teaspoon white pepper
oil for deep frying

Salad:
1 medium lettuce
1 small cucumber
1 small eggplant (optional)
100 g (3½ oz) beanshoots
100 g (3½ oz) pickled vegetables (radish and carrot in vinegar and salt)
small bunch mint leaves
small bunch sweet basil
small bunch *daun kesom*
100 g (3½ oz) rice vermicelli, cooked
24 sheets transparent rice paper, dampened slightly (each about 20 cm or 8 inches square) or use extra lettuce

Sauce:
2 spring onions, finely chopped
2 cloves garlic, crushed
1 fresh red chilli, minced
1 tablespoon lemon or lime juice
4 tablespoons fish sauce
sugar to taste
pinch of white pepper

Soak vermicelli until soft; drain. Boil chicken meat until tender. Cool, then mince finely with onions, drained vermicelli, garlic, ginger and drained mushrooms. Knead to a smooth paste and bind with egg white and cornflour. Season with fish sauce and white pepper.

Divide the mixture between 24 rice paper sheets or spring roll wrappers and roll up tightly into small rolls, about 5 cm (2 inches) long. Stick ends down with a little water, or make a paste by mixing cornflour with boiling water and use to glue ends. Heat oil and deep fry chicken rolls until crisp and a golden brown. Lift out and drain.

Prepare salad. Wash lettuce leaves and dry carefully. Arrange on a plate with rice paper sheets. Peel cucumber and slice thinly. Wipe eggplant and cut into very thin strips. Pour boiling water over beanshoots to soften, splash with cold water and drain well. Shred pickled vegetables. Wash mint, sweet basil and *daun kesom*. Cut rice vermicelli into 5 cm (2 inch) pieces. Arrange all vegetables, herbs and vermicelli on a serving plate.

Mix sauce ingredients in a small saucepan, heat through then allow to cool. Pour into a small bowl.

To prepare salad rolls, line each sheet of rice paper with a lettuce leaf (or use two lettuce leaves instead of rice paper). Put a fried chicken roll on top and add a little of each of the vegetables, herbs, pickles and vermicelli. Roll up and dip into the sauce.

SALAD WITH SEAFOOD AND VEGETABLES

GOI SUG TOM THIT

1 small lettuce
¼ giant white radish
2 medium carrots
1 small red onion
1 medium cucumber
185 g (6 oz) fried or poached fish fillets
6 large prawns, cooked
45 g (1½ oz) crabmeat, cooked and flaked
45 g (1½ oz) lobster, cooked (optional)
45 g (1½ oz) cuttlefish, cooked
60 g (2 oz) tripe or pork sausage, boiled
12 spring onions
5 cm (2 inch) piece fresh ginger
mint and fresh coriander leaves

Sauce:
3 spring onions
1 fresh red chilli
3 cloves garlic
1 tablespoon sugar
2 tablespoons lemon juice or white vinegar
2 teaspoons fish sauce

Prepare sauce by pounding spring onions, chilli and garlic to a paste with sugar, lemon juice or vinegar and fish sauce. Add enough cold water to make a light sauce. Pour into several small bowls.

Wash lettuce and dry leaves carefully. Arrange on a serving plate, using three-quarters of the leaves. Shred remaining leaves and set aside. Wash radish and carrot and grate. Mix with shredded lettuce. Slice red onion thinly. Wipe cucumber and slice. Arrange with onion on the lettuce bed and top with shredded lettuce, radish and carrot.

Cut fish fillets into small pieces. Chop prawns and shred cuttlefish. Dice lobster, if used. Slice boiled tripe or sausage. Pile seafood and tripe or sausage on the vegetables.

Garnish with shredded spring onions, very finely shredded ginger, sprigs of mint and coriander. Serve with the bowls of sauce, or if preferred, pour sauce over salad before serving.

Chicken Rolls with Salad (recipe this page).

MANGO CHUTNEY

NUOC NAM ME

6 small very ripe mangoes
4 fresh red or green chillies, thinly sliced
10 shallots or 3 small red onions, thinly sliced
4 tablespoons fish sauce
3 tablespoons sugar
2 tablespoons dried fish or shrimps, ground
3 teaspoons salt

Peel mangoes, remove stones and slice into thin strips. Put mangoes, chillies, onions and seasonings into a saucepan and cook on low heat, stirring frequently, for 15 minutes. Add a little water when chutney begins to dry up.

Spoon into wide-necked jars, seal and put into a dark cupboard to mature for 5-6 days before using.

NAM PHUONG SALAD

GOI NAM PHUONG

10 cm (4 inch) piece giant white radish
1 tablespoon oil
12 lettuce leaves
3 stalks celery
1 medium red onion
2 large fillets white fish, fried
30 g (1 oz) dried squid (optional), soaked
2-3 cloves garlic, thinly sliced
3 fresh red chillies, thinly sliced
6 spring onions, shredded
2 tablespoons roasted peanuts, crushed
small bunch coriander leaves and mint
12 *krupuk*, freshly fried

Sauce:
3 tablespoons white vinegar or lemon juice
1 tablespoon sugar
1½ tablespoons fish sauce

2.5 cm (1 inch) piece white radish, finely grated
4 cm (1½ inch) piece carrot, finely shredded
1 clove garlic, crushed

Shred white radish and boil quickly in a little water with oil added. Wash lettuce, dry and arrange on a serving plate. Wash celery and slice thinly. Peel onion and cut into thin slices, then break into rings. Arrange celery, onion and radish on top of lettuce.

Cut fish into small, thin slices. Shred dried squid, if used. Place fish on top of vegetables. Scatter garlic, chillies, spring onion, peanuts, coriander and mint leaves over salad. Surround with *krupuk*.

Mix sauce ingredients together and serve separately.

STEAMED RICE MOULD WITH COCONUT CREAM

XOI NUOC DIR A

280 g (9 oz) glutinous rice
3 teaspoons salt
3 cups thin coconut milk
60 g (2 oz) brown sugar
½ cup water
1¼ cups thick coconut milk

Wash rice and put in a saucepan with salt and thin coconut milk. Cover and cook on moderate heat until liquid begins to bubble, then turn heat down and continue to cook until rice softens and forms a thick paste.

Spoon into a lightly greased 25 cm (10 inch) baking tray. Cover tin with a sheet of aluminium foil pierced in two corners. Set over a saucepan of boiling water to steam until firm. Cool, then chill.

Prepare sugar syrup by dissolving brown sugar in water. Bring to the boil, turn heat down and cook without stirring, until syrup becomes slightly sticky. Cool and then chill.

To serve, cut rice mould into serving pieces. Pour a little sugar syrup and thick coconut milk over each.

LAOS & CAMBODIA

I would not hestitate to say that Laotian food is the most unusual I have ever tasted. The cuisine is based on available products harvested from muddy brown fields, collected from native trees and shrubs, or fished from the Mekong River and its tributaries. Large soft mushrooms, crisp bamboo shoots, yams, lettuces, eggplant, chillies and bananas (the vegetable-like flowers and the succulent heart of the trunk are cooked, the sturdy leaves are used as food wrappers in much the same way that Western cooks use aluminium foil) are about the extent of the fresh vegetables available to the Laotian cook, who adds a host of pungent and aromatic herbs and leaves picked from the garden before each meal. Almost any leaf that is neither too bitter nor poisonous is used in the salad bowl or wrapped in lettuce leaves with meat and meatballs similar to those served in Vietnam. Although the few vegetables are used constantly, Laotian food is not monontonously repetitive.

The uncommon, nutty-flavoured Laotian rice is a glutinous type often planted on sloping hillsides instead of in paddys. It is soaked overnight, steamed in bamboo baskets until soft enough to eat, served separately to each diner in a small, covered round basket, and is eaten by rolling a lump of it into a ball to be nibbled like bread. Other dishes are served on a central woven cane table, and one eats with fork and spoon or fingers.

Breakfasts may consist of 'sticky' rice and one or two warm or cold dishes, or a bowl of Fur, a noodle soup similar to those popular throughout Vietnam and Cambodia. Another popular soup dish eaten throughout the day is Khao Phoune, comprising a rich, spicy coconut-milk soup, thin rice vermicelli and a fragrant decoration of sliced banana flowers, sliced chillies and several types of fresh herbs, including mint and coriander. There may be two or three meals a day, but one-bowl meals like Fur and Khao Phoune are eaten whenever one is hungry — be it morning, afternoon or late evening, there is always a noodle seller at hand.

Thin slices of unripe mango or papaya, sold by street vendors as a snack, are sharply seasoned with coarse salt and crushed chillies, and do much to stimulate heat-jaded appetites. Another oddity, through which I slowly worked my way during a boat ride up the Mekong to some holy Buddhist caves, was a kind of chutney made with strips of young buffalo skin (pork skin is also used) dried and preserved in chilli sauce; on this occasion it was served as a topping on crusty French rolls. Snacks are easy to find in Laos, but one generally finds Laotian food only in private homes, for public eating places are rare. The few restaurants in the capital, Vientiane, specialise in surprisingly good French food; farther north at Luang Prabang, the religious capital, there is little more than a couple of cafes where one can sip sweet French-style coffee with an order of Vietnamese Nem Nuong (meatballs served with fresh salad).

One of the best Laotian meals I had was at the home of a teacher in Vientiane. The lunch was prepared by two giggling sixteen-year-olds, disciples of one of the country's leading cooks. After many hours of preparation they presented a stew of buffalo meat and vegetable thickened with pureed eggplant, and containing at least six different types of vegetables including the crunchy 'cloud ear' fungus so often used in Chinese cooking; a fish puree served with a plate of lettuce and assorted herbs; a succulent chicken stuffed with local herbs and boiled until the meat was falling from the bones; plain boiled eggs; baskets of 'sticky' rice; and finally a concoction of small fish pickled in a murky pinkish-brown substance rather like pureed fish roe. It was in fact roe and, as I discovered later, comes from a large fish found in the Mekong. Roe from the same fish is used in another Laotian delicacy, Som Khay, a type of 'caviar' that is stored for a month to ferment and then mixed with fermented cooked rice and fermented minced fish. Som Khay is vaguely reminiscent of the Greek *taramasalata,* and I have included a recipe.

A dish that can usually be afforded only on special occasions is Lap, based on raw meat. Tender young buffalo or venison is finely chopped and mixed into a smooth puree with ground aromatic herbs, Laotian ginger (known as *kha* in Laos and Thailand, *lengkuas* in Malaysia, and *laos* in Indonesia), eggplant, garlic and chillies. The puree is spread onto salad leaves, topped with fresh herbs, rolled into succulent mouthfuls, and served with a flavoured beef stock made from bones. The use of salad leaves as a wrapper for various fish or meat purees, with the addition of herbs such as mint, coriander and sweet basil, is common in both Laos and Cambodia.

Sweets are few. Those available are made with sago, tapioca or bean flour in a small selection of cakes and puddings. Many are served with coconut cream and thick brown palm-sugar syrup, or white sugar syrup. Rice cooked in banana-leaf wrappings is prepared specially as an offering to the monks on religious festival days, but is also eaten at home with accompaniments of banana, slivered coconut and sweet syrup.

In Cambodia, the few dishes that I was fortunate enough to sample revealed the same profusion of unusual flavours found in neighbouring Laos, Vietnam, Thailand and Burma. Many indigenous herbs are blended with the traditional pungent fish sauce (made from dried fermented fish, and known in Cambodia as *nguoc mam*), the juice of local limes and coconut milk, and these ingredients are then added to a base of pounded onion, garlic and chillies to produce creamy curry sauces.

Cambodians eat two main meals a day, consisting of boiled rice (the staple), a soup dish, and several main dishes based on a choice of buffalo meat, poultry, pork and fish cooked in a curry sauce. Barbecued or pureed meat and fish wrapped in aromatic salad greens are as popular here as they are in Laos, though the Cambodians prefer theirs with a dipping sauce of salty, fragrant *nguoc mam* and lime juice flavoured with chop-

ped chilli, garlic and crushed peanuts. The Cambodian cook, like her neighbours in Laos and Vietnam, often uses fresh bacon fat, or pieces of fatty bacon, in her cooking for extra flavour and nourishment. Vegetable oils are rarely used.

Much that is typically Laotian or Cambodian is unlikely to be prepared in a Western kitchen simply because the ingredients are not available or because they strike the fastidious Westerner as unappetising. The recipes included here, which I enjoyed in Laos and Cambodia and have since tried out at home, are mostly easy to prepare and are made with readily available ingredients.

FISH PUREE

TOM PONH

500 g (1 lb) white fish meat
2 large eggplants
4 fresh red chillies
8 spring onions
8 sprigs mint
salt or fish sauce
1 small head lettuce
small bunch of mint
small bunch of fennel
small bunch of *daun kesom*
small bunch of sweet basil
shredded spring onion

In separate saucepans, boil fish and eggplants until soft. Lift out, reserving fish stock. Remove bones from fish and put meat into a blender. Remove skin from eggplants and put with the fish. Add chillies, spring onions and mint and blend to a puree. Add enough of the fish stock to make a smooth creamy sauce. Season with salt or fish sauce to taste.

Wash lettuce and arrange in a salad bowl with washed herbs. To serve, spread fish puree onto a lettuce leaf, add a few sprigs of herbs and a sprinkling of spring onions and roll up.

FISH ROLLS WITH SALAD

KOY TIOUM

1 kg (2 lb) fish fillets (cod, haddock or snapper)
125 g (¼ lb) thin rice vermicelli
10 sprigs mint
6 sprigs fennel
8 sprigs *daun kesom*
8 spring onions

Sauce:
4 cloves garlic
2 fresh red chillies
2 tablespoons fish sauce
3 tablespoons water
3 teaspoons sugar
1 tablespoon finely chopped fresh fennel

Salad:
lettuce leaves
cabbage leaves

1 medium cucumber
6 spring onions
small bunch of mint
small bunch of *daun kesom*

Leave skin on fish and put under a moderately hot grill to cook through. Cool, then remove skin and any bones. Pound meat to a smooth paste.

Steep vermicelli in boiling water until soft. Drain and cut into 1 cm (½ inch) lengths. Chop herbs and spring onions finely. Blend vermicelli, herbs and fish paste together, adding a little water or coconut milk if the resultant puree is too dry. Spoon into a serving dish.

To prepare sauce, grind garlic and chillies to a paste. Add fish sauce, water and sugar and stir well, then add chopped fennel.

To prepare salad, wash lettuce and cabbage leaves. Shred cucumber and spring onions. Break herbs into small sprigs. Arrange lettuce, cabbage, cucumber and spring onion on a plate and top with the herbs.

To serve the fish rolls, place several pieces of herb, cucumber and onions on a lettuce or cabbage leaf. Spread thickly with the fish puree and roll up. Dip into the sauce before eating.

LAOTIAN CAVIAR

SOM KHAY

This is a traditional old Laotian recipe for an unusual fish puree made from the roe of a large freshwater fish caught in the Mekong River. It is included here more for novelty than practicality as it must be prepared at least a month in advance.

500 g (1 lb) fish roe (good cod or mullet roe is suitable)
500 g (1 lb) hot steamed rice
500 g (1 lb) white fish fillets
salt
3 jars each of 500 g (1 lb) capacity
3 tablespoons lemon juice or white vinegar

Wash roe, dry and mix with a generous quantity of salt. Spoon into one of the jars and seal tightly. Fill second jar with rice and seal. Chop fish finely, mix with 1½ tablespoons salt and seal in the remaining jar. It may be necessary to seal the contents with a thin layer of wax if jars are not completely full.

Place jars in a dark, cool cupboard and leave untouched for one month.

To use, mix contents of the three jars together and flavour with lemon juice or vinegar. Blend to a smooth puree. Serve as a spread with thin slices of bread or on lettuce leaves with fresh herbs for added flavour.

Carefully reseal jars before storing remaining caviar.

CHICKEN STUFFED WITH PEANUTS

PHANENG KAI

1.5 kg (3 lb) chicken
6 dried chillies
1 teaspoon fennel seeds

Fish Puree (recipe this page).

90 g (3 oz) roasted peanuts
1 large onion
1 tablespoon oil
90 g (3 oz) minced pork
½ teaspoon powdered cinnamon
1 tablespoon finely chopped fresh mint
¾ cup thick coconut milk
1 tablespoon fish sauce
1 cup thin coconut milk

Toast chillies until crisp then grind to a powder with fennel. Crush peanuts and add chilli and fennel. Peel onion, chop very finely and fry in oil until soft and a light golden brown. Add peanut mixture, minced pork, cinnamon and mint. Saute for 3 minutes, stirring occasionally. Combine thick coconut milk with the mixture and blend well.

Stuff the chicken with the mixture and sew up the opening or secure with toothpicks. Put chicken into a casserole and splash on fish sauce. Add thin coconut milk, cover casserole and cook on moderate to low heat until chicken is completely tender and sauce thick and creamy.

LAOTIAN TARTARE STEAK

LAP

185 g (6 oz) rice
3 medium eggplants
4 cloves garlic
6 fresh red chillies
5 cm (2 inch) piece *lengkuas*
2 teaspoons fennel seeds
12 spring onions
large bunch of mint
750 g (1½ lb) fillet or sirloin steak
2 tablespoons lemon juice
8 cups beef stock
fish sauce
sprigs of mint, sweet basil, fresh fennel and *daun kesom*
2 heads of lettuce

Wash rice and place in a wide pan under the griller or in a moderately hot oven to roast to a light brown. Shake pan occasionally to colour evenly. Leave to cool, then pound to a fine powder in a mortar or spice grinder.

Roast eggplants under a moderately hot grill or in the oven until cooked through. Remove stems and skin. Place in the blender with garlic, chillies, sliced *lengkuas* and fennel seeds. Add a little water and blend to a smooth puree.

Chop spring onions and mint finely and set aside. Chop or mince beef and sprinkle with lemon juice. Add about 2 cups beef stock and blend meat to a smooth cream in the blender.

Blend together rice powder, eggplant puree and beef cream and season with chopped spring onions, mint and fish sauce. Blend well and continue to beat until the mixture is very smooth and creamy, adding a little more beef stock if necessary.

Divide puree between several serving dishes and garnish with mint, sweet basil, fennel and *daun kesom*. Serve with lettuce leaves.

Season remaining beef stock and serve as a soup with a garnish of chopped mint.

MINCED PORK IN SALAD ROLLS

MOU NEM

185 g (6 oz) rice
250 g (½ lb) pork belly with rind
3 tablespoons oil
5 cm (2 inch) piece *lengkuas*
2 teaspoons salt
1½ teaspoons sugar
3 fresh red chillies
6 spring onions
1 small head lettuce
small bunch of watercress
sprigs of mint, sweet basil and *daun kesom*

Wash rice and allow to dry. Place in a wide pan and cook under the griller or in a moderately hot oven until lightly browned. Remove, allow to cool then pound in a mortar or spice grinder to a fine powder.

Remove rind from pork and place rind in a saucepan of boiling, slightly salted water. Boil until very soft, then drain. Mince or chop pork finely. Heat oil and fry pork mince until quite dry. Continue to cook until very dark brown. Blend to a paste in a liquidiser.

Peel *lengkuas*, chop then pound to a smooth paste. Mix rice powder, pork and *lengkuas* together. Cut pork rind into very thin threads and mix in. Season with salt and sugar to taste. Spoon into a serving dish and garnish with shredded spring onions and sliced chillies.

Wash salad greens and dry well. Arrange lettuce, sprigs of watercress and herbs on a serving plate. Prepare salad rolls with the lettuce, herbs and a spoonful of the pork mixture.

Serve with the same sauce as for Fish Rolls with Salad.

TRIPE, LIVER AND PORK STEW

SAMLOR CHAPHECK

375 g (¾ lb) tripe, well washed
250 g (½ lb) beef, pork or calves liver
500 g (1 lb) shoulder or leg of pork
155 g (5 oz) raw shrimp (optional)
4½ cups water or beef stock
1 large onion
4 cloves garlic
3 fresh red chillies
1 tablespoon fish sauce
5 cm (2 inch) piece *lengkuas*, sliced
salt
white pepper

Cut tripe, liver and pork into thin strips and put into a saucepan with stock. Peel onion and garlic and chop coarsely. Slice red chillies. Bring stock to a rapid boil, turn heat down and simmer for 20 minutes, then add onion, garlic, chillies, fish sauce and sliced *lengkuas*. Cover and simmer on low heat for 1 hour.

Season to taste with salt and pepper. If shrimps are used, add in the last 10 minutes of cooking.

VEGETABLE AND MEAT STEW

O LAM

When I had this dish in Laos it was made with buffalo meat which was exceedingly tough and chewy, though the flavour was excellent. Eggplants, which grow profusely in this country, are used in many dishes in pureed form as a thickener.

250 g (½ lb) stewing steak
2 medium eggplants
250 g (½ lb) mixed green vegetables
100 g (3½ oz) green or long beans, sliced
30 g (1 oz) cloud ear fungus, soaked
5 cm (2 inch) piece *lengkuas*
3-4 fresh red chillies
1 heaped teaspoon fennel seeds, lightly crushed
salt
white pepper
6 spring onions
small bunch of fresh mint
small bunch of watercress
sprigs of sweet basil and *daun kesom*

Use green vegetables such as spinach, mustard, cabbage, kale. Cut meat into 2.5 cm (1 inch) pieces and put in a saucepan with sliced eggplant. Cover with water and bring to the boil. Cook until the eggplant is tender, then lift eggplant with a slotted spoon. Continue to simmer meat in the stock until very tender. Add a little more water or beef stock if the level of the liquid becomes too low.

Peel eggplant and mash or pass through a fine wire sieve. Return puree to the stock with washed and chopped vegetables, beans, fungus, sliced *lengkuas*, sliced chillies and fennel. Boil uncovered for 15 minutes. Season with salt and pepper and add chopped spring onions. Continue to simmer until beans are tender and sauce thickened.

Serve with washed sprigs of fresh herbs, or chop the herbs and add to the stew just before serving.

NOODLES WITH MEAT, FISH AND VEGETABLES IN COCONUT SOUP

KHAO PHOUNE

Soups, especially noodle soups like this one, are the most popular breakfast food in Cambodia and Laos. Khao Phoune is similar to the Laksa dishes of Malaysia.

375 g (¾ lb) stewing steak
4 cloves garlic
1 large onion
3 cups water
250 g (½ lb) fish fillets
2 teaspoons salt
3 teaspoons sugar
2 tablespoons tomato paste
1 medium cucumber
2 banana flowers (optional)
1 large slice green papaya or mango
1 white radish or several small red radishes

250 g (½ lb) beanshoots
100 g (3½ oz) green or long beans, sliced
oil
1 medium eggplant
small bunches of mint, fennel and sweet basil
8 spring onions
500 g (1 lb) thin rice vermicelli

Sauce:
1 tablespoon vegetable oil
2.5 cm (1 inch) piece *lengkuas*, shredded
2 teaspoons dried shrimp paste
3 fresh red chillies, chopped
2 heaped tablespoons roasted peanuts, crushed
8 cups thin coconut milk

Cut stewing steak into very small dice and put into a saucepan with garlic and chopped onion. Cover with water and bring to the boil. Turn heat down and simmer until meat is tender, adding a little more water during cooking if necessary. Remove from stock and set aside.

Chop fish into 5 cm (2 inch) pieces and drop into the hot stock. Boil until the meat begins to flake. Return meat and continue to cook until meat and fish combine to make a thickish sauce. Season with salt and sugar and stir in tomato paste. Keep warm while sauce is prepared.

Heat oil and fry shredded *lengkuas* for 2 minutes, then add shrimp paste with chillies and peanuts. Fry for 2-3 minutes, stirring constantly. Pour in coconut milk and heat through. Remove from heat and keep warm.

Wipe cucumber and shred or slice thinly. Shred banana flowers (if used) and green papaya or mango. Shred radish. Steep beanshoots in boiling water for 2 minutes to soften. Boil beans for 3 minutes and drain.

Heat 2.5 cm (1 inch) oil in a pan and fry very thinly sliced eggplant until crisp. Lift out and drain well. Clean and shred spring onions and chop herbs or break into sprigs. Steep vermicelli in slightly salted boiling water to soften.

Drain noodles and divide between six large soup bowls. Top with a little of the vegetables and shredded flowers, and ladle on a serving of the meat and fish sauce. Add coconut and peanut sauce and garnish with fried eggplant, shredded spring onions and fresh herbs.

MOULDED RICE

BAY POUM

375 g (¾ lb) glutinous rice
5 cups water
90 g (3 oz) chicken
75 g (2½ oz) lean pork
375 g (¾ lb) fat pork or bacon
4 cloves garlic
2 medium onions
3 tablespoons fish sauce
salt
pepper
sprigs of fresh herbs (mint, basil, *daun kesom*)
fresh red chilli, finely sliced

Wash rice and pour into a saucepan. Add water, cover

and cook until rice is completely soft and the liquid absorbed. Finely dice all meat. Fry fat pork or bacon until very crisp, then fry chicken and diced pork in the same pan until cooked through. Flavour with fish sauce and stir into the rice. Season with salt and pepper.

Lightly grease a large bowl or several small dishes and press the rice in. Weight the top with a plate and a suitably heavy object and stand in a low oven for 45 minutes.

Turn out onto a serving plate. Garnish with sprigs of fresh herbs and thinly sliced chilli.

BAMBOO SHOOT SALAD

NJUM

375 (¾ lb) canned bamboo shoots, drained
2-3 fresh red chillies, minced
3 cloves garlic, minced
1½ tablespoons lime or lemon juice
3 teaspoons sugar
1 tablespoon fish sauce
2½ tablespoons thick coconut milk
3 spring onions
sweet basil and mint leaves
sprigs of fennel or dill

Boil bamboo shoots for 2-3 minutes in slightly salted water. Drain and rinse in cold water. Slice paper thin.

Prepare the dressing by mixing chillies and garlic with lime or lemon juice, sugar, fish sauce and coconut milk. Put bamboo shoots into a salad bowl and pour on the dressing. Toss lightly.

Shred spring onions and chop basil and mint. Scatter over the salad and stir lightly. Garnish with sprigs of fennel or dill.

RICE ROLLS WITH BAMBOO SHOOTS AND MUSHROOMS

NAM KOW

6 sheets rice flour wrappers or
   fresh uncut *hor fun* noodle dough
100 g (3½ oz) canned bamboo shoots, drained
60 g (2 oz) fresh mushrooms finely chopped, or
   30 g (1 oz) dried mushrooms, soaked
3 cloves garlic
2.5 cm (1 inch) piece *lengkuas*
4 spring onions
100 g (3½ oz) minced pork
1 teaspoon salt

Sauce:
1 tablespoon brown sugar
1 tablespoon fish sauce
3 fresh red chillies, finely chopped
1 heaped tablespoon roasted peanuts, crushed
3 cloves garlic, crushed
1 tablespoon lemon or lime juice
5 cm (2 inch) stalk lemon grass, pounded (optional)

Cut rice wrappers or noodle dough into quarters. Shred bamboo shoots finely. Drain dried mushroom (if used)

and shred. Crush garlic and chop *lengkuas* finely. Shred spring onions. Fry spring onions for ½ minute in a little oil. Add *lengkuas* and garlic and cook briefly, then add minced pork. Saute for 4 minutes, then add mushrooms and bamboo shoots and saute for a further 2 minutes. Cool, then season with salt.

Place a spoonful of the filling in the centre of each piece of pastry and roll up. Place in an oiled plate and steam over high heat for 10 minutes.

Prepare sauce by blending all ingredients. Pour into small bowls. Serve the rice rolls warm or cold with the sauce.

RICE BEANS AND TAPIOCA DESSERT

KHAOLOTE SONG

220 g (7 oz) rice flour
green food colouring
220 g (7 oz) pearl tapioca
7 cups water
pink food colouring
250 g (½ lb) sugar
1½ cups thick coconut milk

Blend rice flour with enough water to make a smooth batter. Colour bright green and bring to the boil. Stir over moderate heat until the mixture thickens and becomes clear. Bring a saucepanful of water to a brisk boil. Turn heat down slightly. Press the rice flour mixture through the holes in a perforated ladle held over the water. The paste should form into samll 'beans' and drop into the water. Cook for at least 10 minutes, then lift out and place in a bowl of ice water.

Wash tapioca and divide between two small saucepans. Cover each with 2½ cups water and add pink food colouring to one lot. Bring to the boil, reduce heat and cook until tapioca clears and is soft enough to squash between the fingers. Drain and rinse with cold water.

Mix sugar with 2 cups water and bring to the boil. Simmer without stirring until the liquid is slightly sticky. Remove from heat and chill with rice beans and tapioca.

To serve the sweet, spoon into glass dessert dishes a large helping each of tapioca, rice beans and sugar syrup. Pour on coconut milk and add a little shaved ice.

COCONUT RICE CAKES WITH BANANA

KHAO TOM

Makes 24

185 g (6 oz) short grain rice
4½ cups thin coconut milk
1 teaspoon salt
4 large ripe bananas
24 pieces banana leaf or aluminium foil
string or cotton

Wash rice well and set aside to drain. Pour coconut milk into a saucepan and bring to the boil. Reduce heat and cook until it thickens and becomes oily. Pour in rice and add salt. Cover tightly and cook on moderate heat for 10 minutes, stirring occasionally.

Peel bananas and slice diagonally. Cut banana leaf or foil into 15 cm (6 inch) squares. Place a spoonful of rice on each piece of leaf or foil and add a slice of banana. Cover with another layer of rice, fold up and tie securely.

When all cakes are prepared place in a steamer and cook for 2 hours, or drop into a large pot of slightly salted boiling water and boil for ¾ hour. Drain and cool.

This type of sweet rice cake is offered to the monks on certain festive days in Laos and Cambodia, but is also enjoyed as a sweet after a meal. Rice cooked in this way, but omitting the banana, can be served in place of the usual baskets of dry steamed rice.

MALAYSIA & SINGAPORE

Faced with the difficult task of accurately separating the foods of Malaysia and Singapore, I opted for the easy way out and combined them in this section. Both countries have three major races (Malay, Chinese, Indian) living side by side in reasonable harmony, and both therefore enjoy three major culinary styles. While traditional Malay, Chinese and Indian foods abound, there are also some unexpected surprises and, indeed, bonuses, in the occasional mingling of styles that has led to some distinctly local dishes and eating habits.

Most Malaysian and Singaporean Chinese were originally from the southern provinces of Kwangtung and Fukien where the food, though tasty, is somewhat bland — but that same style of food, eaten in Kuala Lumpur or Singapore, is likely to be seasoned with hot chillies, or at least served with a chilli *sambal* or a tiny dish of sliced raw chillies as an accompaniment. Indian dishes reflect the cooking of the homeland with creamy rich curry sauces seasoned with spices of every kind; hot dry curries; and the watery but fiery curries of the south. Malay curries, like many in southern India, use creamy coconut milk to achieve smooth sauces made hot with chillies. Other seasonings include plenty of garlic, *bawang merah* (shallots), such local herbs and spices as *serai* (lemon grass), *kunyit* (turmeric), coriander, *daun kesom* and *daun pandan* (both aromatic leaves that grow in profusion), *lengkuas* (greater galangal, a member of the Ginger family) and, for extra pungency and bite, *blacan* (dried shrimp paste) and the sour *asam* (tamarind).

Of all the foods in Singapore and Malaysia, Satay is probably the best known to foreigners. Of Malay-Indonesian origin, it consists of tiny cubes of meat or seafood marinated in a highly spiced sauce, then roasted over charcoal and eaten with a thick sauce of chillies, coconut milk and roasted crushed peanuts. Outdoor Satay-makers do a brisk trade all over the countryside and in every city and town, for eating in the open air is one of the rewards of life in countries where the climate is warm all year round. Throughout Malaysia and Singapore restaurants and foodstalls with access to a small area of garden, a lane or a sidewalk have at least some tables outdoors under canvas awnings or shady banyan trees. Such eating places are usually unsophisticated, but here one pays for the food, not for fancy decor.

Singapore's Orchard Road Car Park is arguably the best-known outdoor eating place in the Far East, at least as far as foreigners are concerned (although there are now many comparable collections of stalls such as those at Newton Circus in Singapore and at Gluttons' Square in Petaling Jaya, a Kuala Lumpur suburb). By day a car park serving the busy Orchard Road area, at night it is transformed into a thriving eating complex aglow with lights, a marvellous selection of Chinese, Malay and Indian dishes being produced at little trolley-mounted 'kitchens', each with its own delectable speciality. It was here that I enjoyed my first meal on Asian soil, and I'll never forget those wonderful smells and flavours.

Along the west coast of Malaysia are two areas with well-developed regional cuisines. Malacca, settled by the Portuguese in the sixteenth century and later held by the Dutch, was a port of call for traders *en route* to the Indonesian islands. Its fiery Devil's Curry, an interpretation of a Portuguese *diable* or devilled dish, is exclusive to this area. *Gula Melaka,* the dark brown sugar extracted from the aren palm, is one of the state's exports and is used extensively all over the country.

Penang, farther north, was once a prosperous trading post and a favourite retreat for British and Chinese rubber planters and tin miners. Now a popular tourist haven, it numbers among its own dishes a crisp-fried chicken, Inche Kabin, burnt almost black on the outside but absolutely tender inside, and served with a sauce made — of all things — with Lea and Perrin's sauce.

From these two areas, and from Singapore, came another specialised style of cooking. Called 'Nonya', it is the traditional food of the Peranakan or Straits-born Chinese, the offspring of marriages between Chinese settlers and Malay women; the children of such unions became known as Nonya (the females, who have given their name to the cuisine) and Baba (the males). Basically Malay in method and ingredients, the Nonya cuisine also utilises Chinese ingredients and cooking styles to produce a truly distinctive range of dishes. This cooking is generally hot and spicy with creamy coconut sauces and plenty of chillies, garlic, onions and fragrant herbs. The Muslim Malays are forbidden pork, but no Chinese worth his soya sauce would be without it; and Nonya cooks use it to make delicious curries. The range of cakes and desserts is enormous and today, four centuries after the first Chinese settlers sought wives in the Malay community, Nonya cooks still pride themselves on these and other Nonya specialities, maintaining a tradition of culinary excellence passed down through many generations.

Bok choy (Chinese cabbage), beanshoots, *brinjal* (eggplant), okra, yams and a hard-fleshed tuber called *bangkuang* (yam bean) are the vegetables most often used in Malaysia and Singapore. Beancurd is popular, and comes soft *(tauhu)* or as a hard cake *(taukwa),* sometimes dyed bright yellow; this is usually fried and shredded, and used as a vegetable.

Rice, usually boiled, is served throughout both countries, but many types of *pillau, biriyani* and fried rice dishes are also prepared. Flat white rice noodles *(kway teow* and *hor fun)* and the thin-thread rice noodles *(bee hoon),* as well as a variety of egg noodles, are as popular as rice.

Sweets and drinks made with coconut milk are sometimes served with meals; the creaminess of the coconut cools the palate after chillies much more effectively than cold water. Indians here also make Lassi, a whisked yoghurt drink that can be either sweet or salty; it is an excellent digestive.

Chinese use the traditional stir-fry method in the *wok,* the local version of which, the *kuali,* is made of

Fried Rice Noodles (recipe page 98).

slightly heavier metal. Clay or earthenware pots for curries and a cast-iron griddle or frying pan for cooking Indian breads will be useful, and a steaming rack that fits inside a large saucepan is an inexpensive and useful addition to any kitchen.

Food is served simply. Plates, or sometimes pieces of banana leaf, are used for curries, which are eaten with fork and spoon or the fingers. Eating with the fingers is quite simple, and not at all messy: simply scoop up a ball of rice using just the first two fingers and the thumb of the right hand, mix in a little of the curry and sop up as much sauce as possible, then pop the lot into your mouth. Chinese food is eaten with chopsticks and the usual array of rice bowls, soup bowls and porcelain spoons.

DRY FRIED FISH

This crispy fish is served as a side dish with curries and other dishes of Malay origin and is accompanied by a chilli and vinegar or onion sambal.

750 g (1½ lb) very small red mullet, herrings or whiting
2 teaspoons salt
2 teaspoons chilli powder
2 tablespoons cornflour
peanut or vegetable oil for deep frying
soya sauce (optional)

Clean fish, leaving heads on. Wash and wipe dry and season inside and out with a mixture of salt and chilli powder. Coat lightly with cornflour, shaking off excess.

Heat oil in a *wok* or large pan and when very hot put in several small fish. Fry to a deep golden brown, turning heat down slightly after first minute.

Remove from oil when cooked and crisp and drain well. Cook remaining fish and set all aside to cool.

Just before serving heat a dry frying pan or *wok* and cook fish for 1 minute on each side, adding a splash of soya sauce if desired.

FISH MOOLEE

750 g (1½ lb) cod, haddock or snapper
1 tablespoon tamarind
1¼ cups boiling water
2 cloves garlic
5 shallots
2 tablespoons oil
2.5 cm (1 inch) piece fresh ginger
1 stalk lemon grass
1 fresh red chilli, thinly sliced
½ teaspoon turmeric powder
1 teaspoon salt
¾ cup thin coconut milk
¾ cup thick coconut milk
fresh coriander leaves, chopped

Cut fish into fillets and remove skin. Cut fillets into pieces about 5 cm (2 inches) square. Soak tamarind in boiling water. Chop garlic and shallots finely. Shred ginger.

Heat oil in a pan and fry garlic and shallots for 2 minutes. Add ginger and cook for another minute.

Add strained tamarind water with lemon grass, chilli, turmeric and salt. Bring to the boil, turn heat down and stir in thin coconut milk. When the sauce is almost boiling drop in fish slices and pour on thick coconut milk. Simmer for about 5 minutes until fish is tender.

Check seasonings, adding more salt if necessary. Spoon into a serving dish and garnish with chopped coriander leaves.

SPICED FISH WRAPPED IN BANANA LEAVES

OTAK OTAK

500 g (1 lb) white fish fillets
4 candlenuts
2 medium onions, minced
2 cloves garlic, minced
¼ teaspoon turmeric powder or 1 teaspoon grated fresh turmeric
2.5 cm (1 inch) piece fresh ginger, minced
½ teaspoon tamarind
1 teaspoon salt
1 tablespoon chilli powder
2 teaspoons coriander, ground
2 teaspoons cummin, ground
½ teaspoon *daun kesom,* chopped
banana leaves (or aluminium foil)

Cut fish into thin slices about 1 cm (½ inch) thick and 10 cm by 5 cm (4 inches by 2 inches). Grind candlenuts and mix to a paste with all the remaining ingredients, except banana leaves. Hold banana leaves over a flame to soften.

Coat each fish slice thickly with the ground ingredients and wrap in a small piece of well-greased banana leaf. Secure with toothpicks. Grill or toast over a charcoal fire for 8-10 minutes.

Serve with the leaf partially torn away to display the fish.

SOUR FISH

IKAN ASAM

375 g (¾ lb) fish fillets
1½ tablespoons tamarind
3 cups boiling water
4 candlenuts
1 stalk lemon grass
1 teaspoon grated fresh turmeric or
    ½ teaspoon turmeric powder
½ teaspoon dried shrimp paste
6 spring onions, chopped
6 fresh red chillies, finely chopped
2 tablespoons peanut or vegetable oil
salt

Cut fish into strips about 2 cm by 5 cm (¾ inch by 2 inches). Soak tamarind in boiling water. Pound ginger and candlenuts in a mortar or spice grinder together with lemon grass, turmeric, dried shrimp paste, spring onions and chopped chillies.

Heat oil and fry pounded mixture for 4 minutes. Pour in strained tamarind water and bring to the boil. Turn heat down and simmer for 8 minutes. Add fish slices and cook on low heat for about 3 minutes until tender.

Transfer fish to a serving plate. Season sauce with salt and strain through a fine sieve over the fish.

Large unpeeled prawns may also be cooked in this way. Serve the fish without the sauce if it is to accompany other dishes with sauce.

STEAMED FISH WITH CHILLI SAUCE

750 g (1½ lb) pomfret, bream or snapper
salt
1 tablespoon oil
1 large onion, finely chopped
2 cloves garlic, crushed
2 teaspoons minced ginger
1 tomato
2-3 fresh red chillies, finely chopped
1 teaspoon chilli powder
1 tablespoon white vinegar
1 tablespoon sugar
½ cup cold water
1 heaped teaspoon cornflour
fresh coriander or parsley sprigs

Clean and scale fish and make several deep diagonal incisions across each side. Rub with salt. Put on a flat, lightly oiled plate and steam over boiling water for 8 minutes, or until cooked through. Test by inserting a toothpick into the thickest part. If no pinkish liquid escapes the fish is done.

Heat oil and cook onion with garlic until soft but not coloured. Add ginger and cook for another minute. Chop tomato and add to the pan with chopped chillies, chilli powder, vinegar, sugar and water. Bring to the boil, turn heat down and simmer for 4 minutes. Season with salt. Mix cornflour with a little cold water and stir into the sauce. Cook until sauce thickens and clears.

Place steamed fish on an oval serving plate and pour on the hot sauce. Garnish with sprigs of coriander or parsley.

FISH ROLLS WITH SATAY SAUCE

This dish of fish rolls prepared Chinese style but served with a typical Malay sauce exemplifies the integration of cuisines in Malaysia and Singapore.

500 g (1 lb) fillets of cod, haddock or snapper
2 medium onions, minced
3 cloves garlic, minced
1 egg
1 tablespoon plain flour
2 teaspoons chopped fresh coriander leaves or parsley
salt
pepper
75 g (2½ oz) browned breadcrumbs
vegetable oil
Satay sauce (see page 95)

Mince or chop fish finely and blend to a smooth paste with onions and garlic. Blend in egg, flour, chopped coriander and season with salt and pepper. Knead till smooth, then form into rolls about 8 cm (3 inches) long and 2.5 cm (1 inch) thick.

Coat generously with breadcrumbs and deep fry in hot oil until a deep golden brown. Lift from oil and drain on absorbent paper.

Prepare Satay sauce as directed and serve in a separate dish. Serve fish rolls hot or cold.

PRAWN AND CABBAGE CURRY

375 g (¾ lb) Chinese cabbage, or white cabbage
6 shallots, finely chopped
1 clove garlic, finely chopped
2 tablespoons oil
250 g (½ lb) peeled raw prawns
1 teaspoon turmeric powder
2 teaspoons salt
¾ cup thin coconut milk
¾ cup thick coconut milk

Chop cabbage roughly, discarding centre stalk. Rinse in cold water and shake dry. Heat oil in a large saucepan or *wok* and fry shallots and garlic until soft but not coloured. Add cabbage and prawns to the pan and saute for 3 minutes, stirring frequently.

Stir in turmeric and salt, then pour on thin coconut milk and bring almost to the boil. Add thick coconut milk, turn down heat and simmer for about 4 minutes. Cabbage should still be slightly crisp.

This is a very mild curry. Sprinkle on 1-2 teaspoons chilli powder for a slightly hotter taste. Halved hard-boiled eggs may be added when curry is almost done.

MALACCAN FISH CURRY, PORTUGESE STYLE

500 g (1 lb) fillets of cod, haddock or snapper
2 medium onions
6 cloves garlic
5 cm (2 inch) piece fresh ginger
250 g (½ lb) tomatoes
3 green chillies
3 tablespoons vegetable or peanut oil
½ teaspoon cummin
2 teaspoons fennel
½ cup water
1 tablespoon tamarind
1 stalk lemon grass
5 curry leaves
2-3 tablespoons curry powder
1 teaspoon chilli powder
½ teaspoon turmeric powder, or
    1½ teaspoons grated fresh turmeric
1½ cups warm water or fish stock
salt
cornflour
dry fried onions (see page 125)

Cut each fish fillet into 2-3 pieces. Peel onions and gar-

lic and chop finely. Shred ginger. Slice tomatoes and chillies.

Heat oil in a large saucepan and fry cummin, fennel, ginger, onion and garlic for 3 minutes. Add tomato and half the chillies and fry for a further 2 minutes. Soak tamarind in water, squeeze, strain and add together with chopped lemon grass and curry leaves. Cook for 2 minutes. Sprinkle on curry powder, chilli powder, turmeric and pour on warm water or fish stock. Stir thoroughly and bring to the boil.

Coat fish fillets lightly with salt and cornflour and drop into the boiling sauce. Cook on moderate heat for 6 minutes, then remove fish and set aside.

Bring sauce to the boil and simmer until it reduces and thickens slightly. Thicken with a little cornflour if necessary. Add salt to taste. Return fish to the sauce, reheat and then spoon onto a serving dish.

Garnish with the remaining sliced green chillies and a little dry fried onion.

TAMARIND PRAWNS

UDANG ASAM

2 tablespoons tamarind
1 cup boiling water
500 g (1 lb) large raw prawns
2 teaspoons chilli powder
2 teaspoons sugar
2 tablespoons oil
185 g (6 oz) mixed pickled vegetables, or
    sliced tomato and cucumber

Soak tamarind in boiling water for 30 minutes. Remove shell from prawns, leaving heads and tails intact. Carefully scrape out dark veins with a sharp knife, then make deep incisions down the centre back of the prawns to make them curl up during cooking. Arrange prawns in a wide flat bowl. Strain tamarind water, and stir in chilli powder and sugar. Pour over prawns and marinate for up to 1 hour, turning occasionally.

Heat oil in a *wok* or large frying pan. Drain prawns and saute on high heat for 2 minutes. Pour on marinade and cook until prawns are tender. Remove prawns from sauce with a slotted spoon. Bring sauce to the boil and cook until well reduced.

Drain pickled vegetables and arrange these, or tomato and cucumber slices, around the edge of a serving dish. Place prawns in the centre and pour on the sauce.

PRAWNS IN GINGER

500 g (1 lb) large raw prawns
2 teaspoons salt
5 cm (2 inch) piece fresh ginger, finely shredded
1 teaspoon finely ground black pepper
2 tablespoons Chinese wine
1 teaspoon sesame oil
vegetable oil for deep frying
pineapple chunks

Clean, peel, and devein prawns, and remove heads. Wash and dry well. Season with salt and roll in shred-

ded ginger, coating well. Allow to stand for 7 minutes to absorb the ginger flavour.

Heat oil in a deep pan and lower prawns in on a slotted spoon. Deep fry until cooked through, then remove and drain. Do not overcook or prawns will become tough and dry.

Pour out all but 1 tablespoon oil and add remaining ingredients to the pan, including any leftover ginger. Boil for 30 seconds, then return prawns and saute for another 30 seconds.

Arrange prawns on a serving plate and garnish with pineapple chunks.

SINGAPORE CHILLI CRAB

2 medium raw crabs
3 teaspoons tamarind
¾ cup boiling water
3 tablespoons oil
2 medium onions, minced
5 cm (2 inch) piece fresh ginger, minced
4 fresh red chillies, finely chopped
1-2 teaspoons chilli powder
2 teaspoons tomato paste
3 teaspoons sugar, or to taste
2 teaspoons cornflour
fresh red and green chillies, sliced
spring onions, chopped

Drop crabs into boiling, slightly salted water and cook rapidly for 4 minutes. Remove, drain and leave to cool. Soak tamarind in boiling water. Chop crabs into large pieces, if possible leaving the legs attached to the body pieces. Remove the spongey grey portion and discard.

Heat oil in a *wok* or very large pan and saute onion, ginger and chopped chillies for 2 minutes. Add crab pieces and sprinkle on chilli powder, then pour in strained tamarind water. Lower heat and simmer for 4 minutes.

Remove crab to a serving plate. Add tomato paste and sugar to the sauce. Thicken with cornflour mixed with a little cold water and cook until sauce thickens and clears slightly. Pour over crab.

Garnish with sliced chilli and spring onion.

CRAB CURRY

KETAM MASAK LEMAK

6 small raw crabs
3-4 green chillies
1 teaspoon turmeric powder
10 cm (4 inch) piece lemon grass, finely sliced
4 cm (1½ inch) piece fresh ginger, shredded
1½ teaspoons salt
1¾ cups thick coconut milk

Wash crabs, wipe dry and crack open shells underneath. Remove all inedible parts and rinse again. Using a heavy knife handle or the flat blade of a cleaver crack shells and claws to allow the seasonings to penetrate the meat.

Chop chillies finely. Arrange crabs in a large saucepan and sprinkle on chopped chilli, turmeric, lemon

Singapore Chilli Crab (recipe this page).

grass, ginger and salt. Pour on coconut milk. Set on moderate heat and simmer, covered, until crabs are cooked and sauce thick and well flavoured.

CRABMEAT OMELETTE

FOO YUNG HAI

4 shallots or 6 spring onions
½ small carrot
30 g (1 oz) bamboo shoot
4 large eggs
1 tablespoon sago or potato flour
2 tablespoons oil
60 g (2 oz) Chinese cabbage, roughly chopped
185 g (6 oz) fresh crabmeat, shredded
2 teaspoons chilli powder (optional)
salt
pepper
monosodium glutamate (optional)
6 sprigs coriander
1 spring onion, shredded

Finely chop shallots or spring onions. Grate or finely chop carrot and bamboo shoot. Beat eggs lightly with sago or potato flour and set aside.

Heat oil in a large frying pan. Fry shallots or spring onions for 2 minutes, then add carrot, bamboo shoots and cabbage. Cook for 3 minutes. Scatter on crabmeat and season with chilli powder (if used), salt and pepper and a pinch of monosodium glutamate (if used). Fry for 1 minute, then pour in eggs and lower heat. Stir gently to mix eggs evenly with vegetables and crabmeat, then cover and cook until just set.

Lift onto a serving plate and garnish with coriander and shredded spring onion. Serve with chilli oil or chilli sauce.

CURRIED CUTTLEFISH

500 g (1 lb) small fresh cuttlefish or squid
1 heaped teaspoon tamarind
¾ cup boiling water
1 small onion, minced
2 cloves garlic, crushed
1 cm (½ inch) piece fresh ginger, minced
1 tablespoon curry powder
2 tablespoons oil
1 tablespoon tomato paste
2 teaspoons sugar
salt
pepper
½ cup thick coconut milk

Clean cuttlefish and remove skin and intestines. Discard heads and ink bags. Soak tamarind in boiling water, then strain and pour liquid over cuttlefish. Marinate for 10 minutes.

Mix together onion, garlic, ginger and curry powder and fry in oil for 5 minutes, stirring frequently. Put in cuttlefish and tamarind water, stir well, then add tomato paste, sugar and salt and pepper to taste. Bring to the boil and simmer for 2 minutes. Pour in coconut

milk, turn heat down low and simmer for a further 1½ minutes.

CAPTAIN'S CURRY

KARI KAPITAN

1.25 kg (2½ lb) chicken
2 teaspoons dried shrimp paste
10 cm (4 inch) stalk lemon grass, chopped
6 candlenuts
1 tablespoon coriander, ground
2.5 cm (1 inch) piece fresh ginger, shredded
1½ teaspoons grated fresh turmeric or
   ¾ teaspoon turmeric powder
3 small red onions, or 6 shallots
3 cloves garlic
2 tablespoons oil
1½ cups thin coconut milk
3 teaspoons sugar
salt
pepper
4 spring onions, shredded

Clean chicken, rinse with cold water and wipe dry. Chop into pieces about 5 cm (2 inches) square, or, if preferred cut all meat from bones.

Make a paste with dried shrimp paste, lemon grass, candlenuts, coriander, cinnamon, ginger and turmeric, grinding ingredients in a mortar or on a grinding stone. Alternatively, grind dry spices in a coffee grinder and add shredded ginger. Chop onions or shallots and garlic finely.

Heat oil in a *wok* or deep saucepan and fry onion and garlic until soft. Add seasoning paste and fry for 3 minutes, stirring frequently. Remove from the heat and stir in coconut milk. Add chicken pieces to coconut milk and seasonings. Sprinkle on sugar and season with salt and pepper. Cover and cook gently until chicken is very tender, literally falling off the bones, and sauce thick.

Garnish with shredded spring onion.

MALAY CHICKEN

1 kg (2 lb) chicken
12 dried chillies, soaked
1 tablespoon curry paste or powder
1 teaspoon turmeric powder
1 teaspoon cummin
1-2 cloves garlic, chopped
5 shallots or 2 medium red onions, chopped
2 tablespoons oil
1 teaspoon sugar
1½ cups thick coconut milk
2 large tomatoes, sliced
1 red onion, thinly sliced
2-3 spring onions, shredded, or
   6 sprigs coriander leaf
sliced tomato
sliced cucumber
dry fried onion (optional — see page 125)

Clean chicken, wipe dry and chop into medium sized pieces. Pound soaked chillies, curry paste or powder, turmeric, cummin, garlic and shallots or onion to a fairly smooth paste.

Heat oil in a heavy saucepan and fry seasonings for 3 minutes. Put in chicken and fry for 8 minutes, stirring to colour evenly. Sprinkle on sugar and pour in coconut milk.

Simmer on a moderate heat until chicken is tender and coconut milk well reduced. Add tomato and onion slices and shredded spring onion or coriander and cook for 5 minutes, stirring frequently.

Spoon onto a serving dish and surround with slices of tomato and cucumber. Sprinkle on fried onion (if used).

FRIED SPICED CHICKEN

1.25 kg (2½ lb) chicken
salt
1 heaped teaspoon cummin, ground
2 heaped teaspoons coriander, ground
1 heaped teaspoon turmeric powder
2-3 teaspoons chilli powder
3 teaspoons sugar
5 cm (2 inch) piece fresh ginger, shredded
2 tablespoons lemon juice or tamarind water
oil for deep frying
lettuce leaves
krupuk or potato crisps

Clean chicken, chop into fairly large pieces and wipe dry. Sprinkle generously with salt. Mix all remaining seasonings into a paste and rub well into the chicken pieces. Allow to stand for 45 minutes to absorb the flavours.

Heat oil in a deep pan and when almost at smoking point carefully lower the chicken pieces into the oil. Turn heat down slightly. Fry chicken until cooked through and well crisped on the surface. Remove from oil and drain thoroughly on absorbent paper.

Serve on a bed of lettuce and garnish with freshly fried *krupuk* or potato crisps.

SWEET CHICKEN CURRY

BEGUM BEHAR

1.25 kg (2½ lb) chicken
3 tablespoons *ghee* or butter
1 large onion, minced
2 cloves garlic, minced
1 cm (½ inch) piece fresh ginger, minced
1 teaspoon turmeric powder
2½ teaspoons coriander, ground
3 cloves
1 teaspoon chilli powder
1½ teaspoons sugar
1 teaspoon crushed peppercorns
1½ teaspoons cummin, ground
1 bay leaf
1 cup water
1 tomato, chopped
30 g (1 oz) sultanas, soaked in water
3 tablespoons thick cream
2 hardboiled eggs, chopped
30 g (1 oz) roasted, slivered almonds

Clean chicken and chop into medium sized pieces. Heat *ghee* or butter and gently fry onion, garlic and ginger for 3 minutes, then add turmeric, coriander, slightly crushed cloves, chilli powder, sugar, peppercorns, cummin and bay leaf. Saute for 2 minutes, then put in chicken pieces. Turn heat up slightly and cook, stirring frequently, until chicken takes on a good colour.

Pour in ½ cup water, turn heat down and simmer for 10 minutes. Add tomato and drained sultanas and another ½ cup water. Cover and cook until chicken is very tender. Stir in cream and chopped boiled eggs. Heat through, then spoon onto a serving dish. Garnish with slivered almonds.

FRIED PENANG CHICKEN

INCHE KABIN

1 kg (2 lb) chicken
2.5 cm (1 inch) piece fresh ginger, sliced
2 teaspoons chilli paste (see below)
2 teaspoons turmeric powder
1 tablespoon lemon or lime juice
1 teaspoon sugar
½ cup thick coconut milk
peanut oil for deep frying
12 large freshly fried *krupuk*

Chilli Paste:
1 fresh red chilli
½ teaspoon salt
½ teaspoon sugar
½ tablespoon oil

Finely chop or mince chilli and mix with remaining ingredients.

Sauce:
¼ cup Lea and Perrins or Worcestershire sauce
2 teaspoons hot mustard powder
sugar to taste
lemon or lime juice

Clean chicken, wipe dry and cut into 6 pieces. Prepare ginger juice by infusing sliced ginger in 1 tablespoon boiling water. Prepare chilli paste and mix with ginger juice, turmeric, lemon or lime juice and sugar. Rub the seasonings into the chicken pieces and stand ½ hour, turning occasionally. Remove from marinade and drain well.

Heat oil and when almost at smoking point fry chicken on very high heat until deep brown in colour. Remove chicken from oil and allow to cool. Turn off heat, but keep the oil in the pan.

When chicken is cool, heat oil until moderately hot and return chicken to the pan. Cook for 8-10 minutes, or until meat is cooked through. Test with a skewer in the thickest parts of the chicken. If no pink liquid runs off the chicken is done. Do not overcook.

Remove chicken from oil and allow to stand for 5 minutes, then return to the marinade. Soak for 10

minutes in this liquid, then drain.

Turn heat up very high and when oil is very hot drop in chicken pieces and cook quickly till the surface of the chicken is very dark brown. Remove from oil, drain and arrange on a serving plate. Surround with freshly fried *krupuk*.

Mix sauce ingredients together in a small bowl, stirring to thoroughly dissolve sugar and mustard. Add a little water and lime or lemon juice to taste.

HAINANESE STYLE CHICKEN

1.25 kg (2 ½ lb) chicken
4 spring onions, minced
2.5 cm (1 inch) piece fresh ginger, minced
2 teaspoons Chinese rice wine
3 teaspoons salt
3 tablespoons vegetable oil
375 g (¾ lb) rice
8 cups light chicken stock
250 g (½ lb) Chinese vegetables (cabbage or spring greens)
salt
soya sauce

Sauce:
2 tablespoons vegetable oil
2 spring onions, finely shredded
5 cm (2 inch) piece fresh ginger, finely shredded

Clean chicken and wipe dry. Mix onions and ginger with wine and salt. Rub outside and cavity of chicken with the seasonings and allow to stand for 1 hour. Place chicken in a covered dish over a steamer and steam on a high heat for 35-40 minutes. Allow to cool slightly, then remove and chop into bite-sized pieces. Arrange on a plate and set aside.

Wash rice well then drain thoroughly. Heat 3 tablespoons oil and fry rice for 5 minutes, stirring to coat each grain with oil. Pour in cold water to cover rice by 4 cm (1 ½ inches). Cover the pan, bring to the boil, then turn heat down to lowest point and cook until rice is tender and liquid completely absorbed.

Bring chicken stock to the boil, add washed vegetables and simmer for 1 minute. Lift out and drain. Season soup to taste with salt and soya sauce. Mix together sauce ingredients and spoon into tiny dishes.

Serve the chicken warm or cold with rice, the hot stock as a soup, the vegetables and the sauce.

CHICKEN LIVER CURRY

RENDANG HATI AYAM

375 g (¾ lb) chicken livers
90 g (3 oz) chicken hearts or giblets (optional)
1 large onion
5 cloves garlic
8 dried chillies, soaked
1 ½ teaspoons grated fresh turmeric, or
    ½ teaspoon turmeric powder
5 cm (2 inch) stalk lemon grass, finely chopped
2.5 cm (1 inch) piece fresh ginger, grated
3 tablespoons oil

2 tablespoons curry paste or mild curry powder
1-2 tablespoons thick coconut milk
2 *daun salam* or bay leaves (optional)
1 medium cucumber
1 ¾ cups thin coconut milk
salt
fresh red and green chillies, sliced

Clean chicken livers and giblets or hearts. Wipe dry and put aside. Mince onion and garlic and pound to a paste with chillies, turmeric, lemon grass and ginger. Fry in oil for 3 minutes. Add curry paste or powder and coconut milk and fry for 2 more minutes.

Put in chicken livers, hearts and giblets with *daun salam* or bay leaves and fry on moderate heat until livers change colour, stirring constantly. Add cubed cucumber and cook until softened. Pour on coconut milk and add salt to taste. Simmer until livers are tender and sauce thickened. Garnish with sliced chilli.

MUTTON AND EGGPLANT CURRY

500 g (1 lb) lean mutton or lamb, shoulder or leg
3 medium eggplants
salt
1 ½ tablespoons white poppy seeds
1 teaspoon fennel seeds, crushed
3 teaspoons coriander, ground
1 ¼ teaspoons cummin, ground
1 ½ teaspoons black peppercorns, crushed
¾ teaspoon turmeric powder or
    1 ½ teaspoons grated fresh turmeric
2.5 cm (1 inch) piece fresh ginger
8 shallots or 3 small red onions
3 cloves garlic
4 tablespoons *ghee* or oil
3 curry leaves, or 1 bay leaf
3 cloves
2 cm (¾ inch) stick cinnamon
2 cups thin coconut milk
½ cup thick coconut milk
lime juice or wedges of fresh lime

Chop meat into 2 cm (¾ inch) cubes. Remove stems from eggplants, wipe with a clean cloth and cut in halves lengthways, then into 5 cm (2 inch) pieces. Sprinkle with salt, cover and allow to stand for 10 minutes to draw bitter juices.

Grind poppy seeds, fennel, coriander, cummin and peppercorns together and mix with turmeric. Peel ginger and shred finely. Mince shallots or onions and garlic. Heat *ghee* or oil in a large pan and fry onions and garlic with ginger for 3 minutes. Add ground seasonings and fry for 5 minutes, stirring frequently. Put in cubed meat, curry or bay leaves, cloves and cinnamon stick. Cook on moderate heat for 10 minutes, stirring to coat meat with seasonings.

Rinse eggplants, wipe and add to the pan, cooking for another 5 minutes. Pour on thin coconut milk and bring almost to the boil. Lower heat and cook for about 25 minutes until meat and eggplant are tender. Stir in thick coconut milk and cook until sauce thickens slightly.

Season to taste with salt and lime juice. Spoon into a serving dish. If serving with lime wedges, arrange

Mutton and Eggplant Curry (recipe this page).

around the edge of the dish.

Note: If using mutton, do not add eggplant when frying meat. Simmer meat in thin coconut milk until almost tender, then add eggplant and cook for another 20-25 minutes before adding thick coconut milk.

LAMB CURRY
KARI KAMBING

625 g (1¼ lb) lamb, shoulder or leg
2 cloves garlic
2 teaspoons peanut oil or *ghee*
4 shallots or 2 small red onions, finely chopped
2½ tablespoons mild curry powder
2 teaspoons salt
1 teaspoon crushed black peppercorns
1½ cups warm water
2 medium potatoes, parboiled
1¾ cups thin coconut milk
½ cup thick coconut milk
90 g (3 oz) cooked peas (optional)
3 hardboiled eggs
fresh coriander leaves, mint or parsley, chopped

Chop meat into 2 cm (¾ inch) cubes. Crush garlic. Heat oil in a deep pan and saute shallots or onion and garlic until soft but not coloured. Add curry powder with salt and peppercorns and fry for 2 minutes. Pour in ½ cup water and stir well. Add cubed lamb and cook for 5 minutes, stirring frequently. Pour in remaining water and simmer on moderate heat, stirring occasionally, until all liquid has evaporated and meat is tender.

Cut potatoes into 2.5 cm (1 inch) cubes and add to the pan with thin coconut milk. Simmer for 5 minutes, then pour in thick coconut milk and add peas and halved boiled eggs. Heat through, remove from heat and let stand for 2 hours. Reheat before serving. Spoon into a serving bowl and sprinkle with chopped herbs.

TAMARIND BEEF
DAGING ASAM

625 g (1¼ lb) chuck, round or topside steak
6 dried chillies, soaked
10 shallots, chopped
2.5 cm (1 inch) piece fresh ginger
4 candlenuts
1 teaspoon dried shrimp paste
½ teaspoon turmeric powder
2 tablespoons oil
3 cups water
2 tablespoons tamarind
sugar
salt
1 fresh red chilli, finely sliced
1 green chilli, finely sliced

Cut beef into small pieces. Chop or mince dried chillies, shallots and ginger and grind to a paste with candlenuts, dried shrimp paste and turmeric.

Heat oil in a large pan and fry seasonings for 4

minutes, stirring constantly. Put in beef and turn several times to thoroughly coat meat pieces with the seasonings. Fry until well browned. Soak tamarind in water. Squeeze and strain into meat. Bring to the boil, then add sugar and salt to taste. Turn heat down and simmer till beef is very tender and gravy slightly reduced.

Remove beef and arrange on a serving dish. Pour on a little of the sauce. Garnish with sliced red and green chillies. Serve the meat without sauce if it is to accompany other sauced dishes.

CHINESE BEEF WITH SPRING ONIONS

250 g (½ lb) rump, sirloin or topside steak
1 tablespoon Chinese rice wine
pinch of monosodium glutamate (optional)
1 tablespoon cornflour
2 cloves garlic
12 spring onions
2 tablespoons oil
4 cm (1½ inch) piece fresh ginger, finely shredded
3 teaspoons sugar
2 tablespoons dark soya sauce
2-3 tablespoons beef stock
1 green chilli, thinly sliced

Slice meat very thinly, then cut into pieces about 5 cm by 2 cm (2 inches by ¾ inch). Sprinkle on Chinese wine and monosodium glutamate (if used) and stand for 10 minutes. Coat lightly with cornflour, shaking off excess.

Chop garlic finely. Clean spring onions, discarding green ends and cut into 5 cm (2 inch) pieces. Heat oil in a *wok* and when very hot put in meat, garlic and ginger. Stir-fry for 2 minutes, then sprinkle on sugar, soya sauce and stock. Add spring onions. Cook until meat is tender and most of the liquid has been absorbed.

Spoon onto a serving dish and garnish with sliced green chilli. This meat dish makes an ideal topping for fried noodles.

DRIED BEEF
DENDENG

375 g (¾ lb) sirloin, round or rump steak
1 large onion
1 stalk lemon grass
4 cm (1½ inch) piece *lengkuas*
2 teaspoons sugar
1 teaspoon salt
oil for deep frying
2 fresh red chillies
1-2 green chillies
4 shallots

Cut beef into paper thin slices with a very sharp knife, cutting across the grain. Peel onion and mince. Chop lemon grass, then pound to a coarse paste with *lengkuas*. Mix in onion, sugar and salt. Coat meat with the seasoning paste and arrange on a wide bamboo or wooden rack. Lay out in hot sunlight for about 30-40 minutes. Alternatively place in a moderate oven for 20 minutes, turning once.

Heat oil and deep fry meat on moderate to high heat until it becomes dry and crisp. Turn heat up during last stages of cooking to thoroughly crisp the meat slices. Remove from oil and drain on absorbent paper.

Shred green chillies and make flowers from red chillies by shredding the ends with a sharp knife and placing in a dish of iced water to make the 'petals' curl. Slice shallots very thinly and fry in a little oil until crisp.

Arrange dried beef slices on a serving plate. Scatter on sliced green chilli and fried shallots and decorate with chilli flowers.

ASSORTED SATAY

A renowned dish in Malaysia, Singapore and Indonesia, this delicious spiced meat or seafood on bamboo skewers is sold at roadside stalls, cafes and restaurants.

Makes 3 dozen.

1 tablespoon coriander, ground
1 teaspoon fennel, ground (optional)
1½ teaspoons cummin, ground
3 cloves garlic, crushed
2-3 dried chillies, soaked
1 stalk lemon grass, chopped
2.5 cm (1 inch) piece fresh ginger, chopped
2 teaspoons sugar
1 teaspoon tamarind
1 teaspoon turmeric powder
1 kg (2 lb) beef, mutton, pork, chicken and raw prawns (mixed)
salt
¼ cup thick coconut milk
1½ tablespoons oil
36 bamboo skewers
2 large cucumbers

Satay Sauce:
2 teaspoons coriander, ground
1 teaspoon cummin, ground
1 teaspoon fennel, ground
6 dried chillies, soaked
2 cloves garlic, chopped
3 shallots or 6 spring onions, chopped
1 heaped teaspoon dried shrimp paste
8 candlenuts
1 stalk lemon grass
1 tablespoon oil
155 g (5 oz) roasted peanuts, coarsely ground
¾ cup thick coconut milk
½ cup tamarind water, made with 2 teaspoons tamarind
sugar
salt

To prepare the Satay marinade, mix together coriander, fennel and cummin and roast briefly in a dry pan or under griller. Grind to a paste with garlic, chillies, lemon grass, ginger, sugar, tamarind and turmeric. Cut all meat into small thin pieces. Peel and devein prawns. Sprinkle with salt. Rub meat and prawns with the sea-sonings and stand for at least 1 hour to absorb flavours.

Prepare sauce. Grind coriander, cummin, fennel, chillies, garlic, shallots or spring onions, dried shrimp paste, candlenuts and lemon grass to a paste. Heat 1 tablespoon oil in pan and fry ground seasonings for 3 minutes. Add ground peanuts and stir in coconut milk slowly. Cook on moderate heat, stirring constantly, for 5 minutes.

Pour in tamarind water and add sugar and salt to taste. Bring almost to the boil, then turn heat down and simmer until oil begins to rise to the surface. Add a little more coconut milk or water if sauce becomes too thick.

Thread various types of meat and prawns onto sepa-rate bamboo skewers. Pour thick coconut milk and oil over the Satay and then place under a griller or over a charcoal fire to roast until done. The surface should be crisp and inside tender and juicy. Brush with a little more of the coconut milk and oil during cooking to pre-vent meat drying out.

Peel cucumbers or scrape with the prongs of a fork and rub with salt. Cut into 2.5 cm (1 inch) cubes and arrange on several plates. Serve cooked Satay with flat plates of sauce and the cucumber.

MALACCAN DEVIL'S CURRY

This recipe came from an old resident of the Portuguese Village on the outskirts of the city of Malacca, where descendants of Portuguese settlers have congregated. Here they still carry on many of the old Portuguese traditions and retain some of the culture their ancestors brought to Malacca in the 16th century. This fiery 'Devil's' curry is an adaptation of the European 'Diable' or devilled dish.

750 g (1½ lb) pork shoulder, boneless
2 tablespoons white vinegar
1 tablespoon dark soya sauce
6 shallots or 3 small red onions
1 tablespoon oil
3 cloves garlic, crushed
4 cm (1½ inch) piece fresh ginger, sliced
2 teaspoons grated *lengkuas* (optional)
1 teaspoon dried shrimp paste
8-10 dried chillies, crushed
1 heaped teaspoon mustard seeds, lightly crushed
1 heaped teaspoon fenugreek seeds, lightly crushed
¾ teaspoon turmeric powder, or
   2 teaspoons grated fresh turmeric
1 stalk lemon grass, very finely chopped
6 candlenuts
1¼ cups veal or light beef stock
salt
pepper

Cut pork into 5 cm (2 inch) pieces and sprinkle with a mixture of vinegar and soya sauce. Leave to stand for 30 minutes.

Peel and chop shallots or onions. Heat oil in a large saucepan and fry shallots with crushed garlic for 2 minutes. Add sliced ginger, *lengkuas* (if used), dried shrimp paste, chillies and mustard and fenugreek seeds. Stir on moderate heat for 3 minutes, then add turmeric, lemon grass and ground candlenuts. Put in cubed meat

and mix well with the seasonings. Turn heat up to brown meat well.

Pour in stock, season with salt and pepper and cover pan tightly. Cook on a moderate heat until meat is tender. Shake pan occasionally to turn meat, but do not open lid for at least the first 20 minutes of cooking.

If liquid dries up too quickly, sprinkle on a little more stock or water to keep meat moist until cooked. When meat is done, the liquid should be completely absorbed and the pan dry.

SPICED ROAST PORK

CHA SIEW

750 g (1½ lb) fat belly pork with rind
1 tablespoon coriander, ground
½ teaspoon black peppercorns, lightly crushed
¼ teaspoon cinnamon, ground
1 heaped teaspoon cummin, ground
1/8 teaspoon Chinese five-spice powder
2 cloves
2½ teaspoons light soya sauce
12 spring onions, finely chopped
2 teaspoons sugar
2 teaspoons salt
vinegar
lard or vegetable oil

Wipe pork and cut deep incisions into the skin diagonally. Grind together coriander, peppercorns, cinnamon, cummin, five-spice and cloves and mix with soya sauce, chopped spring onions, sugar and salt. Rub the seasonings well into the pork meat.

Put meat on a lightly greased baking tray and splash on a little vinegar. Set in a fairly hot oven (220°C/ 425°F/Gas Mark 7) and cook for 20 minutes, then pour in a little oil or melted lard and cover pan with a tightly fitted lid or a sheet of aluminium foil. Turn down oven to moderate (180°C/350°F/Gas Mark 4) and cook for approximately 2 hours until pork is very tender. Baste with a little oil and the pan juices every 15 minutes. If meat appears to be drying up, splash in a little water to keep moist.

When meat is done, remove from the oven and lift out from the tray. Allow to cool slightly, then cut into thin slices and serve immediately, or allow to cool completely and serve cold.

STEWED PORK RIBS

PAI GWAT

375 g (¾ lb) meaty pork ribs
2 tablespoons dark soya sauce
1 tablespoon light soya sauce
½ cup light stock
2-3 fresh red chillies, sliced
5 cm (2 inch) piece fresh ginger, shredded
1 tablespoon sugar
2 tablespoons oil

Trim ribs and chop into 4 cm (1½ inch) pieces. Place in

a large bowl. Mix together all remaining ingredients, except oil. Pour over ribs and marinate for 1-1½ hours.

Drain pork, reserving marinade. Heat oil in a *wok* and stir-fry ribs for 3 minutes, then pour in marinade and cover pan. Simmer on low heat for 20 minutes, adding a little more water or stock if necessary. Serve as a main course or as part of a 'Dim Sum' meal.

Instead of frying, the ribs and marinade may be placed in a shallow dish inside a steamer and steamed over high heat for 25-30 minutes.

FRIED RICE NOODLES

CHA KWAY TEOW

850 g (1¾ lb) fresh rice flour noodles *(kway teow)*
100 g (3½ oz) raw prawns
60 g (2 oz) hard sausages or Chinese sausages
100 g (3½ oz) spinach or mustard greens
250 g (½ lb) beanshoots
vegetable oil or melted lard
60 g (2 oz) shredded cuttlefish or squid
125 g (¼ lb) chicken breast or pork meat, diced
3 cloves garlic
2 heaped teaspoons sugar
2 tablespoons oyster sauce
4 spring onions
2 tablespoons dark soya sauce
2 tablespoons light soya sauce
white pepper
monosodium glutamate (optional)
2 eggs (optional)
fresh chilli, chopped
spring onions, chopped
chilli sauce

Soak *kway teow* noodles in cold water for 3 minutes. Drain and spread on a tray covered with a cloth to dry.

Peel and devein prawns, and cut into small pieces. Dice sausage. Rinse mustard greens or spinach, shake out water and cut into 5 cm (2 inch) pieces. Steep beanshoots in boiling water for 2-3 minutes, then drain well and set aside.

Heat 1 tablespoon oil or lard and fry prawns, cuttlefish, chicken or pork and sausage for 3 minutes. Remove and set aside, keeping warm. Add another tablespoon oil and fry mustard greens or spinach and beanshoots for 1 minute. Remove and mix with the cooked meat.

Add more oil or lard and fry crushed garlic. Cut *kway teow* noodles into 15 cm (6 inch) pieces for easier handling and drop into the pan. Stir-fry for 4-5 minutes until slightly crisped on the edges. Sprinkle on sugar, oyster sauce, shredded spring onions and soya sauce.

Season with white pepper and monosodium glutamate (if used), then add cooked meat and vegetables. Stir all together and cook for a further 2 minutes. If using eggs, break onto noodles and stir in. Turn heat off immediately. Lift onto a large serving plate and garnish with chopped chilli and spring onion. Serve with small dishes of chilli sauce.

Note: If *kway teow* is to be served with several other dishes reduce the quantity by about half.

Ingredients for Steamboat (recipe page 106).

HOKKIEN FRIED NOODLES

8 cups chicken stock
1 kg (2 lb) fresh thick egg noodles or
    375 g (¾ lb) spaghetti
2½ tablespoons peanut oil
1 medium onion, finely chopped
4 cloves garlic, minced
2 tablespoons dried shrimp, soaked overnight
185 g (6 oz) small peeled raw shrimps
250 g (½ lb) beanshoots
2 teaspoons chilli powder
salt
pepper
1 fresh red chilli, shredded
125 g (¼ lb) cooked shrimps or prawns, chopped
2 hardboiled eggs

Sauce:
2 medium onions
2 tablespoons oil
100 g (3½ oz) raw prawns, finely chopped
2 squares soft beancurd, diced
1½ cups chicken or fish stock
1-2 fresh red chillies, chopped
dark soya sauce to taste
salt
pepper
1 teaspoon cornflour

Bring chicken stock to the boil and drop in noodles. Cook for about 8 minutes until tender but not soft. Drain, and spread on a tray to cool and dry.

Prepare sauce. Fry chopped onions in oil for 2 minutes, then add chopped prawns and diced beancurd and cook on moderate heat for 3-4 minutes. Pour in chicken or fish stock and add chopped chilli. Bring to the boil, lower heat and cook for 10 minutes. Season with soya sauce, salt and pepper. Thicken with cornflour mixed with a little cold water, stirring till sauce thickens and clears. Set aside, keeping warm.

Heat oil in a frying pan or *wok* and fry chopped onion and garlic until golden, then add drained dried shrimps and fresh shrimps, both finely chopped. Saute for 3 minutes before adding noodles and beanshoots. Saute for a further 3 minutes, then stir in chilli powder and salt and pepper to taste.

Arrange noodles on a large serving plate, garnish with shredded chilli and cooked shrimp or prawns and arrange sliced boiled eggs around the edge of the plate. Reheat sauce and serve separately, or pour over noodles just before serving.

Note: If Hokkien Fried Noodles is to be served with other main dishes, reduce quantity by at least half.

FRIED RICE NOODLES

BEEHOON

375 g (¾ lb) thin rice vermicelli
2 cloves garlic
1½ teaspoons coriander, ground
½ teaspoon turmeric powder
peanut oil

8 dried Chinese mushrooms, soaked
90 g (3 oz) peeled raw prawns
125 g (¼ lb) white fish
2 medium onions
4 fresh red chillies
salt
125 g (¼ lb) beanshoots
2 eggs, lightly beaten
3 spring onions, chopped
fresh coriander sprigs

Soak noodles in cold water for 5 minutes, then drop into boiling water and steep for about 6-10 minutes until soft. Drain well and rinse in cold water.

Crush garlic and make into a paste with coriander and turmeric. Heat 1 tablespoon oil in a *wok* or frying pan and fry seasoning paste for 2 minutes.

Remove mushroom stems and slice mushrooms thinly. Chop prawns and fish into small dice and add to the pan together with mushrooms. Fry on moderate heat for 4 minutes. Remove from pan and keep warm.

Add 2 tablespoons oil to the pan and fry sliced onions and chillies. Add noodles, season with salt and stir thoroughly. Scatter beanshoots on top and cook, covered, for 1 minute. Mix beanshoots into noodles and remove from pan. Pour in beaten egg, swirling pan to make a very thin omelette. Cook until set, then remove and cool slightly. Shred.

Reheat noodles, adding half the seafood and mushrooms and half of the shredded egg to the pan. Lift onto a flat serving dish and garnish with remaining seafood and mushrooms. Top with shredded egg, chopped spring onions and coriander sprigs.

CHICKEN AND NOODLE SOUP

LAKSA AYAM

1½ tablespoons peanut oil
6 candlenuts, ground
2 teaspoons chilli powder
1 heaped teaspoon cummin, ground
4 cloves garlic, minced
1 large onion, minced
1 large tomato, chopped
1 teaspoon sugar
2½ teaspoons salt
½ teaspoon white pepper
9 cups thin coconut milk
500 g (1 lb) thin rice vermicelli
250 g (½ lb) beanshoots
250 g (½ lb) cooked chicken meat, shredded
60 g (2 oz) fried hard beancurd, shredded
6 spring onions, chopped
¾ cup thick coconut milk
2 green chillies, thinly sliced
fresh coriander leaves, chopped

Heat oil in a *wok* or frying pan and fry ground candlenuts with chilli powder, cummin, garlic and onion for 4 minutes, stirring constantly. Add chopped tomato, sugar, salt and pepper, then pour on thin coconut milk and bring almost to the boil. Turn heat down low and simmer for 6-8 minutes, then set aside, keeping warm.

Pour boiling water over rice vermicelli and leave for

about 8 minutes until softened. Drain and rinse with cold water. Drain again. Steep beanshoots in boiling water for 2 minutes. Drain and rinse. To serve, divide rice noodles between six large bowls. Top each with a serving of beanshoots, shredded chicken, fried bean-curd and spring onion. Pour on a little thick coconut milk and a generous amount of the coconut sauce.

Garnish with sliced chilli and chopped coriander. Soya sauce or extra salt may be added, to taste.

NONYA LAKSA WITH COCONUT SAUCE

LAKSA LEMAK

6 candlenuts
4 fresh red chillies
1 large onion, minced
5 cm (2 inch) piece fresh ginger, minced
2 cloves garlic, minced
1 tablespoon oil
1½ teaspoons turmeric powder
1 teaspoon coriander, ground
1½ teaspoons dried shrimp paste
1 stalk lemon grass, chopped
1 medium tomato, chopped
2 teaspoons sugar
1½ teaspoons salt
½ teaspoon white pepper
185 g (6 oz) white fish fillets
90 g (3 oz) peeled raw shrimp
⅔ cup water
¾ cup thick coconut milk
9 cups thin coconut milk
500 g (1 lb) thin rice vermicelli
185 g (6 oz) beanshoots
90 g (3 oz) fried hard beancurd, shredded
8 cm (3 inch) piece young cucumber, shredded
4 lettuce leaves, shredded
8 spring onions, chopped
sprigs fresh mint
1 fresh red chilli, shredded finely
1 ginger flower, shredded (optional)

Grind candlenuts and red chillies to a paste. Mix with minced onion, ginger and garlic.

Heat oil and fry seasonings for 2 minutes, then add turmeric, coriander, dried shrimp paste, lemon grass, chopped tomato and sugar. Season with salt and pep-per. Cook for 3 minutes then set aside.

Cut fish fillets into 2 cm (¾ inch) dice and place in a small saucepan with shrimp. Cover with water and boil for 10 minutes. Strain, reserving liquid and meat. Set aside to cool.

Pour thick coconut milk into a large saucepan and add fried seasonings. Stir well and when liquid begins to boil, pour in thin coconut milk and fish stock. Bring almost to the boil again, add fish and shrimp and turn heat down. Simmer for 5 minutes. Add salt and pepper to taste.

Place vermicelli in a large bowl and cover with boiling water. Allow to stand for 8-10 minutes to soften. Steep beanshoots in boiling water for 2 minutes, drain and rinse in cold water. Drain noodles and bean-shoots.

Into each bowl place a serving of noodles, then top with beanshoots, shredded beancurd, cucumber, let-tuce and a little shredded ginger flower (if used). Pour on enough coconut sauce to cover and garnish with chopped spring onion, mint leaves and shredded chilli.

NOODLES WITH SOUR FISH SAUCE

LAKSA ASAM

2 cups boiling water
3 tablespoons tamarind
375 g (¾ lb) fish fillets
7 cups cold water
4 fresh red chillies
12 spring onions
1 tablespoon sugar
1½ teaspoons dried shrimp paste
2.5 cm (1 inch) piece lemon grass, finely chopped
2 teaspoons fresh grated turmeric, or
    ¾ teaspoon turmeric powder
salt
pepper
250 g (½ lb) thin rice vermicelli
250 g (½ lb) fresh egg noodles, or
    thick rice flour noodles
8 shallots or 2 medium red onions, thinly sliced
1 ginger flower (optional)
1 small bunch fresh mint leaves
1 small bunch fresh basil leaves (optional)

Pour boiling water over tamarind and allow to stand for at least 15 minutes. Put fish fillets in a saucepan, cover with cold water and bring to the boil. Simmer until fish is soft and flaky. Strain, reserving stock and fish.

Finely slice or mince chillies and spring onions. Add to the fish stock with sugar, dried shrimp paste, lemon grass and turmeric. Bring to the boil, season with salt and pepper and simmer for 10 minutes.

Soak rice vermicelli in boiling water to soften. Soak egg noodles or thick rice noodles in cold water for 10 minutes. Drain, put into a saucepan, cover with slightly salted water and bring to the boil. Reduce heat and cook until tender. Drain and rinse both lots of noodles. Divide noodles between six large bowls and top with flaked fish and sliced shallots or red onion.

Pour fish sauce over noodles and garnish with finely shredded ginger flower (if used), sprigs of mint and sweet basil. Strain tamarind through a piece of muslin and serve tamarind juice in a jug, or pour over noodles before serving.

YELLOW RICE

½ teaspoon saffron strands
2 tablespoons boiling water
345 g (11 oz) long grain rice
3 tablespoons *ghee*
2 teaspoons salt
tomato wedges
fresh coriander sprigs

Steep saffron in boiling water. Wash rice well, drain

and allow to dry for at least 20 minutes, preferably longer.

Heat *ghee* in a large, heavy-bottomed saucepan and put in the rice. Fry on moderate heat for 5 minutes, stirring to coat each rice grain. Cover with 2.5 cm (1 inch) water above the level of the rice, strain saffron and add tinted water to the rice. Add salt and stir well. Bring to the boil, cover and turn heat down very low. Simmer until rice is tender and all liquid absorbed. Leave to stand for a further 10 minutes, covered, but off the heat.

Spoon into a serving dish and garnish with tomato wedges and coriander sprigs.

FRIED RICE
NASI GORENG

6 spring onions, sliced
4 fresh red chillies, sliced
vegetable oil
2 slices ham or bacon
185 g (6 oz) peeled prawns
750 g (1½ lb) cold cooked white rice
2 teaspoons dark soya sauce
salt
2 eggs, lightly beaten
2 tablespoons finely chopped celery leaves (optional)
3-4 spring onions, chopped
100 g (3½ oz) cooked peas
1½ teaspoons chilli powder

Lightly fry spring onions and chillies in 2 tablespoons oil. Chop bacon or ham and prawns and add to the pan. Stir-fry for 2 minutes. Pour in rice, mixing well with meat. Add more oil if necessary. Sprinkle on soya sauce and salt to taste. Stir-fry rice on moderate heat until rice changes colour and is slightly crisp. Remove and keep warm.

Wipe out pan and pour in beaten egg, swirling pan to make a very thin omelette. Cook until set, then remove and shred. Add celery (if used), and a little more oil and stir-fry for 2 minutes. Add chopped spring onions and green peas and heat through, then return rice to the pan and stir in chilli powder. Add salt and more soya sauce if necessary. Stir on high heat for 1 minute, then spoon into a serving dish and garnish with shredded egg.

COCONUT RICE
NASI LEMAK

375 g (¾ lb) long grain rice
½ cup thick coconut milk
2¼ cups thin coconut milk
2 teaspoons salt
2 eggs
sliced onion or onion sambal
sliced cucumber
dried salted whitebait *(ikan bilis)*

Wash rice and pour into a saucepan with thick coconut milk. Cook on moderate heat for 10 minutes, stirring

frequently. Pour on thin coconut milk and salt, cover and bring to the boil. Reduce heat and cook until rice is tender and coconut milk absorbed.

Beat eggs and pour into a very lightly oiled pan. Swirl pan to make omelette as thin as possible. Cook until firm, then remove and leave to cool. Shred finely.

Wash salt fish and dry thoroughly. Fry in hot oil until very crisp. Drain well. Spoon cooked rice into a serving bowl and garnish with fried salt fish and shredded omelette. Arrange sliced onion and cucumber around the rice, and serve onion sambal in a separate dish.

FRUIT AND VEGETABLE SALAD
RUJAK

¼ yam bean *(bangkuang),* or 1 hard green pear
2 tablespoons oil
1 cake hard beancurd
125 g (¼ lb) beanshoots
1 green mango, or 2 slices green papaya
1 star fruit (carambola), optional
1 small cucumber
6 lettuce leaves
6 thin slices pineapple

Sauce:
1 tablespoon tamarind
½ cup boiling water
2 fresh red chillies, minced
1 tablespoon roasted peanuts, crushed
½ teaspoon dried shrimp paste
1-2 teaspoons sugar
2 tablespoons sweet soya sauce

Prepare sauce first by infusing tamarind in boiling water until softened. Mash pulp, then strain into a small saucepan. Add chilli and peanuts, crumbled dried shrimp paste, sugar and sweet soya sauce. Bring almost to the boil. Check flavour and add more sugar if needed. Pour into a sauce boat and set aside.

Shred peeled yam bean (if used), and drop into boiling water. Leave for 10 minutes, then drain. If using pear, peel and shred and sprinkle with a little salt water.

Heat oil and fry beancurd for 2 minutes, lift out and cool. Cut into thin slices. Steep beanshoots in boiling water for 2 minutes, then drain well. Rinse in cold water and drain again. Shred mango or papaya and thinly slice cucumber and star fruit (if used).

Wash lettuce and arrange on a plate. Cut pineapple into small wedges and place around the edge of the dish. Stack all vegetables and fruit in the dish with beancurd on top. Pour on the sauce or serve separately.

VEGETABLES IN COCONUT MILK

185 g (6 oz) green beans
250 g (½ lb) Chinese cabbage or white cabbage
1½ large onions
2 medium tomatoes
2 fresh red chillies
2 tablespoons vegetable oil

Fruit and Vegetable Salad, and Vegetables in Coconut Milk (recipes this page).

2 cloves garlic, crushed
⅓ teaspoon turmeric powder
½ teaspoon chilli powder (optional)
salt
1¼ cups thin coconut milk
1 tablespoon tamarind water, made with 1½ teaspoons
  tamarind

Cut beans into 5 cm (2 inch) lengths. Chop Chinese
cabbage and wash, shake out excess water. Chop onions
roughly, peel and chop tomatoes and slice chillies.

Heat oil in a frying pan and add garlic and chopped
onion. Fry for 2 minutes, then put in beans, turmeric,
chilli powder (if used), sliced chillies and salt. Pour in
½ cup coconut milk and stir well. Cook on moderate
heat for 5 minutes, then add cabbage and cook for a
further 4 minutes.

Pour on remaining coconut milk, bring almost to the
boil and turn heat down low. Add tomato and tamarind water and simmer for 1-2 minutes. Stir continually
to prevent coconut sauce curdling. Add salt to taste.

MALAY VEGETABLE SALAD

PASEMBOR

155 g (5 oz) beanshoots
½ small cucumber
90 g (3 oz) yam bean *(bangkuang)*, or hard green pear
  or apple
12 lettuce leaves
1-2 hardboiled eggs
1 fresh red chilli
1 tablespoon peanut oil
1 cake hard beancurd
4 shallots or 1 medium red onion
sprigs of fresh coriander or mint

Sauce:
2 heaped tablespoons roasted peanuts
4 dried chillies, soaked
1 tablespoon sugar
pinch salt
1 teasooon dried shrimp paste
1 tablespoon tamarind
½ cup boiling water

Prepare sauce first. Grind peanuts coarsely. Pound
chillies and add to the peanuts together with sugar and
salt. Toast dried shrimp paste under a griller for 2 minutes, then mix with other ingredients. Soak tamarind
in boiling water, then strain. Pour all sauce ingredients
except tamarind water into a small saucepan and bring
slowly to the boil. Stir in tamarind water and beat till
sauce is smooth and rather thick. Pour into a sauce jug
and serve separately.

To prepare salad, clean beanshoots and scald with
boiling water. Drain and allow to cool. Wipe cucumber
and shred finely. Peel yam bean and shred very finely.
Sprinkle with a little salt to prevent discolouration.
Shred lettuce, slice boiled eggs and cut red chilli into
very thin strips.

Heat oil in a small frying pan and fry beancurd until
golden. Cool and shred. Peel shallots or onion and slice
thinly. Fry in a very little oil until slightly crisp. Remove

and set aside as garnish. If green pear or apple is used,
peel and slice thinly.

Arrange shredded lettuce in a bed on a flat platter
and top with beanshoots, cucumber, yam bean (or
apple or pear), and shredded beancurd. Decorate with
sliced egg and garnish with strips of chilli, fried shallots
or onion and coriander or mint sprigs. Serve chilled.

CUCUMBER SALAD

2 medium cucumbers
1 small red onion, finely chopped
2 candlenuts
1 teaspoon fresh grated turmeric or
  ⅓ teaspoon turmeric powder
2.5 cm (1 inch) piece fresh ginger, shredded
½ tablespoon oil
2 teaspoons sugar
salt
6 spring onions, shredded
1 tablespoon coarsely ground roasted peanuts
fresh red and green chilli, shredded

Wipe cucumbers and cut lengthways into quarters then
into 2.5 cm (1 inch) pieces. Sprinkle lightly with salt.

Pound onion to a paste with candlenuts, turmeric
and ginger. Heat oil in a saucepan and fry ground seasonings for 3 minutes before adding cucumber, sugar
and salt. Fry on moderate heat until cucumber softens
slightly.

Mix in shredded spring onions and spoon into a deep
serving dish. Garnish with ground peanuts and decorate with shredded red and green chilli. Serve cold.

FRIED EGGPLANT

PAGRI TERONG

3-4 medium eggplants, about 375 g (¾ lb) total weight
salt
oil
6 spring onions, sliced
8 cloves garlic, crushed
2 teaspoons grated *lengkuas*
2 fresh green chillies, thinly sliced
1½ teaspoons cummin, ground
3 black cardamoms, crushed
2.5 cm (1 inch) stick cinnamon
1 teaspoon fennel, crushed
2 tablespoons mild curry paste
1 fresh red chilli, sliced
1 cup thick coconut milk

Wipe eggplants and slice into quarters lengthways,
from base to stem, leaving stem section intact. Sprinkle
with salt and stand for 4-5 minutes to draw bitter juices.
Rinse and wipe dry.

Heat 5 cm (2 inches) oil to smoking point and fry
eggplants until soft, turning heat down after first minute. Drain and cool. Pour off all but 1 tablespoon oil
and fry onions and garlic for 2 minutes. Add ginger
and chillies and fry for a further minute, then add all
spices, curry paste and chilli and fry for 4 minutes. Pour

on coconut milk, add salt to taste and stir well.

Return eggplants to the pan and cook for 10 minutes on low heat. Serve warm or cold as a main course or side dish.

MIXED VEGETABLES WITH SALTED BLACK BEANS

500 g (1 lb) mixed green vegetables
3 cloves garlic
2 tablespoons oil
8 shallots or 3 small red onions, thinly sliced
3 fresh red chillies, sliced
2½ teaspoons salted black beans, crushed
1½ teaspoons sugar
⅓ cup water
3 teaspoons light soya sauce
salt

Use such vegetables as long beans, green beans, green peas, cabbage, Chinese cabbage, spinach. Chop all vegetables, wash and drain well. Parboil peas (if used).

Crush garlic and fry gently in oil, then add shallots or onion. Stir-fry for 2 minutes before adding chillies, crushed black beans and sugar. Pour on water, soya sauce and add the vegetables. Stir-fry for 1 minute, then cover pan and simmer for 4-5 minutes, depending on type of vegetables used.

When ready the vegetables should be lightly cooked but retaining crispness. Add salt to taste. For extra flavour include chopped shrimp or chicken meat.

STUFFED BEANCURD, PEPPERS AND BLACK MUSHROOMS

6 pieces hard beancurd, each 5 cm (2 inches) square
6 green peppers, no more than 5 cm (2 inches) in
    diameter
6 medium sized dried black mushrooms, soaked
250 g (½ lb) lean pork
125 g (¼ lb) small peeled raw shrimp
1 cm (½ inch) piece fresh ginger, shredded
3 spring onions, shredded
1 tablespoon oil or lard
2 egg whites
1½ tablespoons dark soya sauce
2 teaspoons Chinese wine
½ teaspoon white pepper
pinch monosodium glutamate (optional)
vegetable or peanut oil
⅔ cup beef stock
1 teaspoon cornflour
1½ teaspoons sesame oil

Cut beancurd in halves or into triangular pieces and make a slit in each. Wipe peppers and cut in halves horizontally. Remove seeds. Remove stems from mushrooms.

Chop pork and shrimps very finely, or mince, and mix into a paste with ginger and spring onion. Blend in melted lard or oil. Bind with egg white and season with soya sauce, Chinese wine, pepper and monosodium

glutamate (if used). Knead to a smooth paste.

Place about 1 tablespoonful of stuffing into each pepper half, 2 teaspoonsful into each mushroom top and 1 teaspoonful into the slit of each piece of beancurd. Place stuffed mushrooms in a steamer on a piece of waxed paper and steam for 12-15 minutes.

While mushrooms are cooking, heat oil and fry stuffed beancurd and peppers for 5-6 minutes. Remove from oil, drain and keep warm.

Drain oil from pan and pour in stock. Bring to the boil, adjust seasoning if necessary, then thicken with cornflour mixed with a little cold water. Cook until sauce thickens and clears.

Arrange steamed mushrooms, fried beancurd and peppers decoratively on a serving plate. Pour on hot stock and sprinkle with sesame oil.

LADIES FINGERS

375 g (¾ lb) ladies fingers (okra), about 8-10 cm
    (3-4 inches) long
salt
pepper
1 teaspoon chilli powder
1 teaspoon cummin, ground

Wash ladies fingers, wipe dry and remove stems with a sharp knife. Carve tops into a point around the bases of the stems. Make several lengthways incisions in each ladies finger without cutting tops or bottoms. Sprinkle with salt and stand for 5 minutes. Rinse in warm water and wipe dry.

Place ladies fingers in a saucepan with salt, pepper, chilli and cummin. Cover with water and simmer on moderate heat till tender. Drain and serve hot or cold as a side dish.

FRIED BEANCURD SQUARES

TAUKWA GORENG

3 green chillies
1 fresh red chilli
1 clove garlic
2 tablespoons brown sugar
1 tablespoon dark soya sauce
1 tablespoon white wine vinegar
1 teaspoon cummin, ground
½ cup water
155 g (5 oz) roasted peanuts, crushed
salt
6 squares hard beancurd
60 g (2 oz) beanshoots
1 small cucumber
peanut oil

Chop chillies and garlic finely and mix with brown sugar, soya sauce, vinegar, cummin and cold water. Stir in crushed peanuts and add salt. Cook on moderate heat for 10 minutes, stirring frequently. Keep warm while beancurd is prepared.

Cut beancurd squares into 3 slices, horizontally. Heat 1 cm (½ inch) oil and carefully lower in several bean-

curd squares. Fry for 3-4 minutes. Lift out and place on a serving plate and keep warm.

Wash and dry cucumber, rub with salt and shred or grate. Remove roots and tops from beanshoots and scald with boiling water. Arrange a little shredded cucumber and several beanshoots on top of each beancurd slice.

Reheat sauce and spoon a little onto each beancurd square before serving.

MANGO CHUTNEY

6 medium size green mangoes
6 dried chillies
2.5 cm (1 inch) fresh ginger, shredded
1 teaspoon chilli powder
1 teaspoon black peppercorns, crushed lightly
½ cup vinegar
1 cup sugar
3 teaspoons salt
2 cloves garlic, crushed
½ cup water
1 tablespoon raisins, soaked in water

Peel and slice mangoes, discarding stones. Grind or crumble chillies and mix with shredded ginger, chilli and peppercorns.

Boil vinegar, sugar and salt, and add chilli paste, crushed garlic and water. Cook for 2 minutes, then add sliced mango. Simmer for 10-12 minutes, and add drained raisins. Remove from heat and transfer to a wide-necked jar. Seal tightly.

This chutney can be used immediately, but will develop more flavour after several days. Can be stored for many weeks.

COCONUT CHUTNEY

8 dried chillies
3 teaspoons dried fish floss, or powdered dried shrimps
3 shallots or 1 small red onion, chopped
salt
100 g (3½ oz) grated fresh coconut, or
    75 g (2½ oz) desiccated coconut
lemon or lime juice

Grind dried chillies, dried fish or shrimp, shallots and salt to a paste. Add coconut, ground slightly, or desiccated coconut moistened with a little warm water. Moisten with lemon or lime juice and a little water if necessary.

Stir well to thoroughly mix all ingredients. Allow to stand for several hours before using.

SAMBALS

Sambals are accompaniments served in small dishes, usually several at a time, with every Malaysian meal. They add flavour and extra heat to meals. The following three sambals are typical examples.

Other sambals could also be prepared to serve with curries and spiced dishes: grated fresh or desiccated coconut, sliced banana, sliced onion, lemon or lime wedges, raisins, dry fried onions (see page 125), sliced cucumber, roasted peanuts, sliced omelette, fried dry fish, Bombay duck, or wedges of pineapple. Prepare several and serve in small flat dishes or sauce bowls.

ONION SAMBAL

4 medium onions
2 cloves garlic
½ cup white vinegar
2 teaspoons sugar

Peel onions and slice thinly. Pull into rings. Crush garlic and sprinkle over onions. Pour on vinegar and dust with sugar. Marinate for at least 15 minutes before serving. Drain off vinegar before serving, if preferred.

CHILLI SAMBAL

3 green chillies
2 teaspoons salt
1-2 teaspoons sugar
¼ cup white vinegar

Wipe chillies, remove stems and slice thinly. Remove seeds for milder *sambal*. Sprinkle salt and sugar onto vinegar, stirring until dissolved. Pour over chilli and stand for at least 3 hours before using.

TOMATO SAMBAL

4 large tomatoes, diced
1 large onion, minced
2 green chillies, minced
1 tablespoon white vinegar
1½ tablespoons sugar
½ teaspoon salt

Mix all ingredients, adding more salt or sugar to taste. Let stand for 15 minutes before serving.

FISH BALL SOUP

375 g (¾ lb) white fish fillets
1 tablespoon chopped fresh coriander or celery leaves
3 spring onions, chopped
1½ teaspoons salt
¼ teaspoon white pepper
1½ tablespoons oil

Soup:
½ tablespoon oil
1 cm (½ inch) piece fresh ginger, shredded
6 cups fish stock
salt
pepper
1 teaspoon chilli powder
250 g (½ lb) mustard greens, spinach or cabbage
fresh red and green chilli, shredded

Remove bones and skin, if any, from fish and chop

A selection of Sambals (recipes this page).

flesh finely. Mix with coriander or celery leaves, spring onions, salt and pepper. Knead to a smooth paste with oil and a little cold water. With oiled hands form fish paste into small balls by squeezing the paste from a clenched hand out between curled thumb and forefinger. Drop into a bowl of cold, salted water.

Heat oil in a large pot and fry ginger for 1 minute. Pour in fish stock, salt and pepper, chilli powder and add washed vegetables. Drop in drained fish balls and simmer for 12-15 minutes. Garnish with shredded chilli.

MUTTON SOUP

SOP KAMBING

750 g (1½ lb) mutton ribs
2 large onions, chopped
3 cloves garlic, crushed
2 green chillies, sliced
1 heaped teaspoon grated *lengkuas* or fresh ginger
2 teaspoons black peppercorns
3 teaspoons coriander seeds
9 cups water
1 tablespoon oil
4 black cardamoms, lightly crushed
5 cm (2 inch) stick cinnamon
2-3 cloves
2.5 cm (1 inch) piece fresh ginger, grated
3 tablespoons mild curry powder or paste
2 heaped tablespoons white poppy seeds
½ cup thick coconut milk
salt
pepper
dry fried onions (see page 125)
spring onion, chopped
fresh coriander leaves

Chop mutton bones into 5 cm (2 inch) pieces. Put in a large saucepan with onion, garlic, chilli, *lengkuas* or ginger, peppercorns and coriander. Cover with water and bring to the boil. Turn heat down, cover and simmer for 2½-3 hours. Skim off froth as it rises.

Strain stock, reserving liquid (which should be reduced to about 5 cups) and meat. When cool, scrape meat from bones and flake into smaller pieces.

Heat oil in a saucepan and fry cardamoms, cinnamon, cloves and ginger for 1 minute, then add curry powder or paste and fry for 4 minutes. Pour in lightly ground poppy seeds, coconut milk and add reserved stock. Stir well. Season with salt and pepper to taste. Add meat, bring to the boil and cook for 20 minutes.

Serve soup in a tureen or in individual bowls garnished with dry fried onions, spring onion and coriander leaves.

STEAMBOAT

A popular meal in Singapore. Steamboat derives its name from the charcoal-heated pot with funnel chimney in which food is cooked at the table.

10 cups chicken stock

½ teaspoon monosodium glutamate (optional)
2 tablespoons vegetable oil
2.5 cm (1 inch) piece fresh ginger, sliced
1 fresh red or green chilli, sliced
8 spring onions, chopped
12 medium raw prawns
125 g (¼ lb) pork, leg or shoulder
125 g (¼ lb) rump, sirloin or fillet steak
125 g (¼ lb) chicken breast
250 g (½ lb) fish fillets (bream, perch, whiting)
125 g (¼ lb) cuttlefish (optional)
large bunch fresh spinach, lettuce or Chinese cabbage
     leaves
6 eggs (optional)
chilli sauce
3 tablespoons light soya sauce
3 cloves garlic
2.5 cm (1 inch) piece fresh ginger, shredded
2 teaspoons sugar

Bring stock to a rapid boil and add monosodium glutamate (if used), vegetable oil, ginger, sliced chilli and onions. Turn heat down and simmer for 10 minutes, then pour into the Steamboat or other suitable pot which can be heated at the table.

Peel and devein prawns, leaving tails on. Slice pork, beef and chicken thinly. Cut fish fillets into thin strips. Clean and slice cuttlefish. Wash vegetables and shake out excess water. Separate leaves. Arrange meat, prawns and fish attractively on a plate with the vegetables. Keep eggs aside.

Mix soya sauce, crushed garlic, shredded ginger and sugar, stirring till sugar is dissolved. Pour into several small dishes. Spoon chilli sauce into several small dishes.

When stock begins to bubble, the ingredients are cooked individually at the table by each diner, using wooden chopsticks or small wire baskets. Fondue forks could be used. Dip cooked food into either of the sauces.

When all ingredients have been consumed, carefully break the eggs into the stock and poach lightly. These are eaten with the remaining highly enriched soup.

CHINESE SOUP WITH PICKLED VEGETABLES, BEANCURD AND MIXED MEAT

I discovered this delicious soup at an outdoor restaurant on the waterfront in Malacca city.

2 squares soft beancurd
185 g (6 oz) mixed, pickled vegetables (canned)
2 medium tomatoes
1 medium cucumber
6 raw prawns (optional)
2 teaspoons Chinese wine
100 g (3½ oz) chicken, diced
100 g (3½ oz) pork, shredded
8 cups cold water
salt
pepper
pinch monosodium glutamate (optional)
6 spring onions, shredded

small bunch fresh coriander leaves
2 green chillies (optional)

Drain beancurd and cut into thin slices. Drain pickled vegetables and rinse in cold water to remove excess salt. Slice or chop roughly. Wipe tomato and cucumber and cut into even sized pieces. Peel and devein prawns, sprinkle with Chinese wine and marinate for 10 minutes.

Put diced chicken and shredded pork in a large pot with pickled vegetables. Cover with cold water and bring to the boil. Lower heat slightly and simmer for 10 minutes. Add cucumber, tomatoes and prawns and cook for 6 minutes. Season to taste with salt and pepper and add monosodium glutamate (if used).

Just before serving, add sliced beancurd and spring onions. Heat through. Garnish with coriander leaves and shredded chilli.

SPICY YAM RINGS

Makes 18.

500 g (1 lb) yam, taro or sweet potato
2 teaspoons salt
1 teaspoon black pepper
2 heaped teaspoons hot curry powder
½ teaspoon chilli powder
100 g (3½ oz) melted lard (optional)
dry breadcrumbs
oil for shallow frying

Peel yam, taro or sweet potato. Cut into 2.5 cm (1 inch) cubes and place in a steamer to cook until soft. Allow to cool slightly, then mash. Stir in salt, pepper, curry powder and chilli powder and mix to a smooth paste with melted lard. Sweet potato is usually of a much more moist consistency than yam or taro, so if it used, omit lard and substitute a little flour, preferably split pea or gram flour.

Knead for several minutes to distribute the spices evenly, then with oiled hands roll into balls about 4 cm (1½ inches) in diameter. Put on a square of muslin, with space between each. Cover with another piece of cloth and carefully press down to flatten a little. Press the thumb or forefinger through each flattened cake to form a ring. Remove cloth. Smooth edges of each ring and coat thickly with breadcrumbs. Let stand for 15 minutes, in the refrigerator if kitchen is warm.

Heat oil to smoking point, turn heat down very slightly and fry yam rings quickly until crisp on the surface but still soft inside. Lift out and drain on absorbent paper. Serve either warm or cold.

FRIED SEASONED WHITEBAIT

IKAN BILIS

250 g (½ lb) whitebait (dried salted whitebait if available)
1 medium onion
2-3 green chillies
1 tablespoon sugar
2 teaspoons ground black peppercorns

salt (optional)
75 g (2½ oz) peanuts
oil for deep frying

If dried salted whitebait (*ikan bilis*) is used, remove heads and backbones and wash in cold water. Drain well and shake in a cloth to dry. Fresh whitebait should be washed and dried, preferably in the sun, for about 1 hour.

Grind onion, chillies, sugar and peppercorns to a smooth paste. Set aside. Heat oil and fry whitebait until very dry and crisp, then transfer to a rack or plate covered with absorbent paper.

Pour off oil and add chilli paste to the pan. Fry on high heat until seasonings begin to dry, then return whitebait to the pan and cook for a further 6 minutes, stirring continually. Add salt if fresh fish is used.

Roast peanuts under griller until crisp and golden brown. Rub off skins if preferred. Add to the pan and stir on high heat for another minute. Mix with fried whitebait. Spoon into small dishes and serve as a crisp, tasty side dish with meat or vegetable curries, or as a snack with drinks.

CURRY PUFFS

Makes 24.

500 g (1 lb) prepared puff pastry
100 g (3½ oz) beef or mutton
2 medium potatoes
60 g (2 oz) cooked peas
1 medium onion
2 teaspoons finely chopped fresh coriander leaves
1 cm (½ inch) piece fresh ginger, minced
2 cloves garlic, crushed
2 teaspoons coriander seeds
¼ teaspoon fennel (optional)
1½ teaspoon cummin seeds
2 dried chillies
1 cm (½ inch) stick cinnamon
1 clove
1 teaspoon black peppercorns
1 teaspoon turmeric powder
2 tablespoons *ghee*
1 small onion
2 teaspoons salt
oil for deep frying (optional)

If pastry is frozen, allow to thaw. Chop or mince beef or mutton. Peel potatoes, boil until tender, cool and dice. Drain peas. Chop onion finely. Pound all spices and seasonings into a paste.

Heat *ghee* and fry onion for 3 minutes, add seasoning paste and fry for 4 minutes. Stir in minced meat and cook until well coloured. Stir in potato and peas, heat through, then add chopped tomato and salt. Cover and cook for 4-5 minutes on low heat, stirring frequently to prevent sticking. Remove from heat, and cool completely.

Roll out pastry to 2 mm (1/16 inch) thickness. Divide into 24 circles 10 cm (4 inches) in diameter using a pastry cutter. Place a small amount of filling on one side of each pastry circle. Fold over to form semi-circular pastries. Stick edges down with a little milk or water.

Run a pastry wheel around the join, or pinch the wedges into a fluted pattern all around.

Heat oil and deep fry Curry Puffs to a golden brown. Remove from oil, drain and serve either hot or cold. Alternatively, heat oven to 200°C/400°F/Gas Mark 6. Brush pastry tops with a little beaten egg or milk, avoiding sealed edges. Place on a baking sheet and bake for 20-25 minutes. Cool slightly, then remove to a wire rack. Serve hot or cold.

These make excellent hot hors d'oeuvres. Prepare pastry, cutting 5 cm (2 inch) circles, fill and cook as above. Serve on a warming plate or in a chafing dish.

CRISP CORN FRITTERS

6 spring onions
2 fresh red chillies
1 large green pepper
3 young corn cobs, or 1 can (about 315 g or 10 oz) corn kernels
2 stalks celery
60 g (2 oz) raw shrimp
1 egg
2 tablespoons plain flour
2 teaspoons baking powder
salt
pepper
oil for deep frying

Grind spring onions, chillies and green peppers into a coarse paste. Cut corn from cobs, or drain canned corn, and crush slightly. Chop celery into very small dice. Chop or mince shrimps. Place in a mixing bowl with all vegetables. Break an egg on top, add flour and baking powder, salt and pepper. Blend well together with a wooden spoon.

Heat oil in a deep pan or *wok*. When almost at smoking point drop in spoonfuls of the batter and deep fry until crisp and golden. Drain on absorbent paper. Serve either hot or cold.

MALAYSIAN SPRING ROLLS

POPIAH

Popiah are a speciality of Penang but popular throughout Malaysia. They are prepared in two ways, one with a fresh pancake wrapper similar to the Lumpia of the Philippines and the other in spring roll wrappers. The latter is deep fried and is somewhat similar to the Chinese Spring Roll, from which it originated.

Makes about 30 pancakes.

Wrappers:
345 g (11 oz) plain flour
100 g (3½ oz) glutinous rice flour
3 cups water
4 eggs
1½ teaspoons salt

Filling:
185 (6 oz) yam bean *(bangkuang)*, or potato
100 g (3½ oz) bamboo shoots (canned)

8 spring onions
1 small cucumber
2-3 green chillies
3 cloves garlic
155 g (5 oz) pork belly
220 g (7 oz) beanshoots
2 eggs
oil
2 cakes hard beancurd
2½ tablespoons sweet bean paste
155 g (5 oz) raw prawns or shrimps
salt
pepper
1 large lettuce
6 fresh red chillies, pounded
bunch of fresh coriander leaves
2 tablespoons dry fried garlic or onions (see page 125)

Sauce:
1 heaped tablespoon plain flour
3 teaspoons brown sugar
1½ tablespoons dark soya sauce
water

Prepare sauce first by sifting flour into a hot dry frying pan. Fry to a light golden colour. Sprinkle on sugar and allow to melt slightly then remove from heat. Cool briefly, then add soya sauce and enough water to form a sauce of medium consistency. Beat for 2 minutes to remove any lumps then cook for 2-3 minutes. Remove from heat and pour into several small bowls.

To make wrappers, sift plain flour into a mixing bowl with glutinous rice flour and salt. Stir in water to form a thick paste, then gradually blend in eggs. Beat for 10 minutes, adding water a little at a time until batter is of thin consistency and very smooth. Stand for 20 minutes before cooking.

Peel yam bean and grate. Put into a small saucepan and cover with boiling water. Simmer until tender, then remove from saucepan, reserving liquid. If potato is used, peel, grate and place in a bowl. Cover with boiling water and stand for 5-6 minutes. Drain, reserving liquid.

Shred bamboo shoots finely. Thinly slice or shred spring onions. Wipe cucumber and grate. Thinly slice chillies and garlic.

Chop pork into 1 cm (½ inch) dice and put into a small saucepan. Cover with water and bring to the boil. Cook on high heat for 10 minutes, then remove, reserving stock. Mince meat.

Soften beanshoots by steeping in boiling water for 2 minutes. Drain and rinse in cold water. Drain again.

Beat eggs lightly. Oil a small omelette pan and pour in eggs. Cook until firm, turn and lightly brown other side. Remove from pan. Cool and shred finely. Shred beancurd.

Heat 2 tablespoons oil in a large frying pan or *wok* and fry sliced garlic for 2 minutes. Add minced pork and brown well. Add yam bean or potato, bamboo shoots and bean paste. Stir well, then pour on ⅓ cup liquid from the cooked yam bean and ⅓ cup liquid from the pork. Simmer on high heat for 10 minutes, until liquid has dried up. Add prawns in last few minutes of cooking. Stir in cucumber, chilli, beancurd and spring onions. Mix well and cook on low heat, stirring frequently, for 3 minutes. Season with salt and pepper. Wash lettuce leaves and wipe dry.

Cendol, Gula Melaka Pudding, and Sweet Potato Dessert (recipes page 111).

To cook pancake wrappers, brush an omelette pan lightly with oil. Heat and pour in just enough batter to very thinly coat the surface of the pan. Cook on moderate heat until golden underneath with slight specks of brown appearing. Carefully lift up and turn to cook other side. Stack pancakes between pieces of grease-proof paper.

Let pancakes cool slightly, then line each with a lettuce leaf, smear with a little pounded chilli and add several beanshoots. Top with a heaped spoonful of the cooked filling. Garnish with shredded omelette, a few more beanshoots and a sprig of coriander, plus a sprinkling of fried garlic or onion. Roll up tightly, taking care not to tear the pancake. Arrange prepared spring rolls attractively on a wide plate. Serve with the sauce.

If preferred, the lettuce, pancakes, chilli, beanshoots, omelette, herbs and cooked filling may be placed on the table to be individually wrapped.

FRIED MALAYSIAN SPRING ROLLS

POPIAH GORENG

24 sheets prepared spring roll wrappers (frozen), each
   20 cm (8 inches) square
100 g (3½ oz) raw prawns
100 g (3½ oz) chicken or pork meat
100 g (3½ oz) yam bean (bangkuang), or potato
1 medium carrot
vegetable oil
2 eggs
2 squares hard beancurd
8 spring onions
24 lettuce leaves
4 cloves garlic, crushed
4 green chillies, sliced
pinch monosodium glutamate (optional)
salt
pepper
sugar to taste
3 tablespoons sweet bean paste
1 small cucumber, shredded

Sauce:
2 cloves garlic
2 fresh red chillies
1 teaspoon salt
1½ teaspoons sugar
⅓ cup vinegar
1½ teaspoons water

First prepare sauce. Mince garlic and chillies and mix with remaining ingredients, stirring until sugar dissolves. Add water and pour into several small dishes.

Mince prawns and chicken or pork meat and set aside. Peel and grate yam bean or potato. Put into a saucepan, cover with water and boil till tender. If potato is used, put in a bowl and cover with boiling water. Stand till slightly softened.

Grate carrot, cover with boiling water and cook gently for 2 minutes. Reserve liquid. Lightly oil a small omelette pan. Beat eggs and pour into the pan. Cook until firm, remove and cool, then shred finely.

Add a little more oil to the pan and fry beancurd for 2-3 minutes, turning once, then remove from pan.

Cool slightly, then shred. Shred spring onions. Wash lettuce leaves and wipe dry.

Heat 3 tablespoons oil in a large pan and add minced pork or chicken and prawns. Add garlic and fry until meat changes colour. Season with chillies, spring onions, monosodium glutamate (if used), salt and pepper. Cook for 2-3 minutes, stirring occasionally. Add strained vegetables, sugar and bean paste. Cook for 4 minutes, then mix in shredded cucumber and beancurd. Stir continually on high heat for 3 minutes. Pour in a little of the stock in which carrots were cooked, adding just enough to moisten filling. Remove from heat and cool.

Spread a lettuce leaf on each spring roll wrapper. Top with a generous spoonful of filling and garnish with shredded omelette. Roll up carefully and stick edges down by wetting well, or prepare a paste of cornflour and boiling water and use this to stick down the flaps.

Heat 5 cm (2 inches) oil to smoking point, lower heat slightly and put in spring rolls, several at a time. Fry to a deep golden brown. Remove from oil, drain on absorbent paper. Serve with the sauce.

FRIED BANANAS IN BATTER

PISANG GORENG

6 large ripe bananas, slightly firm
4 egg whites
75 g (2½ oz) cornflour
45 g (1½ oz) plain flour
1 heaped teaspoon baking powder
oil for deep frying

Slice bananas in halves, lengthways. Beat egg whites until they begin to stiffen. Make a paste with cornflour, flour and a little cold water, then fold in egg whites and baking powder. Add water a little at a time, beating briskly till batter takes on a smooth creamy texture. It should be of reasonably thick consistency.

Heat oil to smoking point in a wok or deep frying pan. Coat bananas generously with batter and lower carefully into the hot oil. Deep fry for 2-3 minutes, turning to colour evenly. Lift out and drain on absorbent paper.

Serve with a sprinkling of brown sugar and lemon or lime juice or with sugar syrup made by boiling sugar and water until slightly thickened or with thick, slightly sweetened coconut milk.

WAFFLE CAKES

KUEH BELANDA

10 eggs
345 g (11 oz) sugar
575 g (1 1/8 lb) plain flour, sifted
1 teaspoon Chinese five-spice powder
⅓ cup pure coconut oil, or vegetable oil
1¼-1½ cups water

Beat eggs lightly, add sugar and beat firmly. Blend in flour, five-spice powder and coconut or vegetable oil.

Add enough water to form a batter of medium to thin consistency. Stand for at least 5 hours. Stir in very little more water before cooking. Beat for 3 minutes.

Heat a 15 cm (6 inch) waffle pan, oil lightly and pour in enough batter to make a 12-15 cm (5-6 inch) pancake. Cook over high heat until cakes are golden brown, turning once. Serve hot with butter or cold with honey or jam.

SWEET POTATO DESSERT

BUBOR CHA CHA

1 quantity green pea flour 'beans' (see Cendol)
1 medium sweet potato or yam
1 teaspoon salt
3 cups thick coconut milk
8 cm (3 inch) block palm sugar (gula Melaka), or
    185 g (6 oz) brown sugar
1 pandan leaf (optional)
⅔ cup water
shaved or crushed ice

Prepare green pea flour beans and cool.

Steam sweet potato or yam until tender, but not too soft. Cut into 0.5 cm (¼ inch) dice. Chill. Stir salt into coconut milk.

Crumble palm sugar into a saucepan, add water and pandan leaf and simmer until sugar is completely dissolved. Strain and discard leaf. If brown sugar is used pour into a small saucepan with water and bring to the boil. Cook until colour has changed to a deep golden brown and the syrup is very sticky. Remove from heat, cover hand and carefully pour in ⅓ cup cold water. Chill.

Into small glass bowls place a spoonful each of diced sweet potato or yam, green pea flour 'beans' and crushed ice. Pour in a generous amount of sugar syrup and coconut milk.

GULA MELAKA PUDDING

125 g (¼ lb) pearl sago
4½ cups water
155 g (5 oz) crumbled palm sugar (gula Melaka), or
    185 g (6 oz) brown sugar
¾ cup hot water
1 pandan leaf (optional)
1¼ cups thick coconut milk

Wash sago, drain, and put into a saucepan. Add water and bring to the boil. Turn heat down and cook until sago is tender and each grain clear. Rinse with several lots of cold water to separate grains, then divide between small glass bowls or jelly moulds and place in the refrigerator to chill.

Put palm sugar into a small pan, add crushed pandan leaf (if used), and pour on hot water. Simmer for 6 minutes. Strain and discard leaf.

If brown sugar is used, place in a small saucepan with ⅔ cup water and bring to the boil. Stir to dissolve sugar and cook on high heat until syrup is quite sticky and has begun to caramelise to a deep brown. Remove from heat. Carefully pour in ¼ cup cold water, holding saucepan well away to avoid burns from the spluttering syrup. Cover hands with a cloth before doing this. Stir well and allow to cool, then chill.

To serve dessert, pour a little sugar syrup and coconut milk over each dish of sago. Add a little shaved ice if desired. Garnish with a mint leaf.

CENDOL

This is a very special sweet also popular in Indonesia. It can be served as a drink or dessert. The sweet coconut milk makes it a great palate soother after hot dishes.

60 g (2 oz) coloured or plain green pea flour, or
    arrowroot
1⅓ cups water
green or red food colouring (optional)
8 cm (3 inch) block palm sugar (gula Melaka), or
    155 g (5 oz) brown sugar
⅔ cup hot water
1 crushed pandan leaf (optional)
7 cups thin coconut milk
shaved ice

Mix green pea flour or arrowroot with water and cook slowly, stirring to prevent lumps forming, until mixture is very thick and clear. If using plain green pea flour or arrowroot, colour half the mixture pink and the remainder green.

Push through a coarse strainer held over a basin of iced water. The mixture will break up into small bean-shaped lumps. Allow to cool, then drain. Alternatively spread thinly over a slightly chilled flat dish, or baking sheet and allow to set, then cut into very small pieces.

Crumble palm sugar into a small saucepan, add pandan leaf and pour on hot water. Simmer on low heat until sugar is dissolved, discard leaf, strain syrup and cool.

If brown sugar is used, pour into a small saucepan with ½ cup water. Bring to the boil and cook until it turns a deep golden colour and is very sticky. Remove from heat and carefully pour in 2¼ cups water, covering hand first to prevent burns. Stir in, cool and then chill.

Into large tall glasses pour about 1 tablespoon sugar syrup, 2 heaped tablespoons pea flour 'beans', a scoop of shaved ice and fill up with coconut milk. Serve with long straws and long-handled sundae spoons.

INDONESIA

Indonesia, and particularly Bali, which its inhabitants have romantically named the 'Morning of the World', holds special significance for me, for it was here that my interest in Asian cooking graduated from pleasurable hobby to career — and what better place for that to happen than at the heart of the fabled 'Spice Islands'. Bali, strictly speaking, is not one of the Spice Islands, for the term originally applied only to the Moluccan islands of Ambon (with its nutmeg), Ternate and Tidore (with their cloves). From the beginning of the sixteenth century the enormous profits to be earned in Europe from the sale of these two spices attracted the Portuguese, the Spanish and the Dutch to these islands and to others in the Indonesian archipelago, and the phrases 'Spice Islands' and 'East Indies' eventually became mistakenly synonymous — but it was a happy mistake, for Indonesian food is liberally flavoured with a great variety of spices.

Naturally enough, in a country of such size and cultural diversity, there are many distinctive dishes to be found in different regions, but the most impressive and tasty dishes come mainly from Sumatra and Java. Sumatra, Indonesia's westernmost island, has the most inventive cooks, who employ every available ingredient in a richly spiced assortment of curries. Almost every known dried spice is combined with onions, chillies, garlic, masses of fresh herbs, creamy coconut milk, tangy tamarind and ground white nuts to make fragrant, hot, thick curry sauces into which go meat from the buffalo, lungs, brains, liver, poultry, seafood, vegetables and even fruit. The most famous of these curries is 'Padang' food, named after an area of western Sumatra.

Javanese menus are based on sweet and spicy dishes of beef or chicken. Rich brown palm sugar from the aren palm or the coconut palm is combined with garlic, pounded chillies, ginger, candlenuts, soya sauce and a small number of dried spices in this distinctive regional cooking. Fresh green chillies are served as side dishes or are chopped with garlic, onions, tomato, dried shrimp paste, vinegar or soya sauce and sugar to make different-flavoured *sambal,* which accompany every meal in Java and, indeed, in most of Indonesia — dishes are often mildly seasoned, but the hot *sambal* adds as much extra sting as one needs. Some Javanese restaurants specialise in a highly spiced roast chicken, very crisp and extremely delicious. One unusual dish I sampled during a stay in Yogyakarta was introduced as 'cow's skin': it has a jelly-like consistency, and its muddy curry sauce was not particularly appetising to look at, but I hazarded a taste and discovered the delicate flavour of tripe stewed in a spiced sauce.

Most Indonesians observe Muslim beliefs and practices, and among the latter is a ban on eating pig flesh. But in Bali, where the people are Hindu and life revolves around the temples and the many religious festivals, pork is greatly enjoyed (though not, as one might expect of a Hindu culture, to the total exclusion of beef). Babi Guling (Whole Spit-Roasted Pig) is one of the most common specialities. It is always served at the temples after festivities — in Bali this can mean almost every day — and usually outside the markets on market day. The juicy pink meat is cut into bite-sized pieces, served with rice in a cornet of banana leaf and a spoonful of very hot *sambal,* and eaten with the fingers.

Although seafood is plentiful, it is not an important part of the Balinese diet. The Balinese enjoy fish in a mild curry sauce, but beef, buffalo, eggs, poultry and pork predominate. Few vegetables are included in their diet, though an abundance of fresh tropical fruit is available (as it is throughout Indonesia) and is usually served after every meal. Indigenous Indonesian fruits include the furry *rambutan* (Queen Victoria loved them so much that she commanded her sea captains never to return from a voyage to the Spice Islands without a case of *rambutan* for her own use); *salak,* a small fruit with a dark brown snakeskin shell and hard crisp flesh like raw potato or green apple (an acquired taste at first, but then addictive); star fruit (carambola), with a refreshingly astringent taste; and the controversial, evil-smelling *durian,* regarded by many as the king of the tropical fruits.

Rice is the staple in most of Indonesia, though it has not always been so, and even today people in some regions depend on tapioca and sago. The best rice is the medium-grain variety, and, where husked by hand, it has a superb nutty taste. Herbs like *sereh* (lemon grass), coriander and *pandan* or fragrant screwpine (bot. *Pandanus*) grow profusely in this climate; so too do such spices as ginger and *kunyit* (turmeric), while cloves are still plentiful, especially in Maluku (the Moluccas), though most find their way into the distinctive-smelling *kretek* cigarettes. *Kecap manis* (a thick sweet soya sauce) and *terasi* (dried prawn paste) are frequently used seasonings. *Gula Jawa,* the brown palm sugar used by the Javanese in their savoury dishes, is also used to flavour many sweet dishes, when it is usually added along with coconut milk. The coconut has many uses in Indonesian cooking, providing milk for smooth creamy curries, sweets and drinks, shredded coconut for garnishing and *sambal,* and its clear liquid for a refreshing drink.

Snacks of all kinds are eaten, and are available everywhere. On any roadside there will be a vendor set up with makeshift equipment turning out tiny cakes, crunchy peanut crackers, prawn crisps, fritters of jackfruit or banana in crisp batter, shrimp cakes, and sweet corn fritters. Usually the vendor operates with little more than a tin drum containing hot coals that are constantly fanned into flame, and a *kuali* or *wajan* (like a *wok*) of hot oil for frying; carry bags are pieces of banana leaf.

Local alcoholic beverages, made from coconut sap and sugarcane juice, are found in certain parts of Indonesia. A delicious sweet pink wine in Bali, called *brem,* is deceptively mild-tasting and dangerously potent. Water is served with meals, and tea is popular in Java, where it is grown; thick black coffee sweetened with

Shrimp Curry (recipe page 114).

113

large doses of condensed milk is a more expensive but universally enjoyed brew.

Food is served in wide, fairly shallow dishes and is eaten with spoon and fork or fingers from shallow bowls or pieces of banana leaf. Table settings are simple, with no adornments save a few flowers or a *janur* arrangement made with young coconut leaves woven into traditional shapes.

FRIED FISH IN HOT COCONUT SAUCE
IKAN BUMBU RUJAK

500 g (1 lb) fillets of snapper, bream or perch
2 teaspoons chilli powder
2.5 cm (1 inch) piece fresh ginger, shredded
½ teaspoon dried shrimp paste
2 medium onions
2 cloves garlic
vegetable oil
3 small tomatoes
1 red or green pepper
1 fresh red chilli, finely chopped
1½ cups thin coconut milk
1 *daun salam* or bay leaf
1 teaspoon grated fresh turmeric or
   ⅓ teaspoon turmeric powder
2 tablespoons plain flour
salt
vegetable oil for deep frying

Grind chilli powder, ginger and shrimp paste into a paste. Chop onions and garlic and fry in a little oil until golden. Add finely chopped tomato, sliced pepper, chilli and ground seasonings and fry over moderate heat for 4 minutes.

Pour in coconut milk and add bay leaf and turmeric. Bring almost to the boil, turn heat down and simmer until sauce is thick and spicy. Remove from the heat and keep warm while fish is prepared. Cut fillets into pieces about 6 cm (2½ inches) long and season with salt, then coat lightly with flour.

Heat oil and fry fish to a golden brown. Remove from oil, drain and arrange on a serving plate. Reheat sauce, adjust seasonings if necessary and pour over fish.

WRAPPED FISH
PANGGANG BUNGKUS

1 whole fish (pomfret, turbot or sole), weighing about
   410 g (13 oz)
1 teaspoon tamarind, crumbled
2 teaspoons salt
10 candlenuts, ground
¾ teaspoon turmeric powder
½ teaspoon dried shrimp paste
1 cm (½ inch) piece fresh ginger
2 fresh red chillies, finely chopped
1-2 teaspoons chilli powder
2 medium onions
1 clove garlic
1 *daun salam* or bay leaf

4 fresh basil leaves (optional)
banana leaf or aluminium foil
tomato wedges

Clean fish and score diagonally across both sides. Rub with salt and tamarind over skin and inside cavity. Grind candlenuts with turmeric, shrimp paste, ginger, fresh chillies and chilli powder. Chop onion and garlic finely and mix with the ground seasonings.

Coat the fish thickly with the seasoning paste and place *daun salam* or bay leaf and basil (if used), inside cavity.

Hold banana leaf over a flame to soften. Brush with oil. Wrap fish in banana leaf or foil, securing with toothpicks or tieing with cotton. Roast over a charcoal fire or in a moderate oven for about 15-20 minutes.

Test if fish is done by inserting a thin skewer in the thickest part. If the flesh is tender and no pink juices escape, the fish is ready. To serve, tear away the top part of the banana leaf or foil wrapping. Place on a wooden plate and surround with tomato wedges.

SPICED FISH
IKAN PECAL

500 g (1 lb) thick fillets of cod, snapper or haddock
3 medium onions
3 cloves garlic
1 tablespoon chilli powder
½ teaspoon sweet basil, powdered or flaked
1 cm (½ inch) piece fresh ginger, shredded
½ teaspoon dried shrimp paste
4 candlenuts, ground
1 small piece tamarind
2 teaspoons salt
1 cup thick coconut milk
lemon or lime wedges

Chop or mince onion and garlic finely. Mix all ingredients except lemon wedges together and blend well. Slice fish into 12 pieces and arrange in a flat bowl. Pour on the marinade and stand for 20 minutes.

Remove from the liquid and grill fillets, basting with the marinade as they cook. When done, transfer to a warmed serving plate.

Bring the remaining marinade to the boil in a small saucepan and simmer until slightly thickened. Strain over fish. Serve with lemon or lime wedges.

SHRIMP CURRY
KARI UDANG

375 g (¾ lb) peeled raw shrimps
salt
pepper
1 cm (½ inch) piece fresh ginger, shredded
2 teaspoons chilli powder
1 teaspoon grated fresh turmeric, or
   ⅓ teaspoon turmeric powder
8 candlenuts, ground
1 tablespoon coconut oil
2.5 cm (1 inch) piece *lengkuas,* sliced (optional)

Chicken and Tomato Balinese Style (recipe page 116), and Chilli Eggs (recipe page 121).

½ teaspoon dried shrimp paste
¾ cup fish stock
1½ cups thin coconut milk
1 stalk lemon grass
fresh coriander, chopped

Season shrimps with salt and pepper and fry in coconut oil until pink. Remove and set aside.

Grind ginger, chilli powder, turmeric and candlenuts to a paste and fry in oil for 3 minutes. Add sliced *lengkuas* and shrimp paste, then pour on fish stock and bring to the boil. Reduce heat and add coconut milk and lemon grass and boil briefly. Return shrimps and cook for 3-4 minutes on moderate heat.

Season with a salt and pepper to taste and garnish with chopped coriander.

FRIED CHILLI PRAWNS

SAMBAL GORENG UDANG

500 g (1 lb) large raw prawns in shells
salt
pepper
1 medium onion
2 small tomatoes
1½ tablespoons peanut oil
2 cloves garlic, crushed
2.5 cm (1 inch) piece *lengkuas*, minced
2-3 fresh red chillies, thinly sliced
2 teaspoons chilli powder
2.5 cm (1 inch) piece lemon grass
⅔ cup thin coconut milk
2 tablespoons tamarind water, made with ½ teaspoon tamarind
spring onions, chopped

Peel and devein prawns, leaving heads and tails attached. Season with salt and pepper.

Slice onion and tomato. Heat oil in a *wok* or saucepan and fry onion and garlic till soft. Add prawns and cook for 2 minutes. Add tomato, *lengkuas*, red chillies, chilli powder, lemon grass, salt and pepper. Cook for about 3 minutes, stirring occasionally. Turn heat down, pour on coconut milk and simmer for 3 minutes.

Strain tamarind and add liquid and chopped spring onions to the sauce. Heat through and serve immediately.

CHICKEN AND TOMATO BALINESE STYLE

AYAM BUMBU BALI

1 kg (2 lb) chicken
salt
pepper
oil for deep frying
2 medium onions
2 fresh red chillies
2 cloves garlic
¾ cup tomato puree
2 teaspoons brown sugar
1 cm (½ inch) piece fresh ginger, shredded

1 teaspoon dried shrimp paste
3 teaspoons dark soya sauce
2 cups chicken stock
4 medium tomatoes, chopped
¼ cup thick coconut milk
fresh mint or coriander leaves, chopped

Cut chicken into serving pieces. Season with salt and pepper and fry in hot oil until well browned with slightly crisp skin. Remove and drain well. Keep warm.

Chop onions, chillies and garlic finely and fry in 1 tablespoon oil for 3 mintues. Stir in tomato puree and cook on moderate heat for 5 minutes. Mix in brown sugar, ginger, shrimp paste and soya sauce, then pour in chicken stock and season with salt and pepper. Simmer for 10 minutes.

Add chicken and continue simmering until tender. Add chopped tomatoes and coconut milk and cook for a few minutes longer.

Garnish with chopped mint or coriander.

CHICKEN IN COCONUT SAUCE

OPOR AYAM

440 g (14 oz) chicken pieces
2 teaspoons salt
½ teaspoon white pepper
1 medium onion
2.5 cm (1 inch) piece fresh ginger
2.5 cm (1 inch) piece *lengkuas*
2 cloves garlic, crushed
3 black cardamoms, crushed
1 heaped teaspoon coriander, ground
½ teaspoon dried shrimp paste
8 candlenuts, ground
2 tablespoons oil
1 cup chicken stock
½ cup thick coconut milk
2 heaped teaspoons brown sugar
fresh coriander leaf or shredded spring onion

Chop chicken into medium pieces. Season with salt and pepper. Finely chop onion, ginger and *lengkuas* and pound to a paste with garlic, cardamom, coriander, shrimp paste and candlenuts.

Heat oil and fry seasoning paste for 4 minutes, then add chicken pieces and cook till well coloured. Pour in chicken stock, stir well, cover and bring to the boil, then turn heat down and simmer until chicken is tender. Add a little more water or stock if needed.

Pour in coconut milk and sprinkle on brown sugar and cook until sauce thickens. Garnish with coriander leaf or shredded spring onion.

CHICKEN LIVERS IN COCONUT CREAM

HATI AYAM

375 g (¾ lb) chicken livers
2 tablespoons peanut oil
2 medium onions, chopped
3 cloves garlic, crushed

1 heaped teaspoon chilli powder
2 fresh red chillies, sliced
12 candlenuts, ground
2 teaspoons brown sugar
1½ teaspoons salt
¾ cup thin coconut milk
½ cup thick coconut milk
5 cm (2 inch) stalk lemon grass
lemon juice
fried onion flakes (see page 125)
parsley or mint, chopped

Clean chicken livers and cut in halves. Heat oil and fry onions and garlic until soft. Add livers and saute until no pink shows. Sprinkle on chilli powder, and add sliced chillies, ground candlenuts, sugar and salt. Stir well, then pour in thin coconut milk and thick coconut milk and add lemon grass.

Simmer until livers are very tender. Sprinkle on lemon juice to taste and serve garnished with fried onions and chopped parsley or mint.

FRIED CHICKEN WITH TAMARIND

AYAM GORENG ASAM

750 g (1½ lb) chicken
salt
pepper
2 medium onions
3 cloves garlic
40 g (1½ oz) tamarind
½ cup boiling water
oil for deep frying
sweet soya sauce
krupuk or potato crisps

Clean chicken and cut into large pieces. Season with salt and pepper. Grate onions and crush garlic. Soak tamarind in boiling water. Arrange chicken pieces in a flat bowl, sprinkle on grated onion and garlic and strain on tamarind water. Marinate for 20 minutes. Lift up, drain and pat dry with kitchen paper.

Heat oil until almost at smoking point and carefully lower in several pieces of chicken. Deep fry for 2 minutes, then remove from oil and return to marinade while remaining pieces are cooked. Marinate for at least 10 minutes the second time, then drain again and pat dry.

Return to the hot oil and cook again for 2 minutes. Marinate once more, then fry chicken another 2 minutes. It should be crisp on the surface and the meat tender and moist. Serve with soya sauce dip and a plate of freshly fried *krupuk* or potato crisps.

SPICED ROAST DUCK

BEBEK BETUTU

This duck is served on festive occasions in Bali. It is traditionally cooked in a wrapping of banana leaves in a bed of coals under the ground. This simplified recipe can be cooked in the oven and the decorative banana leaf wrapping substituted by aluminium foil.

2 kg (4 lb) duck
2 medium onions
4 cloves garlic
5 cm (2 inch) piece fresh ginger
1 tablespoon coconut or vegetable oil
2 fresh red chillies, chopped
12 candlenuts, ground
2 black cardamoms, ground
1 teaspoon grated fresh turmeric or
   ½ teaspoon turmeric powder
1 teaspoon dried shrimp paste
2 teaspoons salt
1 teaspoon white pepper
banana leaves, or aluminium foil

Clean duck and wash. Wipe dry and set aside.

Mince onion, garlic and ginger and fry in oil for 3 minutes. Grind chilli, candlenuts, cardamom, turmeric, shrimp paste, salt and pepper to a paste and add to the pan, frying for a further 3 minutes.

Stuff into the duck and secure opening with toothpicks or sew up carefully. Rub duck with salt and pepper and a little oil and wrap in several layers of banana leaf or foil. Secure with toothpicks or tie with cotton.

Bake in a preheated moderate oven (180°C/350°F/ Gas Mark 4) for 2 hours. If crisp skin is preferred, remove wrappings, turn heat up and bake for a further 10 minutes.

Serve with Golden Coconut Rice (see page 121).

ROAST SUCKLING PIG

BABI GULING

The most popular Balinese festive dish, Babi Guling is always served at temples during religious festivities. The whole pig is decorated with flowers and surrounded by silver dishes of rice cakes and fruit and is carried to the temple grounds on a large tray balanced on a woman's head.

4-5 kg (8-10 lb) suckling pig
10 cm (4 inch) piece fresh ginger, shredded
3 teaspoons turmeric powder
4 green cardamoms, crushed
1 tablespoon chilli powder
2 tablespoons salt
1 teaspoon grated nutmeg
3 teaspoons dried shrimp paste
1 stalk lemon grass, finely chopped
8 cloves
2 teaspoons black peppercorns
1 tablespoon tamarind
4 tablespoons vegetable oil
2 large onions, chopped
4 cloves garlic, crushed
salt
pepper

Have the butcher clean and prepare the piglet. Wash well and wipe dry.

Grind ginger, turmeric, cardamom, chilli, salt, nutmeg and shrimp paste. Add lemon grass, cloves, peppercorns and tamarind.

Heat oil and fry onion and garlic till soft. Add

ground seasonings and fry for 4 minutes. Stuff into the prepared piglet and sew up opening. Rub skin with salt and pepper mixed with vegetable oil. Bake on a spit over a charcoal fire or in a moderately hot oven for 2½ hours. Test if the meat is done by inserting a skewer into the thickest part. If the liquid runs clear the piglet is cooked. Baste with oil during cooking.

Serve slices of pork with white rice and a hot tomato and chilli *sambal*.

If preparing a larger pig, increase the amounts of ingredients accordingly and allow extra cooking time.

SWEET PORK

BABI KECAP

625 g (1¼ lb) pork belly with rind
2 teaspoons salt
1 teaspoon white pepper
2 tablespoons plain flour
oil for deep frying
3 medium onions
2 cloves garlic
2 teaspoons tomato paste
3 tablespoons chicken stock
1½ tablespoons brown sugar
2½ tablespoons sweet soya sauce
fresh coriander leaves, chopped

Slice pork thinly. Sprinkle with salt and pepper and coat lightly with flour. Stand for 5 minutes.

Heat oil to smoking point and fry pork until well browned. Remove from oil, drain and set aside. Remove all but 1 tablespoon oil from pan.

Peel and chop onions and garlic and fry till soft. Add tomato paste, chicken stock and brown sugar and return pork slices. Sprinkle on sweet soya sauce and simmer for 10 minutes, adding a little water if the liquid dries up. Turn heat up slightly and cook for a further 5-7 minutes until all liquid is absorbed into the meat and pork is very tender.

Sprinkle on chopped coriander to garnish.

BRAISED SPICED BEEF

SEMUR SAPI

625 g (1¼ lb) rump or sirloin steak
2 medium onions
4 cloves garlic
2 tablespoons oil
⅔ cup beef stock
½ teaspoon grated nutmeg
2 teaspoons mixed spice
1½ teaspoons brown sugar
1½ teaspoons salt
1 teaspoon white pepper
2 tablespoons sweet soya sauce
tomato wedges
onion flakes (see page 125)
fresh coriander leaves

Cut beef into 2.5 cm (1 inch) cubes, after removing any fat. Peel and chop onions and garlic. Heat oil in a pan and fry onions and garlic until light brown and soft. Put in beef, turn heat up slightly and fry for 5-6 minutes, turning to brown well. Pour in beef stock, cover and simmer for 10 minutes.

Add nutmeg, mixed spice, brown sugar, salt, pepper and sweet soya sauce. Reduce heat and cook until meat is tender, adding a little more water from time to time as liquid dries up.

Serve with tomato wedges and garnish with fried onion or sprigs of coriander.

COCONUT BEEF

DENDENG RAGI

500 g (1 lb) rump or sirloin steak
1 tablespoon coriander, ground
½ teaspoon powdered sweet basil, or
    2 teaspoons fresh basil, chopped
1 tablespoon brown sugar
2 teaspoons tamarind
3 cloves garlic, crushed
3 medium onions, grated
2 tablespoons oil
2 *daun salam* or bay leaves
155 g (5 oz) freshly grated coconut, or
    100 g (3½ oz) moistened desiccated coconut
salt
pepper

Slice beef thinly. Grind coriander, basil, brown sugar and tamarind to a paste and mix with garlic and onions.

Heat oil in a frying pan and fry seasoning paste for 5 minutes, stirring occasionally. Season beef with salt and pepper and add to the pan. Cook over high heat until very well browned. Remove and keep warm.

In a dry pan pour desiccated or grated coconut and add *daun salam* or bay leaves. Turn heat down low and stir coconut as it cooks. It burns very quickly, so do not stop stirring at any time. When coconut is lightly browned add meat and cook until warmed through.

DEEP FRIED SPICY BEEF SLICES

EMPAL DAGING

500 g (1 lb) round, chuck or sirloin steak
3 teaspoons coriander, ground
2 teaspoons cummin, ground
1 cm (½ inch) piece fresh ginger, shredded
½ teaspoon black peppercorns, crushed
2 teaspoons tamarind
1 tablespoon coriander seeds
vegetable or peanut oil

Make a paste with ground coriander, cummin, ginger, crushed peppercorns, tamarind and a little hot water. Slice beef thinly and rub well with the spices. Put in a flat pan, cover with water and simmer until all liquid has been absorbed, turning meat several times. Remove from pan and keep warm.

Crush coriander seeds and lightly fry in a little vegetable or peanut oil. When ready to serve meat, heat 2.5 cm (1 inch) oil in a pan to smoking point. Dip meat

Coconut Beef (recipe this page).

slices in the fried coriander seeds, pressing in slightly. Place in the hot oil and fry for 1-2 minutes.

For convenience, this dish may be simmered in advance and the meat stored in the refrigerator, wrapped in plastic film, until ready to serve. Remove from the refrigerator half an hour before required, then fry as above.

LAMB WITH COCONUT

GULAI KAMBING

750 g (1½ lb) shoulder of lamb
salt
white pepper
2 teaspoons brown sugar
½ teaspoon turmeric powder
2 heaped teaspoons chilli powder
1 fresh red chilli, chopped
1 teaspoon dried shrimp paste
3 medium onions
2 cloves garlic
2 tablespoons vegetable oil
75 g (2½ oz) freshly grated coconut or
    40 g (1½ oz) desiccated coconut
1½ cups coconut milk
fresh coriander sprigs

Cut lamb meat into 2.5 cm (1 inch) cubes and dust with salt and pepper. Grind brown sugar with turmeric, chilli powder, fresh chilli, and shrimp paste. Peel onions and garlic and chop finely.

Heat oil and fry onions and garlic until soft. Add ground seasonings and fry for 4 minutes. Toss in lamb and cook until well browned, then add coconut. Brown for 10 minutes, stirring continually to prevent coconut burning.

Pour in coconut milk, lower heat and simmer until meat is tender. Season to taste with salt and pepper. Garnish with sprigs of coriander.

CURRIED LIVERS

GULAI HATI

375 g (¾ lb) calves or lambs liver
vegetable oil
1 small onion, chopped
1 clove garlic
1 cm (½ inch) piece fresh ginger, shredded
⅓ cup boiling water
1 teaspoon tamarind
1 teaspoon turmeric powder
1 heaped teaspoon chilli powder
1 cup coconut milk
1 *daun salam* or bay leaf
salt
pepper
fresh red and green chilli, shredded

Slice liver into 1 cm (½ inch) thick slices and fry for 1 minute on each side in a little vegetable oil. Remove from pan and keep warm. Grind onion, garlic and gin-

ger and fry for 2 minutes, stirring frequently. Add liver slices and saute for 1 minute.

Pour boiling water over tamarind, allow to stand for 2 minutes then strain over liver. Turn heat up and cook briefly, adding turmeric and chilli powder, coconut milk and *daun salam* or bay leaf. Reduce heat and simmer until sauce is thick and liver tender, stirring frequently during cooking.

Season to taste with salt and pepper. Garnish with shredded red and green chilli.

BRAINS IN WHITE CURRY

OPOR OTAK

4 sets calves brains
2 teaspoons tamarind
⅓ cup boiling water
1 medium onion
2 cloves garlic
1 tablespoon vegetable oil
2.5 cm (1 inch) piece fresh ginger, shredded
3 heaped teaspoons coriander, ground
1½ teaspoons cummin, ground
½ teaspoon white pepper
10 candlenuts, ground
¾ cup coconut milk
5 cm (2 inch) piece lemon grass
1 teaspoon salt
chilli powder

Clean brains, removing membranes. Place in a saucepan after rinsing in cold water. Steep tamarind in boiling water for 2 minutes. Strain liquid over brains and stand for 10 minutes.

Peel onion and garlic and chop finely. Heat oil in a small pan and fry onion and garlic till golden, then add ginger, coriander, cummin and pepper. Fry for 4 minutes on moderate heat. Add candlenuts and fry for 1 minute. Set aside.

Pour coconut milk into the pan with brains and add lemon grass and salt. Simmer for 3 minutes, then add fried seasonings, stir well and cook for a further 6 minutes, until brains are tender and sauce thick and spicy.

Serve with a sprinkling of chilli powder to garnish.

BOILED EGG IN COCONUT SAUCE

SAMBAL GORENG TELUR

6 eggs
1 medium onion
2 cloves garlic
1 tablespoon coconut or vegetable oil
3 teaspoons chilli powder
1 teaspoon grated fresh turmeric, or
    ⅓ teaspoon turmeric powder
2.5 cm (1 inch) piece fresh ginger, minced
½ teaspoon dried shrimp paste
10 cm (4 inch) piece lemon grass, chopped
1½ teaspoons salt
1¼ cups coconut milk
1 medium tomato, chopped
75 g (2½ oz) cooked peas

Hardboil eggs and put in cold water. Mince or finely chop onion and garlic and fry in oil till soft. Add chilli powder, turmeric, ginger, shrimp paste, lemon grass and salt. Saute for 2 minutes then pour in coconut milk and add tomato. Stir well and simmer on moderate heat for 5 minutes.

Strain sauce through muslin or a fine strainer and return to the pot, adding peas and halved eggs. Simmer for a further 6-7 minutes, then lift out eggs in a slotted spoon and arrange on a serving plate. Pour on sauce.

CHILLI EGGS

TELUR BERLADO

6 large eggs
oil for deep frying
2 medium onions, minced
2 cloves garlic, minced
1 cm (½ inch) piece fresh ginger, minced
1 teaspoon dried shrimp paste
3 teaspoons chilli powder
2 fresh red chillies, finely chopped
5 cm (2 inch) stalk lemon grass, finely chopped
1 teaspoon tamarind
2 tablespoons boiling water
2 teaspoons sugar
¾ teaspoon turmeric powder
salt
pepper
fresh coriander leaves

Hardboil eggs and place in cold water. When cold remove shells and prick eggs with a fork to allow seasonings to penetrate. Heat oil and gently fry eggs to a deep golden colour and slightly crisp on the outside. Remove and set aside.

Pour off all but 1 tablespoon oil and fry onion, garlic and ginger for 2 minutes. Add shrimp paste, chilli powder, chopped chillies, lemon grass and tamarind mixed with boiling water. Stir over moderate heat for 2 minutes, then add sugar and turmeric. Stir well. Replace eggs and cook until the seasonings have dried up and cling to the eggs. Sprinkle on salt and pepper.

Serve eggs either whole or halved. Garnish with sprigs of fresh coriander.

GOLDEN COCONUT RICE

2½ cups coconut milk
½ cup stock
1 teaspoon salt
2½ teaspoons grated fresh turmeric, or
　1 teaspoon turmeric powder
crushed *daun salam* or bay leaf
345 g (11 oz) rice
1 fresh red chilli
1 green chilli

Mix coconut milk with stock, salt, turmeric and crushed *daun salam* or bay leaf in a large saucepan. Bring almost to the boil. Wash rice well and add to the stock, stir and bring to the boil. Cover tightly, turn heat down to lowest point and cook until rice is tender. Stir rice and stand for several minutes with lid removed so grains will dry slightly.

Make flower decorations with the chillies by shredding ends with a sharp knife and placing in a bowl of iced water for the 'petals' to curl.

Spoon rice into an ovenproof serving dish and place in a hot oven or under griller for several minutes to crisp top.

Decorate with the chilli flowers.

INDONESIAN FRIED RICE

NASI GORENG

4½ cups chicken stock
2 teaspoons tamarind
345 g (11 oz) rice
3 medium onions
4 cloves garlic
1 tablespoon oil
1 large tomato, sliced
1½ teaspoons dried shrimp paste
2 teaspoons chilli powder
100 g (3½ oz) lean beef, shredded
salt
white pepper
1 stalk celery, sliced
1 fresh red chilli, finely chopped
2 eggs
dry fried onion flakes (see page 125)

Bring stock to the boil and add the tamarind and well-washed rice. Boil for 12-15 minutes, or until rice is tender but not too soft. Drain, rinse in cold water and set aside to cool. Break up the tamarind and stir well to mix into the rice.

Peel and slice onions and garlic and fry in oil until soft. Add tomato, shrimp paste and chilli powder and cook for 2 minutes. Put in beef and season with salt and pepper. Saute for 3-4 minutes, stirring frequently. Add sliced celery and chopped chilli and cook for a further 2 minutes. Remove and set aside.

Wipe out pan and oil lightly. Beat eggs and pour into the pan. Cook in a thin omelette until set, then break up with a fork and add to the cooked beef mixture.

Add 2 tablespoons oil to the pan and stir-fry rice for 5 minutes, stir in cooked mixture and season with salt and pepper and a little soya sauce if desired.

Garnish with fried onion flakes.

FRIED NOODLES

BAKMI GORENG

250 g (½ lb) thin egg noodles
2 cloves garlic
1 large onion
vegetable oil
100 g (3½ oz) peeled raw shrimp
100 g (3½ oz) chicken, shredded
1 fresh red chilli, chopped

8 spring onions, chopped
100 g (3½ oz) Chinese cabbage, chopped
2 tablespoons dark soya sauce
2 teaspoons sugar
2 teaspoons salt
½ teaspoon white pepper
1 egg, beaten
dry fried onion flakes (see page 125)

Soak noodles for 10 minutes in cold water. Drain and spread on a tray to dry. Peel garlic and onion and chop finely. Fry in a little oil until soft. Put in shrimps and chicken and cook for 5 minutes. Add chilli, spring onions and cabbage and stir-fry for 3 minutes.

Mix soya sauce with sugar, salt and pepper and pour over the vegetables. Remove from heat and keep warm.

Pour 2 tablespoons oil into a pan and when hot fry noodles on high heat until lightly coloured and slightly crisped. Lift onto a serving dish. Reheat vegetable and meat topping and pour on.

Heat pan and fry beaten egg in a thin omelette, swirling pan to make it spread very thinly across the pan. Lift out, cool and shred.

Garnish the noodles with shredded egg and fried onion flakes and serve hot.

BALINESE NOODLES WITH CHICKEN IN COCONUT SAUCE

LAKSA AYAM BALI

9 cups water
1.5 kg (3 lb) chicken
1 tablespoon coriander, ground
1 heaped teaspoon cummin seeds
1½ teaspoons grated fresh turmeric, or
  ½ teaspoon turmeric powder
2.5 cm (1 inch) piece fresh ginger, shredded
3 cloves garlic, crushed
6 spring onions, chopped
4 candlenuts, ground
1 teaspoon dried shrimp paste
3 tablespoons coconut or vegetable oil
125 g (¼ lb) peeled raw shrimp
1 lemon, quartered
10 cm (4 inch) stalk lemon grass
2 lemon leaves (optional)
1¼ cups thick coconut milk
salt
pepper
500 g (1 lb) thin rice vermicelli

Garnishes:
Prawn Fritters (see page 128)
dry fried onion flakes (see page 125)
spring onion, chopped
celery leaves, chopped
fresh sweet basil leaves (optional)
fresh coriander or mint leaves
hardboiled egg, sliced
Tomato Sambal (see page 125)

Pour water into a large saucepan and add the cleaned chicken. Boil for 1½ hours, then remove chicken, drain and set aside. When cool, shred meat. Continue to boil stock until reduced to 6 cups. Set aside.

Pound seasonings from coriander to shrimp paste to a paste and fry in coconut or vegetable oil for 3 minutes, stirring constantly. Add shrimp and fry briefly, then mix into the reserved chicken stock. Add lemon, lemon grass and lemon leaves (if used), and bring to the boil. Reduce heat and simmer soup for 10 minutes. Discard lemon, then pour in coconut milk and season to taste with salt and pepper. Keep warm while garnishes are prepared.

Cover vermicelli with boiling water and leave to soften, then drain. Prepare all other garnishes and arrange on a serving plate. Divide the vermicelli between six large bowls and add a generous serving of coconut soup and shredded chicken.

Serve the garnishes separately to be added to taste.

SHRIMP NOODLES

SOTO UDANG

250 g (½ lb) thin rice vermicelli
250 g (½ lb) beanshoots
8 fresh red chillies, sliced
1 tablespoon oil
4 cups cold water
2 tablespoons sweet soya sauce
salt
white pepper
500 g (1 lb) peeled raw shrimp
90 g (3 oz) roasted peanuts, crushed
2 cloves garlic, crushed
2 medium onions, minced
3 tablespoons tamarind water, made with 1½
  teaspoons tamarind
2 tablespoons brown sugar
2 tablespoons peanut oil

Scald noodles with boiling water. Stand till soft, then drain and rinse in cold water. Steep beanshoots in boiling water for 2 minutes. Drain. Fry sliced chillies until crisp. Reserve 2 for garnish and crush the remaining fried chillies. Divide noodles between six large bowls and top with crushed and fried chilli, and beanshoots.

Bring water to the boil, add soya sauce, sugar, salt and pepper. Toss in shrimps and simmer for 3 minutes, then remove shrimps with a slotted spoon. Cool, then mince.

Mix crushed peanuts with garlic, onion and minced shrimp. Return to the stock and add tamarind water. Add sugar and salt to taste. Add remaining fried chillies and boil for another minute. Pour over noodles and serve hot.

SPICY FRUIT SALAD

RUJAK MANIS

Though this dish is called a fruit salad it is made up of a mixture of fresh fruits and vegetables (any crisp ones will do). The pungent, spicy sauce makes this salad a perfect accompaniment to other main dishes.

Balinese Noodles with Chicken in Coconut Sauce (recipe this page).

3 teaspoons tamarind
½ cup boiling water
3½ tablespoons sweet soya sauce
½ teaspoon dried shrimp paste
salt
3 fresh red chillies, sliced
375 g (¾ lb) peeled mixed fruit and vegetables
(cucumber, green pear, unripe mango, pineapple,
onion, apple, *salak,* partially cooked green beans)

Prepare vegetables and fruit by washing, peeling and
slicing thinly. Soak tamarind in boiling water, then
strain, reserving liquid. Mix tamarind water with sweet
soya sauce, shrimp paste and a pinch of salt. Pour into a
small saucepan and simmer for 2 minutes. Cool.

Arrange vegetables and fruit in a serving dish or salad
bowl. Scatter on sliced chillies and pour on the sauce.
Serve slightly chilled.

INDONESIAN VEGETABLE SALAD

GADO GADO

Sauce: (prepare first)
1 medium onion, minced
2 cloves garlic, minced
155 g (5 oz) roasted peanuts, crushed
2 teaspoons dark soya sauce
1 tablespoon brown sugar
2 heaped teaspoons chilli powder
½ teaspoon salt
1 teaspoon tamarind
3 *daun salam* or bay leaves (optional)
3 tablespoons coconut or vegetable oil
¾ cup thick coconut milk
1 fresh red chilli, finely chopped

Fry all ingredients from onion to *daun salam* or bay
leaves in the coconut or vegetable oil for 5 minutes, stirring frequently. Add coconut milk and simmer until
sauce is thick and aromatic. Add chilli and leave to
cool.

Salad:
2 small carrots
2 medium potatoes
100 g (3½ oz) cabbage, shredded
155 g (5 oz) green beans, sliced
250 g (½ lb) beanshoots
12 lettuce leaves
2 medium tomatoes
3 hardboiled eggs
1 small cucumber
freshly fried *krupuk*
dry fried onion flakes (see page 125)

Scrape carrots and slice thinly, or grate. Peel potatoes
and cut into 1 cm (½ inch) dice or thin slices. Drop into
boiling, slightly salted water and cook for 10 minutes.
Add carrot and cook for 1 more minute. Drain and set
aside. Saute cabbage and beans in a very little oil and
water until partially cooked but still crisp. Put beanshoots in a strainer and pour on boiling water, or steep
in a pot of boiling water for 2 minutes to soften. Drain.
Wash lettuce and dry carefully.

Line a wide plate with the lettuce, top with carrot
and potato pieces, then add beans and cabbage. Stack
beanshoots on top. Cut tomatoes into thin wedges.
Peel and slice cucumber. Slice boiled eggs. Arrange
tomato, cucumber and egg slices attractively around the
edge of the salad.

Pour on sauce and sprinkle with onion flakes. Decorate with freshly fried *krupuk.* Serve slightly chilled.

MIXED VEGETABLES IN COCONUT SAUCE

SAYUR LODEH

1 medium potato
1 medium carrot
60 g (2 oz) green beans, sliced
100 g (3½ oz) cabbage, shredded
100 g (3½ oz) beanshoots
2 medium onions
2 cloves garlic
1 tablespoon oil
½ medium cucumber
1 teaspoon tamarind, crumbled
2.5 cm (1 inch) piece fresh ginger, minced
2 teaspoons coriander, ground
2 teaspoons salt
1½ cups thick coconut milk
krupuk

Peel and slice potato and carrot and parboil for 3
minutes. Add beans and cabbage and cook for 2 more
minutes, then drain. Splash with cold water and allow
to cool.

Steep beanshoots in boiling water for 2 minutes.
Drain. Peel onion and garlic and chop finely. Fry in oil
until soft. Slice cucumber thinly and saute with onions
for 2 minutes.

Mix tamarind with ginger, coriander, salt and coconut milk, then pour over onions and cucumber and
simmer gently for 6 minutes. Add vegetables and beanshoots and simmer for 2 minutes, stirring often.

Serve with freshly fried *krupuk.*

SOYA SAUCE SAMBAL

2 tablespoons dark soya sauce
1 clove garlic, crushed
1 teaspoon sugar
½ fresh red chilli, finely chopped

Pour soya sauce into a bowl. Pound garlic, sugar and
chilli to a paste and add to the sauce. Stir until sugar
dissolves, then leave for 1 hour before using.

GARLIC AND RED CHILLI SAMBAL

3 fresh red chillies
8 cloves garlic
6 spring onions

2 teaspoons salt
1½ tablespoons white vinegar or tamarind water
1½ teaspoons sugar

Mince chillies, garlic and spring onions and mix in salt, vinegar or tamarind water and sugar. Stir until sugar dissolves. Leave to stand for 1 hour before using.

This will keep for up to 3 days in the refrigerator in an airtight jar.

FRESH TOMATO SAMBAL

2 ripe tomatoes, skinned and chopped
1 small onion, finely chopped
½ red chilli, chopped
1 teaspoon salt
½ teaspoon dried shrimp paste, toasted
3 teaspoons water

Mix all ingredients together and pound in a mortar or puree in a blender until smooth. Store in an airtight jar in the refrigerator. This *sambal* will keep for up to 3 days.

If preferred do not pound the *sambal* but serve the ingredients finely chopped.

SHRIMP PASTE SAMBAL

SAMBAL TERASI

1 tablespoon dried shrimp paste, toasted
1 fresh red chilli, finely chopped
1 small onion
1-2 teaspoons sugar
1½ tablespoons oil
lemon or lime juice

Mash shrimp paste and mix with chilli. Mince onion and fry with sugar for 2 minutes. Add to shrimp paste and stir. Add lemon juice to taste.

This *sambal* may be kept in a sealed jar for up to 2 weeks.

DRY FRIED ONION FLAKES

small red onions or shallots

Peel onions and slice as thinly as possible. Pat with kitchen paper to absorb excess moisture.

Heat a heavy-based frying pan and wipe out with an oiled cloth. Turn heat to moderate and put in onion. Cook uncovered until the onion is deeply coloured and dry underneath. Turn and cook other side. Ensure that the onion is completely dried out by placing in a warm oven for ½ hour. Store in an airtight container.

This is a very slow process and the cooking should not be accelerated or the onions will burn and become bitter. Make large amounts at a time and store until needed. If onions become slightly soft after storage, they can be crisped by placing in a warm oven for a few minutes.

FISH SOUP

SOTO IKAN

4 cups water
1 medium onion
1 large carrot
315 g (10 oz) fish trimmings (bones, heads, etc)
10 cm (4 inch) piece lemon grass
½ teaspoon turmeric powder
1 heaped teaspoon chilli powder
2 large potatoes
1¼ cups thin coconut milk
125 g (¼ lb) transparent vermicelli .
100 g (3½ oz) white fish fillets
salt
pepper
1 fresh red chilli, thinly sliced

Bring water to the boil. Peel onion and chop roughly. Scrape carrot and slice. Add vegetables to the pot and boil for 10 minutes. Toss in fish trimmings, lemon grass, turmeric and chilli powder and simmer on moderate heat for 20 minutes. Add diced potato and cook for a further 20 minutes.

Strain through a coarse wire strainer. Pick out all fish bones and return soup to the pot. Pour in coconut milk, add vermicelli and diced fish fillets and stir over moderate heat until noodles are softened. Adjust seasonings to taste. Garnish with sliced chilli.

CHICKEN SOUP

SOTO AYAM

500 g (1 lb) chicken
2 medium onions
3 cloves garlic
1½ teaspoons coriander, ground
1 teaspoon turmeric powder
8 candlenuts, ground
½ teaspoon dried shrimp paste
3 tablespoons oil
salt
white pepper
60 g (2 oz) celery leaves, chopped
½ teaspoon tamarind
60 g (2 oz) cabbage, shredded
60 g (2 oz) beanshoots
4 cups water
60 g (2 oz) thin rice vermicelli
spring onions, chopped
fresh coriander sprigs

Cut chicken into several pieces. Put in a saucepan and cover with water. Peel and chop onions. Pound onion, garlic, coriander, turmeric, candlenuts and shrimp paste. Heat 1 tablespoon oil and fry ground seasonings for 4 minutes. Add to the chicken. Season with salt and pepper, add chopped celery leaves and simmer, covered, until chicken is tender.

Add tamarind, stir and continue to simmer for a few minutes. Remove pieces of chicken, strain stock, then return chicken and stock to pan.

Heat 2 tablespoons oil and fry cabbage and beanshoots lightly. Bring water to the boil in a large sauce-pan, add salt and vermicelli and cook till tender. Add vermicelli and fried vegetables to the chicken stock and heat through.

Garnish with chopped spring onions and coriander.

MIXED VEGETABLE SOUP

SAYUR CAMPUR

90 g (3 oz) beans, sliced
100 g (3½ oz) cabbage, chopped
2 cakes soft beancurd
1 large tomato
1 medium carrot
1 large onion
2 cloves garlic
1 tablespoon oil
1 *daun salam* or bay leaf
1 cm (½ inch) piece fresh ginger, shredded
½ teaspoon white pepper
2 teaspoons salt
1 teaspoon tamarind
8 cups chicken or beef stock
100 g (3½ oz) transparent vermicelli
dry fried onion (see page 125)
fresh coriander leaves, chopped

Wash vegetables. Cut beancurd into 1 cm (½ inch) dice. Slice tomato, scrape and slice carrot. Peel and chop onion and garlic and fry in oil till soft. Add *daun salam* or bay leaf, ginger, pepper, salt and tamarind and cook for 2 minutes.

Bring stock or water to boil in a large saucepan, add fried seasonings and all vegetables. Simmer for 15 minutes, then add noodles and heat through until softened.

Garnish with fried onion and chopped coriander.

KIDNEY BEAN SOUP

SAYUR ASAM KACANG MERAH

315 (10 oz) kidney beans
2 teaspoons salt
6 cups water or beef stock
1 medium onion
3 cloves garlic
1 tablespoon oil
2 teaspoons chilli powder
1 fresh red or green chilli
½ teaspoon dried shrimp paste
1 teaspoon brown sugar
2 teaspoons salt
½ teaspoon white pepper
100 g (3½ oz) beef
4 candlenuts, ground
⅓ cup boiling water
2 teaspoons tamarind
2 tablespoons chopped fresh coriander leaf

Soak beans overnight, then boil until soft in salted water or beef stock.

Chop onion and garlic finely. Heat vegetable oil and fry onion and garlic until golden. Add chilli powder, sliced red or green chilli, shrimp paste, sugar, salt and pepper. Fry for 3 minutes.

Chop beef into small dice or very thin strips and fry for 5 minutes with the seasonings. Stir in ground candlenuts. Add to the beans and stock and bring to the boil. Pour boiling water over tamarind and strain liquid into the soup. Add coriander and boil for 5 minutes.

If soup is too thick, stir in a little more water or stock before serving.

PEANUT CRISPS

REMPEYEK

Makes 30.

155 g (5 oz) peanuts
100 g (3½ oz) rice flour
2 tablespoons cornflour
⅓ cup warm water, or more
1 small onion
2 cloves garlic
3 teaspoons salt
2 teaspoons coriander, ground
1 heaped teaspoon chilli powder
½ cup boiling water
oil for deep frying

Roast peanuts, rub skins off and crush lightly. Mix rice flour, cornflour and warm water. Chop onion and garlic finely and add to the batter. Season with salt, coriander and chilli powder. Beat well, then pour in boiling water and beat to a smooth batter. Stand for 10 minutes. Stir in roasted peanuts and blend thoroughly.

Heat oil to smoking point in a shallow pan. Drop in a tablespoonful of the mixture and cook to a golden brown to test consistency of batter. Remove from oil and drain well. The cooked crisp should have a light, lacy appearance. If not, add a little more liquid to the batter, and cook the remaining crisps.

RICE IN BANANA LEAVES

LONTONG

500 g (1 lb) short grain rice
12 pieces banana leaf or aluminium foil, about 20 cm
   (8 inches) square
string or strong cotton
2 tablespoons sweet soya sauce
2 tablespoons dry fried onion flakes (see page 125)

Wash rice and wrap loosely in banana leaves into rolls about 8 cm (3 inches) long and 4 cm (1½ inches) in diameter. Tie securely. Cook in boiling salted water for 2 hours.

Cut open wrapping and serve hot with a sprinkling of sweet soya sauce and fried onion flakes.

Foil wrapping is an acceptable substitute for banana leaf, but the rice will have a less interesting flavour.

Serve Lontong in place of boiled rice with main courses.

Indonesian Vegetable Salad (recipe page 124).

PRAWN FRITTERS

2 eggs, beaten
1 teaspoon baking powder
75 g (2½ oz) plain flour
salt
pepper
3 spring onions, finely chopped
250 g (½ lb) peeled raw prawns, finely chopped
oil for deep frying

Make a batter with eggs, baking powder and flour. Season with salt and pepper and stir in chopped spring onion and prawns. Beat thoroughly.

Heat oil in a shallow pan and fry spoonfuls of the batter until golden brown and cooked through.

Drain on absorbent paper and serve either hot or cold as a side dish or appetiser.

SWEET CORN FRITTERS

BREGEDEL JAGUNG

440 g (14 oz) can whole kernel sweet corn
5 spring onions
2 cloves garlic
salt
pepper
2 eggs
75 g (2½ oz) plain flour
1½ teaspoons baking powder
100 g (3½ oz) cooked shrimps, chopped (optional)
2 tablespoons celery, finely chopped
oil for deep frying

Drain corn and crush lightly. Mince spring onions and garlic and mix with corn, salt and pepper.

Beat eggs lightly. Sift on flour and baking powder and stir in corn mixture, shrimps and celery. Stir thoroughly with a wooden spoon until batter is well mixed.

Heat oil in a shallow pan and drop in heaped teaspoonsful of the batter, several at a time. Cook to a deep golden brown.

Lift out and drain on absorbent paper. Serve hot or cold.

BANANA FRITTERS

PISANG GORENG

2 tablespoons sugar
2 eggs
100 g (3½ oz) plain flour
½ cup water
4 large bananas, ripe but firm
oil for deep frying

Beat sugar and eggs and blend in flour and enough water to form a smooth batter, not too thick. Beat thoroughly then let stand for 20 minutes.

Slice bananas diagonally. Coat lightly with batter and fry in hot oil until golden brown. Lift out and drain on absorbent paper. Serve hot or cold.

Pieces of pineapple, jackfruit or apple may also be prepared in this way. For variety, roll fritters in toasted coconut or serve with hot sugar syrup.

COCONUT CUSTARD WITH RICE

SERIKAYA KETAN

315 g (10 oz) glutinous rice
2¼ cups thin coconut milk
½ cup water
6 eggs
¾ cup thick coconut milk
1 tablespoon brown sugar
1 teaspoon salt
125 g (¼ lb) palm sugar or brown sugar
water

Wash rice, drain and put into a saucepan with thin coconut milk and water. Bring to the boil, cover, turn heat down and simmer until rice is tender.

Beat eggs lightly and stir in thick coconut milk, sugar and salt. Pour rice pudding into a 1¾ litre capacity (about 3 pints) ovenproof dish and top with the egg and coconut milk batter. Steam over a saucepan of boiling water, or cook in a moderate oven (180°C/350°F/Gas Mark 4) standing the dish in a tray of water. Cook until firm.

Allow to cool then chill well. Serve with sugar syrup made by boiling palm sugar or brown sugar together with water.

FRUIT BASKET

1 large papaya (pawpaw)
2 bananas
1 wedge of watermelon
1 mango
1 *salak*, hard green pear, or apple
4 thin slices pineapple
lemon or lime juice
1 tablespoon brown sugar

Remove two sections from the top half of the papaya to form a basket with handle along the centre. Scoop out seeds. Carefully scoop out the papaya flesh with a melon baller.

Slice other fruit or cut into cubes. Arrange fruit and papaya balls attractively in the basket. Sprinkle with lemon or lime juice and brown sugar and chill before serving.

Serve with cream or thick sweetened coconut milk. For extra flavour add a splash of white rum.

ICED COCONUT WATER

lime juice
syrup made with white sugar and water
coconut water from green coconuts
shaved ice
white rum (optional)
green coconut shells

Mix one part each of lime juice and sugar syrup to four parts of coconut water. Pour into the coconut shells and add a dash of rum (if used). Decorate with flowers and twists of lime or lemon peel.

BANANA CAKES

Makes 24.

5 large bananas
100 g (3½ oz) coloured green pea flour *(tepong hoen kwe)* or substitute arrowroot and green food colouring
75 g (2½ oz) sugar, or to taste
pinch of salt
2½ cups thin coconut milk
1½ cups water
banana leaf or aluminium foil

Steam bananas in their skins for about 10 minutes until soft. Set aside to cool, then slice.

Put flour, sugar, and salt into a saucepan and add coconut milk and water. Bring to the boil, stirring continually, and simmer until the paste turns thick and begins to clear.

Cut banana leaf or foil into 15 cm (6 inch) squares and place a spoonful of the mixture on each. Add a slice of banana and top with a little more batter. Fold leaf or foil around the mixture to make a square shape. Tie with cotton or secure with toothpicks. Set aside to cool, then place in the refrigerator until set completely.

Serve wrapped or with the wrapper torn away at the top.

THE PHILIPPINES

It has been said that the best place to begin a discovery tour of the foods of the Far East is The Philippines, where the food is a magical mixture of East and West. Uniquely Filipino, it combines ideas from China, Thailand, Malaysia and Indonesia, and blends them with flair. It offers dishes that are unmistakably Spanish in origin. And in 'fast foods' it presents a range of delicious snacks and icecreams that put American hamburger stands and icecream parlours in the shade. In a single meal one might meet Sinigang (a sour dish of seafood or vegetables suggesting the tastes of Thailand) and Lumpia (paper-thin egg pancakes stuffed with shredded vegetables and cold meat, possibly adapted from the Popiah of Malaysia). Rice is the staple grain, though white bread is found on most Philippine tables, and one is likely to find a dish of such impeccable Spanish lineage as Paella, fragrant with saffron. Or there is Adobo (originally the Spanish *adobo* or stew), meat marinated in vinegar and cooked with masses of garlic and black pepper.

From the shallow waters surrounding the thousands of islands making up The Philippines come succulent seafoods. Local favourites include *lapu lapu,* a meaty white fish; *bangus* or 'milkfish', moist and white; and the tiger prawns, *sugpo,* almost as big as crayfish and just as flavourful.

For festive occasions — and there are plenty in a country embracing so many ethnic and religious backgrounds — Lechon (Roast Suckling Pig) is the focal point of the banquet highlighting the celebration. A whole piglet is stuffed with fragrant leaves and slowly turned over a charcoal fire, or cooked underground on hot coals, until the skin is crisp and dark and the meat mouthwateringly tender. The skin, *sitcharon,* is served separately and is considered a great delicacy; the meat is served with an almost-too-rich sauce made with pig's liver.

The banquet table groans under the weight of mounds of fresh fruits: pineapple, *atis* (custard apple), *belimbing* (star fruit), pomelos, guavas, persimmons, bananas, mangoes, and payayas of enormous size and superb flavour. The juice of the tiny citrus *calamansi* makes a refreshing drink for those who avoid alcohol; for those who don't, there is the light San Miguel beer, brewed in The Philippines and acclaimed world-wide by beer connoisseurs; and there are the more potent brews such as *tuba,* prepared from the sap of the coconut palm, *tapoy,* a fermented rice wine, and *basi,* a sweeter but equally powerful drink made from fermented sugarcane juice.

Merienda is a social custom peculiar, in Asia, to The Philippines. Served at about five in the evening, this post-siesta snack can take on the proportions of a full-scale meal with a variety of sweet and savoury cookies, sandwiches, small morsels of meat, tiny cakes made from fruit, rice and coconut, and plenty of delicious local coffee or steaming sweet chocolate.

Coconut palms grow in profusion all over the islands. The fruit is used extensively in cooking, while other parts of the palm are used to produce *tuba* as well as a stiff fabric and twine. A particular type of coconut harvested in The Philippines is the *makapuno,* which does not contain inside the shell the usual clear liquid, but which instead is filled with a sticky white flesh used for making jams, sweets and icecreams. The Philippines is renowned throughout the Far East for its superbly creamy icecream flavoured with such ingredients as pineapple, mango and banana — and with such unexpected ingredients as avocado pear, yam, cashew nut and (my favourite) *makapuno.*

Filipinos are renowned for their sweet tooth, and some kind of pudding, cake or biscuit is served at every meal. Once again their choice of unusual ingredients comes to the fore: Bibingka, a rice-flour pudding topped with a mild white cheese; rice flour mixed with mashed yam; salted duck eggs as a garnish for coconut and rice cakes; fresh fruits embedded in milky jellies — these are just a few of the local sweetmeats, and sidewalk stalls do a roaring trade in a hundred and one varieties. Indigenous fruits are also used to make wines and jams (the clear mango, payaya and pineapple jams are delicious, and only in India have I tasted their equal).

Like so much Southeast Asian food, that of The Philippines is made for serving out of doors. I have enjoyed preparing lunches on my roof garden or on a plant-filled balcony where I cooked some of the dishes in cast-iron pans over a charcoal fire and roasted a suckling pig on an improvised spit. The aromatic smoke, flowers, greenery and hazy heat provided the perfect setting for a long, lazy afternoon.

SOUR FISH WITH VEGETABLES

PAKSIW

500 g (1 lb) white fish fillets
1 tablespoon dried shrimps, soaked
75 g (2½ oz) canned or fresh bitter melon
1 small eggplant
2.5 cm (1 inch) piece fresh ginger
2-3 green chillies
¼ cup white wine vinegar
¾ cup fish stock or water
salt
1 teaspoon freshly ground black pepper

Cut fish into pieces about 6 cm (2½ inches) square. Drain shrimp, reserving liquid. Peel bitter melon and eggplant and cut into 2 cm (¾ inch) cubes. Slice ginger and green chillies thinly, removing seeds for milder flavour.

Put eggplant and bitter melon in a saucepan and arrange fish slices on top. Scatter on ginger and chilli and pour on vinegar, stock and shrimp liquid. Add salt and pepper and bring to the boil. Reduce heat and

Vegetable Salad Rolls (recipe page 136).

simmer until fish are tender.

Transfer to a serving dish and serve with rice or noodles.

STUFFED MILKFISH
RELLENONG BANGUS

750 g (1½ lb) milk fish (or pomfret, plaice, sole or
  other flat fish)
1 tablespoon light soya sauce
1½ tablespoons lemon juice
oil
1 onion, minced
4 cloves garlic, crushed
90 g (3 oz) fresh or frozen peas, cooked
1 small tomato, finely chopped
1½ teaspoons salt
½ teaspoon white pepper
1 egg, lightly beaten
tomato slices
lemon or lime slices

Slit fish open and clean thoroughly. Wash and wipe dry. Carefully cut away backbone. Mix soya sauce with lemon juice and pour over the fish. Marinate for 1 hour.

Heat a little oil in a frying pan and saute onion and garlic for 3 minutes. Add peas, remove from heat and stir in tomato, salt, pepper and egg. Stuff this mixture into the cavity of the fish and sew up carefully or secure with toothpicks.

Heat 2.5 cm (1 inch) oil in a large pan and fry fish until golden brown. Turn and fry other side. Skin should be very crisp and meat cooked through but not dry.

Lift out, drain and put on a serving plate surrounded with alternate slices of tomato and lemon or lime.

CRABS IN COCONUT CREAM

2 medium raw saltwater crabs
3 tablespoons grated fresh or desiccated coconut
¾ cup thick coconut milk
10 spring onions, minced
4 cloves garlic, crushed
2 slices fresh ginger, shredded
1 teaspoon salt
pinch of white pepper
2 fresh red chillies, thinly sliced
¾ cup thin coconut milk
½ teaspoon chilli powder
mint or fresh coriander sprigs

Drop crabs into a large pot of boiling, slightly salted water. Cook for 7 minutes, then remove and cool under running water. Remove flesh without breaking top shells. Crack open legs and extract meat. Clean shells, discarding inedible parts. Wash shells with salt water, dry and set aside.

Flake crab meat and mix with one-third of the thick coconut milk, grated or desiccated coconut, spring onion, garlic, ginger, salt and pepper. Fill crab shells with the mixture and scatter on sliced chilli.

Place shells, stuffing side upwards, in a wide sauce-pan. Pour on thin coconut milk, cover and cook gently for 5 minutes, then add remaining thick coconut milk. Season with a little more salt and pepper and add chilli powder. Simmer for a further 5 minutes. Do not allow to boil or sauce may curdle.

Remove crabs to a serving plate and pour on the coconut cream sauce. Garnish with sprigs of mint or coriander.

CHICKEN ADOBO

Adobo dishes, with the pungent flavour of garlic and vinegar, are popular throughout the Philippines. Early Spanish settlers to the Philippine islands introduced this and many other now traditional dishes into the Filipino cuisine.

1½ kg (3 lb) chicken
3 teaspoons salt
1 teaspoon black pepper
2 bay leaves
8-12 cloves garlic, crushed
¾ cup white vinegar
3 tablespoons oil

Clean chicken, rinse and wipe dry. Cut into large pieces and rub with salt and pepper. Put pieces into a deep saucepan and add bay leaves and crushed garlic. Pour on vinegar and marinate for 30 minutes.

Cook on moderate heat until chicken is tender, adding a little water or stock as liquid evaporates, to keep meat moist. When chicken is cooked, turn heat up for a few minutes to dry out any remaining liquid.

Pour oil into the pan and fry on high heat until chicken pieces are dark brown and crisp on the surface. Lift out and drain well before serving.

PRAWNS ADOBO
ADOBONG SUGPO

375 g (¾ lb) large raw prawns
2 cloves garlic, finely chopped
2½ tablespoons white vinegar
½ teaspoon black pepper
1 teaspoon salt
1 bay leaf
¾ cup water
3 tablespoons butter
1 rounded tablespoon plain flour
parsley, finely chopped

Peel and devein prawns, leaving heads and tails on. Mix garlic with vinegar, pepper, salt, bay leaf and water. Arrange prawns in a large saucepan and pour on the marinade. Cover and bring to the boil, then turn heat down and simmer for 3 minutes.

Lift out prawns with a slotted spoon and reduce sauce over high heat. Strain and set aside.

Melt 2 tablespoons of butter in a frying pan. Sprinkle on flour and stir over moderate heat until golden brown. Pour in strained liquid and beat briskly with a wire whisk until sauce is smooth and thick. Keep warm on low heat.

Melt remaining butter and fry prawns quickly on high heat, turning several times. Lift out and place on warmed serving dish. Coat with the sauce and garnish with parsley.

PORK ADOBO WITH COCONUT MILK

1 kg (2 lb) pork shoulder or leg
½ cup white vinegar
6 cloves garlic, crushed
1 teaspoon black peppercorns, crushed
3 teaspoons salt
½ cup beef or chicken stock
½ cup thick coconut milk
3 tablespoons vegetable oil

Cut pork into 5 cm (2 inch) cubes. Put into a large saucepan. Prepare a marinade of vinegar, garlic, pepper and salt and pour over pork. Marinate meat for 1 hour, turning occasionally.

Simmer over moderate heat until all liquid evaporates, then pour in stock a little at a time, simmering on low heat. Cook again until all liquid has evaporated and pork is slightly tender.

Pour in coconut milk and continue cooking on moderate heat until meat is tender and coconut milk completely absorbed into the meat. When pan is fairly dry add oil and fry until meat is deep brown and slightly crisp on the surface.

Note: If using stock cubes, add only 1 teaspoon salt.

BARBECUED SUCKLING PIG WITH LIVER SAUCE

LECHON

6-7 kg (12-15 lb) suckling pig
12 bay leaves
salt
black pepper
750 g (1½ lb) melted lard
2½ cups boiling water

Liver Sauce:
1 pigs liver
1½ cups water
1 whole head of garlic
4 tablespoons lard
¼ medium onion, minced
30 g (1 oz) dried white breadcrumbs
30 g (1 oz) sugar
salt to taste
¼ cup white vinegar
1 teaspoon black pepper

Have the butcher clean and shave the pig. Wash it well and reserve the liver for the sauce. Put bay leaves inside the cavity after sprinkling inside with salt and pepper. Sew up opening or secure with toothpicks or metal pins.

Rub salt and pepper well into the skin. Brush the pig generously with melted lard, then pour on boiling water, allowing the oily liquid to run off into a metal drip tray or baking tin.

Cover the pig with greased paper and roast in a moderate oven (190°C/375°F/Gas Mark 5) for approximately 4½ hours. Lift paper and baste frequently with the pan juices during cooking. When almost done, remove paper and turn oven temperature up very high to slightly crisp the skin.

Suckling pig may be barbecued if preferred. Prepare as above and secure on a heavy metal rotisserie over a charcoal fire. Slowly turn over the coals until meat is done. It should be tender but still quite pink. Cooking time will depend on the heat of the fire and the size of the piglet, but it should be around 4 hours. Brush with melted lard at 15-minute intervals to prevent the skin becoming too dry.

To prepare the sauce, place the liver in a roasting pan and roast until quite brown on the outside. Push the liver through a fine wire sieve or mince finely. Pour on water and strain minced liver and water through a sieve. Discard any coarse pieces of liver or sinew.

Mince garlic and saute in lard until soft. Add onions, saute for 2 minutes, then stir in breadcrumbs, sugar, salt and vinegar. Stir well, then blend in the liver paste and season with pepper. Simmer on moderate heat, stirring continually until sauce becomes quite thick. Check seasonings. Pour into a sauce bowl.

Slice suckling pig into thin pieces and serve with the sauce.

BAKED SPARE RIBS

1½ kg (3 lb) pork or beef spare ribs, trimmed
1 onion, quartered
2 tablespoons light soya sauce
½ teaspoon black pepper
2 teaspoons salt
4 tablespoons oil
2 tablespoons sugar
2 tablespoons dark soya sauce

Sauce:
4 tablespoons brown sugar
1½ teaspoons salt
3 tablespoons dark soya sauce
1 large onion, minced
2 cm (¾ inch) piece fresh ginger, minced

Separate ribs. Put into a very large saucepan with onion, light soya sauce, pepper and salt. Cover with water and boil for 45 minutes. Preheat oven to 190°C/375°F/Gas Mark 5. Drain boiled ribs well and arrange in a lightly oiled baking pan.

Mix oil, sugar and dark soya sauce, stirring to dissolve sugar. Brush ribs with the mixture and bake until crisp and dark. Brush with more of the liquid during cooking.

To prepare sauce, mix all ingredients in a small saucepan. Add enough water to make a thin sauce and bring to the boil. Cook for 5 minutes, or until the sauce thickens slightly.

Serve in several small bowls or pour over the baked ribs before serving.

BEEF TAPA

*This dish of crisply fried slivers of beef is served as a
snack or appetiser, particularly with Merienda.*

500 g (1 lb) beef (rump, sirloin, topside)
1 whole head garlic, crushed
1 cup white vinegar
1 tablespoon salt (or to taste)
2 teaspoons black peppercorns, freshly ground
60 g (2 oz) sugar

Slice beef paper thin. Mix all seasoning ingredients
together and stir until sugar dissolves. Arrange beef
slices in a wide flat pan and pour on the marinade.
Stand overnight, turning several times.

Lift out from the marinade, drain and arrange on a
tray. Put in the sun or in a very low oven to dry for a
whole day.

To cook, heat 2.5 cm (1 inch) oil in a large frying pan
and fry meat slices until dark and quite crisp. Turn
several times during cooking. Drain and serve hot or
warm.

BEEFSTEAK FILIPINO

6 tender steaks (rump or fillet)
½ teaspoon salt
¼ teaspoon black pepper
1½ tablespoons *calamansi* or lime juice
1 tablespoon light soya sauce
2 teaspoons sugar
2 tablespoons olive or vegetable oil
¼ medium onion, minced
3 cloves garlic, crushed
calamansi or lime wedges

Season steaks with salt and pepper. Marinate in a mixture of *calamansi* or lime juice, soya sauce and sugar for
30 minutes.

Heat oil in an iron frying pan, drain steaks and fry as
preferred. Remove to a warmed serving plate. Add garlic and onion to the pan and cook until soft. Pour in the
remaining marinade and bring to the boil.

Pour sauce over the steaks and garnish with wedges of
calamansi or lime.

NOODLES WITH MIXED MEAT AND VEGETABLES

PANCIT GUISADO

1 kg (2 lb) fresh egg noodles, or
    500 g (1 lb) dried noodles
oil
1 large onion, finely chopped
3 cloves garlic, crushed
2.5 cm (1 inch) piece fresh ginger, shredded
100 g (3½ oz) chicken meat, cooked and shredded
100 g (3½ oz) cooked shrimp
100 g (3½ oz) unsmoked ham or bacon, cooked and
    shredded
6 dried mushrooms, soaked in cold water for ½ hour

½ small head cabbage
3 tablespoons light soya sauce
¼ teaspoon white pepper
100 g (3½ oz) green or long beans, sliced
spring onions, chopped
fresh coriander leaves, chopped

Soak fresh or dried noodles in cold water.

Heat 2 tablespoons oil and fry onion, garlic and ginger for 3 minutes. Add chicken, shrimp and ham and
saute for 4 minutes. Lift out and set aside, keeping
warm.

Drain mushrooms and slice very thinly. Shred cabbage. Add mushroom and cabbage to the pan with a
little more oil if needed and fry for 3 minutes, adding
soya sauce, salt and pepper. Turn heat down and return
meat to pan. Cover and keep on very low heat until
needed.

Bring a little water to boil in a small saucepan and
boil beans until slightly tender, but still crisp. Drain
and add to meat and vegetables.

Drain cold water from noodles. Pour boiling water
onto fresh noodles and stand for 5 minutes, then drain.
If using dried noodles, cover with boiling water and
cook until tender but not too soft. Drain and rinse in
cold water. Drain again.

Heat 3 tablespoons oil in another frying pan and fry
noodles for 4 minutes, stirring continually. Transfer to
a serving dish.

Reheat meat and vegetables and spoon onto the
noodles. Garnish with spring onions and coriander
leaves.

Note: Reduce the amount by one-third or half if serving
with several other dishes.

BRAISED CAULIFLOWER AND ASSORTED VEGETABLES

3 dried black mushrooms, soaked in cold water for ½
    hour
2 tablespoons oil
2 cloves garlic, crushed
1 medium onion, minced
light soya sauce
pinch of monosodium glutamate (optional)
salt
250 g (½ lb) cauliflower, broken into sprigs
2 stalks celery, sliced
100 g (3½ oz) fresh or frozen peas, parcooked
3 tablespoons chicken stock
100 g (3½ oz) raw shrimps, peeled
cornflour (optional)

Drain mushrooms and slice thinly. Heat oil and fry
garlic and onion until soft, then add mushrooms and
saute for 3 minutes.

Stir in soya sauce, monosodium glutamate (if used)
and salt. Add cauliflower, celery and peas. Cook for 2
minutes on fairly high heat, then turn down slightly
and add stock. Braise until cauliflower softens. Thicken
sauce if necessary with a little cornflour mixed with cold
water.

Add shrimps and cook on moderate heat until pink

Prawns Adobo, and Stuffed Milkfish (recipes page 132).

and cooked through. If frozen peas are used, add at the same time as shrimps. Adjust seasoning and serve.

VEGETABLE SALAD ROLLS
LUMPIA

Lumpia Wrappers:
315 (10 oz) plain flour
155 g (5 oz) rice flour
1 tablespoon salt
1 tablespoon oil
3 cups water
2 eggs

24 lettuce leaves

Lumpia Filling:
1 tablespoon oil
1 small onion, minced
4 cloves garlic, crushed
125 g (¼ lb) green beans, sliced
2 small carrots, grated
155 g (5 oz) cabbage, shredded finely
1 small sweet potatoes, peeled and grated, or
    90 g (3 oz) thinly sliced palm hearts
100 g (3½ oz) pork, finely diced
¼ cup water
90 g (3 oz) raw shrimps, peeled and finely diced
light soya sauce
salt and pepper

Sauce:
4 tablespoons brown sugar
1½ tablespoons cornflour
1½ tablespoons dark soya sauce
1 teaspoon salt
2 cups beef stock
4 cloves garlic

To prepare wrappers, sift flour, rice flour and salt into a bowl. Beat in oil, water and eggs and beat for 2 minutes. Leave to stand for 1 hour.

To prepare filling, heat oil and fry onion and garlic until soft. Add all vegetables and saute for 2 minutes. Then add pork and stir on moderate heat for 6 minutes. Pour in water, cover and cook for 3 minutes.

Remove lid, add shrimps and season with soya sauce, salt and pepper to taste. Simmer, stirring, until liquid is evaporated and ingredients cooked through. Allow to cool before using.

To prepare the sauce, mix sugar, cornflour, soya sauce and salt in a small saucepan. Pour in stock and bring to a rapid boil. Cook over high heat, stirring frequently, until sauce thickens.

Peel and crush garlic and add to the sauce. Stir in and simmer for a further 2 minutes. Pour into one or two small sauce dishes.

To cook wrappers, heat a well oiled omelette pan and rub base with a paper towel. Pour in just enough prepared batter to thinly coat the pan. Swirl pan so it spreads as evenly as possible. Cook pancake on moderate heat until it can be easily lifted. Lift and turn. Cook other side to a light golden colour. Cook all batter

and stack prepared pancakes between pieces of grease-proof paper.

Wash lettuce leaves and dry thoroughly.

To prepare the salad rolls, line each pancake with a lettuce leaf. Spoon on a generous amount of the filling and roll up. Serve with the sauce.

PRAWNS IN VEGETABLE SOUP
SINIGANG NA SUGPO

6 raw tiger prawns, or 12 raw king prawns
7 cups water
1½ tablespoons tamarind, or
    juice of 2 lemons or limes
⅓ cup hot water
2 large tomatoes, quartered
185 g (6 oz) green beans, sliced
185 g (6 oz) cabbage, chopped
1 teaspoon white pepper
salt

Boil prawns in water for 10 minutes. Remove prawns on a slotted spoon and return stock to the heat to reduce to 4½ cups.

Soak tamarind in hot water for 15 minutes. Strain tamarind water or lemon or lime juice into the pot and add all vegetables. Bring to the boil and cook until tender.

Return prawns and season with pepper. Add salt to taste, and cook for another minute.

Chilli sauce, soya sauce or additional lemon or lime juice may be added, to taste.

SAVOURY SHRIMP SNACKS
UKOY

100 g (3½ oz) raw baby shrimps, peeled
2½ cups water
155 g (5 oz) plain flour
1½ teaspoons salt
2 teaspoons baking powder
2 eggs, beaten
½-1 teaspoon white pepper
1 clove garlic, crushed
6 spring onions, finely chopped
oil for deep frying

Boil shrimps in water for 3 minutes. Drain, reserving ¾ cup liquid.

Sift flour, salt and baking powder into a bowl. Add beaten eggs and ½ cup of shrimp liquid and season with pepper, garlic and spring onions. Beat briskly. Chop shrimp and stir into the batter. Beat again. The batter should be of dropping consistency. If needed, add a little more of the reserved stock.

Heat oil to smoking point and drop spoonsful of the batter into the hot oil. Lower heat slightly. Cook until the cakes rise to the surface, then cook for a further 2 minutes on moderate heat. Lift out and drain.

Serve with dips of vinegar, soya sauce or salt and pepper.

COCONUT RICE CAKE

BIBINGKA

¾ cup thick coconut milk
1 1/8 cups thin coconut milk
220 g (7 oz) rice flour
1 teaspoon salt
250 g (½ lb) brown sugar
¼ teaspoon anise or caraway seed, powdered

Mix ¼ cup thick coconut milk with thin coconut milk, rice flour and salt. Beat until batter is smooth. Cook in a double saucepan until batter is very thick, stirring frequently. Add a little more coconut milk if the mixture becomes too thick. Stir in all but 30 g (1 oz) sugar and beat well.

Grease a 23 cm (9 inch) baking tin and pour in the batter. Pour remaining thick coconut milk on top and sprinkle on remaining brown sugar and anise or caraway seed powder.

Cover with foil and bake in a moderate oven (180°C/350°F/Gas Mark 4) until firm. Cooking time is approximately 25 minutes.

Remove foil and cook until top is lightly browned, or place under a hot grill to brown top.

Serve either hot or cold.

BANANA ROLLS

3 medium very ripe bananas
6 Lumpia wrappers (see recipe page 136, using ¼ of mixture)
2 teaspoons white sesame seeds
2 tablespoons sugar
oil for deep frying

Syrup:
½ cup water
155 g (5 oz) sugar

Put bananas in a preheated moderate oven or under moderate grill and cook until tender (about 12 minutes). Turn frequently if cooking under grill.

Peel and cut into long, thin strips. Put several pieces on each Lumpia wrapper, sprinkle with sugar and sesame seeds and roll up, tucking ends in securely.

Heat oil to smoking point, lower heat slightly and deep fry until golden. Lift out and drain on absorbent paper.

Dissolve sugar in water and bring to the boil in a small saucepan. Simmer until syrup becomes slightly sticky.

Pour over fried banana rolls before serving, or serve in a separate dish to use as a dip. Banana Rolls may be served without the syrup or with a generous sprinkling of white sugar.

Note: Commercially prepared spring roll skins can be used instead of Lumpia wrappers.

THREE-COLOUR CAKE

SAPIN SAPIN

155 g (5 oz) yam or sweet potato, peeled and diced
155 g (5 oz) rice flour
3½ cups coconut milk
315 g (10 oz) brown sugar
green food colouring
red food colouring
grated fresh or desiccated coconut

Cook yam or sweet potato in a little water until soft. Drain and mash.

Combine rice flour, coconut milk and sugar and beat well. Divide batter into three portions. To one portion mix in cooked yam or sweet potato and colour it light green. Colour one portion pink and leave remaining portion white.

Pour pink portion into a lightly greased 20 cm (8 inch) square cake tin, about 4 cm (1½ inches) deep. Place over a steamer or saucepan of boiling water. Lay a sheet of greaseproof paper on top and steam until set.

Pour on green mixture and steam until this layer is set, then add white layer and cook until the whole cake is firm.

Toast coconut lightly under a moderate grill. Sprinkle onto cake, pressing on gently with the fingers.

Leave to cool, then chill and when quite firm cut into squares, or use a decorative cake or pastry cutter to cut into attractive pieces.

FRUIT JELLY

GULAMAN

3½ teaspoons gelatine, or 2 teaspoons *agar agar* powder
1½ cups lukewarm water
155 g (5 oz) sugar
250 g (½ lb) diced fresh fruit (pineapple, banana, mango, apple, etc.)
⅓ cup fresh milk

Bring ⅓ cup water to the boil and sprinkle gelatine powder over it. Dissolve, then pour into lukewarm water, stirring thoroughly.

If using *agar agar* dissolve in water with sugar and bring to the boil. Cook for 2-3 minutes then pour a little into the prepared moulds as described below and keep remainder warm.

Stir sugar into gelatine and water and when completely dissolved pour a little into lightly greased individual jelly moulds of about ⅔ cup capacity. A layer of about 3 mm (1/8 inch) will suffice.

Allow to set, then arrange fruit in the moulds and pour on more of the clear jelly. Set, then place in the refrigerator to chill.

Whisk milk into remaining jelly mixture and when jellies are hard in the moulds pour a little milky jelly onto each. Chill until set.

Turn out onto chilled saucers to serve.

CHINA

Whatever my fondness for other types of Asian food, I have to regard Chinese as my outright favourite — its very greatness demands that it should be so. In Hongkong, where one has access to many of the world's best Chinese restaurants, Cantonese food predominates, but other regional cuisines are well represented: Shanghai, rich and saucy; Peking, sophisticated and very satisfying; Szechwan, with its fiery flavours; and the lesser-known but highly distinctive Chiu Chow and Hunan styles as well as the earthy Hakka. We have a rule in our household that each week we must visit one restaurant that is new to us. This has proved a most enlightening exercise, and I am continually surprised to discover that every restaurant offers at least one dish entirely new to me, such is the endless variety of this food.

One aspect of Chinese cooking that always delights me is the unique blending of such different ingredients as sea scallops with kidney, birds' nests with quail eggs, crisp green vegetables with crabmeat, chicken with ham, or fish with asparagus. Conventional Western concepts of cooking and mixing ingredients have no place in this cuisine, which combines meats, seafoods and vegetables in infinite variations on the principles of harmony and contrast. Each dish, and the meal as a whole, will have a balance of texture, taste and colour with no main ingredient repeated. Smooth textures accompany crisp, sweet flavours complement savoury, wet goes with dry, rich follows bland, and colours blend beautifully; the cooking, seasoning and garnish highlight the main taste, but never overshadow it.

When rice is part of the meal, it is almost invariably polished white rice (usually of the short or medium-grain type), except for dishes requiring the starchy glutinous 'sticky' rice. Methods of preparation differ greatly, but the most common is the absorption method (see page 8). Excess rice can be stored in the freezer and will reheat very successfully in a wire strainer over a pot of boiling water, or it can be used for fried rice.

Unmistakably the most important seasonings are soya sauce (which comes in light and dark types), ginger and spring onions. These are used repeatedly in Chinese cooking and cannot be omitted. Salted black beans, a range of sweet and salty bean pastes, a fragrant spice mix called 'Chinese five-spice powder' and the aromatic star anise also provide unique and distinctive flavours. Chinese rice wine is used frequently, with the light-coloured Shaoshing being suitable for cooking and for drinking (when it is served warm). A pungent brown vinegar, nutty sesame oil, a thick cream-coloured sesame paste and a hot mustard are invaluable as both condiments and seasonings. Fresh coriander leaves (known as 'Chinese parsley') look like overgrown parsley and have a distinct flavour that greatly complements seafoods, soups and meatballs.

With Chinese food one is not restricted to a single choice of dish, but can eat from all the dishes brought to the table. This makes it not only a friendly way to eat, but allows one to enjoy a full range of tastes and in-gredients within one meal. The basic etiquette in serving and eating is straightforward. In most cases several dishes, selected according to the rules of harmony and contrast, are brought to the table at the same time. Each person helps himself using chopsticks or the serving utensils provided. Soup is served at some time during the meal, but never at the beginning unless it has special significance for the occasion or is a culinary masterpiece that must be shown off to advantage — the best sharkfin soup, for instance, is often served first so that it may be fully appreciated.

In everyday meals rice and noodles are served with the other dishes, tea is served and sipped throughout, and there are fruit and a small dessert, for the sweet tooth, to finish. On more formal occasions the rigid etiquette calls for toasts to the guest of honour, host or the food between courses; and one must help neighbouring guests to choice servings from the dishes, which appear in a carefully balanced order. Noodles and rice are not seen until all the main dishes are finished, and then small cakes and fruit are served with cups of tea, which is not usually drunk during such a meal. In Hongkong a good brandy has become the accepted banquet beverage and is an appropriate choice, being, I am told, similar to the best rice wines served on the mainland in the old days. Cold lager beers are also excellent with Chinese food, and light, very slightly sweet white wines are becoming a popular accompaniment; they are refreshing and do not cloy the tastebuds. My choice is still Chinese tea, of which I have several favourites that I drink in great quantity during every meal.

Chinese cooking is best done on gas, for the heat can be increased or decreased without delay — an important factor in fast cooking methods. Much of the cooking is done in the curved shallow *wok;* its shape allows for maximum heat distribution over the cooking area. Food is handled in this pan with wooden chopsticks and the *charn,* a flat miniature shovel. Stir-frying entails cooking on very high heat with a minimum of oil and keeping the ingredients constantly moving to prevent burning. This method quickly seals in all the natural goodness and flavour of any food and is a most respected technique. Deep-frying is also done in the *wok* with plenty of vegetable or peanut oil, which is brought to 'smoking point' (when the oil has a smoky haze over it and a vapour is rising). Foods to be fried are tipped into the oil, stirred with chopsticks to prevent the pieces sticking together, and when done are lifted out on a large perforated metal ladle. Fried foods are usually quickly re-fried at high temperature, before serving, for extra crispness.

Steaming, a popular and healthful cooking method, can be done in the *wok* with the plate of food standing on a bamboo or metal rack over the water. The large deep-sided *wok* lid keeps the steam in and allows plenty of room for it to flow up and around the food being cooked. *Dim sum* and other small steamed foods are cooked in bamboo baskets stacked over a pot of bubbling water.

A selection of Dim Sum (recipes pages 140-143).

The Chinese cleaver is a useful multi-purpose tool used with a chopping board of soft wood. Though large and quite heavy, this 'chopper' can be used for the most intricate and delicate preparation of meat, vegetables and seafoods, yet will happily hack its way through strong bones. Chopping is done by holding the food to be chopped with the fingertips of the left hand and bringing the blade down sharply and squarely on the food. Repeated chopping will make minced foods, which can be quickly reduced to virtually a mashed texture by smashing with the flat side of the cleaver (this is ideal for meatballs). Slicing and shredding are done with a smooth stroke down and away from the body, rather like a light sawing action. The blade of the cleaver should always be kept very sharp.

In most recipes the preparation of ingredients far exceeds cooking time. Everything should therefore be ready before cooking begins, for there is no time to stop halfway to prepare additional ingredients. Good Chinese food, particularly stir-fried dishes, should be cooked quickly and served at once.

There are no absolute rules about the stage in a meal at which certain dishes should be served; the important thing is that the order should be stimulating for the diners. If you were serving Peking Duck, the meal would be spoiled if it were presented first to be followed by a comparatively bland succession of dishes — there should be highlights at various points throughout the meal so that appetites and interest do not flag.

Foods are served on flat oval plates, with deep dishes for soups or dishes with a lot of sauce. Each place should have a rice bowl, a small soup bowl and porcelain spoon, a bowl for eating from (with a saucer underneath), a tea cup, chopsticks, and one or two small sauce dishes containing soya, mustard and chilli sauces. Northen Chinese often eat from a small plate instead of a bowl, but rice will always be served in a bowl as it is difficult (some would say impossible) to eat from a plate if one is using chopsticks. All food should be cut into manageable pieces, or cooked until so tender that it can be broken up with chopsticks. Some dishes, such as Peking Duck with Pancakes or Pigeon in Lettuce Leaves, may be eaten with the fingers and require finger bowls at the table.

SPICED SALT

4 tablespoons table salt
½ teaspoon Chinese five-spice powder

Roast salt in a dry pan on moderate heat until lightly coloured, stirring continually to prevent burning. Remove from heat and leave to cool slightly, then stir in Chinese five-spice powder. Cool, then transfer to a jar. Close jar and shake to mix well. Serve with fried seafoods or poultry, and steamed dishes.

PEPPER AND SALT POWDER

4 tablespoons table salt
1 teaspoon finely ground black peppercorns

Roast salt in a dry pan on moderate heat until lightly coloured. Stir in pepper and heat through briefly. Store in a sealed jar.

ASSORTED MEAT PLATTER

8 thin slices braised beef steak
8 thin slices Chinese roast pork
8 thin slices pressed boiled pork or sausage
90 g (3 oz) boiled chicken, shredded
90 g (3 oz) braised chicken livers, thinly sliced
90 g (3 oz) jelly fish or vermicelli sheets, soaked and shredded
10 spears canned asparagus
salt and pepper powder
sweet bean paste or plum sauce

Arrange the meat and liver in a pattern around a serving dish. Place two spears of asparagus between each different lot of meat. Sprinkle shredded jelly fish or vermicelli with sesame oil and pile into the centre.

Serve with dips of salt and pepper powder and sweet bean paste or plum sauce.

COLD CHICKEN WITH SESAME AND MUSTARD SAUCES

500 g (1 lb) cooked chicken breast
90 g (3 oz) processed jelly fish or vermicelli sheets
2 tablespoons sesame paste
2 teaspoons sesame oil
lemon juice or white vinegar
sugar
salt
2 tablespoons hot mustard powder
3 teaspoons oil
3 teaspoons chilli oil (optional)
3 spring onions, shredded

Slice chicken thinly, then cut into shreds. Shred jelly fish (if used) and drop into boiling water to soften. It may be necessary to boil it briefly to soften, but this will depend on the type used. Soak vermicelli sheets in warm water until softened. Drain well and shred.

Mix sesame paste with sesame oil and add lemon juice or vinegar, sugar and salt to taste. Blend in enough water to make a reasonably thin sauce. Mix mustard with oil and water to make a second thin sauce.

Arrange jelly fish or shredded vermicelli on a serving dish and pile the chicken on top. Sprinkle with chilli oil (if used) and shredded spring onions. Pour on the two sauces or serve them separately in small jugs.

STEAMED SPINACH DUMPLINGS

Makes 30.

Pastry:
125 g (¼ lb) plain flour
⅓-½ cup boiling water
2 tablespoons sesame oil

Filling:
155 g (5 oz) spinach
2 tablespoons sesame oil
1 teaspoon salt
½ teaspoon sugar

¼ teaspoon white pepper
1 teaspoon dark soya sauce

Sieve flour into a mixing bowl and make a well in the centre. Pour in boiling water and stir with a wooden spoon until all water is incorporated. Leave to cool slightly, then transfer to a floured board and knead for 12 minutes until soft and pliable. The more time spent in kneading, the thinner the pastry can be rolled. Cover pastry ball with a damp cloth and set aside.

Wash and dry spinach and chop very finely. Add seasoning ingredients and mix thoroughly.

Roll pastry into a long sausage about 4 cm (1½ inches) in diameter. Cut slices about 0.5 cm (¼ inch) thick. Roll each out very thinly into a circle. Brush one side with sesame oil and place a small mound of the spinach filling in the centre. Fold into a crescent, and press edges together and pinch to seal. Arrange on a piece of greaseproof paper in a steamer and cook over rapidly boiling water for 20 minutes.

PRAWN DUMPLINGS

HAR GOW

Makes 30.

Pastry:
See Steamed Spinach Dumplings (page 140)

Filling:
100 g (3½ oz) raw prawns or shrimp
30 g (1 oz) canned water chestnuts
1 small onion
1 clove garlic (optional)
2 teaspoons oil
1 teaspoon soya sauce
½ teaspoon salt
pinch of white pepper
2 egg whites
cornflour
1 egg, beaten

Prepare wrapper pastry and set aside. Mince prawns and water chestnuts. Mince onion with garlic and fry in oil for about 2 minutes until soft. Allow to cool, then mix with prawn and water chestnut paste and season with soya sauce, salt and white pepper. Bind with egg whites and a little cornflour.

Roll out pastry into thin rounds and place a spoonful of the prawn paste on each. Fold over to form crescent shapes and pinch edges together. Seal with a little beaten egg. Place on a piece of greaseproof paper in a bamboo steamer and steam over rapidly boiling water for 15 minutes. Serve hot.

MEAT DUMPLINGS

SHAO MAI

Makes 24.

Pastry:
1 package frozen or fresh *shao mai* wrappers

Filling:
2 large leaves Chinese cabbage
45 g (1½ oz) canned bamboo shoots
60 g (2 oz) lean pork
2½ teaspoons light soya sauce
pinch of salt
white pepper
pinch of sugar
2 teaspoons cornflour
fresh coriander leaves, finely chopped
crab roe, crumbled

Leave pastry to thaw. Wash cabbage and bamboo shoots and chop very finely. Mince pork and mix with cabbage, bamboo shoots, soya sauce, Chinese wine, salt, pepper and sugar. Bind with cornflour.

Place a spoonful of filling in the centre of each *shao mai* wrapper then gather the sides of the wrapper up to form into a small cup shape. The top should be open. Crimp at the sides to form a slight 'waist' and flatten bottoms to stand upright. Decorate the tops with a little chopped coriander and crab roe. Place in a steamer on a sheet of oiled greaseproof paper and steam over rapidly boiling water for 25 minutes.

SPICY PORK BUNS

Dough:
750 g (1½ lb) plain flour
125 g (¼ lb) sugar
1 tablespoon baking powder
2 tablespoons melted lard
¾ cup water

Filling:
500 g (1 oz) Chinese roast pork
1 cup water
1 teaspoon cornflour
3 teaspoons potato flour (or extra cornflour)
3 teaspoons dark soya sauce
1 tablespoon oyster sauce
pinch of salt
1½ tablespoons sugar
2 cloves garlic, minced
2 spring onions, minced
30 g (1 oz) pork fat, diced
2 tablespoons oil

Sieve flour into a basin and add sugar and baking powder. Make a well in the centre and pour in melted lard. Mix lightly into the flour, then add water and work to a smooth dough. Knead for 8 minutes, then cover with a damp cloth and leave to rise for 30 minutes.

Slice roast pork then cut into small pieces. Put into a saucepan with all filling ingredients except spring onions, pork fat and oil and simmer on low heat for 10 minutes.

Steam pork fat for 10 minutes, and add to the roast pork mixture with spring onions. Fry the mixture in oil on moderate heat for 2 minutes.

Roll the dough out into a long sausage and cut off pieces about 5 cm (2 inches) long. Flatten with the fingers and fill with a spoonful of the mixture. Pull the dough up around the filling and twist the joins to seal

well. Put a piece of plain paper on the joined part of each bun and place paper-side down in a steamer. Cover and leave to rise for a further 10 minutes, then steam over high heat for 20-25 minutes. Serve hot in the steaming baskets.

MEATBALLS ON SPINACH

Makes 24.

500 g (1 lb) beef steak
45 g (1½ oz) pork fat
2 spring onions
4 sprigs fresh coriander
½ teaspoon grated lemon rind
2 teaspoons salt
2 tablespoons dark soya sauce
pinch of white pepper
1½ teaspoons sesame oil
1 teaspoon bicarbonate of soda
3 tablespoons cornflour
3 tablespoons water
24 spinach leaves
2 tablespoons vegetable oil

Mince beef finely with pork fat, spring onions and coriander. Blend in lemon rind, salt, soya sauce, pepper, sesame oil and baking soda and work to a smooth paste. Add cornflour and water and knead until smooth. Form into 24 balls. Leave for 15 minutes.

Wash spinach leaves and arrange on a fireproof plate. Sprinkle on half the oil and place meatballs on top. Sprinkle with remaining oil and place over a steamer to cook for about 12 minutes. Serve with hot mustard.

SPRING ROLLS

Makes 24.

Wrappers:
220 g (7 oz) plain flour
3 eggs
1 teaspoon salt

Sift flour and salt into a mixing bowl and make well in the centre. Break in eggs and stir until the mixture begins to amalgamate. Remove to a floured board and knead gently. When all flour is worked in, knead strongly for several minutes. The more the dough is worked, the more elastic it will be, thereby making the pastry thinner and flakier. Roll out into a long loaf and cut into several pieces to make rolling out easier. While one piece is being rolled, cover remaining pieces with a damp cloth.

Dust a board with flour and with a floured rolling pin press down as hard as possible during rolling to make the pastry paper thin and transparent enough to see the board through. Take care not to break the pastry. Cut into 15 cm (6 inch) squares, cover with a damp cloth and prepare remaining dough. Cut each square into 2 triangular-shaped pieces.

Frozen wrappers may be used for convenience.

Filling:
100 g (3½ oz) minced pork, lightly fried

8 dried Chinese mushrooms, soaked
6 canned water chestnuts, chopped
1 tablespoon finely chopped fresh coriander leaves
4 spring onions, minced
30 g (1 oz) canned bamboo shoot, finely chopped
1 small carrot, grated
45 g (1½ oz) beanshoots
45 g (1½ oz) raw shrimps
1 teaspoon sugar
1½ tablespoons dark soya sauce
1 clove garlic, crushed (optional)
3 teaspoons cornflour
2 teaspoons salt
2 tablespoons oil

Drain mushrooms, remove stems and shred finely. Shred spring onion. Wash beanshoots and steep in boiling water for 2 minutes. Drain and cool. Peel shrimps and rinse. Mix all ingredients except oil in a large bowl. Heat oil and saute filling for 2-3 minutes. Allow to cool completely.

To fill spring rolls, place a heaped tablespoon of the filling on the wrapper. Turn in two ends, fold over and stick last end down with a little water. If using frozen wrappers start down one corner, fold over the filling, fold in two sides, then stick the last flap down with water.

Heat oil for deep frying and fry spring rolls, several at a time, until golden brown. Drain on absorbent paper. Return to the oil briefly before serving to crisp. Serve with soya sauce.

GREEN ONION PASTRIES

Makes 6.

500 g (1 lb) plain flour
¾ cup boiling water
cold water as needed
3 teaspoons salt
1 tablespoon oil
1½ tablespoons sesame oil
20 spring onions
oil for shallow frying

Sieve flour into mixing bowl and make a well in the centre. Pour in boiling water and mix with a wooden spoon until blended as much as possible. Leave to cool, then gradually work in cold water to make a firm dough which should be neither dry nor sticky. Add salt and knead for 3 minutes. Cover with a damp cloth and let stand for 10 minutes, then knead for a futher 3 minutes.

Roll pastry out to about 0.5 cm (¼ inch) thickness and cut into six rectangles. Brush one side with a mixture of oil and sesame oil. Finely chop spring onions and scatter over the cakes. Fold the pieces over to make a tube shape, then twist into a round cake. Roll out flat.

Heat a little oil in a large frying pan and put in several cakes. Cover and cook on moderate heat until golden brown underneath. Turn and cook other side. Shake pan sharply several times during cooking to make the cakes puff up slightly. Remove from the pan, drain and wrap in a cloth until ready to serve. Cut into quarters and serve on a warmed plate.

Eggplant Szechwan Style (recipe page 164), and Ma Po Beancurd (recipe page 166). 143

STEAMED BREAD CRESCENTS

750 g (1½ lb) plain flour
1 tablespoon baking powder
45 g (1½ oz) sugar
1 tablespoon melted lard
¾-1 cup warm water
sesame oil

Sieve flour and baking powder into a bowl. Mix sugar with melted lard and ¾ cup water. Pour into the flour and mix with a chopstick. Gradually add additional water as needed to make a smooth dough. Knead until it is very smooth and elastic. Cover and leave for 25 minutes.

Roll out into a sausage about 3 cm (1¼ inches) in diameter. Cut into 1 cm (½ inch) slices. Brush one side with sesame oil and fold that side over to form a half circle. Place on damp cloth in a steamer and steam over high heat for about 15 minutes, or until light and springy to the touch.

Serve with fried chicken or other dry dishes. Make these crescents larger to serve with Honey Baked Ham. When cooked, prise open with the fingers and insert several slices of ham.

STEAMED HONEY SPONGE

30 g (1 oz) honey
185 g (6 oz) butter
100 g (3½ oz) sugar
5 eggs
1 cup fresh milk
375 g (¾ lb) plain flour
2 teaspoons baking powder

Mix honey with butter, then blend in a quarter of the sugar. Beat until light and smooth. Separate eggs. Beat yolks into butter mixture gradually with remaining sugar. Beat until smooth. Add milk and sift on flour with baking powder. Fold in. Leave to stand for 15 minutes.

Whip egg whites until fairly stiff and fold into the mixture. Line the bottom of a baking tin with grease-proof paper and grease lightly. Line the sides with thin cardboard to aid steam in reaching all around the cake evenly. Pour in batter and steam over rapidly boiling water for 40 minutes. Serve warm or cold.

STEAMED WHOLE FISH WITH GINGER AND GREEN ONION

1 whole bream or perch weighing 500 g (1 lb)
1½ teaspoons Chinese rice wine
½ teaspoon salt
¼ teaspoon white pepper
6 spring onions
4 cm (1½ inch) piece fresh ginger, shredded
1½ teaspoons oil
2 teaspoons light soya sauce
sprigs of fresh coriander

Clean fish, removing scales and intestines. Rinse well, wipe dry, then make several deep diagonal cuts across each side. Sprinkle on Chinese wine and stand for 10 minutes. Rub fish with salt and pepper and put on a lightly oiled plate. Shred spring onions and place half inside the fish together with half of the ginger. Scatter remaining onion and ginger onto the fish. Sprinkle on oil and soya sauce and a very little water.

Cover and cook over high heat in a steamer for about 10 minutes until fish is tender. Test if the fish is done by piercing the thickest part with a thin skewer. If the flesh appears slightly flaky and no pink liquid runs out the fish is done. Do not overcook. Lift onto a serving plate, pour on the cooking liquid and garnish with fresh coriander.

SWEET AND SOUR FISH FINGERS

375 g (¾ lb) thick fish fillets
½ teaspoon salt
pinch white pepper
1 teaspoon ginger wine (see glossary)
2 teaspoons cornflour
1 teaspoon sesame oil
125 g (¼ lb) plain flour
60 g (2 oz) cornflour
2 teaspoons baking powder
2 teaspoons oil
oil for deep frying

Sauce:
½ cup white vinegar
75 g (2½ oz) brown sugar
1 tablespoon tomato paste
1 tablespoon dark soya sauce
¾ cup light chicken stock
2 teaspoons cornflour
4 drops red food colouring
pinch of salt
1 cm (½ inch) piece fresh ginger, shredded
2 cloves garlic (optional)
2 spring onions
½ small carrot
15 g (½ oz) canned bamboo shoot
1 small fresh red chilli
30 g (1 oz) celery

Cut fish into pieces about 10 cm by 2.5 cm (4 inches by 1 inch) and dry with kitchen paper. Sprinkle with salt, pepper, ginger wine, cornflour and sesame oil and leave to marinate for 10 minutes.

Prepare sauce by mixing ingredients from vinegar to salt in a small saucepan. Add shredded ginger. Chop garlic and spring onions finely and add to the pan. Scrape and shred carrot, drain and shred bamboo shoot, slice chilli and shred celery. Add all vegetables to the pan. Bring to the boil, stirring until the mixture clears and thickens. Boil for 4 minutes. Keep hot until needed.

Make a batter with plain flour, cornflour, baking powder, oil and enough water to make a batter of dropping consistency. Heat oil until smoking hot. Lower heat to medium. Dip fish into the batter and fry until cooked. Drain and place on a serving dish.

Serve the sauce separately, or pour over the fish pieces just before serving.

Steamed Whole Fish with Ginger and Green Onion, and Sweet and Sour Fish Fingers
(recipes this page).

FISH WITH HOT BEAN SAUCE

1 whole bream, snapper, or golden carp, weighing
   500 g (1 lb)
oil
1 cm (½ inch) piece fresh ginger
2 cloves garlic
2 tablespoons light soya sauce
1½ tablespoons hot bean paste, or *hoisin* sauce
1 tablespoon Chinese wine
2 teaspoons sugar
½ cup water
cornflour
2 teaspoons Chinese brown vinegar or lemon juice
1 teaspoon sesame oil
spring onion, chopped

Clean and scale fish and make several deep diagonal
cuts across each side. Heat 5 cm (2 inches) oil in a *wok*
and fry fish for 1 minute on each side. Lift out and keep
warm.

Chop ginger and garlic finely. Pour out all but 1
tablespoon oil. Fry ginger and garlic for 2 minutes, then
stir in soya sauce, bean paste or *hoisin* sauce, wine and
sugar. Cook for 1 minute, then add water and bring to
the boil. Return fish to the pan and simmer on moderate heat until fish is done. Turn once during cooking.

Carefully lift fish onto a serving dish. If necessary
thicken sauce with a little cornflour mixed with cold
water. Spoon sauce over the fish and sprinkle with
brown vinegar or lemon juice and sesame oil just before
serving. Garnish with chopped spring onion.

FISH SERVED IN TWO WAYS

1 whole garoupa, mullet, snapper or golden carp,
   weighing 1 kg (2 lb)
salt
light soya sauce
Chinese wine
1 beaten egg
cornflour
oil for deep frying
2 teaspoons oil
2.5 cm (1 inch) piece fresh ginger, shredded
3 spring onions, shredded

Sauce:
2 teaspoons oil
1 cm (½ inch) piece fresh ginger, shredded
½ clove garlic, crushed (optional)
1 spring onion, minced
½ cup water
¼ teaspoon white pepper
1 teaspoon salt
1½ tablespoons white vinegar
2 tablespoons sugar
1 tablespoon tomato paste
1 medium tomato, diced
½ small green pepper, finely chopped
½ fresh red chilli, finely chopped
1 teaspoon cornflour

Clean fish and remove scales. Slice off one fillet. Cut
into serving pieces. Sprinkle a little soya sauce and

Chinese wine onto the fillet remaining on the carcass
and set aside. Coat sliced fillet with beaten egg. Put
cornflour into a plastic bag, drop in fish pieces and
shake vigorously.

Prepare sauce. Heat oil and fry ginger, garlic and
spring onion for 2 minutes. Add water, pepper and
salt, vinegar, sugar and tomato paste and bring to the
boil. Cook for 1 minute, then stir in tomato, green
pepper and chilli. Thicken with cornflour mixed with a
little cold water and cook for another 2 minutes until
sauce thickens and clears. Keep sauce warm until
needed.

Place marinated fish pieces on an oiled plate, splash
with a very little water and oil. Scatter shredded ginger
and onion on top and steam, covered, for about 7
minutes until the fish is very tender.

Heat oil to smoking point and put in fish pieces to
deep fry. Cook to a golden brown. Place on a serving
dish and pour on the sauce. Serve the steamed fish on
the dish in which it was cooked.

FISH AND ASPARAGUS ROLLS

6 white fish fillets
6 large spears canned asparagus
toothpicks
1 teaspoon Chinese rice wine
2 teaspoons sesame oil
1 tablespoon light soya sauce
2 egg whites
1 heaped tablespoon plain flour
1 heaped tablespoon cornflour
oil for deep frying

Wrap fish fillet around each spear of asparagus and
secure with toothpicks. Mix wine, sesame oil and soya
sauce, and marinate fish in this for 5 minutes. Coat fish
rolls with a mixture of flour and cornflour. Dip in the
beaten egg mixture and coat with a little more flour.

Heat oil in a *wok* until almost at smoking point. Fry
fish rolls to a golden brown. Lift out on a slotted spoon.
Drain on absorbent paper. Serve with a small bowl of
soya sauce and spiced salt powder.

SPICY FISH SLICES

375 g (¾ lb) fish fillets
1 tablespoon dark soya sauce
2 tablespoons light soya sauce
1 tablespoon Chinese rice wine
1 cm (½ inch) piece fresh ginger, shredded
2 cloves garlic
6 spring onions, shredded
75 g (2½ oz) sugar
2 teaspoons salt
1 teaspoon Chinese five-spice powder
¾ cup boiling water
oil
6-8 lettuce leaves

Slice fish into 5 cm (2 inch) squares. Prepare a marinade by mixing soya sauce, wine, ginger, garlic and
spring onions. Arrange fish pieces in a shallow flat bowl

and pour on the marinade. Let stand for 3 hours, turning occasionally.

Mix sugar, salt, five-spice powder and boiling water in a small saucepan and bring to the boil. Turn heat down very low and keep warm.

Heat 2.5 cm (1 inch) oil in a frying pan or *wok* and fry fish slices over high heat until a dark golden colour on both sides. Lift out from pan on a slotted spoon and return to the marinade dish. Pour on the warm spiced liquid and marinate in this for 5 minutes.

Dip lettuce into a pot of boiling water to which 1 tablespoon oil has been added. Arrange on a warmed serving plate. Drain fish and place on the lettuce. Serve immediately.

STIR-FRIED SHRIMP IN HOT TOMATO SAUCE

375 g (¾ lb) raw shrimp, peeled
1 egg white
2 teaspoons Chinese rice wine
1 teaspoon salt
1 heaped tablespoon cornflour
oil
1 medium onion
1 cm (½ inch) piece fresh ginger, shredded
2 fresh red chillies, sliced or finely chopped
4 cloves garlic, crushed
2 tablespoons tomato paste
½ teaspoon salt
1 teaspoon sugar
1½ teaspoons cayenne pepper or chilli powder
¾ cup stock
2 teaspoons cornflour
1 teaspoon sesame oil

Rinse shrimp in cold water and shake in a cloth to dry. Mix egg white with wine, salt and cornflour. Coat shrimps lightly with this batter and allow to stand for 1 hour. Heat about 3 tablespoons oil in a *wok* and stir-fry shrimp for 1 minute, lift out and drain. Keep warm.

Chop onion finely and stir-fry with ginger, chillies and garlic for 2 minutes, then add tomato paste, salt, sugar and pepper or chilli powder. Pour on stock and simmer for 2 minutes. Thicken sauce with cornflour mixed with a little cold water.

Return shrimp to the pan and heat through with the sauce. Spoon onto a serving dish and sprinkle on sesame oil.

FRIED SHRIMP BALLS

375 g (¾ lb) raw shrimp, peeled
½ teaspoon salt
30 g (1 oz) pork fat, steamed
2 teaspoons Chinese rice wine
1 teaspoon sesame oil
2 egg whites
1 tablespoon cornflour
¼ teaspoon white pepper
oil for deep frying
sweet soya sauce or *hoisin* sauce

Smash shrimps with the side of a cleaver until reduced to a smooth pulp. Add salt and very finely diced pork fat. Work in remaining ingredients except for oil and sweet soya sauce and knead until smooth and well mixed.

Heat oil to smoking point. To make shrimp balls squeeze a ball of the paste from clenched fist out between thumb and forefinger. Scoop off with a spoon and drop into the oil. Deep fry until golden and crisp on the surface. Lift out and drain.

Serve with a dip of sweet soya sauce or *hoisin* sauce.

CRYSTAL PRAWNS

24 medium sized raw prawns
1 tablespoon ginger wine (see glossary)
1 tablespoon water
¼ teaspoon white pepper
4 spring onions
2.5 cm (1 inch) piece fresh ginger, sliced
1 carrot, sliced
oil

Peel away shells from prawns leaving heads and tails intact. With a small sharp knife cut a deep slit down the back of each prawn and scrape out the dark vein. Cut almost through the prawn. Marinate in ginger wine, water and pepper for 5 minutes.

Clean spring onions and cut into 8 cm (3 inch) pieces. Shred both ends of each piece and drop into a dish of iced water to curl. Cut decorative shapes from carrot and ginger slices using a vegetable cutter.

Heat about 3 tablespoons oil in a *wok* and stir-fry prawns until they turn pink and curl. Cook until flesh is just firm. Do not overcook. Lift onto a serving plate and decorate with spring onion curls, and sliced ginger and carrot. Serve with a bowl of dark soya sauce.

STIR-FRIED SHRIMP ON CRISP RICE

375 g (¾ lb) raw peeled shrimp
1 teaspoon ginger wine (see glossary)
2 teaspoons cornflour
½ teaspoon salt
1 egg white
3 cups shrimp stock or water
1 teaspoon salt
1½ tablespoons tomato paste
1 teaspoon chilli powder
1 fresh red chilli, finely chopped
3 teaspoons sugar
¼ teaspoon white pepper
60 g (2 oz) frozen green peas
1 tablespoon cornflour
185 g (6 oz) dried crisp rice (see Rice, page 214)
oil for deep frying

Marinate shrimp in a mixture of ginger wine, cornflour, salt and egg whites for 5 minutes. Heat about 3 tablespoons oil and fry shrimp until pink. Do not over cook. Remove and drain. Pour in shrimp stock (made by boiling heads and shells in water) or water and add ingredients from salt to white pepper. Boil for 5 minutes. Add peas and thicken with cornflour mixed with a little cold water. Return shrimps and simmer for 1 minute.

Heat oil and deep fry dried rice until puffed and crispy. Drain and place in a deep serving dish or soup tureen. Carry the shrimp and sauce to the table separately and pour over the rice just before serving.

Note: Dried rice vermicelli, deep fried for about 4 seconds, can be substituted for dried crisp rice.

SWEET AND SOUR PRAWNS

12 large raw prawns
cornflour
2 egg whites
oil for deep frying

Sauce 1:
2 spring onions
1 clove garlic
1 cm (½ inch) piece fresh ginger, sliced
½ fresh red chilli
2 teaspoons oil
1 teaspoon pepper
2 teaspoons light soya sauce
75 g (2½ oz) brown sugar
⅓ cup white vinegar
⅓ cup water or chicken stock
3 teaspoons tomato paste
3 teaspoons cornflour
salt

Sauce 2:
¼ cup white vinegar
75 g (2½ oz) sugar
1 tablespoon tomato paste
⅓ cup water or light stock
2 teaspoons cornflour
1 teaspoon salt
2.5 cm (1 inch) piece fresh ginger, shredded
2 spring onions, shredded
30 g (1 oz) Chow Chow fruit pickles, chopped

Peel and devein prawns. Coat lightly with cornflour and brush with beaten egg white. Coat with cornflour again, shaking off excess. Heat oil and deep fry prawns for 2 minutes, or slightly longer if prawns have been frozen.

If preferred, make 'butterfly' prawns by cutting down centre back and pressing sides out flat before coating with cornflour and egg. Cooking time will be slightly shorter.

Keep prawns warm in a covered dish while one of the sauces is prepared. Do not make both. To make Sauce 1, chop spring onions, garlic, ginger and chilli and fry in oil for 3 minutes. Add pepper, soya sauce, sugar, vinegar, water or stock and tomato paste. Stir well, then bring to the boil and simmer for 2 minutes. Thicken with cornflour and continue to cook until sauce thickens and clears. Add salt to taste.

Prepare Sauce 2 by placing all ingredients except Chow Chow pickle in a saucepan and boiling until it thickens slightly. Stir in chopped Chow Chow pickle and keep warm.

Reheat oil and quickly fry prawns for a few seconds to crisp. Arrange on a serving dish and pour on the sauce of your choice.

SHRIMP WITH CASHEW NUTS AND VEGETABLES

250 g (½ lb) raw shrimp
salt
pepper
1½ tablespoons cornflour
75 g (2½ oz) celery, finely diced
60 g (2 oz) baby corn cobs, drained and cut into
    1 cm (½ inch) pieces
60 g (2 oz) cucumber, chopped (optional)
45 g (1½ oz) green pepper, chopped
75 g (2½ oz) button mushrooms or champignons,
    chopped
6 spring onions, finely chopped
60 g (2 oz) bamboo shoots, drained and chopped
oil
45 g (1½ oz) raw cashew nuts
1¾ cups chicken or fish stock
1 teaspoon salt
½ teaspoon white pepper
3 teaspoons dark soya sauce
1 tablespoon Chinese rice wine
fresh coriander leaves

Peel and devein shrimps and sprinkle with salt and pepper. Coat lightly with cornflour.

Put all vegetables in a saucepan and pour in stock, reserving 3 tablespoons. Bring to the boil and season with salt and pepper. Cook for 2 minutes, then remove from heat and drain.

Heat oil and gently deep fry cashews for 5 minutes. Heat 2 tablespoons oil and stir-fry shrimp for 2 minutes. Add vegetables and a little more oil if necessary and stir-fry for 2 minutes on high heat. Add salt, pepper, soya sauce and Chinese wine, stir, then pour in reserved stock. Thicken sauce with a little cornflour mixed with cold water and continue to cook until sauce clears.

Stir in fried cashew nuts. Spoon onto a warmed serving plate and garnish with fresh coriander leaves.

SPICY PRAWNS

8 medium raw prawns
½ fresh red chilli
1 spring onion
1 teaspoon spiced salt
2 cloves garlic
1 teaspoon cornflour
3 tablespoons oil

Soak prawns in cold water for 10 minutes. Slice chillies and spring onion thinly. Trim legs off prawns and wipe dry. Season with half the spiced salt and leave for 15 minutes. Drain and sprinkle on cornflour.

Heat oil and fry garlic for ½ minute. Add prawns and fry until pink and cooked through. Add chilli and remaining spiced salt and stir on moderate heat for ½ minute. Transfer to a serving dish and serve at once.

Scallops with Shrimp and Mushrooms (recipe page 150).

PRAWNS IN RED SAUCE

500 g (1 lb) large raw prawns in shell
1½ tablespoons oil
3 spring onions, shredded
3 cloves garlic, crushed
4 cm (1½ inch) piece fresh ginger, shredded
1 fresh red chilli, finely chopped
3 teaspoons Chinese rice wine
1 tablespoon light soya sauce
1 teaspoon sugar
½ teaspoon salt
1/8 teaspoon white pepper
½ tablespoon tomato paste
4 tablespoons chicken or fish stock
pinch of monosodium glutamate (optional)
few drops red food colouring (optional)
1 teaspoon cornflour

Snip off legs and top of prawn heads. Wash well, dry and set aside. Heat oil and fry onion, garlic, ginger and chilli for 1 minute. Add prawns and cook for 5 minutes, turning to cook prawns evenly. Pour on wine and soya sauce and add sugar, salt and pepper. Stir in tomato liquid and add monosodium glutamate and red food colouring (if used).

Thicken sauce with cornflour mixed with a little water and stir on moderate heat until sauce clears. Lift prawns onto a serving dish and spoon on the sauce.

SCALLOPS WITH SHRIMP AND MUSHROOMS

12 large fresh scallops
220 g (7 oz) raw shrimp, peeled
2 teaspoons Chinese rice wine
2 teaspoons light soya sauce
6 dried Chinese mushrooms, soaked
6 canned or fresh straw mushrooms
1 cm (½ inch) piece fresh ginger, shredded
4 spring onions, shredded
1½ tablespoons oil
1 teaspoon sugar
salt
white pepper
⅔ cup light chicken or fish stock
1 heaped teaspoon cornflour
2 egg whites

Wash scallops in salted water and drain well. Cut shrimps open down the backs and scrape out dark veins. Wash well. Place scallops and shrimp in a dish and pour on wine and soya sauce. Marinate for 10 minutes.

Drain mushrooms and remove stems. Cut in halves. Lightly boil fresh straw mushrooms or drain canned mushrooms and rinse in cold water. Cut in halves.

Heat oil and fry ginger and spring onions for 1 minute. Add scallops and cook for 2 minutes, then add mushrooms and season with sugar, salt and pepper. Add shrimp and cook for another minute on moderate to low heat. Pour in stock and bring to the boil. Thicken with cornflour mixed with a little cold water. Stir in lightly beaten egg whites which will form white threads in the sauce. Do not stir again until egg sets. Transfer to a serving dish and serve at once.

STUFFED CRAB CLAWS

12 crab pincers with meat intact
375 g (¾ lb) raw shrimp, peeled
100 g (3½ oz) fresh breadcrumbs
1 teaspoon salt
¼ teaspoon white pepper
3 teaspoons lemon juice
½ teaspoon dry mustard
2 egg whites
2 eggs, beaten
cornflour
white sesame seeds
oil for deep frying
12 small lettuce leaves
tomato slices

Break shell away from meat on pincers leaving meat attached to the claw. (It will cling to the central sinew.) Pound shrimp meat to a paste and add fresh breadcrumbs, adding a little water if the mixture is too dry. Season with salt, pepper, lemon juice and mustard and bind with egg whites. Press mixture around the crab meat to form a smooth ball with the claw tip exposed. Coat very lightly with cornflour, then brush with beaten egg. Dip the end of each ball into toasted sesame seeds, coating thickly. Coat again with cornflour.

Heat oil and fry several claws at a time for about 2½ minutes until golden brown. Drain well. Place lettuce on a serving plate and put a crab claw in the curl of each leaf. Decorate the plate with sliced tomato.

BAKED STUFFED WHELKS

6 large whelks in the shell
1 teaspoon caustic soda
1 small onion
2 teaspoons oil
60 g (2 oz) raw shrimp
30 g (1 oz) chicken livers
60 g (2 oz) chicken
30 g (1 oz) lean pork
30 g (1 oz) canned bamboo shoots
1 tablespoon dark soya sauce
¼ cup thick coconut milk
salt
white pepper
1 egg
dry breadcrumbs

Wash shells and place in a large saucepan. Cover with water, bring to the boil and cook until meat is tender. Remove shells from liquid, drain and let cool. Scrape out meat, wash well, chop very finely and set aside.

Scrape shells to remove all traces of meat, return to saucepan and add caustic soda. Soak shells for 10 minutes, then rinse thoroughly in cold water and dry. Discard liquid and wash saucepan thoroughly.

Mince onion and fry in the oil until soft. Finely chop all seafood and meat with bamboo shoots and mix with chopped whelk, soya sauce, coconut milk and salt and pepper. Stuff the mixture into the whelk shells and brush top with beaten egg. Coat lightly with breadcrumbs and bake in a slow oven for 45 minutes, raising heat for the last 10 minutes to brown tops.

LOBSTER WITH SALTED BLACK BEANS AND CHILLI

750 g (1½ lb) fresh lobster
3 teaspoons salted black beans
2 cloves garlic
1 teaspoon sugar
3 tablespoons oil
2 fresh red chillies, thinly sliced
1 cm (½ inch) piece fresh ginger, thinly sliced
¼ cup light chicken stock
1 tablespoon light soya sauce
pinch of white pepper
1 teaspoon ginger wine (see glossary)
1 teaspoon cornflour
1 spring onion, finely chopped

Cut lobster in half and discard inedible parts. Scoop flesh from tail and scrape out shell. Drop head and shell into a saucepan of boiling water and cook to a bright red. Drain and brush gently to clean.

Cut lobster meat into bite-sized cubes. Crush black beans with garlic and sugar and fry in oil for 2 minutes. Add lobster and stir-fry until pink. Add chillies, ginger, chicken stock, soya sauce, pepper and ginger wine, cover and simmer for 3 minutes. Mix cornflour with a little cold water and stir into the sauce to thicken. Spoon cooked lobster into the lobster shell and pour on the sauce. Garnish with chopped spring onion.

ABALONE IN OYSTER SAUCE

375 g (¾ lb) canned abalone
12 lettuce leaves
2 tablespoons oil
2 teaspoons sesame oil
⅓ cup chicken stock
2 teaspoons Chinese rice wine
1 tablespoon dark soya sauce
3 tablespoons oyster sauce
sugar
white pepper
cornflour

Drain abalone and cut into thin slices. Drop into a saucepan of boiling, slightly salted water and simmer for 2 minutes. Drain well. Drop lettuce into a pot of boiling water to which 1 tablespoon oil has been added. Remove at once and drain well. Arrange on a serving plate and sprinkle with sesame oil and remaining oil.

Bring remaining ingredients from chicken stock to oyster sauce to boil and season to taste with sugar and white pepper. Thicken with a little cornflour mixed with cold water if necessary. Put in abalone and simmer for 2 minutes, then spoon onto the lettuce and serve hot.

FRIED OYSTERS

12 large Chinese oysters, or
    24 small oysters
60 g (2 oz) plain flour
30 g (1 oz) cornflour
1 egg
1 egg white
2½ teaspoons baking powder
1 teaspoon salt
pinch of white pepper
1½ tablespoons oil
water
oil for deep frying
spiced salt or sweet and sour sauce

Wash oysters in salted water and rub lightly with salt and set aside. Make a batter by mixing ingredients from plain flour to oil, then blend in enough water to make a smooth, fairly thick batter. Leave for 10 minutes.

Heat oil to smoking point, then reduce heat. Drop large oysters into a pot of boiling water and leave for 30 seconds. Do not soak small oysters. Lift out and drain well. Coat thickly with batter and put several at a time into the hot oil. Deep fry to a golden brown. The batter should be very puffy and crisp. Drain on absorbent paper. Serve hot with the spiced salt or a dish of hot sweet and sour sauce.

BRAISED EEL WITH SPRING ONION SHOOTS AND GARLIC

500 g (1 lb) fresh eel
1½ tablespoons dark soya sauce
2 teaspoons Chinese rice wine
1 teaspoon sugar
pinch of white pepper
4 cm (1½ inch) piece fresh ginger, shredded
6 cloves garlic, sliced
2 tablespoons oil
12 fresh spring onion shoots, sliced
3 tablespoons fish or beef stock
1 teaspoon cornflour
sesame oil

Remove skin from eel and wash well. Wipe dry and cut into 5 cm (2 inch) pieces. Mix ingredients from soya sauce to ginger and pour over the eel pieces. Leave to marinate for 15 minutes.

Heat oil and fry garlic for 1 minute, then put in eel and marinade and cook until tender, adding spring onion shoots and fish stock. Thicken sauce with cornflour mixed with a little cold water. Transfer to a serving dish and sprinkle on a generous amount of sesame oil. Sprinkle with white pepper before serving.

SAUTEED EEL WITH BAMBOO SHOOTS AND MUSHROOMS

500 g (1 lb) fresh eel
30 g (1 oz) fat pork
3 tablespoons oil
6 spring onions, sliced
4 cm (1½ inch) piece fresh ginger, thinly sliced
90 g (3 oz) canned bamboo shoots
8 dried Chinese mushrooms, soaked
1 tablespoon Chinese rice wine
2 tablespoons dark soya sauce
3 teaspoons sugar
¾ cup water, fish or chicken stock

3 teaspoons Chinese brown vinegar
3 teaspoons sesame oil
2 teaspoons cornflour
6 spring onion shoots or chive shoots

Clean and skin eel and drop into a pot of boiling water. Remove after 10 seconds. Wipe dry and cut into 2.5 cm (1 inch) pieces. Dice fat pork and saute in oil with onion and ginger. Drain and slice bamboo shoots and mushrooms thinly and add to the pan. Saute for 2 minutes, then season with wine, soya sauce and sugar. Add eel and water or stock and simmer until eel is tender.

Add vinegar and sesame oil and thicken sauce with cornflour mixed with a little cold water. Cook until sauce thickens and clears. Spoon onto a serving dish and garnish with chopped spring onion or chive shoots.

SAUTEED FROGS LEGS WITH SESAME AND CHILLI

375 g (¾ lb) frogs legs
3 teaspoons Chinese rice wine
2 teaspoons cornflour
3 tablespoons oil
1 fresh red chilli, thinly sliced
3 spring onions, shredded
1½ tablespoons light soya sauce
1 teaspoon sugar
½ teaspoon salt
pinch of white pepper
1 tablespoon sesame oil
fresh coriander leaves

Divide frogs legs at the central joint. Sprinkle with Chinese wine and cornflour. Leave for 10 minutes. Heat oil and stir-fry frogs legs until light gold in colour. Add sliced chilli and shredded onions and fry briefly, then add soya sauce and remaining seasonings and cook on lowered heat for 3 minutes.

Sprinkle on sesame oil and heat again briefly. Transfer to a serving dish and garnish with fresh coriander.

PAPER-WRAPPED CHICKEN

375 g (¾ lb) chicken
3 teaspoons sesame oil
2 teaspoons salt
1 teaspoon Chinese five-spice powder
¼ teaspoon crushed star anise
heavy-duty cellophane or greaseproof paper
oil for deep frying

Cut chicken into small dice. Mix remaining ingredients and pour over the chicken. Mix well and leave to marinate for ½ hour. Cut cellophane into 20 cm (8 inch) squares. Divide meat between the paper sheets and fold up, tucking the last end in securely.

Heat oil to smoking point and carefully lower in the packages. Deep fry for 1½-2 minutes. Lift out and drain thoroughly before serving, still in paper wrapping. Each diner unwraps his chicken just before eating.

LEMON CHICKEN

1½ kg (3 lb) chicken
salt
white pepper
1½ teaspoons sugar
½ tablespoon Chinese rice wine
2 tablespoons custard powder
2 egg yolks
oil for deep frying

Sauce:
¼ cup lemon juice
¾ teaspoon white vinegar
½ cup light chicken stock
60 g (2 oz) sugar
3 teaspoons cornflour
3-4 drops yellow food colouring
lemon slices

Prepare chicken and pat dry. Mix salt and pepper with sugar and Chinese wine and rub into the chicken inside and out. Leave for 15 minutes. Place in a steamer and cook for 45 minutes. Leave to cool. Coat the bird with custard powder, then brush with beaten egg.

Heat oil and carefully lower in the bird. Deep fry until skin is golden brown and crisp. Lift out and drain well, then cut into serving pieces.

Put all sauce ingredients into a small saucepan and bring to the boil, stirring until it becomes clear. Check taste and add more sugar or lemon as preferred. Pour over the chicken and garnish with lemon slices.

CHICKEN WITH WALNUTS

375 g (¾ lb) chicken breast
1 egg white
1 tablespoon cornflour
1 tablespoon ginger wine (see glossary)
½ teaspoon salt
pinch of white pepper
1 teaspoon sesame oil
1 teaspoon vegetable oil
185 g (6 oz) shelled walnuts
salt
oil for deep frying
2 spring onions, chopped in 2.5 cm (1 inch) lengths
1 cm (½ inch) piece fresh ginger, sliced
1½ teaspoons Chinese rice wine
1½ teaspoons soya sauce
pinch of white pepper
½ teaspoon sesame oil
1½ tablespoons water
cornflour

Skin chicken and cut into 2.5 cm (1 inch) cubes. Put into a basin and add egg white and cornflour. Mix well. Pour on ginger wine, salt, sesame oil, and vegetable oil and stir well. Leave to marinate for 10 minutes.

Put walnuts into a saucepan, cover with water and add 1 teaspoon salt. Bring to the boil, then reduce heat and simmer for 10 minutes. Drain and dry on a kitchen towel. Heat oil to smoking point and lower in walnuts on a perforated ladle. Fry until deep golden brown. Lift out and drain well.

Reheat oil and put in the chicken pieces. Deep fry

Lemon Chicken (recipe this page).

until lightly coloured, then lift out and drain. Pour off all but 2 tablespoons oil and add spring onions and ginger. Fry for one minute, then add chicken pieces and remaining seasonings. Stir-fry for 30 seconds. Add walnuts and cornflour mixed with water. Stir until the sauce thickens slightly and becomes clear. Check seasonings.

Note: Dried chillies, bamboo shoots, carrots or cashew nuts may be used in place of walnuts.

STIR-FRIED CHICKEN AND GREEN PEPPERS

375 g (¾ lb) chicken breast
1 egg white
1 tablespoon cornflour
1 tablespoon soya sauce
2 teaspoons ginger wine (see glossary)
2 teaspoons sesame oil
½ teaspoon salt
¼ teaspoon white pepper
2 green peppers
1 fresh red chilli
2 cloves garlic
2½ tablespoons oil
2 teaspoons white vinegar
1 teaspoon sugar
2 teaspoons Chinese rice wine
1 teaspoon sesame oil
2 tablespoons water
salt
cornflour

Skin chicken and cut into 2.5 cm (1 inch) cubes. Put into a basin and add egg white and cornflour. Mix with a chopstick. Mix ingredients from soya sauce to white pepper and pour over the chicken. Stir well and leave to marinate for 15 minutes.

Cut peppers into 2.5 cm (1 inch) pieces, discarding seeds. Seed and slice chilli. Chop garlic finely. Heat oil and stir-fry peppers, chilli and garlic for 2 minutes. Remove and set aside. Add chicken and stir-fry until lightly coloured. Add remaining ingredients except cornflour and continue to stir on moderate to high heat until chicken is cooked through. Return peppers, chilli and garlic to the pan.

Mix a little cornflour with cold water and pour into the pan. Stir until the sauce thickens slightly and becomes clear. Check seasonings.

CHICKEN WITH MANGO

375 g (¾ lb) chicken breast
1 teaspoon salt
¼ teaspoon sesame oil
pinch of white pepper
1 tablespoon oil
3 teaspoons water
1 tablespoon cornflour
2 ripe mangoes
2 spring onions
3 tablespoons oil
lemon juice

Skin chicken and cut into thin slices, then into strips. Put into a basin and pour on a mixture of the ingredients from salt to cornflour. Leave to marinate for 10 minutes. Peel and stone mangoes and cut into dice. Cut spring onions into 2.5 cm (1 inch) pieces.

Heat oil and saute marinated chicken until lightly coloured. Add spring onion and cook until chicken is done. Add mango and splash in a little water. Stir on moderate heat until mango pieces are warmed through. Spoon onto a serving dish and add a sprinkling of lemon juice.

ONE-POT CHICKEN WITH RICE AND CHINESE SAUSAGE

375 g (¾ lb) short grain rice
3 cups light chicken stock
185 g (6 oz) chicken breast
3 dried Chinese mushrooms, soaked
1 dried Chinese sausage
2 spring onions, shredded
pinch of salt
white pepper
½ teaspoon sugar
1 tablespoon light soya sauce
1 teaspoon sesame oil
1 teaspoon cornflour
1 tablespoon water

Wash rice and put into a casserole with chicken stock. Bring to the boil, cover and reduce heat. Cook until beginning to soften and water reduced to the level of the rice. Cut chicken into 2.5 cm (1 inch) cubes and scatter over the rice. Drain and slice mushrooms, wash and slice sausage. Add to the pot with remaining ingredients. Cover and continue to cook until the rice is done and meat tender. Any liquid in the pot should be absorbed into the rice. Stir with chopsticks to distribute meat through the rice. Serve at once.

CRISP FRIED PEKING CHICKEN

1½ kg (3 lb) chicken
2 tablespoons Chinese rice wine
1 teaspoon salt
1 teaspoon sugar
2 teaspoons sesame oil
¼ teaspoon white pepper
¼ teaspoon Chinese five-spice powder
2 eggs
2 tablespoons cornflour
oil for deep frying

Wash and wipe chicken. Rub all over with a mixture of ingredients from rice wine to five-spice powder and leave to marinate for ½ hour. Brush with beaten egg and coat fairly thickly with cornflour.

Heat oil to smoking point and lower in the bird. Reduce to moderately low and cook until golden brown, lift out and drain well. Reheat oil and return chicken to cook until well browned, about 5 minutes.

Drain and cut into serving pieces. Serve with spiced salt and steamed bread crescents *(page 144)*.

BEGGAR'S CHICKEN

2 kg (4 lb) chicken
12 dried Chinese mushrooms, soaked
155 g (5 oz) Tientsin preserved vegetables
100 g (3½ oz) fat pork
3 tablespoons oil
1 tablespoon dark soya sauce
2 teaspoons Chinese rice wine
2 teaspoons sugar
pinch of white pepper
4 lotus leaves (or use spinach or cabbage)
newspaper or plain paper
1½ kg (3 lb) clay or plain flour

Wash and wipe chicken. Drain and chop mushrooms and preserved vegetables. Dice pork finely. Saute pork in oil until cooked through. Add mushrooms, vegetables and all seasonings and stir-fry for 5 minutes. Cool slightly. Stuff the mixture into the cavity of the bird and secure the opening with toothpicks or sew up carefully.

Cover chicken with lotus leaves, or other leaves. Wrap in newspaper or plain paper and encase in the prepared clay. If using flour, make into a stiff dough with water and wrap the paste around the bird after first wrapping in paper. Ensure there are no cracks which will allow the juices to escape. Place on a baking sheet in a moderately hot oven for 1¾-2 hours. The bird should be so tender that the flesh falls from the bones.

Break open casing and tear away paper and leaves before serving.

BRAISED CHICKEN WINGS IN OYSTER SAUCE

12 chicken wings
1 tablespoon dark soya sauce
8 stalks Chinese cabbage or spring greens
oil for deep frying
½ teaspoon sesame oil
pinch of salt
pinch of white pepper
1½ tablespoons oyster sauce
1 teaspoon sugar
1 teaspoon sesame oil
½ cup water
2 teaspoons cornflour

Cut chicken wings in halves at the joint. Pour on dark soya sauce and rub well into the skin to colour. Leave for 10 minutes, then deep fry until golden brown.

Cut vegetables into 8 cm (3 inch) sections and drop into a saucepan of boiling salted water. Cook until tender, then lift out and drain very well. Heat 3 tablespoons oil and stir-fry vegetables for 2 minutes. Season with sesame oil, salt and pepper and arrange on a serving dish. Keep warm.

Put chicken wings back into the pan, cover and simmer until cooked through. Add remaining ingredients except cornflour and simmer for 4 minutes. Mix cornflour with a little water and add to the pan. Stir until sauce thickens and begins to clear. Check seasoning. Arrange the chicken wings on the vegetables. Pour on sauce.

SLICED CHICKEN AND HAM WITH VEGETABLES

1½ kg (3 lb) chicken
1 tablespoon Chinese rice wine
2 teaspoons salt
pinch of white pepper
1 teaspoon sugar
2 spring onions, shredded
2.5 cm (1 inch) piece fresh ginger, shredded
125 g (¼ lb) Chinese or unsmoked ham
3 teaspoons sugar
1 tablespoon Chinese rice wine
500 g (1 lb) broccoli spears or Chinese cabbage
1 tablespoon oil
2 tablespoons water
1 teaspoon cornflour

Clean and wipe chicken and rub inside and out with a mixture of wine, salt, pepper and sugar. Put onions and ginger inside the cavity and place chicken over a steamer and cook for about 25 minutes until done.

Slice ham thinly and place in a dish over a steamer. Sprinkle on sugar and wine and steam for 20 minutes. Drop broccoli or Chinese cabbage into boiling water and leave until tender. Drain and splash with oil.

Cut chicken into pieces the same size as the ham. Arrange in alternate layers on the serving dish and surround with vegetables. Heat the dish in which the chicken was steamed and add any drippings from the ham dish. Add water mixed with cornflour and bring to the boil. Stir until sauce thickens and clears. Check seasonings. Pour over the chicken and ham, and serve immediately.

DUCK IN LEMON SOUP

1 kg (2 lb) duck pieces
6 cups water
2 lemons
2 dried tangerine peels (optional)
1 teaspoon salt
pinch of white pepper
fresh coriander sprigs

Clean duck and wipe dry. Put into a deep casserole and add water, halved lemons and tangerine peel. Add salt and white pepper. Cover and cook over low heat for about 4 hours until duck is very tender. Adjust seasonings to taste and garnish with fresh coriander before serving.

DUCK WITH CHINESE SPICES

1½ kg (3 lb) duckling
1 tablespoon spiced salt
¼ teaspoon ground Szechwan peppercorns
2 teaspoons Chinese rice wine
3 teaspoons dark soya sauce
oil for deep frying
1 tablespoon dark soya sauce

Clean and wipe duck inside and out. Combine all seasonings and rub well into the duck. Leave for 2 hours to absorb the flavours. Place on a plate over a steamer and cook on moderate heat for 2 hours. Remove from heat and rub with 1 tablespoon dark soya sauce.

Heat enough oil to cover the duck in a deep pan. Lower in the duck and deep fry until very dark brown and crisp. Serve with spiced salt.

PEKING DUCK WITH PANCAKES

This simplified version of the long and involved traditional recipe gives good results.

3 kg (6 lb) fat duck
¾ cup boiling water
1 cup golden syrup
3 star anise
1 heaped teaspoon Chinese five-spice powder

Pancakes:
185 g (6 oz) plain flour
½ cup boiling water
sesame oil

Garnishes:
spring onion curls
sweet bean paste or *hoisin* sauce

Clean and wash duck. Dry thoroughly inside and out. Dilute golden syrup in the boiling water then bring to the boil. Add crumbled star anise. Rub the bird inside and out with Chinese five-spice powder. Hold the duck oven a large bowl and pour the boiling syrup into the cavity and over the skin.

Tie a strong string around the neck and hang the duck over a drip tray in a draughty place to dry for 5 hours. If necessary, direct an electric fan onto the bird to hasten the drying. This process makes the skin crisp when cooked.

Brush the bird with remaining syrup solution and place on a rack in a baking tin. Roast in a preheated moderately hot oven for 1 hour. Turn and roast for a further ¾ hour or until cooked through. Test if done by inserting a skewer into the thickest part of the thigh. If no pink liquid escapes the bird is done. Peking Duck should not be overcooked.

To prepare pancakes, sieve flour into a mixing bowl and pour in water. Work with a wooden spoon until dough is completely amalgamated. Add a little more water if needed. When cool enough to handle transfer to a floured board and knead briskly for 10 minutes. Cover with a damp cloth and leave to stand in a warm place for 15 minutes. Roll on a floured board into a long sausage. Cut off walnut-sized pieces and press flat. Brush one side with sesame oil and stick two pieces together, oiled sides meeting. Roll out the two pancakes together until paper thin.

Heat a heavy frying pan or hot plate and cook pressed-together pancakes on moderate heat until brown flecks appear. Turn and cook other side, then peel apart. Do not cook the inside surfaces. Cook all pancakes in this way and keep wrapped in a cloth until ready to serve.

To prepare spring onion curls, cut off the lower white section and shred with a sharp knife at each end, discarding green tops. Drop into a bowl of very iced water to make them curl.

To serve Peking Duck, first slice off the skin, then the meat. Arrange on a serving plate. Serve pancakes and spring onions on another plate and pour sauce into small dipping dishes.

FRIED STUFFED DUCKLING

This recipe is not nearly as complicated as it may look.

1½ kg (3 lb) duckling
2 spring onions, shredded
1 cm (½ inch) piece fresh ginger, shredded
3 teaspoons Chinese rice wine
2 tablespoons dark soya sauce
1 teaspoon sugar
2 star anise, crushed
½ teaspoon Chinese five-spice powder
½ teaspoon crushed black peppercorns
375 g (¾ lb) cooked taro yam or sweet potato
4 spring onions, finely chopped
4 dried Chinese mushrooms, soaked
2 tablespoons finely chopped fresh coriander leaves
1 teaspoon sesame oil
2 teaspoons Chinese rice wine
1 teaspoon salt
1 teaspoon sugar
1 tablespoon softened lard
1 tablespoon cornflour
1-2 egg whites
pinch of Chinese five-spice powder
pinch of white pepper
beaten egg
cornflour
oil for deep frying

Clean duck and wipe inside and out. Put spring onions and ginger inside and rub skin with a mixture of rice wine, soya sauce, sugar, anise and five-spice powder. Put remaining anise and peppercorns into the cavity. Leave to absorb flavours for 15 minutes, then put onto a plate over a steamer and cook for about 2 hours until tender. Leave to cool, then cut in half down the centre back. Carefully cut away all bones and press the duck out flat.

Mash cooked taro or sweet potato and mix with spring onions, finely chopped mushrooms, coriander and seasonings from sesame oil to sugar. Work in lard, cornflour and egg whites to bind the stuffing. Spread thickly over the duck and press on gently with the fingers. Sprinkle on five-spice powder and white pepper. Brush all over with beaten egg then coat in cornflour.

Heat oil to smoking point, then lower heat slightly. Carefully lift the duck into the oil and deep fry until dark brown and the skin very crisp. Lift out and drain well. Cut into serving pieces and arrange on a plate. Serve with small dishes of sweet soya sauce and chilli sauce.

MINCED PIGEON IN LETTUCE LEAVES

2 pigeons, each weighing 750 g (1½ lb)
4 dried Chinese mushrooms, soaked
100 g (3½ oz) canned bamboo shoots

Minced Pigeon in Lettuce Leaves (recipe this page and overleaf).

1 egg
1 tablespoon dark soya sauce
1½ teaspoons cornflour
3 tablespoons oil
60 g (2 oz) chicken livers, chopped
3 spring onions, chopped
1 tablespoon sweet bean paste
2.5 cm (1 inch) piece fresh ginger, shredded
pinch of monosodium glutamate (optional)
salt
white pepper
1 head of lettuce
3 tablespoons sweet bean paste or *hoisin* sauce

Clean pigeons and put into a large saucepan. Cover with water and bring to the boil. Simmer until meat is tender, then lift out and drain well. Allow to cool, then slice off meat and mince or chop finely. Drain mushrooms and remove stems, chop very finely. Drain and finely dice bamboo shoots, then mix with the mushrooms.

Beat egg lightly and combine with soya sauce and cornflour. Toss pigeon meat in this mixture and marinate for 10 minutes. Heat oil and fry pigeon meat for 3 minutes. Add chicken livers, mushroom and bamboo shoots and stir-fry for 2 minutes. Add spring onions, bean paste, ginger, monosodium glutamate (if used), salt and pepper. Lower heat and saute gently for several minutes. Pour on a little water if the mixture becomes dry. Spoon onto a serving plate and keep warm.

Wash lettuce and shake out water. Separate leaves, discarding very small ones. Arrange on another serving plate. Pour sauce into a small dish. Prepare the lettuce rolls at the table by coating each leaf with sauce and topping with a helping of minced pigeon meat. Roll up and serve.

TWICE-COOKED PORK

250 g (½ lb) pork belly with skin
1 green pepper
8 chive shoots
6 cloves garlic
4 tablespoons oil
2 teaspoons Chinese rice wine
1 tablespoon hot bean paste
1 tablespoon sweet bean paste
1½ tablespoons dark soya sauce
2 tablespoons chicken stock or water
1 teaspoon sugar
¼ teaspoon white pepper
1 teaspoon cornflour
1 teaspoon sesame oil
white pepper

Place pork piece in a saucepan and cover with water. Bring to the boil then reduce heat and simmer for 45 minutes. Lift out and drain well. Slice very thinly. Cut pepper into 2.5 cm (1 inch) squares. Cut chive shoots into 5 cm (2 inch) pieces and slice garlic.

Heat oil and fry sliced pork over high heat for 3 minutes. Add chive shoots and garlic and fry for another 2 minutes. Add bean pastes, Chinese wine, soya sauce and pepper squares and simmer, stirring continually, for 3 minutes. Add stock or water with sugar and white

pepper. Boil for about 5 minutes until pork is tender.

Thicken with cornflour mixed with a little cold water and stir until sauce clears. Sprinkle with sesame oil and season with white pepper before serving.

BARBECUED SPARE RIBS

1¼ kg (2½ lb) pork spare ribs
3 tablespoons dark soya sauce
1 tablespoon sweet bean paste
2 tablespoons sugar
3 cloves garlic
1 tablespoon Chinese rice wine
¼ teaspoon Chinese five-spice powder

Separate ribs and trim each neatly at the ends. Mix remaining ingredients together and pour over the ribs. Allow to marinate for 2 hours.

Place ribs on a rack and cook under a moderate grill until cooked through and crispy on the surface, or cook over a charcoal barbecue. Brush with the marinating liquid during cooking to keep meat moist.

SWEET AND SOUR PORK

375 g (¾ lb) pork belly
2 egg whites
45 g (1½ oz) plain flour
30 g (1 oz) cornflour
½ teaspoon salt
1 teaspoon baking powder
1 tablespoon Chinese rice wine
3 teaspoons light soya sauce
pinch of monosodium glutamate (optional)
pinch of salt
pinch of white pepper
1 cm (½ inch) piece fresh ginger, shredded
oil for deep frying

Sauce:
60 g (2 oz) brown sugar
2 teaspoons dark soya sauce
¼ cup white wine vinegar
2 tablespoons tomato paste
3 teaspoons cornflour
¼ cup light chicken stock or water
1 spring onion
1 cm (½ inch) piece fresh ginger, shredded
1 medium carrot
1 green pepper
1 red pepper
1 medium onion
2 slices canned pineapple
1 fresh red chilli (optional)

Cut pork belly into 2.5 cm (1 inch) cubes. Mix Chinese wine with soya sauce, monosodium glutamate (if used), salt, white pepper and ginger and pour over the meat. Rub in well and leave to stand for 10 minutes.

Beat egg whites with plain flour, cornflour, salt and baking powder adding just enough water to make a smooth, fairly thick batter.

Heat oil to smoking point and lower heat slightly. Coat pork pieces with the batter and put into the oil to cook for 4 minutes. Remove and drain. Turn off heat and prepare sauce.

Mix brown sugar, soya sauce, vinegar, tomato paste, cornflour and stock or water in a small saucepan. Add shredded spring onion and ginger. Bring to the boil and simmer for 4 minutes. Scrape and slice carrot thinly. Cut peppers and onion into 2.5 cm (1 inch) squares. Cube pineapple and slice chilli thinly. Drop carrot, onion and pepper pieces into a small saucepan of boiling water to blanch for 1 minute. Drain and add to the sauce with pineapple and chilli. Simmer on low heat for 5 minutes.

Reheat oil and return pork pieces to fry for a further minute. Place on a serving dish and pour on the piping hot sauce.

SHREDDED PORK WITH VERMICELLI IN SESAME BUNS

125 g (¼ lb) lean pork
90 g (3 oz) transparent vermicelli
3 tablespoons oil
1 cm (½ inch) piece fresh ginger, finely shredded
3 spring onions, finely shredded
3 teaspoons hot bean paste
1 teaspoon salt
2 tablespoons dark soya sauce
1 teaspoon sugar
1 cup beef stock
2 teaspoons cornflour
2 teaspoons sesame oil

Slice pork thinly, then cut into thin shreds. Soak vermicelli in warm water to soften. Drain and cut into 2.5 cm (1 inch) pieces. Heat oil and fry pork until well coloured. Add ginger and spring onions and fry for 2 minutes, then add bean paste and stir on moderate heat for 1 minute. Add vermicelli and salt, soya sauce, sugar and stock. Bring to the boil and simmer until pork and vermicelli are tender and liquid almost absorbed.

Mix cornflour with a very little cold water and stir into the meat. Leave to thicken slightly, then sprinkle on sesame oil. Serve with crispy sesame buns. Cut the buns in halves and stuff with the pork and vermicelli mixture.

Sesame Buns:
1 cup plain flour
¾ cup vegetable oil
750 g (1½ lb) plain flour
1½ cups boiling water
cold water
1½ teaspoons salt
30 g (1 oz) white sesame seeds

Pour 1 cup plain flour and vegetable oil into a pan and fry on moderate heat, stirring, until the flour is coloured a rich golden brown and is very fragrant. Leave the flour oil to cool.

Sieve remaining 750 g (1½ lb) flour into a mixing bowl and add boiling water. Work with chopsticks until incorporated, then add cold water and salt to make a smooth, fairly stiff dough. Knead for 10 minutes on a lightly floured board. Cover with a damp cloth and leave for 15 minutes, then knead for a further 5 mi-

nutes. Roll out to about 2 mm (1/16 inch) thick. Spread the flour oil thickly over the dough and roll up into a long tube. Cut into 2.5 cm (1 inch) lengths.

Roll each piece out across the folds, fold two ends in and turn the dough to one side. Roll out again, working away from the body. Continue rolling, folding and rolling for about five times. Press sesame seeds onto each piece and roll out into a 13 cm (5 inch) long cake, about 4 cm (1½ inches) wide. Place on a floured baking sheet and bake in a preheated hot oven for 7 minutes, turn and cook the other side for about 3 minutes. Cool slightly before cutting in halves.

STEWED SPARE RIBS WITH SALTED BLACK BEANS

375 g (¾ lb) pork spare ribs
2 tablespoons salted black beans
4 cloves garlic
3 spring onions
1 cm (½ inch) piece fresh ginger
1 fresh red chilli
3 tablespoons oil
1 teaspoon sugar
2 tablespoons dark soya sauce
2 tablespoons water
1 tablespoon Chinese rice wine
2 teaspoons sesame oil

Separate ribs and cut into 2.5 cm (1 inch) pieces. Crush black beans with garlic. Finely chop spring onions, ginger and chilli. Heat oil and fry spare ribs until well coloured. Add crushed bean paste and fry for an additional minute, then add onion, ginger and chilli and stir on moderate heat for 1 minute.

Pour in sugar, soya sauce, water and Chinese wine. Cover pan and turn heat down very low. Stew for about 45 minutes until ribs are very tender. Check seasonings and sprinkle on sesame oil.

STEWED PORK AND TARO YAM

500 g (1 lb) pork belly with rind
½ cup dark soya sauce
500 g (1 lb) peeled taro yam or sweet potato
oil for deep frying
5 cloves garlic
3 cubes fermented beancurd 'cheese' (see glossary), each 2.5 cm (1 inch) square
3 teaspoons Chinese rice wine
2 teaspoons sugar
pinch of white pepper
⅓ cup water
3 spring onions
185 g (6 oz) Chinese cabbage

Put pork into a saucepan and cover with water. Bring to the boil and lower heat. Simmer for 2 hours. Drain and cool, then rub with soya sauce. Cut taro yam or sweet potato into 5 cm (2 inch) squares about 0.5 cm (¼ inch) thick.

Heat oil and deep fry pork until dark brown with crisp skin. Lift out, drain and cut into pieces the same size as the taro. Add taro or sweet potato to the oil and deep fry until lightly coloured.

Heat a little oil and fry thinly sliced garlic and crumbled beancurd 'cheese' for 2 minutes. Add remaining soya sauce, Chinese wine, sugar, pepper and water and boil for 2 minutes.

Arrange alternate layers of pork and taro in a basin. Pour on the prepared sauce. Shred spring onions and sprinkle over the dish. Cover tightly and steam over fairly high heat for at least 1¼ hours.

Separate leaves of Chinese cabbage and cut each leaf in half. Bring a saucepan of water to the boil and drop in Chinese cabbage. Boil for 1 minute, then drain and arrange on a serving dish. Turn the meat and taro out onto the vegetables.

HONEY BAKED HAM

750 g (1½ lb) middle section of uncooked ham
3 tablespoons honey
45 g (1½ oz) sugar
3 tablespoons oil
1 large sheet cellophane paper
2 lotus leaves (optional)
aluminium foil

Steam ham for 30 minutes, then remove skin, fat and bone and cut into thin slices. Mix honey, sugar and oil. Arrange ham slices on the cellophane paper in a block and pour on the honey mixture. Wrap cellophane around the ham, then wrap in lotus leaves or foil.

Place ham on a baking tray and bake in a moderate oven for 2 hours. Leave to cool for 15 minutes before removing the wrappers. Serve with steamed bread crescents (page 144).

SZECHWAN BEEF STEW

AU LAM

1 kg (2 lb) stewing beef, preferably shin or flank
3 whole star anise
1 large onion, sliced
2.5 cm (1 inch) piece fresh ginger, sliced
1 dried tangerine peel or 1 lemon rind
2 tablespoons oil
6 cloves garlic
2 teaspoons black peppercorns, crushed
2 teaspoons Chinese brown peppercorns
¾ cup dark soya sauce
¼ cup Chinese rice wine
3 tablespoons sweet bean paste or hoisin sauce

Cut meat into 5 cm (2 inch) cubes. Place in a deep pot and cover with water. Add star anise, onion, ginger and tangerine peel or lemon rind. Cover and bring to the boil, then reduce heat and simmer for at least 2 hours.

Heat oil in a small saucepan and add chopped garlic and peppercorns. Fry for 1 minute, then add soya sauce, wine and bean paste or hoisin sauce. Bring to the boil and remove from the heat. Skim off any froth and pour the sauce into the meat. Cover and cook for a further 1 hour. Remove star anise and peel before serving.

CHINESE STEAK AND PEPPERS

375 g (¾ lb) frying steak
3 teaspoons Chinese rice wine
2 tablespoons dark soya sauce
1 teaspoon sugar
½ teaspoon salt
¼ teaspoon white pepper
1½ teaspoons cornflour
1 red pepper
1 green pepper
2 cloves garlic
3 spring onions
1 cm (½ inch) piece fresh ginger, sliced
3 tablespoons oil
2 tablespoons beef stock
sprigs of fresh coriander

Cut meat into 0.5 cm (¼ inch) slices, then into strips about 4 cm (1½ inches) wide. Put into a basin with ingredients from wine to cornflour. Toss to mix well and leave to marinate for 10 minutes.

Cut peppers into 2.5 cm (1 inch) squares, discarding seeds. Chop garlic finely and cut spring onions into 2.5 cm (1 inch) pieces. Shred ginger.

Heat oil and stir-fry peppers for 1½ minutes. Remove and keep warm. Put in garlic, onions, ginger and meat and stir-fry together for about 1½ minutes until meat is cooked through. Pour on any remaining marinade and add stock. Bring to the boil and return peppers. Cook briefly, then transfer to a serving dish. Garnish with fresh coriander.

SHREDDED BEEF WITH BAMBOO SHOOTS

250 g (½ lb) topside beef
125 g (¼ lb) canned bamboo shoots
4 spring onions
2.5 cm (1 inch) piece fresh ginger, sliced
1 clove garlic (optional)
1 tablespoon dark soya sauce
3 teaspoons oil
2 teaspoons Chinese rice wine
2 teaspoons cornflour
½ teaspoon salt
pinch of white pepper
pinch of monosodium glutamate (optional)
1 teaspoon sugar
3 tablespoons oil

Slice meat thinly across the grain, then into strips about 4 cm by 0.5 cm (1½ inches by ¼ inch). Drain and shred bamboo shoots. Cut spring onions into 2.5 cm (1 inch) pieces and shred ginger slices. Crush garlic (if used). Mix ingredients from soya sauce to monosodium glutamate and pour over meat. Leave to marinate for 15 minutes.

Heat oil in a wok and stir-fry beef until well coloured. Add bamboo shoots, spring onion, ginger and garlic and pour on any remaining marinade. Add a little water and cook for another minute. Add sugar and if necessary thicken sauce with a little cornflour mixed with cold water. Stir on moderate to high heat until sauce thickens and clears.

Honey Baked Ham (recipe this page).

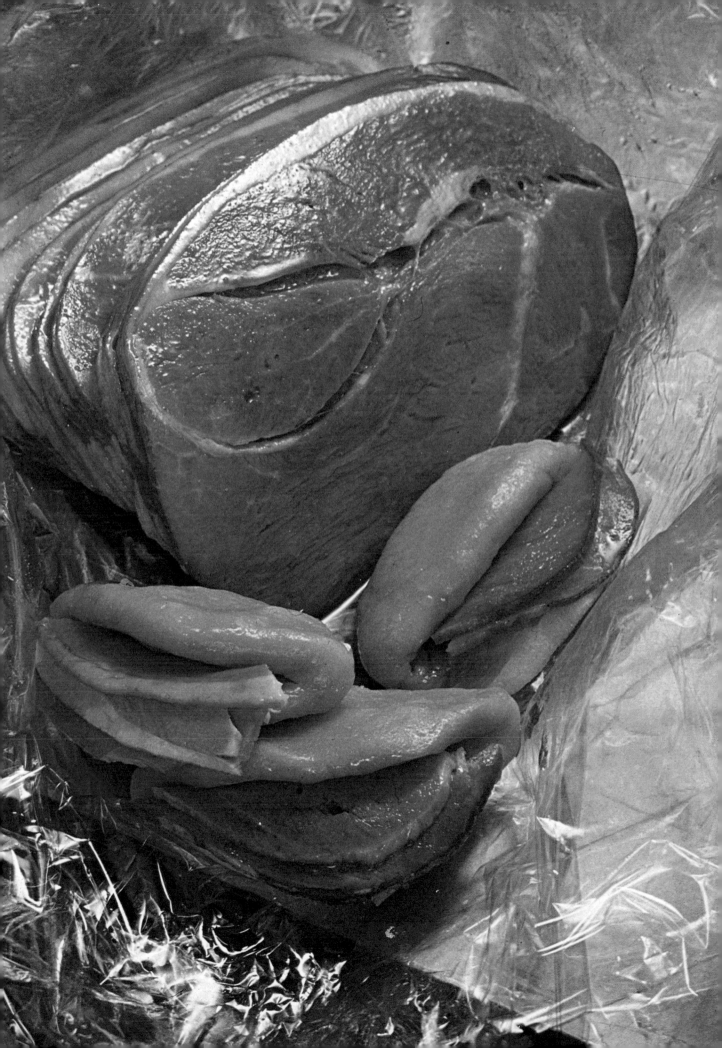

SHREDDED BEEF COUNTRY STYLE

250 g (½ lb) frying steak
3 tablespoons dark soya sauce
1 tablespoon Chinese rice wine
2 teaspoons sugar
1 teaspoon ginger juice
1 tablespoon cornflour
2 egg whites
125 g (¼ lb) celery
125 g (¼ lb) green beans
1 small carrot
1 small onion
2-3 fresh red chillies
oil for deep frying
2 teaspoons sesame oil
white pepper

Slice beef across the grain, then cut into fine shreds. Mix ingredients from soya sauce to egg whites and pour over the meat. Stir well and leave for 10 minutes to marinate.

Cut celery and green beans into matchstick pieces. Scrape carrot and cut into strips. Slice onion and chillies thinly.

Heat about 10 cm (4 inches) oil in a pan. Place shredded meat in a wire frying basket and lower into the hot oil. Fry until dark and crisp. Lift out and drain well. Pour off most of the oil. Put in vegetables and fry until cooked but still crisp. Put with the meat, mix well and sprinkle on sesame oil and white pepper.

BEEF IN OYSTER SAUCE

500 g (1 lb) flank steak or topside
2 teaspoons sugar
2 tablespoons cornflour
2 tablespoons dark soya sauce
1½ teaspoons sesame oil
2 teaspoons Chinese rice wine
1 tablespoon water or beef stock
12 dried Chinese mushrooms, soaked
1 green pepper
1 red pepper
6 spring onions
3 tablespoons oil
3 tablespoons oyster sauce
1 teaspoon cornflour
¼ teaspoon white pepper
1½ teaspoons sesame oil

Slice meat very thinly across the grain, then cut into strips about 2.5 cm (1 inch) wide. Marinate in a mixture of sugar, cornflour, soya sauce, sesame oil, wine and water or stock for 15 minutes.

Drain mushrooms and reserve 3 tablespoons of the soaking liquid. Remove stems from mushrooms. Wipe peppers and cut into 2.5 cm (1 inch) squares. Cut spring onions into 2.5 cm (1 inch) lengths.

Heat oil in a *wok* and fry meat for 1½ minutes. Lift out and keep warm. Reheat oil and fry peppers, spring onions and mushrooms for 1½ minutes, adding a little more oil if necessary. Add oyster sauce and mushroom liquid mixed with cornflour and white pepper. Bring to the boil and simmer until sauce thickens. Return meat

and heat through. Sprinkle on sesame oil and transfer to a warmed serving plate.

FRIED BEEF WITH PINEAPPLE AND YOUNG GINGER

250 g (½ lb) frying steak
pinch of salt
½ teaspoon sugar
1½ teaspoons ginger wine (see glossary)
2 teaspoons light soya sauce
4 drops sesame oil
pinch of white pepper
3 tablespoons water
1 heaped teaspoon cornflour
4 thick slices canned pineapple
10 cm (4 inch) piece fresh young ginger
1 fresh red chilli
1 clove garlic
3 tablespoons oil
3 teaspoons ginger juice
2 teaspoons dark soya sauce
sugar to taste
salt
¼ cup canned pineapple juice
1 teaspoon cornflour

Trim and slice meat very thinly across the grain. Put into a basin and sprinkle on salt, sugar, ginger wine, soya sauce, sesame oil, white pepper and water mixed with cornflour. Toss meat in this marinade to mix evenly, then leave to marinate for 20 minutes.

Drain and slice pineapple or cut into wedges. Peel and cut ginger lengthways into long, very thin slices. Slice chilli, discarding seeds. Crush garlic. Heat oil and fry meat until coloured but not completely cooked. Add pineapple, ginger, chilli and garlic and continue to cook on fairly high heat for another minute.

Mix ginger juice, soya sauce, sugar, salt, pineapple juice and cornflour and add to pan. Stir until the sauce thickens slightly and becomes clear.

SAUTE OF GREEN VEGETABLES WITH CRABMEAT DRESSING

500 g (1 lb) Chinese cabbage or Chinese long leaf lettuce
4 cups water
2 tablespoons oil
½ teaspoon salt
90 g (3 oz) cooked or canned crabmeat
2 teaspoons cornflour
⅓ cup water
2 egg whites
salt
white pepper
1 teaspoon light soya sauce
½ teaspoon sesame oil
3 teaspoons crab roe, crumbled (optional)

Wash cabbage or lettuce and shake out water. Break leaves from stem, discarding centre core. Bring water to boil with 1 tablespoon oil and when bubbling put in cabbage or lettuce. Reduce heat slightly and cook cabbage for 30-40 seconds, lettuce for a maximum of 20 seconds. Lift out and drain well. Arrange vegetables on a serving dish and splash with remaining oil.

Flake crabmeat and put into a small saucepan with cornflour mixed with water. Bring to the boil and stir until slightly thickened. When sauce is just bubbling slowly, pour in beaten egg white so it forms white threads in the sauce. Do not stir until the egg sets. Season with salt, white pepper and soya sauce. Pour dressing over the vegetable and sprinkle on sesame oil and crab roe.

TWO-COLOUR MUSHROOMS

10 dried Chinese mushrooms, soaked
1 teaspoon Chinese rice wine
1½ tablespoons dark soya sauce
1 teaspoon sugar
2 tablespoons chicken stock
1 tablespoon oil
15 canned white straw mushrooms or champignons
salt
¼ cup chicken stock
¼ cup fresh milk
1½ teaspoons cornflour

Remove stems from dried mushrooms and place in a dish with rice wine, soya sauce, sugar, chicken stock and oil. Cover and steam on high heat for 30 minutes.

Drain straw mushrooms or champignons. Boil with a little salt and chicken for 3 minutes. Drain well. Arrange black dried mushrooms on one side of a serving dish and white mushrooms on the other side.

Pour juices from black mushrooms into a small saucepan and add chicken stock and milk. Thicken with cornflour mixed with a little cold water. Bring to the boil and cook until thick. Add salt to taste and pour over the vegetables. Serve at once.

MIXED GREEN VEGETABLES WITH SALTED BLACK BEANS

500 g (1 lb) mixed green vegetables
2 cloves garlic
1 tablespoon salted black beans
1½ teaspoons sugar
3 tablespoons oil
6 spring onions, coarsely chopped
white pepper
1 teaspoon sesame oil

Choose vegetables such as long or green beans, snow peas, Chinese cabbage, kale, *bok choy*. Wash and slice vegetables. String snow peas and leave whole. Crush garlic and mash with salted beans and sugar.

Heat oil in a *wok* and fry the crushed beans for 1 minute. Put in harder green vegetables with spring onions and cook until beginning to soften, then add softer vegetables. Cover pan and allow vegetables to cook in their own steam for about 4 minutes on moderate to low heat. Splash in a very little water if the pan begins to dry. Season with white pepper and sesame oil. Serve at once.

STIR-FRIED VEGETABLE ASSORTMENT

8 dried Chinese mushrooms
250 g (½ lb) snow peas (*mange-tout*)
250 g (½ lb) canned bamboo shoots
1 small carrot
90 g (3 oz) frozen green peas
2 tablespoons oil
½ teaspoon salt
½ teaspoon sugar
1½ teaspoons dark soya sauce
2 teaspoons Chinese rice wine
¼ cup chicken stock
½ teaspoon cornflour
½ teaspoon sesame oil

Soak mushrooms in cold water for ½ hour. Wash snow peas and remove strings. Drain bamboo shoots and slice thinly. Scrape and slice carrot and cut into decorative shapes with a vegetable cutter. Thaw peas. Drop carrots into a small saucepan of boiling water to simmer for 2 minutes. Drain well. Drain mushrooms and slice thinly.

Heat oil in a *wok* and fry bamboo shoots with carrots for 1½ minutes. Season with salt, sugar, soya sauce and Chinese wine and add mushrooms and snow peas. Stir-fry for another 1½ minutes, then put in peas and add chicken stock. Bring to a rapid boil and continue to stir vegetables until the liquid is reduced.

Thicken sauce with cornflour mixed with cold water and sprinkle on sesame oil before serving.

CHINESE VEGETABLE OMELETTE

4 eggs
60 g (2 oz) Chinese roast pork
60 g (2 oz) canned bamboo shoots
3 dried Chinese mushrooms, soaked
1 small carrot
1 cm (½ inch) piece fresh ginger
8 chive or spring onion shoots
1 spring onion
pinch of salt
white pepper
1 teaspoon sesame oil
1 teaspoon cornflour
2 tablespoons water
3 tablespoons oil
fresh coriander leaves or fresh red chilli

Beat eggs lightly and set aside. Cut roast pork and bamboo shoots into thin shreds. Drain mushrooms and cut into thin shreds. Scrape carrot and cut into matchstick pieces. Shred ginger, chive or spring onion shoots and cut spring onion into 2.5 cm (1 inch) lengths.

Season eggs with salt and pepper. Add sesame oil, cornflour mixed with water and set aside. Heat oil and fry meat and vegetables until slightly softened. Pour in egg and stir vegetables evenly through the egg. Cook on low heat until egg is set underneath. Cut in halves or quarters and turn. Cook other side, then slide onto a serving plate. Garnish with sprigs of fresh coriander or shreds of red chilli.

SEASONED BAMBOO SHOOTS

500 g (1 lb) canned young bamboo shoots
oil for deep frying
2 tablespoons sweet bean paste
2 tablespoons dark soya sauce
1 tablespoon sugar
3 teaspoons Chinese rice wine
2 tablespoons water
pinch of white pepper
250 g (½ lb) leaf spinach
2 teaspoons sesame oil

Drain bamboo shoots and cut into 2 cm (¾ inch) cubes. Place in a large perforated ladle or strainer and lower into hot oil to fry until well coloured. Lift out and drain.

Place bamboo shoots in a dry pan with bean paste, soya sauce, sugar and rice wine. Add 2 tablespoons oil from the other pan and bring sauce to the boil. Add water and simmer until sauce is well reduced and bamboo shoots tender. Season with white pepper.

Drop spinach into boiling water to soften. Drain. Stir-fry in 1 tablespoon oil for 2 minutes, then arrange on a serving dish. Place seasoned bamboo shoots on top and sprinkle with sesame oil.

DRY-COOKED BEANS WITH BACON

500 g (1 lb) fresh or frozen broadbeans
30 g (1 oz) fatty pork belly
oil for deep frying
1 tablespoon light soya sauce
1½ teaspoons sugar
1 tablespoon water
2 spring onions, minced
2 cloves garlic, minced
1 teaspoon sesame oil

Chop pork belly finely and place with beans in a perforated ladle or strainer. Heat oil and lower in the beans and bacon. Cook until pork is crisp and beans cooked through. Lift out and drain well.

Cook beans with pork and remaining ingredients in a dry pan for 5 minutes on moderate heat. Raise heat a little at the end of cooking to dry off any liquid.

EGGPLANT SZECHWAN STYLE

375 g (¾ lb) eggplants
4 tablespoons oil
2 teaspoons sesame oil
6 spring onions
8 cloves garlic
1 cm (½ inch) piece fresh ginger
2 tablespoons *hoisin* sauce
1½ teaspoons sugar
2 tablespoons dark soya sauce
1½ teaspoons Chinese brown vinegar
⅓ cup chicken or beef stock
2 teaspoons cornflour
2 teaspoons sesame oil

Wipe eggplants, remove stalks but do not peel. Cut into 2.5 cm (1 inch) thick slices. Heat oil, add sesame oil and fry both sides of sliced eggplant for 1 minute. Turn heat down and cook until soft, then remove from pan and drain on absorbent paper.

Chop spring onions, garlic and ginger finely. Add to the pan with a little more oil if needed and fry for 1 minute. Add remaining ingredients except cornflour and sesame oil and bring to the boil. Simmer for 3 minutes, then return eggplant and cook for 10 minutes on moderate to low heat. Thicken sauce with cornflour mixed with a little cold water and cook until clear. Sprinkle on sesame oil.

Thinly sliced red chilli can be added at the same time as the spring onions to make this dish more piquant.

SZECHWAN PICKLE

1 carrot
250 g (½ lb) Chinese cabbage
2 medium cucumbers
1 giant white radish
4 fresh red chillies
2.5 cm (1 inch) piece fresh ginger
3 tablespoons Chinese rice wine
5 cups boiling water
1 tablespoon lightly crushed black peppercorns
45 g (1½ oz) salt
15 g (½ oz) sugar

Scrape and slice carrot. Wash and chop cabbage coarsely. Wipe and slice cucumbers (peel if preferred). Peel and slice radish. Slice red chillies and ginger. Put all ingredients into several large jars. Add remaining ingredients, seal jars and shake well. Leave for about 4 days in a dark, dry cupboard.

To use, remove pickles from the liquid and transfer to smaller jars. Store tightly sealed until needed. The pickling liquid may be used for a second pickling.

HOTPOT OF VEGETABLES AND BEANCURD

This hotpot is made in the kitchen in an earthenware cooking pot and carried to the table steaming hot.

8 squares soft beancurd
1 medium carrot
12 dried Chinese mushrooms, soaked
4 spring onions
60 g (2 oz) canned bamboo shoots
30 g (1 oz) 'cloud ear' fungus, soaked
100 g (3½ oz) chicken livers or pigs liver
8 cups water or chicken stock
soya sauce to taste
Chinese brown vinegar to taste

Slice or dice beancurd and set aside. Scrape carrot and slice thinly. Drain mushrooms and cut each in half. Chop spring onions. Thinly slice bamboo shoots. Drain 'cloud ear' fungus. Clean and slice chicken livers or pigs liver.

Bring stock to boil in an earthenware pot and drop in

Hotpot of Vegetables and Beancurd (recipe this page).

the carrot, mushrooms, spring onions, bamboo shoots, fungus and pigs liver (if used). Boil for 10 minutes, then add beancurd and chicken livers. Simmer gently for a further 10 minutes. Season to taste with soya sauce and/or Chinese brown vinegar.

BRAISED BEANCURD WITH CHINESE MUSHROOMS

4 squares soft beancurd
oil for deep frying
6 dried Chinese mushrooms, soaked
4 spring onions
½ cup chicken stock
1 tablespoon dark soya sauce
1 tablespoon oyster sauce
1 teaspoon sugar
1 teaspoon cornflour
1 teaspoon sesame oil

Choose firm pieces of beancurd. Cut each square of beancurd into quarters and place on a large perforated ladle. Heat oil to smoking point and lower in the beancurd to deep fry to a dark brown. Remove and drain well.

Drain mushrooms and remove stems. Cut spring onions into 2.5 cm (1 inch) pieces. Heat about 3 tablespoons oil in a *wok* and fry mushrooms and spring onions for 3 minutes. Add chicken stock, dark soya sauce, oyster sauce and sugar and bring to the boil. Add beancurd and cover. Braise until the mushrooms are completely tender and sauce well reduced.

Thicken with cornflour mixed with a little cold water and stir carefully until the sauce clears. Sprinkle on sesame oil and serve hot.

MA PO BEANCURD

½ cup oil
6 squares soft beancurd
90 g (3 oz) minced beef
90 g (3 oz) minced pork
8 cloves garlic, finely chopped
4 spring onions, finely chopped
1½ tablespoons hot bean paste
¼ teaspoon white pepper, or
    1½ teaspoons chilli oil
3 tablespoons dark soya sauce
½ cup beef stock
2 teaspoons cornflour
pinch of monosodium glutamate
1½ teaspoons sesame oil

Choose well-drained firm pieces of beancurd. Heat oil in a frying pan. Drain beancurd and hold in the palm of the hand. Carefully cut into cubes, then transfer to a slice and lower into the pan. Fry the beancurd without stirring to avoid breaking the cubes. Cook to a light golden brown. Lift out and set aside.

Add minced beef and pork to the pan and fry to a light brown before adding garlic, onion, bean paste, pepper or chilli oil and soya sauce. Cook for 3 minutes, then add beef stock mixed with cornflour, and mono-

sodium glutamate. Bring to the boil, reduce heat and simmer until sauce is thickened and meat is well seasoned. Return beancurd and cook for 2 minutes. Transfer to a serving dish and splash with sesame oil.

COLD BEANCURD SALAD

I have never eaten this delicious dish at any Chinese restaurant and I suspect that it is not an authentic Chinese recipe. It was taught me by an American woman who lived for over 30 years in Shanghai.

6 squares soft beancurd
6 lettuce leaves
1½ tablespoons light soya sauce
1 teaspoon sesame oil
2 teaspoons sugar
¼ teaspoon white pepper
2 spring onions, finely minced

Choose well-drained, fairly firm pieces of beancurd. Rinse beancurd and cut into thin slices. Wash and shred lettuce and place on a serving dish.

Mix remaining ingredients together, stirring to dissolve sugar. Place sliced beancurd on lettuce and pour on the dressing. Serve slightly chilled.

FRIED BEANCURD

8 squares soft beancurd
vegetable or peanut oil
2 tablespoons light soya sauce
1 tablespoon spiced salt powder

Choose well-drained, fairly firm pieces of beancurd. Wrap beancurd in a towel, put in dish, and place flat weight on top. Leave to drain and firm for at least 8 hours.

Wipe beancurd and place several pieces on a large perforated ladle. Heat oil to smoking point, then lower heat slightly. Carefully lower the ladle into the oil and leave until beancurd has cooked to a light golden colour. Lift out and drain thoroughly, then transfer beancurd to a serving dish. Cook remaining beancurd pieces and add to the plate.

Sprinkle with soya sauce and serve with a dip of spiced salt.

CLEAR MUSHROOM SOUP

18 large dried Chinese mushrooms, soaked
8 cups water or light beef and vegetable stock, mixed
1 teaspoon salt
2 teaspoons dark soya sauce
¼ teaspoon white pepper
8 spinach leaves or other green vegetables
4 spring onions
60 g (2 oz) chicken giblets (optional)

Drain mushrooms, remove stems and put into a saucepan with water or stock, salt, soya sauce and white pepper. Bring to the boil, then cover and reduce heat. Simmer for 3 hours until liquid is reduced by one-third. Put in spinach or vegetables, sliced spring onions and sliced giblets and simmer for a further 25 minutes. Add extra soya sauce and white pepper to taste.

WINTER MELON POND

4 kg (8 lb) winter melon
salt
375 g (¾ lb) chicken
100 g (3½ oz) chicken livers
100 g (3½ oz) chicken giblets
60 g (2 oz) fresh crab meat
60 g (2 oz) frozen peas
12 dried Chinese mushrooms, soaked
30 g (1 oz) dried lotus seeds (optional)
50 g (1¾ oz) raw smoked Yunan ham
2 tablespoons cornflour
2 tablespoons oil
salt
light soya sauce

Remove the top of the melon and cut edge in a zig-zag or scalloped design. Carve decorative figures and patterns on the sides. Scoop out seeds and fill the melon with salted water. Stand upright in a steamer and steam over gentle heat for ½ hour.

Remove any skin and bones from chicken and cut into small dice. Clean and slice livers and giblets. Cut crab meat into pieces. Thaw peas. Drain and soak mushrooms. Boil lotus seeds until tender. Shred ham finely and set aside as garnish. Coat chicken pieces lightly in cornflour and fry in oil until lightly coloured. Put into the melon pond and continue to steam.

Scoop a little water from the melon and put into a small saucepan with chicken livers and gizzards, crab meat, peas, mushrooms and lotus seeds. Boil until all are tender, then add to the melon pond. Season to taste with salt and light soya sauce. Stand the melon upright in a large bowl or rack which will hold it securely in place. Scatter on shredded ham before serving.

HAM AND MELON SOUP

250 g (½ lb) winter melon
125 g (¼ lb) unsmoked ham
2 chicken livers (optional)
6 dried Chinese mushrooms, soaked
5 cups chicken stock
2 cm (¾ inch) piece fresh ginger, sliced
2 teaspoons salt
1 teaspoon Chinese rice wine
2 teaspoons dark soya sauce
1 teaspoon vegetable oil

Peel melon and cut into 2.5 cm (1 inch) cubes. Slice ham thinly, then cut into threads. Slice chicken livers, (if used). Put melon, ham, livers and quartered mushrooms (stems removed) into a saucepan and add stock, ginger, salt, wine and soya sauce. Cover and bring to the boil. Simmer until melon is tender. Skim once or twice during cooking. Check seasoning. Pour into a serving dish and sprinkle on vegetable oil.

SHARKS FIN SOUP

185 g (6 oz) dried sharks fin
5 cups water
125 g (¼ lb) chicken breast
6 dried Chinese mushrooms, soaked
60 g (2 oz) smoked ham
6 cups chicken stock
2 teaspoons dark soya sauce
salt
white pepper
3 teaspoons cornflour
Chinese brown vinegar or mustard

Soak sharks fin overnight in cold water. Rinse in several lots of cold water and pick out any debris with tweezers. Cover with water and bring to the boil. Cook on low heat for 1 hour.

Slice and shred chicken finely. Drain mushrooms and shred. Shred ham. Bring chicken stock to the boil and add chicken, mushrooms and ham. Strain sharks fin and add to the soup with soya sauce. Bring to the boil and simmer until the meat and sharks fin are tender.

Season with salt and white pepper and thicken with cornflour mixed with a little cold water. Stir until the soup thickens and clears. Serve with bowls of Chinese brown vinegar or hot mustard.

FISH SOUP WITH CELERY

375 g (¾ lb) white fish fillets
4 sticks celery
1 teaspoon salt
pinch of white pepper
1 teaspoon Chinese rice wine
½ teaspoon sugar
1 tablespoon light soya sauce
2 tablespoons cornflour
1 tablespoon dried shrimps, soaked for 3 hours
2 cm (¾ inch) piece fresh ginger, sliced
5 cups boiling water
1 fish head (optional)

Cut fillets into thin slices. Quarter celery. Mix salt, pepper, wine, sugar and soya sauce together and rub into sliced fish. Leave for 10 minutes. Put cornflour into a plastic bag and drop in fish slices. Shake bag to coat fish thickly with cornflour.

Put dried shrimps and ginger into a large saucepan with celery, boiling water and the fish head (if used). Bring to boil and simmer for 2 minutes. Drop in fish slices and simmer for 4 minutes. Discard head before serving, if preferred. Check seasoning and serve hot.

STEAMED MINCED PIGEON IN BAMBOO SOUP CUPS

4 fresh small pigeons
90 g (3 oz) canned water chestnuts
4 cups chicken stock
30 g (1 oz) pickled turnip or cabbage
¼ teaspoon white pepper
light soya sauce
2 cm (¾ inch) piece fresh ginger, shredded

Clean pigeons and cut meat from bones. Mince meat finely with water chestnuts. Divide the meat into six portions and form into balls. Place one in the bottom of each bamboo bowl or individual soup ramekin. Pour on chicken stock. Add a piece or two of pickled turnip or cabbage, a sprinkling of white pepper, soya sauce and a few shreds of ginger. Place in a steamer and cook on moderate heat for 1 hour.

SOUR AND HOT SZECHWAN SOUP

125 g (¼ lb) frying steak
60 g (2 oz) chicken
2 teaspoons light soya sauce
2 teaspoons Chinese rice wine
3 eggs
3 cloves garlic
1 cm (½ inch) piece fresh ginger
7 cups beef stock or water
pinch of monosodium glutamate (optional)
2 tablespoons dark soya sauce
1 teaspoon salt
1 teaspoon chilli oil
1 teaspoon ground black pepper, or crushed Chinese
   brown peppercorns
1 tablespoon cornflour
6 dried Chinese mushrooms, soaked
2 squares soft beancurd
Chinese brown vinegar

Slice beef and chicken paper thin, then cut into shreds and sprinkle with light soya sauce and Chinese wine. Leave to stand for 10 minutes. Beat eggs lightly and set aside. Mince garlic and ginger and sprinkle over the beef and chicken.

Bring stock or water to the boil, add monosodium glutamate (if used), dark soya sauce, salt, pepper, chilli oil and cornflour mixed with a little of the cold stock or water. Cook for 3 minutes over high heat, then add beef and chicken and cook until the meat is very tender.

Slowly pour in beaten egg to form threads in the soup. Flavour to taste with vinegar, then add thinly sliced mushrooms and diced beancurd. Cook for 2 minutes. Transfer to a serving bowl. Serve with additional Chinese brown vinegar.

BIRDS NEST SOUP WITH QUAIL EGGS

125 g (¼ lb) prepared birds nests
6 cups chicken stock
1-2 teaspoons light soya sauce
1 teaspoon salt
¼ teaspoon white pepper
pinch of monosodium glutamate (optional)
185 g (6 oz) spinach, watercress or other green
   vegetables
1 teaspoon cornflour
2 egg whites
12 poached or boiled quail eggs (see below)

Soak birds nests for 4-5 hours in cold water. Pick out debris with tweezers, rinse well and drain. Pour into a saucepan, cover with water and bring to the boil. Cook for 2 minutes, then drain. Rinse with cold water.

Return birds nests to the saucepan and pour on chicken stock. Add seasonings from light soya sauce to monosodium glutamate. Bring to the boil, then reduce heat and simmer for 5 minutes. Add vegetables and boil until softened.

Beat egg whites and slowly pour into the soup. They will form into white threads. Do not stir until the egg sets. Add poached or boiled eggs and heat through before serving.

Note: To poach quail eggs wipe 12 small soya sauce dishes out with an oiled paper and break an egg into each. Place in a steamer and cook until set, about 2½ minutes. To boil put into a saucepan of cold water and bring to the boil. Cook for 5 minutes, then drain and cover with cold water.

WONTON SOUP

375 g (¾ lb) chicken pieces
6 cups water
8 Chinese dried mushrooms, soaked
12 spinach leaves
90 g (3 oz) chicken livers (optional)
1 tablespoon light soya sauce
pinch of monosodium glutamate (optional)
1 teaspoon sugar
salt
white pepper
1 teaspoon sesame oil
4 spring onions

Wonton:
1 package frozen or fresh *wonton* wrappers
155 g (5 oz) lean pork
4 spring onions
2 tablespoons chopped fresh coriander leaves
1 cm (½ inch) piece fresh ginger
1 clove garlic
2 teaspoons cornflour
2 teaspoons dark soya sauce
½ teaspoon sugar
½ teaspoon salt
pinch of white pepper
3 teaspoons peanut oil

Chop chicken pieces and put into a saucepan with water. Quarter mushrooms and add with spinach leaves and quartered livers. Season with soya sauce, monosodium glutamate (if used), sugar, salt and white pepper and bring to the boil. Cover, reduce heat and simmer for 40 minutes.

Thaw frozen wrappers and set aside. Mince all remaining *wonton* ingredients together, then knead to a smooth paste. Leave to stand for 10 minutes before preparing *wonton*.

Place a spoonful of filling towards the side of circular wrappers, or in one corner of square wrappers. Fold closest edge or corner over the filling. The two other corners should be pinched together, using a little water to stick them. The 'tail' can be either folded backwards or pinched into a waist close to the wonton filling to form a tail-like shape. Stick all joins with water or a

Birds Nest Soup with Quail Eggs, and Sour and Hot Szechwan Soup (recipes this page).

paste of cornflour and boiling water.

Strain soup through fine mesh and return to the pot with mushrooms and vegetables. Discard chicken pieces, or remove meat from the bones and add to the soup. Bring soup to the boil and drop in *wonton*. Reduce heat when it begins to bubble again and simmer for 5 minutes. Transfer to a soup tureen and sprinkle on sesame oil and finely chopped spring onions.

EGG SOUP WITH TOMATO

3 large tomatoes
1 small onion
1 tablespoon oil
5 cups chicken stock
1 tablespoon light soya sauce
2 teaspoons Chinese rice wine
salt
sugar
¼ teaspoon white pepper
3 egg whites
sprigs of fresh coriander

Drop tomatoes into boiling water, count to eight, then remove and peel off skin. Cut into wedges. Peel onion and chop finely and fry in oil until very soft and transparent. Put into a large saucepan with chicken stock, soya sauce, rice wine, salt and sugar to taste and white pepper. Bring to the boil and simmer for 10 minutes.

Lightly beat egg whites and slowly pour into hot stock to form white threads. Do not stir soup or it will go cloudy. Leave for 1 minute until egg sets, then put in tomato and cook gently for 3 minutes. Add fresh coriander and cook for a further minute. Check seasonings and transfer to a serving dish.

CHICKEN AND SWEET CORN SOUP

375 g (¾ lb) chicken breast
375 g (¾ lb) canned cream-style sweet corn
2 teaspoons salt
1 tablespoon light soya sauce
¼ teaspoon white pepper
2 egg whites
3 spring onions
1 clove garlic (optional)
4 cups chicken stock
cornflour
chopped fresh coriander leaves

Remove skin from chicken breast and cut into very small dice. Pour sweet corn into a saucepan and season with salt, soya sauce and white pepper. Gently heat through. Lightly beat egg whites. Chop onions and garlic very finely.

Bring chicken stock to boil in a large saucepan and add onion, garlic and chicken pieces. Boil for 3 minutes, then pour in beaten egg white. Stir gently so egg forms white strings in the soup. Add warmed cream-style sweet corn and stir thoroughly. Thicken soup if necessary with cornflour mixed with a little cold water. Check seasonings. Garnish with chopped fresh coriander and serve with extra soya sauce.

SOUP NOODLES WITH MEATBALLS

375 (¾ lb) lean pork
2.5 cm (1 inch) piece fresh ginger, sliced
6 spring onions, chopped
1 heaped tablespoon cornflour
3 teaspoons Chinese rice wine
1 teaspoon salt
¼ teaspoon white pepper
oil for deep frying
5 cups chicken stock
12 spinach leaves, or 8 cabbage leaves
6 dried Chinese mushrooms, soaked
155 g (5 oz) transparent vermicelli
soya sauce

Chop pork until very smooth. Mince ginger and onions and blend with pork, cornflour, wine, salt and pepper. Knead to a smooth paste, then form into walnut-sized balls.

Heat oil and deep fry balls to a light golden colour. Drain. Bring stock to boil and add pork balls and remaining ingredients. Add soya sauce to taste and simmer for 10 minutes.

FRIED EGG NOODLES WITH BEEF AND GREEN VEGETABLES

125 g (¼ lb) frying steak
1 tablespoon dark soya sauce
2 teaspoons Chinese rice wine
2 teaspoons cornflour
1 teaspoon sesame oil
pinch of sugar
pinch of white pepper
185 g (6 oz) thin egg noodles
3 tablespoons oil
100 g (3½ oz) green vegetables such as snow peas, celery, green pepper, beans, cabbage
3 spring onions
1 cm (½ inch) piece fresh ginger
½ cup beef stock
1 teaspoon cornflour
2 teaspoons dark soya sauce
½ teaspoon sugar

Slice beef thinly, then cut into strips and marinate in a mixture of dark soya sauce, Chinese wine, cornflour, sesame oil, sugar and white pepper. Leave for 15 minutes.

Drop egg noodles into boiling water to soften. Drain well. Heat 2-3 teaspoons oil in a *wok* and fry noodles until dark and crisp on the edges. Turn over in one piece and fry other side. Do not cook noodles with too much oil or they will become very greasy. Lift onto a serving plate and keep warm.

Drop vegetables into boiling water and leave to soften. Hard vegetables can be boiled briefly. Drain and add to the pan with remaining oil, spring onions cut into 2.5 cm (1 inch) lengths and shredded ginger. Stir-fry for 2 minutes, then pour over noodles.

Fry marinated beef for 2-3 minutes, then add beef stock mixed with cornflour and dark soya sauce. Sprinkle on sugar and simmer until sauce thickens. Spoon over noodles and serve at once.

HOR FUN NOODLES WITH BEEF AND BROCCOLI

500 g (1 lb) *hor fun* rice flour noodles
250 g (½ lb) frying steak
3 teaspoons Chinese rice wine
1 teaspoon sugar
2 tablespoons dark soya sauce
2 tablespoons sweet bean paste or *hoisin* sauce
6 tablespoons oil
8 broccoli spears
4 spring onions, shredded
¾ cup beef stock
cornflour
1½ teaspoons sesame oil

Drop noodles into a pot of boiling water. Remove from heat and leave to soften for 10 minutes. Drain well and allow to dry.

Slice beef thinly across the grain, then into small pieces. Marinate in a mixture of wine, sugar, soya sauce and bean paste for 10 minutes. Heat 2 tablespoons oil and fry meat for 3 minutes. Keep warm.

Cook broccoli in salted water until tender but still crisp. Heat 4 tablespoons oil and fry broccoli with spring onion for 1 minute. Remove and add noodles, frying until slightly crisp. Remove to a serving plate. Return meat and vegetables to the pan and pour on stock. Bring to the boil, then thicken with a little cornflour mixed with cold water. Spoon over noodles and sprinkle with sesame oil.

THICK AND THIN NOODLES IN SOUP

250 g (½ lb) *hor fun* rice flour noodles
250 g (½ lb) thin rice vermicelli
90 g (3 oz) pigs liver
90 g (3 oz) lean pork
60 g (2 oz) raw peeled shrimp
90 g (3 oz) green beans (optional)
125 g (¼ lb) green vegetables such as spinach, cabbage, lettuce
3 tablespoons oil
2 cloves garlic, crushed
¼ cup light soya sauce
sugar
white pepper
6 cups chicken or beef stock
2 teaspoons cornflour

Put *hor fun* noodles in a basin and cover with boiling water. Cover thin rice noodles with cold water. Leave to soften. Slice liver thinly and remove any membrane. Finely shred pork. Chop shrimps, beans and vegetables.

Heat oil and fry garlic for 1 minute. Add drained *hor fun* noodles and fry for 2 minutes. Transfer to a serving bowl. Add liver and pork to the pan and fry for 5 minutes, adding a little more oil if needed. Add shrimp, beans and remaining seasonings. Pour on stock and bring to the boil. Add vegetables and simmer for 3 minutes, then thicken soup slightly with cornflour mixed with a little cold water. Finally, drop in thin rice vermicelli. Heat through and pour over the *hor fun* noodles.

CRISPY RICE VERMICELLI WITH CHICKEN AND VEGETABLES

185 g (6 oz) rice vermicelli
90 g (3 oz) chicken breast
30 g (1 oz) chicken livers
6 dried Chinese mushrooms, soaked
60 g (2 oz) canned bamboo shoots
90 g (3 oz) *bok choy* cabbage
2 teaspoons Chinese rice wine
1 tablespoon light soya sauce
white pepper
2 teaspoons cornflour
3 tablespoons oil
¾ cup chicken stock
1 teaspoon sesame oil
salt
white pepper
2 spring onions, shredded
oil for deep frying

Break vermicelli into 5 cm (2 inch) pieces. Slice chicken thinly and chop livers. Drain and slice mushrooms and bamboo shoots and cut *bok choy* into 5 cm (2 inch) pieces. Heat a saucepan of water until boiling and put in *bok choy*. Cook until tender, then drain.

Marinate chicken in a mixture of rice wine, soya sauce, white pepper and cornflour for 5 minutes. Heat oil and fry chicken until lightly coloured. Add livers and cook until no pink shows, then add mushroms and bamboo shoots, *bok choy* and chicken stock. Boil for 1 minute, then season with sesame oil, salt and pepper. Thicken sauce slightly with a little cornflour mixed with cold water if necessary. Add spring onions.

Heat 5 cm (2 inches) oil in a deep pan and when very hot put in noodles. They will immediately expand and become very crisp. Cook for about 30 seconds. Lift out and drain. Place on a serving plate and pour on the chicken and vegetables.

COLD E FU NOODLES

375 g (¾ lb) thin egg noodles
2 tablespoons vegetable oil
1 tablespoon sesame oil
125 g (¼ lb) beanshoots
125 g (¼ lb) celery
125 g (¼ lb) cooked chicken
3 tablespoons sesame paste
2 tablespoons dark soya sauce
2 tablespoons lemon juice or
    1 tablespoon white vinegar
1 fresh red chilli
4 shallots
1 cm (½ inch) piece fresh ginger
1 tablespoon sesame oil
sugar to taste
2-3 teaspoons toasted white sesame seeds

Cook noodles in boiling salted water until just tender. Drain and rinse in cold water. Drain again and pour into a serving dish. Splash on vegetable and sesame oil.

Steep beanshoots in boiling water for 2 minutes to soften. Drain. Shred celery and steep in boiling water for 4 minutes, or simmer gently, until softened but still crisp. Shred chicken. Pile beanshoots, celery and chicken onto noodles.

Mix sesame paste with soya sauce, lemon juice or vinegar and enough water to make a thin sauce. Shred chilli, shallots and ginger and add to the sauce with sesame oil and sugar to taste. Mix well and pour over the noodles. Scatter sesame seeds on top. Serve cold.

STIR-FRIED MILK CUSTARD ON CRISPY NOODLES

8 egg whites
1¼ cups fresh milk
2 tablespoons cornflour
1 teaspoon salt
pinch of monosodium glutamate (optional)
oil
2 tablespoons pine nuts or cashews, chopped
90 g (3 oz) rice vermicelli
⅔ cup melted pure lard
45 g (1½ oz) cooked ham, finely diced
sprigs of fresh coriander
tomato, sliced

Beat egg whites until foamy. Stir in milk, cornflour, salt and monosodium glutamate (if used). Beat until well mixed, then set aside.

Heat about 5 cm (2 inches) oil in a deep pan or *wok* and when very hot put in chopped nuts on a perforated ladle. Cook to a light golden brown then remove and drain. Do not overcook as they will continue to darken after being removed from oil.

Reheat oil and put in noodles which will very quickly puff up to at least double the volume. Remove quickly to avoid burning. Place on an oval serving dish. Keep warm in an open oven.

Pour lard into a *wok* and when warm stir in the egg and milk mixture. Cook on moderate to low heat until it begins to curdle, then continue to stir until the mixture has completely amalgamated and is fairly thick. Drain off any excess lard and pour the milk custard over noodles. Sprinkle with diced ham and fried nuts and garnish with coriander sprigs and sliced tomato. Serve quickly or noodles will soften.

SINGAPORE-STYLE NOODLES

This is a Hong Kong speciality created for those who like a bit of curry flavour.

250 g (½ lb) thin rice vermicelli
4 tablespoons oil
3 shallots, sliced
2 cloves garlic, thinly sliced
1 cm (½ inch) piece fresh ginger, shredded
1 fresh red chilli, thinly sliced
1 green chilli, thinly sliced
100 g (3½ oz) raw shrimp, peeled
1 medium onion, thinly sliced
3 spring onions, shredded
100 g (3½ oz) beanshoots
30 g (1 oz) frozen green peas

1 tablespoon mild curry powder
½-1 teaspoon chilli powder
2 teaspoons dark soya sauce
salt
white pepper
1 egg, beaten
fresh coriander leaves, chopped

Soak vermicelli in cold water to soften. Drain and leave to dry. Heat 2 tablespoons oil and fry shallots and garlic until soft. Add ginger, shrimp and chillies and stir-fry for 3 minutes. Add onion and spring onion and cook until soft. Remove and set aside.

Heat remaining oil and add noodles with beanshoots and peas. Cook on lowered heat for 5 minutes, then remove and keep warm. Add curry powder, chilli powder and soya sauce to the pan and return first lot of cooked ingredients. Add salt and pepper to taste. Stir-fry for 1 minute. Return noodles and stir to mix well. Lift onto a serving plate and keep warm.

In another pan wipe with an oiled cloth and pour in beaten egg. Turn pan to make omelette as thin as possible and cook until firm. Lift out and shred finely.

Garnish noodles with shredded egg and chopped coriander.

RICE CONGEE WITH LIVER

500 g (1 lb) glutinous rice
100 g (3½ oz) pigs liver
100 g (3½ oz) lean pork
2 egg whites
salt
white pepper
3 Chinese doughnut pastries (optional)
45 g (1½ oz) sliced salted turnip or other salted vegetables
4 spring onions, chopped
oil for deep frying

Rinse rice in cold water, place in a large saucepan and cover with water rising to 10 cm (4 inches) above the level of the rice. Bring to the boil, reduce heat and simmer, covered, until rice becomes a thick, starchy soup.

Slice liver and pork into thin strips. Beat egg whites lightly. Add meat and liver to the soup and cook until tender. Stir in beaten egg white and leave to form white strings in the soup. Season with salt and pepper.

Slice Chinese doughnut and fry until deep golden brown. Ladle congee into large soup bowls and top with chopped spring onions, fried doughnut pastries and slices of salted vegetable.

This can be reheated several times and improves in flavour with keeping.

FRIED CANTONESE RICE

750 g (1½ lb) cooked white rice
3 tablespoons lard
2 eggs
60 g (2 oz) raw peeled shrimp
60 g (2 oz) roast pork
1 large onion

Toffee Apples (recipe page 175).

4 spring onions
60 g (2 oz) frozen green peas
4 dried Chinese mushrooms, soaked
1 tablespoon dark soya sauce
1 teaspoon sugar
white pepper
salt
1 teaspoon sesame oil
finely chopped fresh coriander leaves

Fry rice in lard until grains are well coated. Set aside. Beat eggs and drop into the pan. Swirl pan so egg forms a very thin pancake. Cook until firm, then lift out. Allow to cool then shred finely.

Put in shrimps and cook until pink, then remove from pan and spoon over the rice. Cook pork for 1 minute adding more lard if needed. Add finely chopped onion and spring onions and cook for another minute. Put in peas and thinly sliced mushroom and stir-fry for a further 2 minutes. Splash in soya sauce and add sugar. Stir, then return rice and shrimps to pan. Season with white pepper and salt, if needed, and stir on moderate heat until warmed through.

Transfer to a serving dish. Sprinkle an oil. Decorate with finely shredded egg and fresh coriander.

LOTUS RICE

6 dried scallops, soaked
8 dried Chinese mushrooms, soaked
30 g (1 oz) dried duck, soaked (optional)
30 g (1 oz) dried shrimp, soaked
45 g (1½ oz) canned bamboo shoots
45 g (1½ oz) canned water chestnuts
185 g (6 oz) Chinese roast pork
2 small Chinese sausages (optional)
5 cups water
2 tablespoons oil
250 g (½ lb) glutinous rice
2 tablespoons peanut oil
45 g (1½ oz) roasted peanuts
1 tablespoon sesame oil
salt
white pepper
4 spring onions, chopped
1 tablespoon finely chopped fresh coriander
1 dozen lotus leaves or aluminium foil

Bring a small saucepan of water to boil and drop in scallops, mushrooms, dried duck and dried shrimps. Cook until softened. Drain, reserving liquid. Cut all into very fine dice. Drain bamboo shoots and water chestnuts and dice finely. Shred roast pork and dice sausage.

Bring water to boil and put in diced dried ingredients and oil. Add washed rice and boil until rice softens. Add diced meat and vegetables, reserved liquid, peanut oil, sesame oil and roasted peanuts and continue to cook until rice is almost done. Season to taste with salt and pepper and stir in chopped spring onion and coriander. Mix well.

Divide the mixture between the lotus leaves or pieces of foil. If using lotus leaves brush surface with oil to soften. Wrap rice and tie bundles with strong string. Place in a steamer and cook for about ½ hour. Serve hot or cold.

ALMOND JELLY WITH MIXED FRUITS

1 tablespoon gelatine
1½ cups lukewarm water
1 teaspoon almond extract, or to taste
45 g (1½ oz) sugar
¾ cup evaporated milk
canned fruit cocktail in syrup

Soften gelatine in lukewarm water and heat until dissolved. Mix in almond extract, sugar and evaporated milk and heat through, stirring to dissolve the sugar. Pour into a greased tray and leave to set.

When firm cut into diamond shaped pieces. Serve in glass dessert dishes topped with mixed fruit. Pour on a generous amount of the syrup. Serve chilled.

SWEET PEANUT SOUP

185 g (6 oz) raw peanuts
2 tablespoons white sesame seeds
8 cups water
125 g (¼ lb) white sugar
4 tablespoons cornflour
½ cup thick cream

Place peanuts in a hot oven or under a moderate grill to roast until lightly coloured. Place in a cloth and rub off skins. Toast sesame seeds lightly and grind peanuts and sesame seeds to a fine powder in a heavy-duty blender, adding a little water if needed.

Pour into a saucepan with water and sugar and simmer until smooth and creamy. Strain to remove any large pieces of peanut and bring to the boil again. Mix cornflour with thick cream and stir into the soup. Heat through until thickened. Serve warm.

CANDIED YAM

625 g (1¼ lb) yam or sweet potato, peeled
flavourless vegetable oil
45 g (1½ oz) white sesame seeds
½ cup water
60 g (2 oz) sugar

Use a melon baller to scoop out balls of yam or sweet potato. Heat oil for deep frying and drop in the balls to cook until golden brown. Remove and drain. Place in a steamer and cook over high heat until soft.

Toast sesame seeds lightly and set aside to cool. Pour water and sugar into a saucepan and bring to the boil, stirring to dissolve sugar. Cook until slightly sticky. Put in yam balls several at a time and roll in the syrup until well coated. Remove from syrup, sprinkle with sesame seeds and leave to cool or serve warm.

RED BEAN SOUP

250 g (½ lb) small red beans
8 cups water
1 cup sugar

1 dried tangerine peel
30 g (1 oz) dried lotus buds (optional)

Place red beans with water, tangerine peel and lotus buds in a saucepan and simmer for about 2 hours until beans are completely tender. Add sugar and heat through until completely melted. Cook for a further 10 minutes on high heat. Serve warm.

TOFFEE APPLES

2 medium sized eating apples
100 g (3½ oz) plain flour
1 egg
1⅓-1½ cups water
250 g (½ lb) sugar
1 tablespoon oil
2 tablespoons white sesame seeds
flavourless vegetable oil for deep frying
iced water
ice cubes

Oil a serving plate lightly and have all ingredients and utensils on hand as this dish requires precision timing.

Peel apples, remove cores and cut each into 8 pieces. Lightly beat egg and combine with ⅓ - ½ cup water and flour to make a smooth, fairly thick batter. Put oil for deep frying on to heat.

Mix sugar with 1 cup water and 1 tablespoon oil and bring to the boil. Simmer until it forms a thick, light coloured toffee. Test if toffee is ready by dropping a spoonful into iced water. If it hardens immediately the toffee is done. Add sesame seeds to the toffee and set near the cooker.

When oil is almost at smoking point coat several pieces of apple with the batter and put into the oil. Fry to a golden brown. Lift out with wooden chopsticks and place in the toffee syrup. When coated transfer to the iced water to harden. Place on the oiled serving plate. Cook all apple in this way and serve immediately with the bowl of ice water. Dip into the water again to harden if the toffee has begun to soften.

Firm ripe banana may be used in this way also, either sliced or whole.

BIRDS NEST WITH COCONUT

185 g (6 oz) birds nests
5 cups boiling water
45 g (1½ oz) dried lotus seeds
45 g (1½ oz) sugar
¼ cup thick coconut milk

Soak birds nests in cold water for 5 hours. Pick out impurities with tweezers. Drain and soak in hot water for ½ hour. Drain again. Boil lotus seeds in a little slightly sweetened water until soft. Drain.

Put birds nests, lotus seeds and water into a saucepan and bring to the boil. Pour in sugar, stirring to dissolve. Boil for 4 minutes. Pour in coconut milk and heat through. Serve immediately.

For other sweets using birds nests, simply boil cleaned birds nests with sugar and water, chill thoroughly and add such fruits as grapes, melon balls, slices of apple, orange or mandarin.

JAPAN

Japanese cuisine has developed largely independently of other Asian countries, including its close neighbours Korea and China. The food is unique in its delicacy of taste, splendid in its simplicity, and quite unlike the food of any other nation. Nevertheless, the Japanese are always ready to adopt a style that appeals to them and fits in with their way of life, and some aspects of their food have been subject to agreeable influences from outside. Curry with rice, for instance, is a national favourite though it bears little resemblance to a genuine Indian dish; the Nagasaki area specialises in food with a noticeable Chinese leaning, the result of its centuries as the main trading port of Japan; in Kyoto, vegetarian dishes are popular; while resident Koreans have introduced into local dishes such aspects of their own cooking as garlic and chilli. The popular Tempura was apparently devised by Portuguese living in Japan, and even Sukiyaki is a relatively recent innovation, being introduced, it is believed, to encourage the Japanese to include more meat in their low-protein diet.

But these new elements are only minor changes in a cooking style that has remained consistent over the centuries. It may take some time to learn to appreciate the delicate flavours of Japanese food, to accept the small quantities of meat — but, believe me, it is well worth the effort! Japanese cooking is essentially a system of undercooking and of moderation in seasoning, with little blending of flavours. The food is intended to be appreciated for its own natural qualities, unmasked by heavy sauces, rich spices or strong seasonings.

Its visual qualities are of the utmost importance, and the almost austere simplicity of presentation calls for care, time and dedication to achieve just the right degree of apparently casual 'non-arrangement' that is a Japanese hallmark. A good chef is a master of form and shape, and possesses an innate sense of colour co-ordination as well as the ability to combine good basic ingredients with a minimum of garnish to create outstandingly delicious dishes.

Japan being an island country, much of its cooking focuses on fish, shellfish and seaweeds, used with pork, poultry and fresh vegetables and supplemented by protein-rich beancurd. Red meat has always been prohibitively expensive here, though special milk-fed cattle, massaged into plump tenderness, are bred for the famed Kobe steaks. Top quality beef is also used in dishes like Shabu Shabu (Hotpot), Sukiyaki and Teppan Yaki (barbecued food), which are popular with the Japanese and are also thought to be most amenable to the Western palate.

Throughout Japan I found very small restaurants (often consisting of just a counter and stools), which, I learned, were specialised eating places serving one particular dish or a very limited menu of select foods. I quickly learned to pick out a Sushi bar, where one sits facing a refrigerated display cabinet filled with different raw fish, prawns, omelette and shellfish; the Sushi chef prepares the rice balls with one's choice of toppings and passes them across the counter with a bowl of soya sauce and a spoonful of hot horseradish paste. Tempura (Fried Vegetables and Seafood in Crisp Batter), Sashimi (Raw Fish), Yakitori (Charcoal-Grilled Chicken) and different types of noodles served plain, in bowls of steaming soup, or cold in scrubbed wooden boxes, were all to be had in these speciality establishments. A warming bowl of noodles on the way home from work or *en route* to a movie house on a cold winter's night promotes a wonderful feeling of wellbeing. One feature (invaluable to tourists) of Japanese restaurants is the illuminated display case, near the entrance, which houses plastic replicas of the restaurant's specialities — a fashion that has crept into Japanese eating places in many parts of the world.

The Japanese like their food to taste slightly sweet, and add sugar and *mirin* (rather like a sweet sherry) to most savoury dishes. I have reduced the quantities of sugar suggested in these original recipes to what I believe will better appeal to Western tastes. The few basic ingredients that give Japanese food its unique qualities are absolutely necessary to achieve authenticity of flavour. Most are now readily available overseas, and include *shoyu,* a light soya sauce (buy genuine Japanese *shoyu* for best results); *wasabi,* hot green horseradish powder; *mirin,* a sweet *sake;* and *sake* itself, the dry rice wine served warm as Japan's most popular drink and used generously in cooking. *Miso* is a thick yellowish- or brownish-red paste made from fermented soya beans, somewhat similar to the bean pastes used in Chinese cooking, and is used as a flavourer, thickener, sauce and filling. It is available in pressure-sealed containers and keeps indefinitely, even after opening, but I have included a recipe for an acceptable substitute using chickpeas.

Many forms of seaweed are used. *Kombu,* a large-leafed kelp, and *wakame* (similar to *kombu,* and usually sold in strips, often salted) are used to make delicate stocks for simmering meats and as the base for soups. *Nori,* sea laver compressed in sheets, has a crisp fragrance that is heightened by a brief toasting before use. It is used as a garnish, as a nibbler, and as the wrapping for Norimaki Zushi, rolled cakes of vinegared rice that are a traditional part of the Sushi assortment. Seaweeds, especially *nori,* should be stored in an airtight container to prevent mould or softening; toasting will restore crispness, and the larger-leafed seaweeds can be washed and re-dried in a low oven or hot sunlight if they are beginning to spoil as a result of incorrect storage. *Kombu* and paper-thin shreds of *katsuobushi,* dried bonito fish, are boiled together to make *dashi,* an aromatic stock; *dashi* is now available in dehydrated and powdered form and is indispensable for soup making *(see page 178).*

Fresh spring onions, thin white *negi* (Japanese leeks) and *daikon* (giant white radish) are used in many savoury dishes. Raw *daikon* has a delightful piquancy, and it is often used as a shredded salad accompaniment, but when cooked it has the sweet taste of a young mar-

White Radish with Sweet Miso Filling (recipe page 194).

row. Much of the protein in the Japanese diet is derived from *tofu*, soft beancurd made from soaked and ground soya beans. Powdered 'instant' *tofu* is now available; it sets in minutes and is a good substitute for fresh bean-curd. Eggs are another good source of protein and are used to make a variety of soft steamed custards. A sweetened omelette flavoured with *mirin* is cooked in layers and compressed into a roll as a tasty cold dish, and the same omelette is also used as a topping for Sushi.

There are many types of Japanese mushroom. Dried black and brown varieties with large round caps are used as a vegetable and for decoration, the caps being carved with floral motifs. Tiny golden long-stemmed mushrooms and types similar to the French *morilles* are used fresh or preserved in brine, and give certain soup and hotpot dishes an unusual musky taste. Citrus juice (especially that of the *yuzu*, a tangerine-like fruit) gives a sweeter and more subtle flavour than lemon juice to many savoury dishes.

Japanese cooks use several main cooking methods, and a meal will normally be made up of a balanced selection of foods cooked by various methods. Most dishes are cooked on top of the stove using water or stock rather than oil, resulting in food that is lighter and more easily digested than many other Asian foods; if deep-frying is called for, the foods to be fried are often coated with batter which is sealed quickly in the hot oil, thus preventing too much oil seeping into the food. Steaming, charcoal barbecueing, grilling and boiling are also applied. Normal Western kitchenware can be used for most dishes, but a pair of long-handled cooking chopsticks can be useful as these perform many duties — once you get the hang of them! A heavy iron frying pan or an electric frying pan is needed for barbe-cued dishes and Sukiyaki.

It is in presentation that Japanese food stands specta-cularly apart. There are innumerable rules applicable to the order in which dishes should be served, the style of the serving bowls, the number of dishes to be served at a particular meal, and the dishes to be served together. While the intricacies of Japanese table etiquette are far too involved to be included here, presentation cannot be ignored.

'European food, every blasted plate is round.' So wrote a Japanese poet, for the Japanese never cease to be amused by Westerners wanting to serve everything on round plates. Japanese tableware, by contrast, com-prises an extraordinary array of bowls, small plates, dishes, cups without handles and tiny pots for drinking tea and *sake*. These are made of porcelain, china, plain scrubbed wood or lacquered wood, and are chosen both to harmonise with the food and to be admired for their artistic quality. Japanese provincial ware is particularly attractive, for it is made of sturdy clay and has a kind of naive artistry that will appeal to the lover of ethnic arte-facts.

Rice is served in a small- or medium-sized lidded bowl (the lid can be upturned and used to hold the pickles that should be served with rice at the end of a meal). Soup comes in lidded lacquer bowls. Large- or medium-sized plates and dishes (round, square, rectan-gular or oval) will be used to serve boiled, grilled or fried foods. Small dishes are used for serving small por-tions of dressed vegetables, seafood salads, and vege-tables and pickles. Lacquered boxes with lids hold dressed rice dishes, while compartmented boxes are used for the *bento* or 'lunchbox' meals. Noodles come in large china bowls or wooden boxes, depending on whether or not they are served in soup. Small wooden chopsticks (each pair in an individual paper envelope) or slightly longer, pointier lacquer chopsticks are used. Soups are sipped straight from the bowl, and spoons are only used for soft custards and similiar dishes.

Soup is served first, to be sipped throughout the meal, and is followed by several dishes cooked by diffe-rent methods and containing a variety of main ingre-dients. Last comes plain boiled rice of the short-grain type, sticky enough for the grains to cling together easily. Small pickled foods, such as salted plums, are served with the rice. Sweets are not served with meals, but are eaten between meals. A fragrant green tea is served before and after the meal; warmed *sake*, at around 42°C (108°F), can be served throughout.

BASIC STOCK
DASHI

1 piece dried kelp *(kombu)*, about 5 cm (2 inches) square
4 cups water
15 g (½ oz) dried bonito flakes *(katsuobushi)*

Simmer *kombu* and water together for 3 minutes. Re-move *kombu* and sprinkle dried bonito flakes over the water. Let stand undisturbed for 2 minutes, then strain. Will keep in the refrigerator for 2-3 days.

SOYA BEAN PASTE
MISO

Thick, salty Miso paste prepared from fermented soya beans is used in many Japanese dishes. It is obtainable in most countries in sealed containers and will keep for a very long time, even unrefrigerated and unsealed. However, if it is difficult to obtain locally, this recipe (which makes 315 g or 10 oz) will provide a suitable substitute. It does not keep for more than a few days, so prepare just as much as is needed.

200 g (6½ oz) canned chick peas, drained
3 tablespoons white vinegar
2 tablespoons lager beer
1 tablespoon salt
1 tablespoon sugar
1 tablespoon light soya sauce
1 tablespoon dark soya sauce

Blend together in a liquidiser or pound to a smooth puree in a mortar. This makes a dark *miso*. When white *miso* paste is needed, omit dark soya sauce and add 2 tablespoons more salt.

RICE CAKES WITH RAW FISH
SUSHI

I tasted my first Sushi in a tiny bar somewhere in the

centre of Tokyo's sparkling entertainment centre, Shinjuku. The restaurant was the typical small room with a long counter and stools. Behind the counter the chefs faced a selection of chilled seafood which they deftly sliced on order, preparing the tiny rice cakes with a great deal of showmanship. As each Sushi was prepared it was passed across the counter to be eaten with shoyu *(soya sauce), and* wasabi, *a fiery pale green horseradish paste.*

Traditionally, sake or cups of green tea form the accompanying beverage. Sushi can be eaten with chopsticks, but enthusiasts often prefer to use the fingers, which makes it very much easier and a lot of fun.

The account at the end of a meal is calculated from the number of pieces of Sushi served, and the corresponding cost of the toppings, some of which can be astronomically expensive. Certain types of fish are so special that a single Sushi can cost more than a normal meal.

Rice for Sushi is of a slightly moister type than that served with Japanese meals, and is very delicately flavoured with vinegar.

375 g (¾ lb) short grain rice
salt
2 tablespoons white vinegar
1½ teaspoons sugar

Wash rice well in cold water and put into a heavy-based saucepan. Cover with cold water to 4 cm (1½ inches) above the level of the rice. Add a little salt, cover the saucepan tightly and bring to the boil. When the steam begins to rise, turn heat down to the lowest point and cook until rice is tender and liquid completely absorbed (about 14 minutes normally, though this will depend on the type of rice used).

For extra flavour, add a leaf of kelp *(kombu)* to the water before cooking. Remove it half-way through the cooking. When rice is done, turn heat up high and shake pan for several seconds. This will help the rice grains to fluff up. Leave to stand in the saucepan, covered but off the heat, for 10 minutes.

Spoon rice into a large mixing bowl. Sprinkle on vinegar, sugar and 1 teaspoon salt and stir rice lightly with a chopstick. Leave stand for 15 minutes. Prepare the garnishings, using the above quantity of rice to make 36 pieces of Sushi.

Garnishings:
45 g (1½ oz) raw or smoked salmon
45 g (1½ oz) raw tuna
45 g (1½ oz) white fish fillets (trout, whiting or perch)
ginger juice
lemon juice or white vinegar
salt
sugar
1 small cucumber
6 medium raw prawns
90 g (3 oz) Japanese omelette (see recipe page 192)
powdered green horseradish *(wasabi)* made into a paste with water
2 sheets dried laver *(nori)*, each 20 cm (8 inches) square
sweet pickled ginger
pickled gourd (optional)

Chill the fish in the freezer for 15 minutes to make it firm and easier to slice thinly. Using a very sharp knife slice salmon thinly across the grain. Sprinkle with a few drops of ginger juice or lemon juice. Cut tuna into 0.5 cm (¼ inch) slices and season with a few drops of vinegar mixed with a little salt and sugar to mask the raw taste (optional). Slice white fish thinly. Cut all fish pieces into sections of 5 cm by 3 cm (2 inches by 1¼ inches) to fit the rice cakes.

Wash the cucumber and rub with salt. Cut into thin slices lengthways, then into matchstick pieces. Marinate in a mixture of 1 tablespoon vinegar, 2 teaspoons sugar and 1 teaspoon salt.

Prawns may be used raw, but are preferable if lightly steamed or boiled. Remove heads and shells but leave tail fins intact. Trim tails square.

Prepare omelette and when cool, cut into pieces to fit the Sushi. Shred pickled ginger and gourd, if used.

Hold the dried laver over a flame to crisp, then place on a napkin or ideally a small flexible bamboo mat. Cover with a 1 cm (½ inch) layer of rice, pressing on with wet hands. Leave a 1 cm (½ inch) border of uncovered laver on one end. Drain cucumber and arrange strips down the centre of the rice, adding a few shreds of ginger and gourd. Lift napkin or bamboo mat and roll over. Roll forward to form the laver-wrapped rice into a roll. Press down firmly, then roll again and remove napkin or mat. If necessary, stick edge of laver down with a little water. Dip a knife blade into water and cut each roll into 6 pieces. Set aside.

Make rice cakes with the remaining rice, to fit garnishings. Keep hands wet during working to prevent rice sticking. Select a piece of fish and with a wet hand, take a ball of rice. Work the rice into an oval shape, pressing firmly in a kneading motion in the palm of the hand. Spread a smear of horseradish paste on the fish and press down on the rice cake. Prepare all rice, making slightly longer cakes to fit the prawns.

An alternative method of preparation is to press rice into a square cake tin or box with removeable sides. Put in a 2.5 cm (1 inch) layer. Pat down firmly, then remove sides. Cut rice into cakes to fit the fish and omelette.

To serve Sushi, arrange a selection of wooden platters or lacquered boards. Decorate with available greenery such as chrysanthemum leaves, parsley, finely grated cucumber skin, fresh horseradish or shredded lettuce. Serve with small dishes of soya sauce and horseradish paste.

If preferred, fish for Sushi and other raw fish dishes may be very lightly cooked by steeping in boiling water for 25 seconds, then draining, refreshing with cold water and draining again. This will remove the very fishy taste. Pat dry on kitchen towels before using.

ASSORTED RAW FISH PLATE

SASHIMI NORIAWASI

90 g (3 oz) tuna fillet
90 g (3 oz) bream
60 g (2 oz) salmon
60 g (2 oz) freshwater trout
3 medium cuttlefish (squid)
2 pieces dried laver *(nori)*, each 15 cm by 10 cm (6 inches by 4 inches)

6 medium raw prawns
6 raw scallops or clams (optional)
1 small cucumber
¼ giant white radish
white vinegar
salt
sugar
lemon peel
8 cm (3 inch) piece fresh ginger
small lettuce leaves
watercress sprigs
powdered green horseradish (wasabi), or freshly grated
　horseradish
lemon juice
light soya sauce

For good Sashimi it is essential that all fish and shellfish are absolutely fresh, preferably bought live from the market where possible. Though the dish calls for raw fish, in the interest of hygiene, any surface bacteria can be eliminated by dipping the sliced portions of fish or shellfish into a bowl of very hot water and then into a dish of iced water. Drain well and wipe with a kitchen towel before using.

Remove skin from tuna and cut diagonally to the grain into 1 cm (½ inch) thick slices, then into pieces about 4 cm by 2.5 cm (1½ inches by 1 inch). Slice salmon and bream thinly and cut into 2.5 cm (1 inch) squares. Skin may be left on bream. Remove any bones from trout, skin, then cut into narrow strips and tie into simple knots.

Wash cuttlefish, peel off skin and cut away head and ink bag. Clean out and rinse well. Using a sharp knife, cut one cuttlefish into thin circles, discarding tentacles if these are not considered appetising. Cut the other two open and press flat. Score with a criss-cross pattern on one side.

Hold dried laver over a flame to crisp slightly, then press onto the cuttlefish on the unscored sides. Roll up tightly and cut into 2.5 cm (1 inch) pieces. When serving, stand these on end to expose the alternate colours of white and green.

Shell prawns, leaving tail fins intact. Remove dark veins and slit open underneath the prawns. Press flat. Parboil or sprinkle with a little lemon or ginger juice. Rinse scallops or clams in salted water and cut into thin slices.

Wash cucumber and rub with salt. Shred finely and marinate in a sweet mixture of 1 tablespoon vinegar, 3 teaspoons sugar and ½ teaspoon salt for 5 minutes. Drain.

Peel white radish, cut into 2.5 cm (1 inch) blocks. With a small sharp knife shred the top section to form 'chrysanthemum flower' decorations. Place a sliver of lemon peel in the centre of each 'flower'.

Peel and shred ginger. Wash lettuce and watercress and shake out water.

On a large platter or several smaller ones, arrange the fish and shellfish attractively. Decorate with shredded cucumber and ginger, the radish flowers and sprigs of watercress. Place lettuce leaves beneath prawns, scallops and clams.

Prepare sauces by mixing the following:

Sauce 1:
¼ cup light soya sauce
2 tablespoons lemon juice

Sauce 2:
⅓ cup light soya sauce
1 tablespoon powdered green horseradish, or
　freshly grated horseradish

Serve the sauces in small bowls. Dip fish into one of the sauces before eating.

SALMON SAUTEED WITH LEMON

LEMON YAKI

This classic Japanese dish has a touch of artistry in the garnish of cucumber fans and lemon slices carved into butterfly shapes. Much of the joy of Japanese cooking is in making the dishes look attractive.

750 g (1½ lb) salmon or salmon trout
1 teaspoon salt
oil or butter
2 lemons
2 small cucumbers, about 13 cm (5 inches) long

Cut salmon into six streaks, across the body. Sprinkle with salt and let stand for several minutes. Rinse off and wipe dry. In a heavy-based pan heat oil or butter and saute fish gently for 4 minutes on each side. Sprinkle with juice of 1 lemon during cooking. When fish is cooked, lift each slice onto a small plate, preferably rectangular, and decorate with cucumber fans and lemon butterflies prepared as follows.

Wash cucumbers and cut each into 3 pieces. Slice each piece lengthways into 0.5 cm (¼ inch) slices, discarding end pieces. To make cucumber fans, use a very sharp knife to cut each slice into strips, leaving the end 0.5 cm (¼ inch) uncut. Gently press the 'fan' ribs open.

Slice remaining lemon into thin slices and make butterfly shapes by cutting away a small triangle from two opposite sides, leaving wing-like shapes.

TUNA GLAZED WITH MISO

GYODEN

1 medium cucumber
1 tablespoon white vinegar
2 teaspoons sugar
1 teaspoon salt
6 small red radishes (optional)
6 thick slices tuna, about 90 g (3 oz) each
90 g (3 oz) dark *miso* paste
2 tablespoons sugar, or to taste
1½ tablespoons *mirin*
¼ cup water
1 tablespoon white sesame seeds

Wipe cucumber and rub with salt. Cut into fan shapes (see previous recipe) or cubes and marinate in a mixture of vinegar, sugar and salt for 3 minutes. Wash radishes and carve into flower shapes. Dip into iced water to open the 'petals'.

Clean fish slices and trim off any loose skin. Grill fish on both sides until lightly browned and cooked through.

Salmon Sauteed with Lemon (recipe this page).

Mix *miso* with sugar, *mirin* and water and cook in a small saucepan on low heat until thick. Stir frequently. Spread *miso* thickly over each slice of fish and continue grilling until the sauce is firm and shiny like a glaze. Lift onto a serving plate and keep warm.

Toast sesame seeds lightly under the grill and sprinkle over fish. Decorate each plate with a radish flower and several pieces of cucumber.

FRIED WHOLE FISH WITH PON-ZU SAUCE

1 fresh bream, about 625 g (1¼ lb)
salt
2 tablespoons plain flour
1 egg
oil for deep frying

Pon-zu Sauce:
½ cup lemon or orange juice
½ cup *dashi* stock
½ cup light soya sauce
½ giant white radish
1 fresh red chilli

Clean fish and scale. Cut away fillets leaving backbone, head and tail in one piece. Place carcass on a baking tray, sprinkle with salt and roast in a warm oven (150°C/300°F/Gas Mark 3) for 30 minutes.

Cut fillets into 2.5 cm (1 inch) cubes and sprinkle with a little salt. Mix flour, egg and ½ teaspoon salt with enough cold water to make a batter of medium consistency. Heat oil in a deep frying pan. Dip fish pieces in the batter and fry to a golden colour. Fish should be cooked through, but still moist. Do not over-cook. Remove from oil and drain well. Arrange fish pieces in the prepared carcass and keep warm.

Mix lemon juice with *dashi* and soya sauce and pour into small sauce bowls. Grate radish and chilli together. Put fish on a serving plate and decorate with the radish and chilli, or serve grated mixture in small sauce dishes.

FISH AND BAMBOO SHOOTS

NITSUKE

This is a typical Nimono (boiled) dish which is usually served near the beginning of a meal. Nimono dishes are flavoured with combinations of soya sauce, sugar, mirin, dashi and miso.

1 medium carrot, thinly sliced
salt
6 thick slices white fish (cod, snapper, haddock)
1 cup *dashi* or fish stock
⅔ cup *mirin*
1 tablespoon sugar
2 tablespoons light soya sauce
155 g (5 oz) canned bamboo shoots, thinly sliced

Place carrot in a small saucepan and cover with slightly salted water. Bring to the boil, turn heat down and sim-mer until cooked but still crisp. Drain and cool. Set aside.

Arrange fish in a wide pan, pour on stock and *mirin* and simmer on low heat for 3 minutes, then sprinkle on sugar and soya sauce, shaking pan to dissolve the sugar and mix the sauce. Cook until fish is tender, then lift onto a heated plate. Add bamboo shoots to the pan and simmer in sauce for 2-3 minutes.

Place one piece of fish and several pieces of bamboo shoot in small bowls. Dip carrot pieces in the remaining sauce, then add to the bowls. Pour about 1 tablespoon sauce over each fish slice.

SEAFOOD HOTPOT

YOSENABE

A favourite winter dish. This hearty seafood hotpot is served in an earthenware pot taken straight from the fire to the table.

3 small potatoes, or 2 small sweet potatoes
24 gingko nuts (optional)
500 g (1 lb) white fish fillets
90 g (3 oz) raw shrimp or prawns
90 g (3 oz) raw clams or scallops
250 g (½ lb) *kamaboko* (fish cake) or mild flavoured
  sausage
½ head Chinese cabbage
250 g (½ lb) spinach or mustard greens
8-10 dried Japanese black mushrooms, soaked in cold
  water for ½ hour
1 carrot, thinly sliced
100 g (3½ oz) *shirataki* noodles
6 cups *dashi* stock
light soya sauce
salt

Peel potatoes or sweet potatoes and cut into 1 cm (½ inch) thick slices. Parch gingko nuts, if used, in a hot oven or under the grill, then rub off skins, holding the hot nuts in a kitchen towel.

Slice fish into pieces about 5 cm (2 inches) square. Peel and devein shrimp or prawns. Wash clams or scal-lops in slightly salted water and cut in halves.

Slice *kamaboko* or sausage thinly. Rinse vegetables and chop coarsely. Drain soaked mushrooms and cut a cross in the cap of each.

Pour *dashi* stock into a large earthenware or fireproof pot and bring to the boil. (A very light chicken stock can be used in place of *dashi*, but the essential seaweed and fish flavour would be missing, making this a rather tasteless dish by comparison.) When stock begins to bubble, add potato and cook on high heat for 8-10 minutes, or until the vegetable begins to soften. Sweet potato will require less cooking time.

Add the green vegetables, carrot, gingko nuts and mushrooms. Turn heat down slightly and cook for 5 minutes, then add noodles, fish, shrimp, clams or scal-lops and *kamaboko* or sausage. Cover the pot and turn heat down very low. Simmer for about 4 minutes, then take the pot to the table and set it over a portable fire or fondue spirit fire.

Season to taste with soya sauce and salt. If available, Japanese *sansho,* a blend of powdered Japanese pep-pers, should be sprinkled over the dish.

GRILLED EEL

UNAGI KABAYAKI

This delicious glazed eel dish is eaten mainly in August, when its health-giving properties are believed to ensure against the debilities caused by summer heat.

750 g (1½ lb) fresh eel
2 tablespoons oil
¼ cup *mirin*
¼ cup light soya sauce
shredded cucumber or giant white radish

With a sharp knife cut skin around the head of the eel and pull off the skin in one piece. Slice eel open, cut away backbone and cut meat into 8 cm (3 inch) pieces. Flatten and brush with oil.

Place under the grill and cook on moderate heat, for at least 5 minutes on each side, brushing occasionally with oil. Combine *mirin* and soya sauce in a small saucepan and bring to the boil. Dip eel pieces in the sauce and return to the grill to cook until the glaze begins to dry. Brush with more glaze and continue cooking, adding more glaze until the eel is done and the sauce used up.

Place eel pieces on a serving dish and garnish with shredded cucumber or radish.

PRAWNS BAKED IN SEA SALT

24 very large raw prawns
2 tablespoons *sake*
625 g (1¼ lb) sea salt
bamboo or metal skewers

Sauce:
For each serving mix the following:
½ teaspoon powdered green horseradish *(wasabi)*
2 teaspoons *dashi* stock
2 tablespoons light soya sauce

Peel prawns, leaving heads and tail fins intact. Devein. Arrange on a flat platter and sprinkle with *sake*. Stand for 2 hours.

Wipe prawns with paper towels and insert skewers along the bodies from tail to head. Coat each thickly with salt, pressing on firmly. Put on a baking tray which is covered with a thin layer of salt. Sprinkle a little more salt on top and bake for about 12 minutes in a fairly hot oven (220°C/425°F/Gas Mark 7). Alternatively cook over a charcoal barbecue for about 10 minutes.

Wipe off salt and arrange prawns on a serving dish. Put sauce in individual sauce dishes and serve with the prawns.

BAKED CRAB ON THE SHELL

6 small raw crabs
salt
3 Japanese leeks, or 6 spring onions
6 gingko nuts (optional)
2 eggs
1 tablespoon *mirin*

1 tablespoon light soya sauce
30 g (1 oz) lightly toasted breadcrumbs

Sauce:
For each serving mix the following:
¾ teaspoon hot mustard powder
2 teaspoons dark soya sauce
1 teaspoon *dashi* stock or water

Drop crabs into a large pot of briskly boiling, lightly salted water. Cook for 10 minutes, then remove and allow to cool. Break open the underpart of each shell and scrape out meat and yellow yolk. Discard all inedible parts. Crack open legs and claws and remove meat. Shred crabmeat and put in a mixing bowl with yolks.

Chop leeks or spring onions finely. Slice gingko nuts, if used, and add to the crabmeat with onions. Bind with eggs and season with *mirin,* salt and soya sauce.

Wash crab shells and wipe dry. Spoon mixture into the shells, rounding the top smoothly. Coat lightly with breadcrumbs, pressing on with the fingers. Bake in a moderate oven (190°C/375°F/Gas Mark 5) for 15 minutes, then serve with the prepared sauce.

CRAB HOTPOT

KANI CHIRI

1 large raw saltwater crab
4 squares soft beancurd
250 g (½ lb) green vegetables (Chinese cabbage, mustard greens, spinach)
1 medium carrot
6 dried black mushrooms, soaked in cold water for ½ hour
12 small Japanese golden mushrooms, or champignons
3 Japanese leeks or 6 spring onions, cut into 4 cm (1½ inch) pieces
6 cups *dashi* stock

Sauce and Dips:
15 cm (6 inch) piece giant white radish
1 fresh red chilli

Mince together.

1 large onion
1 teaspoon salt

Mince onion and mix in salt.

⅔ cup lemon juice
⅔ cup *dashi* stock
⅓ cup light soya sauce

Mix together, heat slightly and allow to cool.

Clean crab and remove inedible parts. Rinse crabs and chop into several large pieces leaving legs attached to the body pieces.

Slice beancurd into 3-4 pieces each. Wash green vegetables, shake out water and chop roughly. Scrape carrot and slice thinly, or cut into decorative shapes with a vegetable cutter. Drain dried mushrooms, discard stems and cut a cross on the top of each with a sharp knife.

Heat stock in a large earthenware pot, put in all vegetables and crab pieces and simmer for about 7 minutes. Add beancurd. Set over a portable fire on the table and continue to simmer until ready to set. Serve together with the sauces in small bowls.

COLD LOBSTER WITH CUCUMBER

6 very small raw lobsters, or crayfish
salt
1 medium cucumber
4 tablespoons lemon juice
1½ tablespoons light soya sauce
1½ tablespoons sugar, or to taste

Drop lobsters into boiling, slightly salted water and cook for about 8 minutes until meat firms and shells are bright red. Cut lobsters in halves, remove meat and rinse in cold water. Drain then cut into 2 cm (¾ inch) cubes.

Wipe cucumber and use a vegetable cutter to make decorative shapes, or cut into 2 cm (¾ inch) cubes. Rinse out lobster shells, scraping away any flesh. Sprinkle on a little salt. Arrange lobster meat and cucumber pieces in the shells and place two half shells on each rectangular or oval platter.

Mix lemon juice and soya sauce with sugar, and pour over the lobsters. Chill slightly before serving.

DEEP FRIED SEAFOOD AND VEGETABLES

TEMPURA

1 small sweet potato or 1 slice pumpkin
1 medium carrot
6 green beans
2 small green peppers
1 small eggplant
salt
12 spring onions
6 chrysanthemum leaves (optional)
125 g (¼ lb) thin white fish fillets
125 g (¼ lb) cuttlefish
12 medium raw prawns, in shells
1½ teaspoons ginger juice
½ teaspoon sugar
pinch of salt
cornflour
vegetable oil
1 teaspoon sesame oil

Batter:
500 g (1 lb) plain flour
3 tablespoons cornflour
3 eggs
cold water

Sauce:
1 cup *dashi* stock
½ cup light soya sauce
½ cup *mirin*
2 tablespoons grated giant white radish
sesame seeds (optional)

Peel sweet potato or pumpkin and cut into 0.5 cm (¼ inch) slices. Rub with a little salt. Peel and slice carrot. Cut beans into 5 cm (2 inch) lengths. Wipe peppers and cut into 2.5 cm (1 inch) squares. Wipe eggplant and cut into 0.5 cm (¼ inch) slices and sprinkle with salt. Cut 10 cm (4 inch) pieces from white part of spring onions. Wash and wipe chrysanthemum leaves (if used).

Cut fish into 5 cm (2 inch) squares. Skin cuttlefish and cut into thin circles or flatten and score a criss-cross pattern across one surface. Remove heads and shells from prawns leaving tail fins on. Clip fins. Sprinkle fish, cuttle fish and prawns with a mixture of ginger juice, sugar and salt.

Make a medium to thin batter with flour, cornflour, eggs and cold water. Beat for 1 minute, but leave very slightly lumpy. Set aside for 10 minutes.

Pour *dashi*, soya sauce and *mirin* into a saucepan and heat gently, then remove and leave to cool. When cold, add grated radish and a sprinkling of sesame seeds and pour into small dipping dishes.

Heat oil for deep frying. Add sesame oil. Dip vegetable pieces into the batter and place several at a time in the hot oil. Fry until well coloured and cooked through. Drain on absorbent paper. Coat fish, prawns and cuttlefish with cornflour, shake off excess and coat with the batter. Fry until golden and cooked through.

Arrange the seafood and vegetables attractively on a serving dish and serve at once. Ideally, Tempura should be eaten piece by piece as it is cooked. If possible fry in a portable pan on or near the table. Dip the Tempura in sauce before eating.

TURBO IN THE SHELL

12 raw turbos (in shells), or 6 large raw whelks or
    abalone
1 teaspoon caustic soda
6 dried black mushrooms, soaked in cold water for ½
    hour
1½ teaspoons sugar
2½ tablespoons light soya sauce
¾ cup *dashi* stock
1 Japanese leek, or 3 spring onions
6 canned water chestnuts, or gingko nuts
30 g (1 oz) watercress or mustard greens
1 tablespoon *mirin*

Place turbos or other shellfish in a deep saucepan and cover with boiling water. Set on high heat and boil for 15 minutes. Drain and open shells, using an oyster knife if necessary. Scrape out meat and clean shells with a knife and plenty of salt water. Slice shellfish into very small pieces. Return empty shells to the pot and add caustic soda. Cover with water and boil again, then rinse very thoroughly and wipe dry.

Drain mushrooms, discard stems and slice thinly. Marinate shellfish and mushrooms for 3 minutes in the sugar, soya sauce and *dashi*.

Wash leek or spring onions and chop finely. Parch gingko nuts under the grill, rub off skin and slice thinly, or finely chop water chestnuts. Wash green vegetables and chop finely. Mix shellfish and mushrooms with leek and vegetables, adding gingko or water chestnuts. Put in a small saucepan with the mari-

Crab Hotpot (recipe page 183).

nade from the shellfish and mushrooms and a little more water and simmer for 6 minutes.

Divide cooked ingredients between the cleaned shells. Mix remaining soya sauce and *dashi* and *mirin* and pour into the shells. Place filled shells in a wide, flat-based pan and cook on moderate heat until shellfish is tender, then transfer shells (two turbo or one whelk per serving) to small bowls which have been lined with tiny pebbles to hold the shells upright. Serve while contents are still bubbling.

Traditionally this dish is cooked at the table over a small alcohol fire with each turbo in a small earthenware bowl containing pebbles.

QUAIL EGGS, CHICKEN MEATBALLS AND PICKLED CUCUMBER ON SKEWERS

Chicken meatballs:
250 g (½ lb) minced, cooked chicken
2 egg whites
½ teaspoon salt
pinch of pepper
vegetable oil
1 teaspoon sugar
3 teaspoons dark soya sauce
2 teaspoons *mirin*
1 tablespoon orange juice

For skewers:
1 medium cucumber
2 tablespoons vinegar
1 teaspoon salt
12 quail eggs (or 6 small hen eggs)
12 thin bamboo skewers
shredded lettuce or cabbage (optional)

To prepare chicken meatballs, blend the minced chicken and egg whites thoroughly. Season with salt and pepper. Using wet hands form the paste into 24 small balls. Heat about 2.5 cm (1 inch) oil in a frying pan and fry meatballs to a deep golden colour. Remove from the pan and drain on absorbent paper.

Remove oil from the pan and pour in sugar, soya sauce, *mirin* and orange juice. Stir on low heat till sugar dissolves, then return the meatballs to the pan and turn slowly in the sauce. Simmer gently, shaking the pan to turn meatballs constantly, until sauce forms a glaze on the meatballs. Turn off heat and allow meatballs to cool.

To prepare skewers, wipe cucumber and cut into 12 pieces. Put in a flat dish and sprinkle on vinegar and salt. Stand for 10 minutes, turning once. Put quail eggs in a saucepan, cover with cold water and bring to the boil. Turn heat down a little and boil eggs for 6 minutes. If using small hen eggs boil for 8 minutes. Drain off hot water, then cover with cold water. When eggs are cold, drain and shell. Cut small eggs in halves (if used).

Thread onto each skewer one meatball, a piece of cucumber, a quail egg (or half a small egg) and another meatball. Arrange on a bed of finely shredded lettuce or cabbage, or place on attractively folded paper napkins. Serve as part of the main meal, or as *hors d'oeuvres*.

GRILLED CHICKEN
YAKITORI

6 chicken thighs
⅓ cup *sake*
⅓ cup dark soya sauce
60 g (2 oz) sugar
¼ cup *mirin*
2 teaspoons powdered ginger
¼ giant white radish or 1 small cucumber
salt
6 bamboo or metal skewers

Wash chicken thighs, wipe dry and insert skewers securely along bones. Cook over a charcoal barbecue or under a moderate grill until partially done.

Mix *sake*, soya sauce, sugar and *mirin* and pour into a wide, flat bowl. Lay the chicken thighs in the sauce for 5 minutes, turn and marinate other side for 5 minutes. Return to the griller or barbecue and cook for 2 minutes on each side.

Return to the sauce, then grill again, this time brushing the chicken with the remaining sauce while chicken cooks and sauce forms a dark, shiny glaze. Sprinkle on powdered ginger.

Shred radish or cucumber and sprinkle with salt. Arrange chicken thighs on small plates and garnish each with a small mound of radish or cucumber.

JAPANESE BARBECUE
TEPPANYAKI

375 (¾ lb) sirloin or striploin steak
1 clove garlic, crushed
6 large raw prawns
6 large oysters in half shell
1 large sweet potato
salt
2 green peppers
2 small onions
butter or oil

Sauce: (choose 2 or 3)
½ giant white radish
2 fresh red chillies

Mince finely.

60 g (2 oz) Japanese leek

Mince finely.

1 tablespoon hot mustard powder
2 teaspoons *sake*
5 tablespoons dark soya sauce

Mix ingredients together.

To prepare barbecue first slice steak thinly, then cut into bite-sized pieces. Rub with crushed garlic. Remove shells and legs from prawns, leaving heads and tails intact. Rinse oysters in clean salt water, remove from shell then replace.

Peel sweet potato and cut into 1 cm (½ inch) thick slices, rub with a little salt. Wash peppers, slice into quarters. Remove seeds and stems. Peel onions and slice.

Heat a little oil or butter in a heavy iron griddle or skillet, preferably over a charcoal fire. Cook several pieces of the meat, seafood and vegetables at a time and serve immediately. Dip into one of the sauces before eating. Pon-zu Sauce *(page 182)* can also be used.

Variations on ingredients can be made according to season and preference, using sliced chicken (marinated in a little *sake* and soya sauce), lobster, clams or scallops in the shell, fresh mushrooms, fillets of fresh fish or very thin pork chops.

GOURMET BEEF

TSUKIYAKI

6 fillet steaks, about 155 g (5 oz) each
½ cup light soya sauce
⅓ cup *mirin* or *sake*
½ teaspoon *sansho* or ½ teaspoon ginger juice
butter
vegetable oil
eggplant or green pepper, sliced

Sauce:
hot mustard powder
dashi stock or water

Place fillet steaks in a large bowl. Prepare a marinade of soya sauce, *mirin, sansho* or ginger juice and pour over steaks. Stand for 45 minutes, turning several times.

Heat a little butter and oil in a heavy-based frying pan or skillet and when pan is very hot quickly seal steaks on both sides. Pour in marinade and simmer on moderate heat for 4-5 minutes, according to preference. Do not overcook. Turn steaks several times during cooking to absorb most of the sauce.

Saute slices of eggplant or green pepper in a little oil to serve as a garnish. Serve with dips of hot mustard powder mixed to a paste with a little *dashi* or water.

FRIED MEAT, VEGETABLES AND NOODLES

SUKIYAKI

750 g (1½ lb) sirloin, striploin or rump steak
3 squares soft bean curd
12 spring onions
6 dried Japanese black mushrooms, soaked in cold
   water for ½ hour
500 g (1 lb) watercress or spinach
2 onions, thickly sliced
185 g (6 oz) *shirataki* noodles, pre-cooked
45 g (1½ oz) suet
6 eggs (optional)

Warishita Sauce:
1 cup light soya sauce
75 g (2½ oz) sugar
⅓ cup *sake* or *mirin*
1¼ cup *dashi* stock

Cut meat into wafer-thin slices. Cut beancurd into 2.5

cm (1 inch) cubes. Remove roots and green tops from spring onion and cut remaining portion into 5 cm (2 inch) pieces. Remove mushroom stems and slice caps in halves. Wash watercress or spinach and break leaves into 5 cm (2 inch) pieces. Arrange all vegetables, meat, noodles and beancurd on a wooden platter.

Heat a heavy-based frying pan on a portable fire (or use an electric frying pan). Rub with suet until thoroughly oiled. Put beef in the pan and brown, turning once. Push meat to the side of the pan.

Mix sauce ingredients and pour into a small jug or teapot. Add some vegetables, beancurd and noodles to the pan and pour on some of the sauce. Cook on moderate heat until vegetables are cooked through but still crisp and meat is done to individual taste. Add more sauce and ingredients to the pan when cooked ingredients are served.

If using eggs, break one into each bowl, beat lightly. Dip food into beaten egg before eating.

BEEF HOTPOT

SHABU SHABU

This meal is similar to the Mongolian Rinsed Mutton Hotpot. Thin slices of meat are cooked in a bubbling stock, heated at the table over a charcoal fire. The soup is then eaten with noodles and chilli pepper powder dressing. A great winter dish and an interesting change from the traditional Sukiyaki.

1 kg (2 lb) steak (sirloin, rump or striploin)
500 g (1 lb) spinach, watercress, cabbage or lettuce
12 fresh mushrooms
250 g (½ lb) canned bamboo shoots, drained
2 medium carrots
12 spring onions
3 squares soft beancurd, quartered
6 cups *dashi* or soup stock
1 large piece dried kelp *(kombu)* (optional)
500 g (1 lb) thick egg noodles or spaghetti, partially
   cooked
3 tablespoons spring onion or Japanese leek, finely
   chopped
chilli powder, or *sansho* to taste

Sauce 1:
3 teaspoons light soya sauce
1 teaspoon powdered green horseradish *(wasabi)*

Mix well and serve in individual bowls.

Sauce 2:
45 g (1½ oz) white sesame seeds
1 cup *dashi* stock
¾ cup light soya sauce
2 teaspoons sesame oil
2 tablespoons lemon juice
2 teaspoons finely chopped red chilli

Toast sesame seeds under a griller, then grind and mix with all other ingredients in a small saucepan. Bring to the boil, remove from heat and cool. Pour into small bowls.

To prepare Shabu Shabu, slice beef across the grain into wafer-thin slices. Clean green vegetables and cut leaves in halves. If using watercress break into sprigs. Remove mushroom stems and peel or wipe caps. Slice bamboo shoots thinly and cut carrots into thin discs. Remove roots and green tops from spring onions and cut into 5 cm (2 inch) pieces.

Divide meat between six wooden platters and place vegetables and beancurd on one or two serving dishes in the centre of the table near the hotpot. Pour stock into the pot, add kelp and bring to the boil. If the fire is not strong enough, bring stock to the boil before bringing to the table. Using wooden chopsticks or fondue forks, hold meat in bubbling stock until cooked to individual taste, ideally very rare. Dip in either of the sauces before eating.

When most of the beef is cooked, add some vegetables and beancurd and cook briefly. When all meat and vegetables are finished, remove kelp and add noodles to the broth. Cook until soft, then spoon into soup bowls. Sprinkle on chopped spring onion or leek and chilli powder or *sansho* and add ladle of the enriched soup.

MINCED PORK BALLS ON SKEWERS

NIKU DANGO NO KUSHI ZASHI

3 dried Japanese black mushrooms, soaked in cold
    water for ½ hour
4 spring onions
500 g (1 lb) pork tenderloin, finely minced
2 eggs
1½ tablespoons light soya sauce
2 teaspoons sugar
2 teaspoons *mirin*
½ teaspoon salt
pinch of monosodium glutamate
60 g (2 oz) breadcrumbs
oil for deep frying
bamboo skewers

Sauce:
⅓ cup *sake* or *mirin*
⅓ cup dark soya sauce
1 tablespoon sugar
⅓ cup *dashi* or soup stock
sansho or chilli powder
juice of one lemon

Remove mushroom stems and chop caps. Peel onions, remove green tops and roots and chop finely. Combine mushrooms, onion, minced pork, eggs, soya sauce, sugar and *mirin* in a large mixing bowl. Season with salt and monosodium glutamate and knead to a smooth paste. Blend in half the breadcrumbs, knead again, then form mixture into 4 cm (1½ inch) balls. Roll mince meat balls in remaining breadcrumbs, pressing on lightly.

Heat 2.5 cm (1 inch) oil in a *wok* and fry meatballs until golden brown and cooked through. Drain and keep warm.

Pour sauce ingredients, except lemon juice, into a small saucepan and bring to boil. Cool, add lemon juice and transfer to small sauce bowls.

Thread several meatballs on each skewer. Line a ser-

ving dish with lettuce leaves and arrange skewers on top. Serve with the sauce.

BRAISED PORK AND LEEK ROLLS

TERIYAKI

6 leeks or 12 Japanese leeks
6 very thin slices pork shoulder or leg
⅓ cup light soya sauce
⅓ cup *sake* or *mirin*
2 tablespoons sugar
vegetable oil
2 small cucumbers
2 tablespoons white vinegar
2 teaspoons salt
3 teaspoons sugar

Wash leeks, remove roots and green tops and cut pieces the same length as the width of each slice of pork. Wrap pork securely around one piece of leek or two pieces of Japanese leek and secure with toothpicks.

Mix soya sauce, *sake* or *mirin* and sugar, stirring until sugar dissolves. Heat 2.5 cm (1 inch) oil in a frying pan and cook rolls on moderate heat, turning to brown evenly.

Wash and dry cucumbers, cut into wedges about 2.5 cm (1 inch) long and sprinkle with a mixture of vinegar, salt and sugar. Set aside to marinate for a few minutes.

Drain oil from pan when pork is partially cooked and pour in prepared sauce. Simmer on low heat for 6-7 minutes, turning pork frequently. Remove Teriyaki from the pan and cut each piece into two or three pieces. Stand these upright on small, flat plates and garnish each with several pieces of drained cucumber.

Bring remaining sauce to the boil and cook until reduced to a thick glaze. Spoon a little over each portion of Teriyaki before serving.

NOODLES WITH CHICKEN AND VEGETABLES

NABEYAKI UDON

750 g (1½ lb) *udon* noodles, or spaghetti
6 cups *dashi* or chicken stock
6 dried Japanese black mushrooms, soaked in cold
    water for ½ hour
12 spring onions
90 g (3 oz) chicken breast
½ teaspoon monosodium glutamate (optional)
⅔ cup light soya sauce
⅔ cup *mirin* or *sake*
1½ teaspoons sugar
60 g (2 oz) fish cake (*kamaboko*), sliced (optional)
6 eggs
sansho or chilli powder

Soak noodles for 20 minutes in cold water. Drain. Bring stock to the oil. Add noodles and cook till tender. Remove noodles from the stock, drain and spread on a tray to dry slightly.

Drain mushrooms and remove stems. Clean spring

Braised Pork and Leek Balls (recipe this page).

onions and cut into 2.5 cm (1 inch) pieces. Remove any skin and bones from chicken and slice thinly. Return stock to moderate heat. Add chicken and mushrooms and cook until chicken is tender. Remove chicken and mushrooms from soup with a perforated spoon and set aside. Season soup with monosodium glutamate (if used), soya sauce, *mirin* and sugar. Add spring onions and *kamaboko,* if used.

Return noodles, reheat, then divide noodles and soup between six large bowls. Add a mushroom and several pieces of chicken to each bowl. Break an egg on top of the noodles and add a sprinkling of *sansho* or chilli powder. Cover bowls and put in a hot oven, or on warming plate for 5 minutes before serving.

NOODLES WITH FRIED PRAWNS AND FISH
TEMPURA SOBA

625 g (1¼ lb) *soba* noodles
6 large raw prawns
125 g (¼ lb) thin white fish fillets
1½ cups Tempura batter (see page 184)
cornflour
oil for deep frying
125 g (¼ lb) beanshoots
9 cups *dashi* stock
6 pieces lemon or tangerine peel
light soya sauce
monosodium glutamate (optional)
6 eggs (optional)

Place noodles in a large cooking pot and add boiling water. Set over high heat and bring to the boil. Cook until tender but not too soft. Drain well then rinse with cold water. Drain again.

Remove heads and shells from prawns leaving tail fins intact. Clip fins. Cut fish into six pieces. Prepare Tempura batter. Coat fish and prawns lightly with cornflour and dip into the batter. Fry in moderately hot oil until cooked through and golden brown. Lift out and drain well.

Steep beanshoots in boiling water for 2 minutes. Drain. Bring stock to the boil. Divide the noodles between six large bowls and add a serving of beanshoots and a twist of lemon or tangerine peel to each. Place one prawn and a piece of fish on each bowl and pour on the boiling stock. Season to taste with soya sauce and monosodium glutamate (if used). Break an egg onto each portion of noodles, cover with a lid and leave for 5 minutes before serving.

STEAMED RICE

Japanese rice is slightly more starchy than most Asian rice. As the particular varieties favoured are difficult to obtain outside of Japan, the most suitable substitute is Australian short grain white rice.

To cook, first wash rice well and pour into a large heavy pot. Add sufficient cold water to cover the rice by about 4 cm (1½ inches) and set on high heat. Bring rapidly to the boil, cover pot and turn heat down to lowest point. Steam rice gently for about 15 minutes until it is tender and all liquid has been absorbed. Turn heat off, allow rice to stand, still covered, for another 10 minutes before using. If your cooker cannot be turned to a very low temperature, stand the pot on an asbestos mat.

For Sushi rice, use a little less water and cover the saucepan before bringing to the boil, then proceed as above. With a traditional Japanese meal, plain white rice is generally served as the last course, to be eaten with little savoury nibbles such as pickled plums, but special rice dishes may be served separately or at any time during a meal.

VINEGARED RICE
CHIRASHI ZUSHI

375 g (¾ lb) short grain white rice
3 cups water
1 small cucumber
salt
white vinegar
sugar
90 g (3 oz) white fish fillet
2 eggs, beaten
vegetable oil
90 g (3 oz) cooked peas
1 tablespoon shredded preserved ginger

Seasoning Sauce:
4 tablespoons white vinegar
2 tablespoons sugar
1½ teaspoons salt

Wash rice, put into a heavy-based saucepan, cover with water and cook, covered, on low heat till tender. Set aside.

Wipe cucumber and rub with a little salt. Shred or grate, then marinate in a mixture of 3 teaspoons vinegar and 1 teaspoon sugar.

Steam or boil fish fillet till soft, then flake or chop coarsely. Sprinkle on a mixture of 3 teaspoons vinegar, 1½ teaspoons sugar and ½ teaspoon salt.

Mix eggs with 2 teaspoons sugar and ½ teaspoon salt and pour into a hot, lightly oiled pan. Cook until firm, turn and cook other side, then remove and cool. When cool, shred with a sharp knife.

Mix seasoning sauce, stirring until sugar is completely dissolved. Pour into rice and mix in with a chopstick, then fold in fish, cucumber, shredded egg and peas. Garnish with shredded ginger.

RICE WITH GREEN TEA, TUNA AND SESAME SEEDS
CHAZUKE

This sounds the most unlikely dish and I was horrified the first time I was served it. My companion mentioned that she'd ordered a rice dish for me, and when it came the waitress picked up the teapot and poured the contents over my rice. I sat speechless until I realised this was how the dish should be. It's absolutely delicious, and I often make it now as a lunchtime snack, using leftover rice.

625 g (1¼ lb) cooked white rice
185 g (6 oz) canned or poached fresh tuna
1 tablespoon *sake*
3 tablespoons white sesame seeds
2½ cups boiling hot Japanese green tea

Spoon cooked rice into deep bowls. Flake tuna and sprinkle with *sake*. Stand for 2-3 minutes, then scatter over rice. Toast sesame seeds lightly under the grill until they begin to pop, then sprinkle on the rice and tuna.

Prepare tea, allow to draw for 3-4 minutes, then pour onto the rice. Cover bowls and stand for 2-3 minutes for rice to absorb the flavour and fragrance of the tea before serving.

Other green teas will not give the same slightly smoky taste, so important to this dish, as Japanese tea.

RICE-FILLED EGG PANCAKES

FUKUSA ZUSHI

440 g (14 oz) cooked white rice
white vinegar
sugar
salt
6 dried Japanese black mushrooms, soaked in cold
    water for ½ hour
sake
light soya sauce
4 large eggs
1 tablespoon milk
90 g (3 oz) raw baby shrimps, chopped
90 g (3 oz) finely minced ham
red food colouring (optional)
vegetable oil

Put rice in a large mixing bowl and sprinkle on a mixture of ¼ cup vinegar, 2 tablespoons sugar and 2 teaspoons salt. Mix in well with chopsticks.

Drain mushrooms and slice into thin threads. Simmer in a small saucepan with 1 tablespoon *sake*, 2 tablespoons soya sauce, and 1 tablespoon sugar for 4 minutes, then stir into rice.

Beat eggs until smooth, add milk, 1 teaspoon salt, 2 teaspoons sugar and 2 teaspoons *sake*. Beat until slightly frothy. Heat a little vegetable oil in a large omelette pan and pour in one-sixth of the mixture. Swirl so egg covers as much of the base of the pan as possible and is very thin. Cook on a low heat and when firm, flip over and cook other side. Remove from pan and put on a plate. Cook remaining pancakes in this manner, stacking cooked pancakes with pieces of greaseproof paper in between. Keep warm until needed.

Cook chopped shrimps with ham in a little vegetable oil, adding a dash of red food colouring to brighten up the colour. Warm rice by stirring in a large saucepan on a moderate heat.

To fill pancakes, place some of the shrimp and ham mixture in the centre of each pancake and divide the rice between them. Fold over to form square packages and turn, so folds are underneath. Using a very sharp knife make several diagonal slits on the top of each filled pancake to expose the red shrimp and ham filling.

Serve warm or cold.

CHICKEN ON RICE

TORI GOHAN

250 g (½ lb) chicken
2 tablespoons *sake*
2 teaspoons sugar
⅔ cup light soya sauce
375 (¾ lb) short grain white rice
6 dried Japanese mushrooms, soaked in cold water for
    ½ hour
90 g (3 oz) frozen peas

Chop chicken into medium-sized pieces. Make a marinade of *sake,* sugar and soya sauce and pour over chicken. Stand at least 10 minutes.

Wash rice thoroughly, pour into a large heavy-based saucepan and cover with sufficient water to rise about 4 cm (1½ inches) above the level of the rice. Cover saucepan and bring to the boil on high heat. Drain mushrooms and slice thinly. Drain chicken, reserving marinade. When rice begins to boil, add chicken pieces with peas and mushrooms. Turn heat down low and cook gently for about 15 minutes, or until rice is tender. Test after 12 minutes.

Remove chicken pieces from the rice and mince or chop finely. Simmer for 3 minutes in the reserved marinade, then return to the saucepan and stir chicken, peas and mushroom slices into the rice, distributing evenly.

As an alternative do not stir chicken, peas and mushrooms into the rice. Spoon the rice into small lacquer boxes or onto plates, and the chicken and vegetables on top.

RICE WITH SHREDDED NORI AND BONITO

375 g (¾ lb) short grain white rice
1½ teaspoons salt
3 cups fish stock
1 large sheet dried laver *(nori)*
2 tablespoons dried bonito shavings *(katsuobushi)*
1 teaspoon powdered green horseradish *(wasabi)*
½ teaspoon monosodium glutamate (optional)

Wash rice thoroughly, add salt and fish stock and bring to the boil in a deep saucepan. Cook, covered, on low heat until tender. Remove from heat and let stand, covered, for 10 minutes.

Hold laver over a flame to crisp, then shred finely. Scoop rice into a deep lacquered bowl, sprinkle with green horseradish powder and monosodium glutamate (if used), then top with shredded laver and bonito shavings.

Serve with meat, fish or vegetable dishes.

OMELETTE ROLL

DASHIMAKI TAMAGO

6 eggs
3 tablespoons sugar
1 teaspoon salt
1½ tablespoons *mirin*
½ cup *dashi* stock
pinch of monosodium glutamate (optional)
1 teaspoon light soya sauce
vegetable oil
6 sprigs watercress or parsley
½ small cucumber
salt
white vinegar

Beat 3 eggs lightly and add half the sugar, salt, *mirin*, *dashi*, monosodium glutamate (if used) and soya sauce. Beat for 2 minutes. Heat a little oil in an omelette pan and pour in one-third of the mixture. Cook on moderate to low heat and when omelette is just set, carefully lift onto a plate or a piece of greaseproof paper. Cook remaining batter in two parts and stack the three omelettes together. Roll up carefully and return to the pan to cook on low heat for a further 2 minutes. Lift from pan and wrap in a piece of clean muslin, tying securely to form a firm roll. Cool.

Repeat the process with the remaining eggs and seasonings, and wrap in another piece of muslin. When both rolls are completely cool, remove cloth and cut each roll into three pieces.

Wash watercress or parsely. Rub cucumber with a little salt, then steep in boiling water for 2 minutes. Drain, cool and cut into 5 cm (2 inch) pieces. Sprinkle with a little salt and vinegar. Stand pieces of omelette roll on end on a serving dish, garnish each with a sprig of watercress or parsley and decorate the plate with cucumber.

Serve as a breakfast dish or as the first course of a main meal.

EGG CUSTARD SQUARES

TAMAGO TOFU

6 eggs
1¾ cups *dashi* stock
2 teaspoons *mirin*
1 teaspoon sugar
½ teaspoon salt
1 teaspoon light soya sauce
pinch of monosodium glutamate (optional)
6 pieces crystallised peel

Sauce:
¾ cup *dashi* stock
½ teaspoon salt
1 teaspoon sugar
2 teaspoons light soya sauce

Beat eggs lightly with *dashi*. Add *mirin*, sugar and salt and beat till very smooth, then stir in soya sauce and monosodium glutamate (if used). Line a 18 cm (7 inch) square baking tin with a piece of muslin cloth and pour in the egg mixture. Cover with another square of cloth, then cover tin with lid or a piece of aluminium foil, making a small hole in the centre to allow steam to escape. Steam over boiling water, or in the oven set in a tray of water, until custard is firmly set. This will take approximately 25 minutes.

Remove muslin top and cut custard into six squares. Using a wide spatula or slice, lift each square into a small bowl. Garnish with crystallised peel.

Prepare sauce by mixing ingredients together in a small saucepan. Heat through, but do not boil. Pour a little sauce over each custard square.

EGG CUSTARD IN TEACUPS

CHAWAN MUSHI

6 eggs
6 dried Japanese black mushrooms, soaked in cold water for ½ hour
90 g (3 oz) chicken
1 tablespoon light soya sauce
½ small cucumber
salt
1¾ cups *dashi* stock
2 teaspoons *mirin*
pinch of monosodium glutamate (optional)
30 g (1 oz) fish or raw clams, diced
6 small peeled raw shrimp
6 sprigs parsley or watercress leaves

Beat eggs lightly in a mixing bowl. Remove stems from mushrooms. Dice chicken and marinate in soya sauce for 10 minutes. Rub cucumber with a little salt, then slice lengthways into 6 pieces, remove seeds.

Add *dashi*, 1 teaspoon salt, *mirin* and monosodium glutamate to eggs and beat again. Put chicken, fish and 1 mushroom into 6 Japanese teacups or small ramekins and pour in egg mixture. Set in a steamer and cook over high heat until almost set.

Press a shrimp and a parsley sprig or watercress leaf onto the top of each custard and cook for a further 10 minutes. Serve with sliced cucumber.

EGG AND ASSORTED MEATS STEAMED IN PUMPKINS

TAKARA MUSHI

2 small pumpkins, about 1 kg (2 lb) each
2 tablespoons *sake*
3 teaspoons salt
12 dried Japanese black mushrooms
90 g (3 oz) chicken breast
75 g (2½ oz) ham
6 eggs
⅓ cup *dashi* or chicken stock
75 g (2½ oz) canned or frozen peas
1 tablespoon light soya sauce
2 tablespoons sugar

Slice the tops from the pumpkins and scoop out seeds. Sprinkle the insides with 2 teaspoons salt and the *sake*. Let stand for 10 minutes, then set over a pan of boiling

Noodles with Fried Prawns and Fish (recipe page 190), and Noodles with Chicken and Vegetables (recipe page 188).

water and steam for 10 minutes. Remove from heat before that time if shells are becoming too soft.

Soak mushrooms in hot water for 10 minutes, drain and remove stems. Slice mushrooms, chicken and ham finely. Beat eggs lightly and mix with the sliced meat, vegetables, 1 teaspoon salt, and all remaining ingredients.

Pour into pumpkins and place pumpkin tops in position. Steam over high heat for 20 minutes, or until egg custard is set and pumpkins are soft. Serve hot or cold. Any fleshy melon or squash can be used instead of pumpkin, with the cooking time depending on the size of the melon and the hardness of the flesh.

SPINACH SALAD

1 large bunch fresh young spinach
1½ tablespoons white sesame seeds
1½ tablespoons light soya sauce
2 tablespoons sesame oil

Wash spinach thoroughly, shake out excess water and put in a saucepan. Cover and steam on very low heat for about 6 minutes until tender. Add a very little water during cooking if necessary.

Put sesame seeds under the griller and toast lightly. Grind to a fairly smooth paste with soya sauce and sesame oil.

Chop spinach into 5 cm (2 inch) lengths and arrange a little in 4-6 small bowls. Spoon on a little of the dressing, lightly mixing in with chopsticks, or put all spinach in a salad bowl and toss with the dressing. Serve cold.

CUCUMBER SALAD

KYURIMOMI

3 small cucumbers
2 teaspoons salt
2 tablespoons white vinegar
1 tablespoon water
1 teaspoon light soya sauce
½ teaspoon salt
2 teaspoons sugar
½ teaspoon dried chilli flakes
1 teaspoon sesame oil
pinch of monosodium glutamate (optional)

Wash cucumbers and rub with salt. Slice or cut into thin strips as preferred. Mix remaining ingredients together, stirring to dissolve sugar. Put cucumber in a salad bowl and pour on dressing. Toss well, then let stand for 30 minutes in the refrigerator before serving.

PICKLED VEGETABLES

SU ZUKE

The best pickling vegetables are giant white radish, turnip, white Chinese cabbage, spinach, trefoil, eggplant, cucumber and pumpkin. The vegetables should be young and fresh for best results.

½ giant white radish
½ head white Chinese cabbage
1¼ cups white vinegar
½ cup *sake*
1 tablespoon sugar
1 teaspoon salt
½ teaspoon monosodium glutamate
light soya sauce

If using turnip, eggplant or pumpkin, steam until slightly softened before pickling.

Cut vegetables into bite-sized pieces and put into a wide jar or bowl. Radish may be peeled or unpeeled as preferred. Mix vinegar with *sake*, sugar, salt and monosodium glutamate and pour over the vegetables. Press down with a heavy weight, cover and stand for at least one day in a cool place. Splash pickles with soya sauce before serving.

Serve Su Zuke or commercially produced pickles (available canned or in pressure-sealed containers) with Japanese meals to aid digestion, particularly after fried foods.

FRIED EGGPLANT IN MISO SAUCE

345 g (11 oz) eggplant
2 teaspoons salt
1 cup vegetable oil
2 teaspoons sesame oil
100 g (3½ oz) white *miso* paste
¼ cup water
3 tablespoons *mirin*
2 tablespoons sugar
1½ tablespoons light soya sauce
1 tablespoon white sesame seeds

Cut eggplant into 0.5 cm (¼ inch) thick slices, sprinkle with salt. Cover and stand for 5 minutes, rinse and pat dry. Heat vegetable and sesame oil in a frying pan and saute eggplant until partially cooked. Drain off excess oil.

Mix *miso* with water, *mirin*, sugar and soya sauce. Pour into the pan over eggplant and simmer on very low heat for 5 minutes, or until eggplant is soft. If the sauce begins to dry up, add a little more water.

Toast sesame seeds lightly under the griller and sprinkle over eggplant before serving.

WHITE RADISH WITH SWEET MISO FILLING

HORIFUKI

I discovered this at a fairytale restaurant and guesthouse, the Oushukuzen-Ryori Nishiki, on the outskirts of Kyoto.

100 g (3½ oz) white *miso* paste
3 tablespoons *mirin*
2 tablespoons sugar, or to taste
⅓-½ cup water
5 white radishes, about 220 g (7 oz) each

Choose round, squat radishes, or cut top sections from

giant white radish. Put radishes in a large saucepan and boil for 10 minutes. Remove and drain. Allow to cool, then with a very sharp vegetable knife remove skin and slice off top, leaving stem attached. Cut a hollow in the centre of each radish for the filling. Remove the centre, taking care not to damage the sides of the radishes. Carve the top to fit as a lid, leaving the stem attached as the handle.

Mix *miso, mirin* and sugar in a small saucepan, adding enough water to make a paste of medium consistency. Bring to the boil, turn heat down and simmer for 2-3 minutes, stirring continually. Remove sauce from heat and cool slightly, then pour into the radish cups. Set lids in position and carefully place the filled radishes in a steamer or on a dish over a saucepan of boiling water. Steam for 10 minutes over high heat, serve in small flat bowls, decorated with small blossoms or leaf sprigs.

The flavour of the sweet *miso* should permeate the radish, giving this usually sharply flavoured vegetable a delicate, slightly sweet taste. If radishes are unavailable substitute turnips or small squash.

GREEN BEANS WITH SESAME DRESSING

INGEN NO GOMA-AE

250 g (½ lb) young green beans
3 tablespoons white sesame seeds
1 tablespoon sesame oil
½ teaspoon sugar
1 teaspoon *mirin*

Cook beans, left whole, in boiling, slightly salted water until tender, but not too soft. Drain and cool. Cut into 5 cm (2 inch) pieces and place in small dishes or a salad bowl.

Toast sesame seeds lightly, then grind to a paste with sesame oil, sugar and *mirin*. Spoon over the beans, stirring lightly with a chopstick to mix. Serve cold.

LOTUS ROOT FILLED WITH MUSTARD

KARASHI RENKON

This recipe requires advance preparation.

1-2 sections of lotus root, weighing a total of about 345 g (11 oz), or canned lotus root
2 teaspoons salt
1 tablespoon white vinegar
30 g (1 oz) white *miso* paste
1½ tablespoons hot mustard powder
3 teaspoons sugar
¾ cup Tempura batter (see page 184)
oil for deep frying

Peel fresh lotus root and rub with salt to prevent discolouration. Put in a saucepan with white vinegar and cover with water. Boil until partially cooked, then remove and drain well. If using canned lotus root, drain and simmer in water for 10 minutes.

Mix *miso* paste with mustard and sugar, adding enough water to produce a smooth paste of running consistency. Cut top from lotus root to expose holes and fill with the sauce. Wrap in plastic or aluminium foil and place in the refrigerator for at least 5 hours, but preferably overnight.

Prepare Tempura batter. Heat oil until almost at smoking point. Coat lotus root thickly with the batter and fry until cooked through and a deep golden colour. Drain, allow to cool completely, then slice thinly.

Serve as an appetiser or *hors d'oeuvres*.

MISO SOUP

MISO SHIRU

1 piece dried kelp *(kombu)* 2.5 cm (1 inch) square (optional)
2¾ cups *dashi* stock
100 g (3½ oz) diced chicken or fish
75 g (2½ oz) diced beancurd
4 tablespoons white *miso* paste
2 teaspoons sugar
pinch of monosodium glutamate (optional)
4 spring onions, finely chopped
6 sprigs watercress

Put *kombu* in a large pot with stock and bring to the boil. Add chicken and boil for 5 minutes. Remove *kombu* and discard, then add diced beancurd. If fish is used instead of chicken, add at this time. Simmer for 2 minutes.

Scoop out ½ cup of the hot stock and blend with *miso* and sugar. Stir this into the soup with monosodium glutamate (if used). Simmer for 4 minutes. Serve in covered lacquered soup bowls, garnished with shredded spring onions and a sprig of watercress.

CLAM SOUP

12 raw clams, in shells
6 spring onions, or 2 Japanese leeks
6 dried Japanese mushrooms, soaked in cold water for ½ hour
3 cups *dashi* stock
5 cm (2 inch) piece fresh ginger, shredded
1 teaspoon light soya sauce
2 teaspoons *mirin* or *sake*
pinch of monosodium glutamate (optional)
60 g (2 oz) soft beancurd, diced

Steam clams over a pot of boiling water to open shells. Remove beards, wash clams in salted water, loosen from shell, but do not remove. Clean spring onions or Japanese leeks and shred finely. Remove stems from mushrooms and slice into three or four pieces, or leave whole and cut a cross into each cap.

Bring stock to rapid boil. Add mushrooms and ginger and boil for 2 minutes. Season with soya sauce, *mirin* or *sake* and monosodium glutamate (if used). Add diced beancurd and clams, simmer for 2 minutes then remove from heat. Pour into soup bowls and garnish with shredded spring onion or Japanese leeks.

Crab pieces may be used instead of clams.

CHICKEN AND LEEK SOUP

TORI NO MIZUDAKE

155 g (5 oz) chicken breast
3 cups light chicken stock or water
2 Japanese leeks, or 1 leek
1 tablespoon light soya sauce
1½ teaspoons salt
2 teaspoons *sake*
2 teaspoons sugar
juice of 1 lemon
6 very thin, small pieces lemon or tangerine peel

Boil chicken in water or stock until tender. Remove and cut into very small dice, discarding any bones. Strain stock and return to the pot with chicken. Wash Japanese leeks and slice into 1 cm (½ inch) pieces. Add to the pot.

Mix soya sauce, salt, *sake*, sugar and lemon juice and pour into the soup. Simmer until leek is cooked through but not too soft. Pour soup into six bowls. Add a twist of peel to each and serve immediately.

DEEP-FRIED SALTED GINGKO NUTS

GINNAN AGE

185 g (6 oz) gingko nuts, shelled
3 heaped teaspoons salt
oil for deep frying

Place gingko nuts in a dry pan and roast until skins begin to lift. Allow to cool slightly, then rub skins off, holding hot nuts in a kitchen towel. Heat oil to smoking point and put in nuts. Deep fry to a golden colour. Remove from the oil and put on a sheet of greaseproof paper. Sprinkle with salt, rolling nuts on the paper to coat evenly. Serve cold as a snack or a nibble with drinks.

These may also be served as a garnish for meat and vegetable dishes. Thread several onto thin bamboo skewers, toothpicks or pine needles to make an attractive garnish for simple dishes.

PLUMS PICKLED IN SALT

UMEBOSHI

750 g (1½ lb) barely ripe, small plums
345 g (11 oz) rock or sea salt

Wash plums. Select a large flat-bottomed dish into which a plate can be tightly fitted to weight the plums. Arrange the washed fruit in the dish, cover with water and stand overnight. Drain off water and remove fruit. Spread a layer of salt in the bowl and top with a layer of plums. Use more salt and more plums until all plums are in place. Finish with a layer of salt.

Press a plate on top of the plums and weight with a suitably heavy object. After 5 days double the weight. Stand undisturbed for another 14 days, then drain off salt liquid which has accumulated. Reserve the liquid in an airtight bottle.

Dry plums on a tray in the sun for 2 days, or in a very, very low oven for 1 day. Put into a warm part of a room and stand for another day. Arrange plums in large, wide-necked jars and seal tightly. Store for 3 weeks, then pour on reserved salt liquid. Seal jars and store for another week, then drain off liquid and dry plums again in the same way.

Serve these salted, dried plums as a pickle with meat dishes, as an appetiser, or to complete a meal, Japanese style, with the final bowl of rice. Also serve as a snack with drinks, especially *sake*.

JAPANESE LUNCHBOX

BENTO

Bento is traditionally served in a special lacquered box with three layers, or two drawers and an open top shelf. Each level is filled with a variety of small portions of cold meat, seafood, vegetables, tiny rice cakes or preserved fruit and seaweed.

Below is a suggested selection, but a Bento may be prepared with a choice of many other items.

For 6 boxes.

1 medium carrot
1¾ cups *dashi* stock
6 knots lobe leaf seaweed *(wakame)* salted and dried (optional)
light soya sauce
mirin
12 green beans
3 tablespoons lemon juice
sugar
18 small spinach leaves
6 small sheets dried laver *(nori)*, each 8 cm (3 inches) square
3 teaspoons white sesame seeds, toasted and crushed
18 gingko nuts
100 g (3½ oz) rice flour
few drops pink colouring
250 g (½ lb) fish fillets
12 raw clams, removed from the shell
cornflour
sake
18 small shrimp, boiled
6 slices lemon
6 blocks cooked pork sausages or pickled pork, each 2.5 cm (1 inch) square
shredded white radish
12 chrysanthemum, mint or small lettuce leaves
toothpicks or small bamboo skewers

If a flower-shaped vegetable cutter is available, cut carrot into 18 thin slices and drop into a small saucepan with about ⅔ cup stock and bring to the boil, cooking till carrot slices are tender. Alternatively, carve rounded indentations down the sides of the carrot so the slices will have four rounded petals. Slice and cook as above. Drain 'Plum Flowers' carrots and reserve stock.

Rinse salt from *wakame* seaweed and put into the carrot stock, adding a little more *dashi* if needed. Boil for 2 minutes, drain, reserving stock, and marinate in a little soya sauce and *mirin*.

Chicken and Leek Soup (recipe this page), Miso Soup, and Clam Soup (recipes page 195).

Cut green beans into 5 cm (2 inch) lengths, drop into boiling water and cook until they just begin to soften. Drain off water and add lemon juice mixed with 1 tablespoon sugar. Stir on low heat, cooking until sugar and lemon juice form a light glaze on the beans. Cool.

Wash spinach and steam until leaves soften. Remove moisture by patting leaves with a kitchen towel, then place three leaves on each square of dried laver which has been crisped by holding over a flame for a few seconds. Roll up, sticking edges with a little water. Cut each roll in halves and dip one end into the toasted sesame seeds, coating thickly. Stand with sesame-covered ends upwards.

Drop gingko nuts into boiling water to loosen skins, then transfer to a dish of cold water and rub to remove skins. Place nuts in a small saucepan and pour on 2 tablespoons *mirin* and 2 teaspoons sugar. Cook, stirring continually, on low heat until nuts are glazed. If preferred the nuts can be skinned, deep-fried and coated lightly with salt. Thread three nuts onto each of 6 small bamboo skewers, toothpicks or pine needles.

Sift rice flour into a small bowl and add water, a little at a time, to make batter of firm but workable consistency. Colour with a few drops of pink food colouring, then roll into six balls and press with the palm of the hand to flatten slightly. Bring *dashi* reserved from *wakame* seaweed to the boil and add rice flour balls. Boil until the balls rise to the surface, turn heat down slightly and continue to cook for a further 5 minutes. Remove and drain.

Mince fish finely, season with 3 teaspoons *sake* and 2 teaspoons soya sauce, then blend in 1 heaped tablespoon cornflour. Knead to a smooth, thick paste. Form into 12 balls. Place on a sheet of greaseproof paper and set over a steamer to cook for about 15 minutes. Cool.

Wash clams and slice thinly. Cut each lemon slice into three triangular pieces and set aside with shrimp and pork.

To arrange Bento Boxes:
Top layer: Place one washed and dried chrysanthemum, mint or lettuce leaf in a corner with a sliced clam on top. Add one skewer of gingko nuts and a bundle of spinach.

Second layer: Two fish balls separated by one chrysanthemum, mint or lettuce leaf, glazed beans, one rice ball and a knot of *wakame* seaweed.

Bottom layer: One cube pork sausage or pickled pork, three 'Plum Flower' carrots, three shrimps alternated with slivers of lemon and a mound of finely shredded radish.

PICKLED SWEET KUMQUATS

KINKAN

500 g (1 lb) ripe kumquats
1½ cups *sake*
500 g (1 lb) sugar
2½ cups water

Wash kumquats. Pour *sake* and sugar into a saucepan and add water. Stir until sugar dissolves and add washed kumquats. Bring to the boil, lower heat and simmer for 5-6 minutes, turning fruit occasionally. Spoon kumquats into wide-necked jars, packing tightly. Reduce syrup on high heat and pour thickened syrup over kumquats. Seal carefully using a little wax to make jar absolutely airtight if necessary.

Stand for at least one month, undisturbed, then strain off liquid and reserve. Dry fruit a little in the sun or in a low oven. Return to the jars, without liquid. Serve as a sweet or as a nibble with sweet drinks.

The sweet liquid may be blended with a little brandy or sherry and served as a liqueur or poured over ice-cream or other desserts as a sweet topping.

SHAVED ICE WITH RED BEANS AND FRESH FRUIT

shaved ice
2 apples, sliced
2 pears, sliced
2 slices pineapple, cut into wedges
18 cherries or other berries
2¾ cups red bean sauce

Red Bean Sauce:
250 g (1 lb) cooked or canned red beans
75 g (2½ oz) sugar
1½ cups water

First prepare the red bean sauce by slightly crushing cooked beans and heating through on moderate heat with water and sugar. Stir till sugar is completely dissolved. Remove from heat and chill.

Mound shaved ice into six glass dessert dishes. Garnish with fresh fruit and pour on red bean sauce. Serve immediately.

YAM BALLS ROLLED IN SESAME SEEDS

YAMA-IMO NO AME-DAGI

Though the Japanese are inveterate sweet-tooths, they rarely serve a dessert or sweet with meals, reserving this pleasure for between-meal snacks.

Sweets made with yam or sweet potato are common and popular throughout Asia.

Makes 24.

625 g (1¼ lb) yam or sweet potato, peeled
1 teaspoon salt
2 tablespoons oil
250 g (½ lb) sugar
3 heaped tablespoons lightly toasted white sesame seeds

Chop yam or sweet potato into 2.5 cm (1 inch) cubes and steam until soft. Cool, then mash with a fork and work in salt and oil, then half the sugar. If using sweet potato, which is usually of a much more moist consistency than yam, it may be necessary to delete the oil and add a very little flour if the paste is difficult to work.

Using oiled hands, form paste into walnut-sized balls. The easiest method is to squeeze little balls of the paste from the palm of the hand between curled thumb and forefinger.

Prepare a sugar syrup by boiling remaining sugar with an equal quantity of water until it becomes slightly sticky. Coat yam balls one at a time with the syrup, dipping them in on a slotted spoon. Spread sesame seeds on a piece of greaseproof paper and roll each ball in the seeds after coating with syrup.

PANCAKES FILLED WITH RED BEAN JAM

DORAYAKI

Makes 18.

155 g (5 oz) plain flour
²/₃ cup milk
¼ cup water
2 tablespoons butter or oil
2 eggs
1 teaspoon salt
3 teaspoons sugar
1 quantity *yokan* (red bean jam)

Yokan (red bean jam):
220 g (7 oz) mashed cooked red beans
7/8 cup water
125 g (¼ lb) sugar
½ teaspoon salt
3 tablespoons cornflour

Make *yokan* first. Mix mashed beans with water, sugar and salt in a saucepan, stir in cornflour mixed with a little water and cook on low heat for about 10-12 minutes until it becomes a thick paste. Allow to cool while pancakes are prepared.

Blend all pancake ingredients together, beating well. Set aside for 10 minutes. Heat a heavy-based iron skillet or omelette pan and wipe with an oiled cloth. Pour in enough batter to make 8 cm (3 inch) pancakes and cook lightly on both sides. Cook all the batter in this way.

When all pancakes are cooked, spread half with the *yokan* and sandwich with the remaining pancakes. Serve warm or cold. A little sugar may be sprinkled over pancakes before serving.

MANDARIN ORANGES WITH ORANGE JELLY

MIKAN

1 dozen small mandarin oranges
5 teaspoons gelatine, or 3 teaspoons *agar agar* powder
1 ¾ cups lukewarm water
²/₃ cup boiling water
155 g (5 oz) sugar

Remove top sections of mandarins and carefully scoop out centres, taking care not to break the skin. Divide flesh of four mandarins into segments and mash the remaining eight. Put pulp in a piece of muslin and squeeze to obtain as much juice as possible. Set aside.

Dissolve gelatine in boiling water, then stir in lukewarm water. Add mandarin juice and sugar and stir till completely blended. Cool slightly. If *agar agar* powder is used, stir into water, bring to the boil, add mandarin juice and sugar and cook for 1-2 minutes, then cool.

Arrange several mandarin segments in each shell and pour the jelly on top. Place in the refrigerator to chill and set firmly.

KOREA

Korean food is as robust, wholesome and warming as the country's severe climatic conditions demand. It has a rich spiciness, is hot from an abundance of chillies and pepper, and pungent with an all-pervading flavour of garlic and sesame, the seasoning ingredients used in almost all Korean dishes.

In the cities, Korean food has lost some of its originality, being influenced to some extent by neighbouring Japan and northern China, as well as by the introduction of some Western concepts, but out of the cities one finds that the eating habits of the Korean have changed little over the centuries. No meal is considered complete without boiled rice and Kim Chi (pickled vegetables). Even when there are noodles on the table, rice is generally served as well. Many vegetables (the most usual being cabbage, white radish and cucumber) and some types of seafood go into Kim Chi, which is prepared in the autumn for winter consumption. The vegetables are cut up, washed and seasoned with salt, pepper, garlic and chilli and sealed in large jars for storage underground or beneath the floorboards of the family home. They are brought up in varying stages of fermentation throughout the winter, and by the change of season can be astonishingly pungent; in fact, Kim Chi ranges in taste from quite bland to extremely hot, depending on the length of fermentation and the amount of chillies added. It serves as the main source of vegetable protein during the hard winter months when fresh vegetables are not readily available. During the summer it may take only a few days to mature.

Many sea products are used in Korean cooking: squid, octopus, shellfish, edible molluscs, fish, several types of seaweed and some of the world's best abalone are cooked in stews and soups and made into salads. Seafood is often eaten raw, particularly in the coastal regions where it is plucked straight from the sea, cut into manageable pieces and eaten on the spot with an indescribably hot gruel of rice and chilli to wash it down.

The Koreans also have an inordinate fondness for beans, a good source of protein. Mung beans are cooked whole, or are ground into a thick paste to make a stodgy fried pancake flavoured with Kim Chi; soya beans are eaten whole or made into beancurd; and small red beans are used in sweets and desserts. Red meat is used sparingly, being barbecued in thin slivers or boiled in a thick stew. A favourite soup, Yukkai Jang Kuk, has thin slices of beef and young spring onions in a fiery chilli stock seasoned with plenty of garlic and ground sesame seeds.

Shinsulro is one of those great serve-yourself meals with vegetables, meat and seafood simmering in a tasty seaweed-based soup kept hot in a large copper hotpot over a gas ring or charcoal burner in the centre of the table; it is accompanied by a dip of vinegar and soya sauce *(see page 215)*. Bulgogi, another example of Korean table-top cooking, is done on a conical plate mounted over the gas ring or charcoal fire, with slivers of well-marinated beef, pork, poultry and seafood be-ing cooked quickly on the hot surface. Served with the barbecue are several styles of Kim Chi and a variety of other side dishes of vegetables (Na Mool), including boiled seasoned beans, beanshoots, cooked cucumber and eggplant, shredded seaweed and tiny crispy fried fish (smaller than whitebait) heavily seasoned with chilli.

A Korean banquet can be a lavish affair with an enviable selection of up to thirty main dishes, side dishes, rice, soup and noodles served at low tables with guests seated on comfortable cushions. *Kisaeng* girls, hostesses like the Japanese *geisha,* use silver chopsticks to offer tidbits to guests, sing traditional songs, dance, and generally make sure everyone is happy. Wine is almost always served (though Koreans rarely drink wine without food), and the local wines are potent enough to compete with the strongly flavoured dishes typical of Korea. *Jungjong* is a rice wine similar to *sake,* and *soju,* made from grain and potatoes, can be likened to vodka. *Ginseng* wines, renowned for their restorative powers, have an unusual, rather medicinal taste, but are drunk in great quantities; the red *ginseng* root is also used for preparing a strong-tasting tea, and is dried and marketed as an aphrodisiac. Koreans rarely drink tea, preferring the *ginseng* brew or an infusion made from roasted barley. They also have a number of sweet fruit teas.

There are many cakes, sweets and desserts in this cuisine. Most are made with red beans, rice and nuts, and are often sweetened with honey instead of sugar. I took a particular fancy to Song Pyun, which combines mashed chestnuts and red beans as a filling for small rice cakes steamed on an aromatic bed of fresh pine needles.

Ingredients and cooking methods employed by Korean cooks are not unusual and no special equipment will be needed. Table-top cooking is fun, and Bulgogi can be prepared in an electric frying pan while a meat fondue pot will do well for Shinsulro. Food is eaten from small bowls using thin chopsticks, the best ones being made of silver. Main courses are all served together with a selection of side dishes, including Kim Chi. Soya sauce, sometimes mixed with vinegar, should be on the table.

FRIED BATTERED FISH IN SESAME OIL

TOMI CHUN

2 whole fish, each weighing 500 g (1 lb) (perch, bream,
    whiting)
salt
white pepper
2 eggs
3 tablespoons plain flour
1 heaped tablespoon cornflour

sesame oil
white sesame seeds
lettuce leaves
cucumber slices
onion slices

Scale fish and slice off fillets leaving heads and backbones in one piece. Sprinkle a little salt on bones and place in a baking tray. Bake in a moderate oven for 15 minutes. Keep warm when done.

Cut fillets into thin slices. Sprinkle with salt and pepper. Beat eggs lightly with ½ teaspoon salt. Coat fish pieces with cornflour mixed with flour, then dip into the beaten egg.

Heat 2 cm (¾ inch) sesame oil in a large frying pan and fry fish pieces until tender and a deep golden colour on each side. Sprinkle lightly with sesame seeds.

Place roasted fish bones on a bed of shredded lettuce on a large serving dish. Arrange fried fish on top of the bones and surround with slices of cucumber and onion.

STEWED CRABS

KE CHIKAI

Stock:
100 g (3½ oz) beef (round, chuck, topside)
3 teaspoons sesame oil
2 cloves garlic, minced
1 teaspoon white sesame seeds, ground
3¾ cups water
1 teaspoon red pepper paste *(kochujan)* (see page 213)
2 teaspoons white *miso* paste
3 tablespoons light soya sauce

6 small raw saltwater crabs
100 g (3½ oz) soft beancurd, diced
60 g (2 oz) lean beef, minced
1 egg
1 tablespoon light soya sauce
4 spring onions, minced
3 cloves garlic, minced
1½ tablespoons white sesame seeds, ground
1 tablespoon sesame oil
2 cm (¾ inch) piece fresh ginger, minced
1 teaspoon salt
¼ teaspoon white pepper
chilli powder
3 spring onions

Make stock by sauteeing chopped beef with sesame oil, garlic and sesame seeds until well browned. Add water and boil for 30 minutes, then stir in red pepper paste, *miso* paste and soya sauce. Boil for a further 5 minutes.

Break crabs open without damaging the top shells. Scrape out meat and yellow yolks. Wash well in a little salt water and set aside. Chop crab meat. Crack open legs and claws and extract meat. Retain shells.

Put diced beancurd, minced beef, crab meat and yolk in a mixing bowl and add remaining ingredients except chilli powder and 3 spring onions. Blend thoroughly and spoon into the cleaned shells. Sprinkle on chilli powder. Chop 3 remaining spring onions and sprinkle over crabs. Place crab legs and claws in the bottom of a large saucepan and arrange stuffed crabs on top. Pour stock into the pan taking care not to upset the crabs. Cover pot and simmer for 10 minutes. Carefully lift out crabs and place on a serving dish.

Strain sauce and discard all shell pieces. Pour sauce into a pan and reduce over high heat by at least half. For extra flavour add chopped clams, cuttlefish, scallops or octopus to the crabmeat filling.

STUFFED CUTTLEFISH

OJINGU CHIM

12 small cuttlefish or squid, each about 10-13 cm (4-5 inches) long
2 cabbage leaves
90 g (3 oz) beanshoots
2 dried mushrooms, soaked in cold water for ½ hour
90 g (3 oz) lean beef, minced
1 tablespoon light soya sauce
½ teaspoon salt
6 spring onions, minced
3 cloves garlic, minced
1 tablespoon sesame oil
1 tablespoon white sesame seeds, ground
pinch of white pepper
pinch of monosodium glutamate (optional)
vinegar and soya sauce dip (see page 215)

Clean cuttlefish and remove head and tentacles. Peel off skin and wash thoroughly with salt water. Chop tentacles finely. Drop cabbage leaves and beanshoots into a pot of boiling water and stand for 3 minutes. Drain well. Chop vegetables, including mushrooms finely.

Mix minced beef with chopped mushrooms, cabbage, beanshoots and the chopped cuttlefish tentacles. Season with remaining ingredients. Blend well, then saute on moderate heat for 5 minutes, stirring frequently. Stuff the mixture into the prepared cuttlefish bodies and secure openings with toothpicks.

Put on a plate inside a steamer and cook over boiling water for 15-20 minutes. Cut into thick slices and serve with the sauce dip. Alternatively steam for 12 minutes, then deep fry until lightly golden in vegetable oil mixed with a little sesame oil.

BOILED CHICKEN WITH VEGETABLES

TAK CHIM

750 g (1½ lb) chicken
1 green pepper
1 small carrot
6 dried mushrooms, soaked in cold water for ½ hour
18 gingko nuts
1 tablespoon light soya sauce
1½ teaspoons sesame oil
2 teaspoons white sesame seeds, ground
2 teaspoons salt
½ teaspoon white pepper
3 spring onions, minced
1 teaspoon chilli powder
⅔ cup cold water
1¾ cups warm water

Wash chicken, clean and wipe dry. Remove bones, if preferred, and chop meat into 4 cm (1½ inch) pieces. Remove seeds and stem from pepper and cut into 2.5 cm (1 inch) squares. Scrape carrot and slice or cut into small dice. Drain mushrooms, remove stems and cut in halves. Parch gingko nuts under griller and rub off skins.

Mix soya sauce, sesame oil, sesame seeds, salt, pepper, spring onions and chilli powder with cold water. Arrange chicken pieces in a pan and pour on half the seasoned water. Cook on moderate heat for 10 minutes, turning chicken several times. Pour in warm water, add mushrooms and gingko nuts and cook a further 10 minutes, then add carrots and remaining seasoned water. Cook until chicken is tender, then add green pepper. Lower heat and simmer for a further 5 minutes.

Arrange chicken pieces on a serving dish. Pile vegetables on top and pour on a little of the reduced sauce.

KOREAN BARBECUE

BULGOGI

This popular traditional dish is cooked at the table over charcoal or gas fires with everyone helping themselves. The barbecued meat is always accompanied by a selection of spiced dishes, salads and pickles known as Na Mool and Kim Chi.

Beef Barbecue:
500 g (1 lb) lean beef (rump, sirloin, topside)
1½ tablespoons dark soya sauce
1½ tablespoons light soya sauce
1 spring onion, minced
4 cloves garlic, minced
2.5 cm (1 inch) piece fresh ginger, minced
2 tablespoons white sesame seeds, ground
pinch of white pepper
3 tablespoons sesame oil

Chicken Barbecue:
500 g (1 lb) chicken breast meat
2 tablespoons sugar
1½ tablespoons light soya sauce
6 spring onions, minced
2 cm (¾ inch) piece fresh ginger, minced
6 cloves garlic, minced
2 tablespoons white sesame seeds, ground
pinch of pepper
2 tablespoons sesame oil

Pork Barbecue:
500 g (1 lb) pork shoulder, leg or tenderloin
1½ teaspoons red pepper paste *(kochujan)*
  (see page 213)
2½ tablespoons sugar
4½ tablespoons light soya sauce
6 spring onions, minced
2.5 cm (1 inch) piece fresh ginger, minced
8 cloves garlic, minced
2 tablespoons white sesame seeds, ground
1 tablespoon sesame oil

Cut beef into 0.5 cm (¼ inch) slices, then into small pieces. Sprinkle with soya sauce, then marinate in a mixture of remaining ingredients for 5 minutes.

Cut chicken into small, thin slices discarding skin. Rub with sugar, then marinate in a mixture of remaining ingredients, except sesame oil, for 5 minutes. Sprinkle on sesame oil and stand another minute.

Rub pork with red pepper paste then sprinkle on sugar. Mix all ingredients and marinate meat in this sauce for at least 10 minutes.

Heat a griddle, ideally a slightly convex one, over a portable fire on the table. (Protect table top with an asbestos mat). Cook beef to preference, ideally rare, then serve chicken and cook to taste, and lastly cook the pork. Serve with a selection of side dishes and dips of soya sauce and Vinegar Soya Sauce Dip *(page 215)*.

Prawns may also be cooked on the barbecue. Marinate in the preparation for chicken, omitting sugar. Spare ribs may be substituted for pork. Cut meaty ribs into 5 cm (2 inch) lengths and marinate in the same way. Cook until meat is well done.

KOREAN HOTPOT

SHINSULRO

185 g (6 oz) liver
salt
pepper
sesame oil
90 g (3 oz) tripe
100 g (3½ oz) minced beef
1 egg
½ medium carrot
6 dried mushrooms, soaked in cold water for ½ hour
1 green pepper
1 fresh red chilli
100 g (3½ oz) canned bamboo shoots, drained
100 g (3½ oz) beef steak
12 gingko nuts
4 walnuts
4½ cups beef stock
3 teaspoons light soya sauce

Slice liver thinly. Rub with salt and pepper and fry for 2 minutes on each side in a little sesame oil. Slice tripe and boil for 5 minutes in slightly salted water. Drain. Mix minced beef with egg and a little salt and pepper and roll into small balls. Fry in sesame oil until lightly browned.

Scrape carrot and cut into long thin strips. Drain mushrooms, remove stems and cut into quarters. Remove seeds and stem from peppers and slice thinly. Remove seeds from chilli and slice. Slice bamboo shoots.

Cut beef into wafer-thin slices, season with salt and pepper and fry for 2 minutes in a little sesame oil. Arrange liver, tripe and beef in a charcoal hotpot or metal fondue pot (use an electric frying pan on lowest heat setting). Add vegetables and then meatballs, gingko nuts and walnuts. Pour on the stock and add 1 teaspoon salt and soya sauce. If stock is made from a stock cube, do not add extra salt. Bring to the boil and simmer for 12-15 minutes.

Serve straight from the pot using wooden chopsticks. Small bowls of soya sauce and Vinegar Soya Sauce Dip should be placed on the table. When all meat and vegetables have been eaten, serve the soup in small bowls.

SEAWEED AND CRABMEAT SALAD

SAING MUIK MUCHIM

8 pieces dried kelp *(kombu)*
125 g (¼ lb) shredded cooked crab meat
1½ tablespoons light soya sauce
½ tablespoon white wine vinegar
1½ teaspoons sesame oil
2 teaspoons white sesame seeds, ground
red chilli powder
monosodium glutamate (optional)
salt

Soak seaweed in warm water for several hours, changing water when it begins to cool. When soft, drain and cut into thin strips. Drop seaweed into a pot of boiling water and let stand for 5 minutes then drain. Chop seaweed and arrange with shredded crab meat on a large seashell or small salad bowl.

Prepare the dressing by mixing all remaining ingredients together. Pour over salad and let stand for ½ hour in refrigerator to chill slightly before serving. Lobster, chopped clams or scallops may be substituted for the crab meat.

VERMICELLI WITH BEEF AND CUCUMBER

KUKSOO BUBIM

345 g (11 oz) dried vermicelli, or
    500 g (1 lb) spaghetti
185 g (6 oz) lean beef
2 medium cucumbers
salt
sesame oil
6 spring onions, minced
1 tablespoon light soya sauce
1 teaspoon chilli powder
1 tablespoon white sesame seeds, ground
pinch of monosodium glutamate (optional)
1 egg

Marinade:
2 teaspoons sugar
1½ tablespoons light soya sauce
12 cloves garlic, minced
2 cm (¾ inch) piece fresh ginger, minced
½ teaspoon white pepper
1 tablespoon sesame oil

Sauce:
2 tablespoons dark soya sauce
1½ tablespoons sugar
1½ tablespoons sesame oil
1 tablespoon white sesame seeds, ground
1 teaspoon chilli powder
monosodium glutamate (optional)

Boil vermicelli or spaghetti in salted water to which a few drops of sesame oil have been added. When soft, splash on cold water and drain well. Set aside.

Cut beef into thin strips. Prepare marinade and pour over meat in a flat bowl. Stand for 15 minutes. Fry meat with marinade for 5 minutes on high heat, remove from pan and keep warm.

Wash cucumbers and cut into thin slices. Sprinkle with a little salt and let stand for 5 minutes. Dry with a cloth then saute for 2 minutes in 1 tablespoon sesame oil. Add onion and cook for a further 2 minutes, then season with soya sauce and chilli powder. Stir on high heat for a few seconds, then remove from heat and stir in sesame seeds and monosodium glutamate (if used).

Beat egg lightly. Heat a little sesame oil in a small pan and pour in the egg. Swirl pan to spread omelette as thinly as possible. Cook until firm, then lift out and allow to cool. Shred thinly.

Put drained noodles, cucumber and beef in a large frying pan and warm through on moderate heat, stirring to mix thoroughly. Prepare the sauce by mixing all ingredients together. Pour over the noodles, reheat again and lift onto a serving dish. Garnish with shredded omelette. This dish may be served hot or cold.

Note: Reduce amounts by one-third or half if serving with several other dishes.

KOREAN PANCAKES

BINDAE DUK

Makes 6.

315 g (10 oz) dried mung beans or soya beans, or use
    about 750 g (1½ lb) cooked canned soya beans or
    chick peas
100 g (3½ oz) raw ham
250 g (½ lb) *kim chi* (preferably made with Chinese
    cabbage)
2 tablespoons sesame oil
2 tablespoons dark soya sauce
10 spring onions, chopped
4 cloves garlic, minced
1 tablespoon white sesame seeds, ground
¾ teaspoon white pepper
salt
3 eggs

Put beans in a heavy-duty blender and grind to a coarse powder. Cover with boiling water and soak overnight. Rinse in cold water and drain well. Put soaked bean paste back in the blender and grind to smooth paste, adding a little water as needed. If using canned chick peas or soya beans, drain and mash or grind in the blender. Soaking is unnecessary.

Chop ham and *kim chi* finely and stir into the bean paste. Season to taste with remaining ingredients, binding with the eggs. Allow to stand for 1 hour before cooking. When ready, beat for 3 minutes with a wire whisk. The batter should be fairly thick. If too thin beat in 2-3 tablespoons plain flour or split pea flour.

Heat a little sesame oil in a 18 cm (7 inch) omelette or pancake pan and pour in about 2 cm (¾ inch) of batter. Cover and cook on moderate heat until brown and set. Turn carefully and cook other side. Remove to a warmed serving plate and keep in a warm oven until ready to serve. Cut the pancakes into quarters if difficult to turn.

Serve with chilli and soya sauce.

Korean Barbecue (recipe page 203).

EGGPLANT STUFFED WITH BEEF

KA JI CHIM

6 small eggplants, about 15 cm (6 inches) long
salt
185 g (6 oz) lean beef, minced
small bunch parsley
1 tablespoon garlic, minced
1 tablespoon dark soya sauce
2 teaspoons white sesame seeds, ground
2 teaspoons sesame oil
pepper
1½ tablespoons light soya sauce
1 tablespoon sugar
monosodium glutamate (optional)
2½ cups chicken or veal stock

Cut stems from eggplant. Wipe with a damp cloth and make several deep slits down the sides, taking care not to sever tops or bottoms of the vegetables. Sprinkle with salt and leave to stand for 10 minutes to draw off the bitter juices.

Mix minced beef with finely chopped parsley, garlic, dark soya sauce, sesame seed, sesame oil and pepper. Knead to a smooth paste. Wipe eggplants again and press the prepared meat stuffing into the slits, filling tightly.

Pour light soya sauce into a large saucepan. Add sugar, monosodium glutamate and stock. Put in eggplants, cover pot and bring to the boil. Turn heat down and simmer until eggplants are cooked through and tender. Lift out from the stock and arrange on a serving plate.

Reduce sauce by boiling for several minutes and pour over the eggplants before serving. Minced clams, scallops or cuttlefish may be substituted for beef.

RADISH PICKLES

NABUK KIM CHI

Kim Chi and Na Mool are two types of pickled or cooked vegetables which are served cold, usually several at a time, with every Korean meal. Kim Chi is usually very hot and is made in advance, often being stored for several months in large pots. Na Mool dishes are made when needed, but several hours in advance to allow time for the flavours to develop. They include vegetable and seafood dishes.

1 kg (2 lb) giant white radish
100 g (3½ oz) watercress
1 small onion, minced
10 cloves garlic, minced
2.5 cm (1 inch) piece fresh ginger, minced
3 teaspoons chilli powder
3 tablespoons salt
2½ cups boiling water

Peel radish and cut into 1 cm (½ inch) cubes. Rinse watercress under cold water and cut into small pieces. Dry well. Mix minced onion, garlic, ginger, chilli powder and 2 tablespoons salt. Place vegetables into a large bowl and pour on the seasonings, tossing to mix in well. Spoon into a large, wide-necked jar.

Dilute remaining salt in water and pour over pickles. Cool slightly, then seal jar and stand in a warm dark place for 5-6 days. Add a little sugar for a slightly sweet taste if preferred.

CHINESE CABBAGE PICKLES

BAICHU SAING KIM CHI

Traditionally this pickle is prepared several weeks in advance and allowed to mature in large jars. This simplified recipe can be made a day or two before it's needed and can be stored for 5-6 days in the refrigerator.

1 kg (2 lb) Chinese cabbage
1 tablespoon salt
75 g (2½ oz) small oysters (optional)
½ Chinese pear, hard green pear or cooking apple
250 g (½ lb) watercress
1 tablespoon sesame oil
1 tablespoon white sesame seeds, ground
1 tablespoon chilli powder
4 spring onions, minced
3 cloves garlic, minced
1 cm (½ inch) piece fresh ginger, minced
1½ tablespoons light soya sauce
1½ tablespoons white wine vinegar
1 tablespoon sugar
pinch monosodium glutamate (optional)

Discard outer leaves of cabbage, wash well and drain. Cut into 5 cm (2 inch) pieces and sprinkle with salt. Stand for 3-4 hours, turning occasionally. Squeeze out excess moisture.

Wash oysters and cut into small pieces. Rinse in salt water. Peel pear or apple and cut into thin strips. Wash watercress, shake out water and break into sprigs. Put cabbage, pear or apple, and cress in a large bowl and sprinkle on sesame oil.

Mix together remaining ingredients, including chopped oysters (if used), and pour over the vegetables. Toss to distribute all seasonings evenly. Spoon into large jars, seal and allow to stand for at least 24 hours before using. Flavour will improve after 2-3 days.

GREEN VEGETABLE PICKLES

PUT KIM CHI

1 kg (2 lb) mustard greens or spinach, cut into 5 cm (2 inch) pieces
3 tablespoons salt
2 small onions
10 cloves garlic
2.5 cm (1 inch) piece fresh ginger, minced
3 teaspoons chilli powder
2 tablespoons anchovy essence
2½ tablespoons sugar
1½ cups hot water

Wash vegetables, discarding any limp leaves. Dry well and sprinkle with 2 tablespoons salt. Stand for 5 hours until greens become soft and wilted. Wash and wipe dry.

Chop onions finely and put into a large bowl with garlic, ginger, chilli powder, anchovy essence and remaining salt. Mix well. Add vegetables and toss with the seasonings. Place in a wide-necked jar and pour on hot water and sugar. Seal tightly and store in a cool dark place for 3-4 days.

MARINATED CABBAGE SALAD

YANG BAI CHU NA MOOL

155 g (5 oz) Chinese cabbage
1 small cucumber
1½ tablespoons sesame oil
3 spring onions, minced
2.5 cm (1 inch) piece fresh ginger, minced
1 tablespoon white sesame seeds, toasted and ground
1½ tablespoons white vinegar
2½ tablespoons light soya sauce
1 tablespoon sugar
1½ teaspoons chilli powder
2 teaspoons salt (or to taste)
pinch of monosodium glutamate (optional)

Wash each leaf of cabbage and wipe dry. Shred coarsely. Wipe cucumbers, remove ends and cut into thin strips. Pour sesame oil over prepared vegetables and stand for 15 minutes. Mix remaining ingredients together and pour over salad. Let stand for at least 5 hours before serving.

MARINATED EGGPLANT

KA JI NA MOOL

220 g (7 oz) eggplant
3 spring onions, minced
3 cloves garlic, minced
1 tablespoon white sesame seeds, toasted and ground
1 tablespoon sesame oil
1 tablespoon white vinegar
1 tablespoon light soya sauce
1 tablespoon sugar
1½ teaspoons chilli powder
monosodium glutamate (optional)

Wipe eggplants with a clean damp cloth and cut off stems. Slice thinly and put in a dish. Steam over boiling water for 10 minutes. Press out liquid and cut eggplant into smaller pieces. Put into a serving bowl.

Mix remaining ingredients, stirring well. Pour marinade over the eggplant and allow to stand for at least 4 hours before serving.

TOASTED SEA LAVER

KIM KUI

10 sheets dry sea laver (nori)
1 tablespoon sesame oil
1 teaspoon salt

Brush laver sheets lightly with sesame oil. Sprinkle on salt and toast under griller until the colour turns bright green. Remove from grill and cut into small pieces. Serve with rice, meat or vegetables, or as a side dish or with drinks.

COOKED CUCUMBER SALAD

OI BOK KUM NA MOOL

1 large cucumber
1 tablespoon salt
1½ tablespoon sesame oil
2 spring onions, minced
1½ tablespoons light soya sauce
1½ teaspoons sugar
2 teaspoons chilli powder
pinch of monosodium glutamate (optional)
1 tablespoon white sesame seeds, toasted and ground

Cut cucumber into thin strips or slices and sprinkle with salt. Stand for 10-15 minutes, then press out excess liquid.

Heat sesame oil in a small frying pan and fry cucumber with onion, soya sauce, sugar, chilli powder and monosodium glutamate (if used). Stir on moderate heat for 7 minutes. Spoon into a small serving dish and sprinkle on ground sesame seeds. Stir lightly into the salad. Serve warm or slightly chilled.

COLD CUCUMBER SOUP

NAING KUK

2 medium cucumbers, about 15 cm (6 inches) long
2 tablespoons light soya sauce
1½ tablespoons white vinegar
2 spring onion shoots, finely chopped
½ teaspoon sugar
2 teaspoons white sesame seeds, toasted and ground
½ teaspoon chilli powder
1½ teaspoons sesame oil
5 cups water

Slice cucumber very thinly and marinate in a sauce made by mixing all remaining ingredients together. Stand for at least 15 minutes, stirring occasionally. Pour on cold water or light beef or chicken stock or water and chill soup thoroughly before serving.

BEANSHOOT SOUP

KONG NAMOOL KUK

500 g (1 lb) beanshoots
185 g (6 oz) lean beef
1 piece dried kelp (kombu)
3 cloves garlic, minced
2 teaspoons white sesame seeds, ground
1 tablespoon sesame oil
½ teaspoon white pepper
6 cups water
2 tablespoons dark soya sauce
monosodium glutamate (optional)
2 spring onions, finely chopped

Remove roots and pods from beanshoots. Wash well and drain. Cut beef into very thin strips and put in a saucepan with kelp, garlic, sesame seeds, sesame oil and pepper. Saute on moderate heat till meat changes colour, then pour in water. Bring to the boil and simmer, covered, for 25 minutes.

Add beanshoots and cook for a further 5 minutes, then stir in soya sauce, monosodium glutamate (if used). Garnish with chopped spring onion.

BEEF AND GREEN ONION SOUP

YUKKAI JANG KUK

This is a very hot soup which, it is traditionally accepted, should be taken on the hottest days of summer for heat relief.

500 g (1 lb) beef shank or flank
8 cups water
1½ tablespoons chilli powder
2 tablespoons sesame oil
18 spring onion shoots
6 cloves garlic, minced
1 tablespoon white sesame seeds, ground
1 teaspoon sugar
½ teaspoon white pepper
1½ tablespoons dark soya sauce
monosodium glutamate (optional)

Chop beef into large pieces and boil in water for 2 hours. Skim several times during cooking. When meat is very tender, lift out from stock with a slotted spoon and cut into smaller pieces. Strain stock and reserve.

Mix chilli with sesame oil and set aside. Clean onions and chop into 2.5 cm (1 inch) lengths. Put meat in a small pan with oil and chilli mixture. Toss well to thoroughly coat the meat, then saute on moderate fire until meat changes colour. Add minced garlic, sesame seed, sugar, pepper, soya sauce and monosodium glutamate (if used). Fry for 3-4 minutes, stirring constantly. Bring stock to the boil, cook until reduced by half. Add onions, meat and seasonings and boil for 5 minutes. Serve piping hot.

SPICED SEAFOOD

JEOTKAL

125 g (¼ lb) whitebait, or sliced small white fish
1 egg
1 teaspoon salt
1 teaspoon white sesame seeds, ground
1 heaped teaspoon chilli powder
3 teaspoons sesame oil

Wash whitebait and pat dry. Beat eggs lightly and add salt. Mix in ground sesame and chilli powder. Coat whitebait or sliced fish in this mixture. Heat oil in a shallow pan and fry fish until dark brown, crisp and quite dry.

Serve cold as a side dish with Korean Barbecue or as an accompaniment to Na Mool and Kim Chi at any meal. This can be prepared in larger amounts and stored in an airtight container in a cool dry cupboard.

Re-fry before serving if necessary.

RICE CAKES COOKED ON PINE NEEDLES

SONG PYUN

75 g (2½ oz) red beans
75 g (2½ oz) chestnuts
salt
1 tablespoon brown sugar or honey
75 g (2½ oz) raisins
250 g (½ lb) rice flour
3 tablespoons plain flour
pine needles
sesame oil
granulated sugar

Soak red beans in warm water for 5 hours. Rub off skins and rinse well. Grind red beans coarsely. Retain water in which beans were soaked. Cook beans in this water, adding a pinch of salt. When completely soft, drain and mash. Form into small balls about 1 cm (½ inch) in diameter.

Cook chestnuts, peel and mash, adding sugar or honey. Form into small balls the same size as the red beans. Soak raisins until soft, then drain.

Mix rice flour and plain flour with enough hot water to make a firm dough. Work until pliable, then roll into walnut-sized balls. Press a finger into the centre of each ball and insert a ball of red bean, one of chestnut and several raisins. Pull the dough up around the filling to seal. Roll with hands greased with a little sesame oil.

Spread pine needles in the bottom of a steaming pan and arrange the cakes on top. (If pine needles are unavailable place cakes on a greased plate). Steam for 25 minutes over boiling water. Brush with a little sesame oil and roll in sugar.

SWEET RED BEAN PORRIDGE WITH RICE DUMPLINGS

PAT JUK

185 g (6 oz) red beans
6 cups water
185 g (6 oz) short grain rice
1 teaspoon salt
155 g (5 oz) rice flour
sugar

Wash red beans and pour into a saucepan with water. Bring to the boil then reduce heat and simmer until completely softened. Pour into a wire strainer and push through using a wooden spoon. Pour the liquid off the beans into another saucepan. Add rice and bring to the boil with salt. Simmer until rice is tender. Add more water if the mixture is thick; it should be the consistency of a soup. Add sieved beans and bring to the boil.

Mix rice flour with enough water to make a soft dough. Break off small pieces and drop into the boiling porridge. Cook until they rise to the top, then cook for a further 10 minutes. Remove from the heat and add sugar to taste. Serve after a meal or as a sweet snack.

Japan: Egg Custard in Teacups (recipe page 192), Quail Eggs, Chicken Meatballs and Pickled Cucumbers on Skewers (recipe page 186), and Green Beans with Sesame Dressing (recipe page 195).

GLOSSARY

NOTE. Local names are identified by language as follows: Burmese (B); Chinese, generally Cantonese (C); Filipino (F); Indian, generally Hindi (H); Indonesian (I); Japanese (J); Korean (K); Laotian (L); Malay (M); Thai (T); Vietnamese (V).

AGAR AGAR: A gelatinous seaweed, sold dried in powdered or strip form. It is used instead of gelatine for sweets, and because it sets without refrigeration it is suited to hot climates. *Gulaman* (F), *kanten* (J).

ALLSPICE: A West Indian spice of the Myrtle family, its pods are similar to peppercorns in appearance and have a flavour resembling a combination of nutmeg, mace and cloves. Not to be confused with Mixed Spice, which is a blend of sweet spices.

AMCHUR (H): Powdered seasoning made from dried green mangoes. It has a sharp, slightly tangy taste, and is used as condiment on roasted foods and frequently in pickles.

ANISEED: Similar to caraway seed, it has a light licorice flavour, and is used in sweet and savoury cooking.

ASAFOETIDA: Gum-like substance used in Indian cooking. Can be omitted if unavailable.

ASAM (I, M): *see* tamarind

ATTA (H): *see* flour

AZUKI (J): *see* red beans

BAMBOO SHOOTS: Cream-coloured spear-like shoots of the bamboo plant. Fresh shoots must be peeled to the firm heart and then boiled. Also sold canned in water or in a sauce usually based on soya. Store in the refrigerator in a dish of fresh water, changing the water daily, for up to ten days. Winter bamboo shoots have a better flavour than the common variety.

BANANA LEAVES: Young pale-green banana leaves are used as fragrant wrappers for food cooked by steaming or roasting. Leaves must be softened by holding over a flame or plunging into boiling water, and should be greased lightly to prevent food sticking. Older leaves are sometimes used as plates. Aluminium foil can be substituted.

BANGKUANG (M): *see* yam bean

BANGUS (F): *see* milkfish

BARBECUE SAUCE: *see* hoisin sauce

BASIL, SWEET: Pungent herb used in fresh (leaf), powdered or flaked form in many Southeast Asian dishes.

BASMATI RICE: *see* rice

BAY LEAVES: Dried leaves of the Bay Laurel.

BEAN PASTE, HOT: A thick spicy paste, reddish-brown in colour, made from chillies and soya beans. *Lap do ban jiang* (C).

BEAN PASTE, SALTED: A brown paste of soya beans, also known as yellow bean paste. *Taucheo* (C).

BEAN PASTE, SWEET: Either a thick flavourful black paste made from fermented flour and spices, *tien mien jiang* (C); or a similar sweet paste made from soya beans, *do dan jiang* (C). *See also* hoisin sauce.

BEANCURD: Soft beancurd is prepared by setting a liquid of ground soya beans with gypsum. Hard bean-curd, or beancurd cake, is soft beancurd compressed to remove most of the water content. *Dofu* (C), *tofu* (J), *tahu* (M). *See also* taukwa.

BEANCURD 'CHEESE', FERMENTED: Cubes of medium-hard beancurd fermented in brine with chillies, wine and spices. Used as a seasoning and condiment. *Dofu ru* (C).

BEANCURD SKIN: A byproduct of making beancurd, it is a yellowish, almost transparent sheet. Sold in strips or sheets, it is used in soups or as a wrapper for small meatballs and rolls.

BEANS, RED: *see* red beans

BEANS, SALTED BLACK: *see* salted black beans

BEANSHOOTS (BEANSPROUTS): Young sprouts or shoots of mung or soya beans, about 5-7 cm long. Bought fresh, they can be stored in fresh water in the refrigerator for up to seven days if the water is changed daily. Canned beanshoots should be rinsed in cold water before use. Roots and pods can be removed.

BEEHOON (C): *see* noodles, Chinese

BESAN (H): *see* flour

BIRD'S-EYE CHILLIES: Very small and *very* hot red or green chillies used particularly in Thai cooking and in sauces. Substitute sliced long green chilli.

BIRD'S NESTS: A glutinous, fibrous substance, an almost transparent cream in colour, produced by a certain kind of swallow for building nests. The best come from Thailand.

BITTER MELON: These sour vegetables, resembling a wrinkled cucumber, are sometimes available fresh in Oriental supermarkets, but are also sold canned in water. Substitute choko (chayote), unripe melon or squash.

BLACAN (M): *see* dried shrimp paste

BOK CHOY (C): *see* Chinese cabbage

BOMBAY DUCK: *see* dried fish

BONITO SHAVINGS: *see* katsuobushi

BRINJAL (H, M): Eggplant or aubergine.

BROWN PEPPERCORNS: *see* peppercorns, Chinese brown

BUAH KERAS (M): *see* candlenuts

CALAMANSI (F): Small citrus fruit with distinctive sweetish juice found in the Philippines, Malaysia and Indonesia. Substitute tangerine or orange. *Limau kesturi* (I, M).

CANDLENUTS: White waxy nuts similar to macadamia nuts. Used to add body and flavour to many sauces. *Buah keras* (M), *kemiri* (I).

CARAMBOLA: Also known as star fruit, a slightly bitter yellow tropical fruit with a waxy appearance. Cross-sections of the fruit have a star-like shape. Very unripe pear, mango or papaya (pawpaw) can be substituted.

CARDAMOM: An aromatic spice of the Ginger family available in two forms, 'black' and 'green'. The darker, larger pods, about 2 cm in length, contain clusters of small black seeds, and are used as an important curry spice in the Indian *garam masala* and as a fragrant spice in sweets. The smaller, greenish pods have a mild lemony fragrance and are also used in sweet and savoury dishes. Cardamom is sold whole or powdered.

CASSIA: *see* cinnamon

CELERY CABBAGE: *see* Chinese cabbage

CHANNA (H): Also known as chickpeas or garbanzos, these pale creamy-gold dried peas are used extensively in Indian cooking. A fine yellow flour, *besan* (H), is made from the ground peas and used in many sweet and savoury dishes.

CHAT MASALA (H): A combination of spices, including ground mango powder or *amchur* (H) and ground pomegranate seeds, with a sharp, almost astringent taste. Used with fruit and vegetables as a condiment and seasoning.

CHICKPEAS: *see* channa

CHILLI OIL: Made by steeping chilli powder in boiling oil and water. Also known as pepper oil or *la yu* (C).

CHILLIES: Members of the Capsicum family, sometimes known as hot peppers, chillies can be used fresh, flaked or powdered. Fresh chillies are green (unripe) or red (ripe). The seeds, which are the hottest part, can be removed before use.

CHINESE BROWN VINEGAR: Fermented rice vinegar, mild but pungent. Use white vinegar or malt vinegar as a substitute.

CHINESE CABBAGE: Also known as Tientsin cabbage or celery cabbage, it has long pale-green thick stems with light-green leaves and grows, tightly packed, up to 40 cm high. *Bok choy* (C), another cabbage-like vegetable known in some countries as 'Chinese cabbage', has white stems and dark-green leaves; it can be substituted for genuine Chinese cabbage in most recipes.

CHINESE DUCK, DRIED: De-boned and pressed flat before being dried, these ducks are used for flavouring stocks and soups.

CHINESE FIVE-SPICE POWDER: *see* five-spice powder

CHINESE PARSLEY: *see* coriander

CHINESE PEARS: Crisp, hard-fleshed fruit with yellow skin and slightly tart taste. Substitute cooking apples or unripe pears.

CHINESE RICE WINE: The pale, clear Shaoshing is most suitable for cooking, though it is not readily available. Rose Wine Spirits, if available, can be substituted, but use no more than half the quantity recommended for rice wine. Pale dry sherry is a good substitute.

CHINESE SAUSAGE: Thin dried sausages filled with pork fat and ham or cured liver. Should be steamed before use.

CHIVE SHOOTS: Pale-green shoots produced by growing chives under a cover so that they do not turn dark green. They have a subtle onion flavour, and are ideal with fish.

CHOW CHOW (C): *see* pickled/preserved vegetables

CINNAMON: True cinnamon originates from Sri Lanka, is pale golden-brown in colour, and is sold in stick or powder form, though powder does not keep as well as sticks. It is used in sweet and savoury cooking. Cassia, similar to cinnamon bark, is a less expensive spice with a coarser flavour, and is often used in Chinese, Malay and Indonesian dishes.

CITRONELLA GRASS: *see* lemon grass

CLOUD EAR FUNGUS: A dark-brown, almost black, crinkly gelatinous fungus, about 3 cm in diameter, which gives a musky flavour to many Chinese dishes

and is a common ingredient in vegetarian cooking. Store in an airtight container.

COCONUT MILK: The thick and creamy liquid made from the ground flesh of ripe coconuts mixed with water. Not to be confused with coconut water, which is the almost clear liquid found inside the nut. Coconut milk can be bought as compressed cakes, which should be dissolved in warm water to the required thickness. This type of coconut milk (or cream, as it is usually labelled) is readily available and keeps indefinitely. The milk can also be made from fresh or desiccated (dried shredded) coconut.

Using an electric blender: Prise the white flesh away from the shell, and peel or scrape off the brown skin. Break flesh into small chunks, put into electric blender with 1 or 2 cups of milk or water, and pulverise at high speed to make a smooth liquid. Strain liquid through muslin or a fine-meshed strainer to obtain *thick* coconut milk.

Using fresh grated coconut: Grate the flesh finely instead of breaking into chunks. For every 125 g (¼ lb) of grated coconut, add 1 cup of hot milk or water and blend thoroughly. Pour blended liquid through muslin, and squeeze hard to extract as much milk as possible. This will make 1¼-1½ cups of *thick* coconut milk. For *thin* coconut milk, blend the squeezed pulp with another 2 cups of hot milk or water and squeeze liquid through muslin.

Using desiccated coconut: Follow the same blending and squeezing process as for fresh grated coconut (above), but use double the amount of desiccated coconut to make a good, rich coconut milk.

Fresh coconut milk should not be chilled, or it will go solid. However, it can be frozen. I freeze fresh coconut milk in ice-cube trays, then use as many cubes as necessary for a recipe.

CORIANDER: Used extensively in Asian cooking, the dried seeds being a common spice in curry powders and many savoury dishes. The leaves, sometimes known as Chinese parsley, have a strong, distinctive taste and fragrance. The roots are used in Thai cooking. Fresh coriander is sometimes available, and it can be grown at home from the dried spice seeds.

CORNFLOUR (MAIZE FLOUR): *see* flour

CUMMIN, BLACK: More peppery than white cummin (below), it is in fact a totally different spice. It is used in certain Indian dishes. *Kalonji (H)*.

CUMMIN, WHITE: Actually light brown in colour, it is a seed resembling caraway but with a completely different flavour. It is an important ingredient in the Indian *garam masala*, and is used whole or powdered in most spiced dishes.

CURRY LEAVES: A fragrant dried leaf indispensible to a good curry. Bay leaves can occasionally be suggested as a substitute, but the flavour is quite different.

CURRY PASTE: Commercially prepared curry paste containing a mixture of spices in an oil or coconut-milk base.

CURRY POWDER: In most countries where curry is a main part of the diet, cooks prepare fresh spices daily and seldom used commercially prepared spice mixtures. The exceptions are special mixtures for specific dishes such as Dhansak or Sambar Masala.

DAHI: *see* yoghurt

DAIKON (J): *see* giant white radish

DAN MIEN (C): *see* noodles, Chinese

DASHI (J): A Japanese stock based on dried fish and seaweed, available powdered in single-serving packets. A recipes for *dashi* is given in the Japanese section.

DAUN KESOM (I, M): A very pungent dark-green leaf, sometimes called Vietnamese mint, used in Indonesia, Malaysia and Thailand.

DAUN PANDAN (I, M): *see* pandan leaf

DAUN SALAM (I): A type of bay leaf used in Indonesia.

DHAL or DAL (H): *see* lentils

DILIS (F): *see* dried fish

DO DAN JIANG (C): *see* bean paste, sweet

DOFU (C): *see* beancurd

DRIED CHINESE DUCK: *see* Chinese duck, dried

DRIED FISH: Many types of dried fish are used in Asia. Small sprats, anchovies or whitebait, 'Bombay duck', and many types of larger fish are salted and dried in the sun to be used for flavouring, fried as side dishes or pounded as a sauce ingredient. Tiny dried fish, about 2-4 cm long, used extensively in Malayo-Indonesian areas, are known as *ikan bilis* (M), *ikan teri* (I) and *dilis* (F). *See also* fish floss.

DRIED MUSHROOMS: Dried Chinese black mushrooms should be softened by soaking before use. Japanese dried black mushrooms, *shiitake*, are similar in appearance but have a slightly different flavour, though they are interchangeable in recipes.

DRIED PRAWNS: Small dried prawns are used for flavouring soups and savoury dishes, and are soaked and ground before being added to sauces. They are strong tasting, though milder than dried shrimp paste.

DRIED SHRIMP PASTE: A pungent seasoning paste made from fermented prawns pressed into blocks. Store in a well-sealed container. *Blacan* (M), often seen commercially as 'blachan', *terasi* or *trasi* (I), *kapi* (T), *ngapi* (B).

DUCK, DRIED CHINESE: *see* Chinese duck, dried

EE MIEN (C): *see* noodles, Chinese

EGG NOODLES: *see* noodles, Chinese

FENUGREEK: Dried fenugreek seeds smell of burnt sugar and have a slightly bitter taste; they are used in Indian cooking, especially pickles. The fresh leaves are also used in India as a vegetable, being interchangeable with spinach thought slightly more bitter. *Methi* (H).

FISH, DRIED: *see* dried fish

FISH FLOSS: Shredded dried salt fish, or fish cooked to dryness in coconut milk and then finely shredded. Sold in small quantities in Oriental provision stores.

FISH SAUCE: A salty, thin sauce made with fermented salt fish, used instead of soya sauce. Substitute light fish sauce (available at Chinese provision shops) to which has been added a little fried dried prawn paste or anchovy essence. *Ngan pya ye* (B), *nam pla* (T), *nuoc mam* (V).

FIVE-SPICE POWDER: A blend of star anise, fennel, aniseed, cloves and cassia (similar to cinnamon stick). The spices are roasted before grinding. *Ng heung fun* (C).

FLOUR: The many kinds of flour used in Asia are made from a variety of grains, pulses and tubers.

    Atta (H): Fine wholewheat flour, used in Indian breads.

    Besan (H): A fine yellow flour made from *channa*.

    Cornflour: Finely ground maize flour used as a thickener in Chinese cooking. Arrowroot can be substituted, but *not* wheat flour.

    Gram (H): A general term for flours made from lentils, including *channa*.

    Green pea: Made from mung beans. Often light green in colour, but sometimes white or pink, it is used for sweets in Malaysia and Indonesia. Arrowroot is a suitable substitute. *Tepong hoen kwe* (M-C).

    Maida (H): Finely ground white wheat flour. Substitute all-purpose or plain flour.

    Maize: *see* cornflour (above).

    Potato: Often added to batters to give more elasticity.

    Rice: Made from finely ground white rice and used in sweets and some batters.

    Rice, glutinous: Becomes almost clear and sticky when cooked, and is used in sweets and batters. Has more elasticity than ordinary rice flour.

Sago: Often added to batters to give more elasticity.

FUN SIE (C): *see* noodles, Chinese

GALANGAL, GREATER: A member of the Ginger family with a similar though more delicate flavour and a creamy or pinkish flesh. *Lengkuas* (M), *laos* (I), *kha* (L, T).

GARAM MASALA (H): A blend of spices prepared as a curry powder or condiment for Indian cooking. Unlike commercial curry powders, the mixture contains neither powdered turmeric nor chilli powder. Store in an airtight container for up to a month.

GHEE (H): Clarified butter used as the main cooking medium in the Indian kitchen, giving a richness to sweet and savoury dishes. It is high in cholesterol, and vegetable oils can be substituted.

GIANT WHITE RADISH: A very large white radish with a mild flavour, almost sweet when cooked. Sold at Chinese and Japanese food stores. *Loh bak* (C), *daikon* (J).

GINGER: Fresh root ginger is essential in all Asian cooking, and dried powdered ginger is *not* a substitute. Fresh ginger should be peeled or scraped to remove the thin flaky skin, and the flesh sliced, finely shredded or grated. Sweet pickled and preserved ginger, often dyed bright pink, are used as garnishes in Japanese cooking.

GINGER JUICE: Used as a marinade or seasoning ingredient. Mince or shred fresh root ginger, then squeeze in a piece of muslin to extract juice.

GINGER WINE: An infusion of shredded fresh ginger in Chinese rice wine, dry sherry or dry white wine. Leave for at least 1 hour before use. To preserve fresh ginger root in wine for future use, clean the whole root, put it in a jar, cover with wine or dry sherry, seal, and store until needed. Will keep indefinitely in the refrigerator.

GINGKO NUTS: Small white nuts, a little larger than peanuts, with a distinctive taste. Available canned or dried, they are fried or cooked in various foods (usually Chinese or Japanese). *Ginnan* (J).

GINNAN (J): *see* gingko nuts

GLUTINOUS RICE: A rice of very short grain that becomes very sticky when cooked, and is therefore also known as 'sticky' rice. Used for sweets and certain savoury rice dishes and stuffings. *See also* rice.

GLUTINOUS RICE FLOUR: *see* flour

GRAM (H): *see* flour

GREEN PEA FLOUR: *see* flour

GULA MELAKA (M): *see* palm sugar

GULAMAN (F): *see* agar agar

HOISIN SAUCE: A sweet brownish-red sauce made

with garlic, chillies, spices and soya beans. Often labelled 'Barbecue Sauce'. Available in cans and jars, it keeps indefinitely in the refrigerator. *See also* bean paste, sweet.

HOKKIEN NOODLES: *see* noodles, Chinese

HONG DOW (C): *see* red beans

HOR FUN (C): *see* noodles, Chinese

HWA CHIAO (C): *see* peppercorns, Chinese brown

IKAN BILIS (M): *see* dried fish

IKAN TERI (I): *see* dried fish

IMLI (H): *see* tamarind

JAGGERY (H): *see* palm sugar

JELLY FISH, PROCESSED: Gelatinous dried shreds of jelly fish are used in Chinese cooking. Substitute pea-flour vermicelli (transparent vermicelli) or shredded agar agar.

KALE: *see* mustard greens

KALONJI (H): *see* cummin, black

KAMABOKO (J): Japanese processed sausage made from fish, available in cans or vacuum packs. Substitute Chinese fishballs or mildly flavoured pork sausage.

KANTEN (J): *see* agar agar

KAPI (T): *see* dried shrimp paste

KAS KAS (H): *see* poppy seeds, white

KATSUOBUSHI (J): Dried bonito fish, available pre-flaked. An essential Japanese flavouring ingredient, it keeps indefinitely.

KECAP MANIS (I, M): Sweet, slightly thick soya sauce used in Indonesian cooking. Substitute dark soya sauce sweetened with dark brown sugar.

KELP: A wide-leafed seaweed used in making *dashi* stock and for flavouring soups and stocks in Japanese and Korean cooking. Shredded cooked kelp is also used as a vegetable. *Kombu* (J).

KEMIRI (I): *see* candlenuts

KHA (L, T): *see* galangal, greater

KHOYA (H): A reduced whole milk producing a thick dry cream used in stuffings, sweets and sauces in Indian cooking. A substitute is suggested in the Indian section.

KIM CHI (K): Pungent hot pickles, usually made with cabbage, served with all Korean meals.

KOCHUJAN (K): A hot Korean sauce made by mixing 2 tablespoons soya bean paste or *miso* (J), 2 tablespoons dark soya sauce and 1½-2 teaspoons chilli powder. Leave to stand for 1 hour before using.

KOMBU (J): *see* kelp

KRUPUK (I, M): Small crisp wafers, generally made of prawns. Fry in hot oil for a few seconds until they puff up.

KUNYIT (I, M): *see* turmeric

KWAY TEOW (C): *see* noodles, Chinese

LA YU (C): *see* chilli oil

LAOS (I): *see* galangal, greater

LAP DO BAN JIANG (C): *see* bean paste, hot

LEMON GRASS: A grass native to Asia but also found in Africa, Australia and America, and sometimes known as citronella grass. The leaves grow in clumps of which the white bulbous part is used for its lemony fragrance. It is sold dried in strip form, chopped, or powdered. More dried lemon grass is needed than fresh to produce the same flavour. Substitute lemon peel. *Serai* (M), *sereh* (I).

LENGKUAS (M): *see* galangal, greater

LENTILS: Dried beans and peas used in Indian cooking to make various vegetarian dishes, sauces and savoury snacks. *Dhal* or *dal* (H).

LIMAU KESTURI (I, M): *see* calamansi

LOH BAK (C): *see* giant white radish

LOTUS ROOT: The tubular root of the lotus plant with a series of round holes running lengthways. Sold in cans or dried slices that can be used for flavouring, and sometimes available fresh. Used as a vegetable in Thai, Chinese and Japanese cooking and occasionally in curried dishes.

MAIDA (H): *see* flour

MALAI (H): A thick creamy substance made by reducing full cream fresh milk, and used in Indian cooking. Substitute is given in the Indian section.

MAIZE FLOUR: *see* flour

MANGE-TOUT: *see* snow peas

MANGO POWDER: *see* amchur

MEI GAN TSAI (C): *see* pickled/preserved vegetables

METHI (H): *see* fenugreek

MIE FUN (C): *see* noodles, Chinese

MILKFISH: Sweet soft-fleshed fish used in the Philippines. *Bangus* (F).

MIRIN (J): Sweet *sake* (J) used in Japanese cooking. Similar to sweet sherry (which can be substituted), it is used only for cooking, not as a beverage.

MISO (J): A thick salty paste made with fermented soya beans. High in protein, it is used in sauces and soups. *Miso* varies in colour from light creamy-yellow to dark red-brown, depending on the degree of saltiness.

MONOSODIUM GLUTAMATE: Crystals or powder used as a tenderiser or to highlight flavours. Although used extensively in Japanese and Chinese cooking, it is not necessary if the ingredients are good and the seasonings are used properly. The medical profession discourages its use. Well-known brands include Aji-No-Moto and Vetsin. It is often referred to simply as M.S.G.

MUSHROOMS, DRIED: *see* dried mushrooms

MUSTARD GREENS: A leafy green vegetable used in Chinese cooking. More frequently known as kale.

MUSTARD POWDER: Hot yellow mustard powder is used in Japanese cooking, and is made into a sauce with water as a condiment for certain Chinese dishes. Hot dry English mustard can be used.

MUSTARD SEEDS: Small black seeds used as a pungent spice in Indian cooking.

NAM PLA (T): *see* fish sauce

NG HEUNG FUN (C): *see* five-spice powder

NGAN PYA YE (B): *see* fish sauce

NGAPI (B): *see* dried shrimp paste

NOODLES, CHINESE: Chinese noodles vary greatly in size, shape, colour and texture, and are made from a variety of flours. They are long, thin and round (like Italian *spaghetti*) or flat (like *tagliatelle*), but some types are available fresh (i.e. 'wet' or 'soft') rather than dried.

Beehoon: The name given in Malaysia and Singapore to *mie fun* (below).

Dan mien: Also known as egg noodles, these are thin dried yellow noodles, either round or flat. They are sold in small bundles, which must first be soaked to soften and separate the strands. Used in soups, fried noodle dishes and boiled dishes. Known simply as *mee* in Malaysia and Singapore.

Ee mien: Fresh, fat, yellow egg noodles, either round or slightly flattened. They should be rinsed and then left to dry slightly before being fried. Like all fresh noodles, they should not be kept for more than a day before use or they will go heavy. Served hot or cold, depending on the sauce and accompaniments. Known as Hokkien noodles in Singapore.

Fun sie: Also known as transparent vermicelli or cellophane noodles, these are fine threads of glass-like dried noodles made from mung bean flour. Generally used in soup dishes and in braised dishes with plenty of sauce. Called *sohoon* or *tunghoon* in Malaysia and Singapore, and *sotanghoon* in Indonesia.

Hor fun: Fairly thin rice-flour noodles cut into flat strands about 0.5 cm wide, and available fresh or dried; the dry type must be soaked for up to 30 minutes to soften. They are boiled or fried.

Kway teow: Similar to *hor fun* (above), but about twice the width and slightly thicker. They are best bought fresh, if available, and should be simmered briefly in water before being fried or added to soups.

Mie fun: Very fine threads of rice vermicelli. When deep fried they puff up quite dramatically and become very crisp. Also served in soups and in well-sauced dishes. Known as *beehoon* in Malaysia and Singapore.

NOODLES, JAPANESE: In Japan, as in China, there are several kinds of noodles.

Shirataki: Translucent vermicelli-like noodles made from a starchy, tuberous root.

Soba: Fine buckwheat noodles.

Somen: Fine wheat-flour noodles, for which fine semolina vermicelli can be substituted.

Udon: Thick wheat-flour noodles resembling spaghetti, which can be substituted.

NORI (J): Dried laver, a paper-thin edible seaweed of purplish-green colour, used as a flavouring and garnish in Japanese cooking and occasionally in Chinese and Korean. It should be crisped over a low flame before use. Store in an airtight container to prevent softening.

NUOC MAM (V): *see* fish sauce

OYSTER SAUCE: A thick brown sauce made from oysters, soya sauce and salt. It gives a delicate, fishy flavour to many Chinese dishes.

PALM SUGAR: Compressed cakes of rich brown sugar from the aren palm, or less commonly, the coconut palm. Substitute dark-brown sugar. *Jaggery* (H), *gula Melaka* (M).

PANDAN LEAF: The long, deep-green leaf of Fragrant Screwpine (a species of the Pandanus family), it has a musky fragrance and adds a bright-green colour and a distinctive flavour to Malay and Indonesian sweets. There is no substitute, though vanilla approximates the flavour in certain dishes. *Daun pandan* (I, M).

PATNA RICE: *see* rice

PEPPER, BLACK: Whole peppercorns, a vital ingredient in the Indian *garam masala* spice mixture and in many Southeast Asian dishes.

PEPPER, WHITE: Powdered white pepper is used in Chinese and Vietnamese cooking.

PEPPER OIL: *see* chilli oil

PEPPER SALT: *see* spiced salt

PEPPERCORNS, CHINESE BROWN: Used in stewed and braised dishes from northern and western China. Also known as Szechwan Pepper (bot: *Xanthoxylum piperitum*), it is not the same as black pepper, and the latter cannot be substituted. *Hwa chiao* (C).

PICKLED/PRESERVED VEGETABLES: Certain dishes throughout Asia call for pickled and preserved vegetables. These vary from country to country, and include the Korean *kim chi;* the Chinese *mei gan tsai,* a salted dried mustard cabbage used with braised meats; the Chinese *tai tau tsoi,* a heavily salted preserved turnip sold in cans or by weight; the Japanese *takuan,* a pickled giant white radish; and the Chinese *chow chow* preserves, a mixture of fruit, ginger and vegetables used in sweet and savoury dishes. There are other types of pickled and moist-preserved cabbage and related greens that add saltiness and flavour to soups, stewed and braised dishes, and stuffings.

PLUM SAUCE: A Chinese sweet thick sauce, slightly hot and spicy, made with dried plums and used as a dip. Sold in cans and jars, it keeps indefinitely.

POMEGRANATE SEEDS: Small shiny dark-red to black seeds of the pomegranate, used to give a tangy flavour to Indian dishes. Lemon juice can be substituted.

POPPY SEEDS, WHITE: Used as a flavouring and thickening ingredient in Indian cooking. *Kas kas* (H).

POTATO FLOUR: *see* flour

PRAWNS, DRIED: *see* dried prawns

RED BEANS: Small dried red beans used in many types of Chinese, Japanese and Korean sweets. No suitable substitute. *Azuki* (J), *hong dow* (C).

RICE: Basmati and Patna are the best-known and most expensive types of long-grain rice, and are most suitable for savoury rice dishes.

Short-grain rice is preferred in Japan, and should be a slightly sticky type that holds together when cooked. It is used for most sweet dishes, except when glutinous rice is needed (*see* glutinous rice).

Dried Rice Cakes, Popped Rice Cakes and Glutinous Rice Cakes are some of the names given to pieces of cooked rice that are deep fried to a light golden colour and served with sauce. They can be made by overcooking rice until a layer at least 1 cm thick lines the pan. Leave layer to dry, then scrape off pan. When completely dry and cool, deep fry in hot oil.

RICE FLOUR: *see* flour

RICE PAPER, TRANSPARENT: A type of thin, edible paper-like sheet made from glutinous rice or potato and used as a wrapper for small fried foods. *See also* spring roll wrappers.

RICE WINE: *see* Chinese rice wine

ROSE WINE SPIRITS: *see* Chinese rice wine

ROSEWATER: Fragrant, delicate essence of roses used as a flavouring for Indian sweets and occasionally in rich savoury dishes and *biriyani.*

SAFFRON: Powdered and strand saffron are commonly used in Indian cooking to impart a delicate flavour and a bright orange-yellow colour. Turmeric is often substituted as a colouring agent, though its flavour is strong and lacks the subtlety of saffron. Do not use turmeric in sweet dishes.

SAGO FLOUR: *see* flour

SAKE (J): Japanese rice wine, the popular national liquor warmed to about 40°C in small porcelain jars and served in square pinewood boxes or thimble-sized cups. It is also used extensively in cooking. Light dry sherry is a reasonable substitute, though *sake* is now readily available and moderately priced.

SALAK (I): A fruit, indigenous to Indonesia, with a dark-brown snakeskin-like peel and a nutty hard flesh rather like raw potato. Substitute hard unripe pear.

SALT AND PEPPER POWDER: *see* spiced salt

SALT FISH: *see* dried fish

SALTED BLACK BEANS: Preserved, fermented salted soya beans used as a well-flavoured seasoning ingredient in Chinese and Malaysian cooking. If unavailable, add more salt and soya sauce.

SANSHO (J): A commercial blend of chilli powder, salt and sesame seeds used as a condiment with certain Japanese foods.

SCALLIONS: *see* spring onions

SERAI (M): *see* lemon grass

SEREH (I): *see* lemon grass

SESAME OIL: A nutty dark-brown oil made from sesame seeds, and used in Korean, Chinese and Japanese cooking to give a rich flavour and nutty aroma. Never used alone for deep frying, for it burns at a relatively low temperature and has too strong a taste.

SESAME PASTE: A thick, strongly flavoured yellowish paste made from ground sesame seeds and used for flavouring northern Chinese and Korean dishes and occasionally some Japanese dishes. It keeps indefinitely with or without refrigeration. Substitute *tahina,* a similar sesame paste from the Middle East.

SESAME SEEDS: White sesame seeds are used as a garnish for many types of Asian sweets, and are ground for use in Indian savoury cooking. Black and white seeds are favoured by Japanese and Korean cooks as a savoury garnish. High in protein.

SHALLOTS: Small purple onions that grow in clusters similar to garlic heads, they are used extensively in Asian cooking. Quantities given here as, say, '4-5 shallots', mean four or five pieces or cloves and *not* whole heads. Brown or white onions can be substituted, but being milder in flavour their amounts should be increased. *See also* spring onions.

SHAO MAI WRAPPERS: Small circular or square wheat-flour wrappers sold frozen or fresh in packs, and used for used for *wonton* and other *dim sum.*

SHARK FIN: Clear 'needles' of gelatinous shark fin are sold in packets and need to be soaked before use. Whole shark fin requires longer soaking before cooking.

SHIITAKE (J): *see* dried mushrooms

SHIRATAKI (J): *see* noodles, Japanese

SHRIMP PASTE: *see* dried shrimp paste

SINGKAMAS (F): *see* yam bean

SNOW PEAS: Flattish bright-green peas pods used as a vegetable in Chinese cooking. Also known as *mange-tout.*

SOBA (J): *see* noodles, Japanese

SOMEN (J): *see* noodles, Japanese

SOYA SAUCE: Available in light, dark and sweet types. 'Light' is a thin watery liquid, is quite salty, and is most often used in Chinese cooking. 'Dark' is used when sauces or meats need additional colour, and is usually less salty than the light type. For 'sweet', *see* kecap manis.

SPICED SALT: Two kinds of spiced salt are used as condiments with Chinese food, particularly dry-cooked food.

Salt and pepper powder is made with finely ground white salt, slightly roasted until just beginning to colour, then cooled and mixed with finely ground Szechwan pepper.

Five-spice salt is similarly prepared, but uses five-spice powder instead of pepper.

SPINACH: *see* fenugreek

SPRING ONION SHOOTS: Like chive shoots, these are grown under cover to prevent the leaves turning green. They look insipid, but have a delicate onion flavour and a subtle fragrance. Best bought fresh in quantities as needed, but will keep two or three days in the vegetable compartment of a refrigerator. They can be grown at home by covering spring onion shoots with a tall tin and watering normally. Substitute the white portion of slender spring onions.

SPRING ONIONS: Tall dark-green leafy onions, of which the small white bulb section is the part most often used. Common in all Asian cooking. Substitute white onion in slightly smaller quantities. Spring onions are often called scallions, and in Australia are often known incorrectly as shallots.

SPRING ROLL WRAPPERS: Also known as rice paper wrappers or rice doilies, these paper-thin skins are made with flour dough that is wiped across a hot metal pan to leave a very thin layer of batter attached. This is cooked until it becomes dryish and begins to lift off. Sold frozen in packs of 25 or 50, they must be thawed before use. After thawing, cover with a damp cloth until you are ready to use them; if allowed to dry out, the wrappers crack and become impossible to fold.

STAR ANISE: An eight-pointed star-shaped fragrant Chinese spice with a rich anise flavour.

STRAW MUSHROOMS: Delicately flavoured mushrooms grown in Taiwan, and available in cans. Similar in taste to button mushrooms, which can be substituted.

SZECHWAN PEPPER: *see* peppercorns, Chinese brown

TAHU (M): *see* beancurd

TAI TAU TSOI (C): *see* pickled/preserved vegetables

TAMARIND: Semi-dried flesh from the seed pods of the tamarind tree. Mix with hot water to make a strongly flavoured acidulating liquid for tenderising meats and for adding a sourish tang to many dishes. Available in vacuum packs. Substitute vinegar, lime or lemon juice mixed with a little water. *Asam* (I, M), *imli* (H).

TAUCHEO (C): *see* bean paste, salted

TAUKWA (C): Hard beancurd.

TIEN MIEN JIANG (C): *see* bean paste, sweet

TIENTSIN CABBAGE: *see* Chinese cabbage

TRASI or TERASI (I): *see* dried shrimp paste

TOFU (J): *see* beancurd

TURMERIC: Fresh root turmeric is used for colouring and flavouring. Powdered turmeric, a bright-yellow spice with a musky fragrance and a distinctive taste, is also used for colouring and flavouring many curried dishes and some rice dishes. Powdered turmeric is stronger than fresh: substitute one-third to one-half powder to fresh. *Kunyit* (I, M).

UDON (J): *see* noodles, Japanese

VERMICELLI: *see* noodles, Chinese

VERMICELLI SHEETS: Transparent sheets of mung bean flour, which can be shredded and used as a vegetable or garnish. *See also* jelly fish, processed.

VIETNAMESE MINT: *see* daun kesom

VINEGAR AND SOYA SAUCE DIP: A sharp-flavoured Korean accompaniment made by blending ¾ cup light soya sauce, 3 tablespoons white wine vinegar, 3 tablespoons ground sesame seeds and 2 teaspoons finely chopped spring onions. Serve in individual sauce bowls.

VINEGAR, CHINESE BROWN: *see* Chinese brown vinegar

WAKAME (J): Lobe-leafed seaweed used in Japanese

and Korean cooking. Sold dried and lightly salted.
WASABI (J): Powdered green horseradish used in Japanese cooking and as a highly pungent garnish. Available in small cans. Substitute hot mustard powder or fresh, grated horseradish.
WATER CHESTNUTS: Brown-skinned crisp white nuts, available fresh or canned, and used as a vegetable in Chinese cooking.
WINE: *see* Chinese rice wine, ginger wine, mirin, sake
WINTER MELON: Large white-fleshed melon similar in external appearance to watermelon. Used, when in season, in Chinese and Malaysian soups and stewed

dishes. Available canned. Substitute squash.
WONTON WRAPPERS: Prepared rice-flour skins for *wonton*. Sold fresh or frozen.
XANTHOXYLUM PIPERITUM: *see* peppercorns, Chinese brown
YAM BEAN: A large tuberous root much used as a vegetable in Malaysia, Singapore and the Philippines. *Bangkuang* (M), *singkamas* (F).
YELLOW BEAN PASTE: *see* bean paste, salted
YOGHURT: Plain unflavoured yoghurt is used extensively in Indian cooking as a tenderiser, enricher, thickener and sweets ingredient. *Dahi* (H).

INDEX